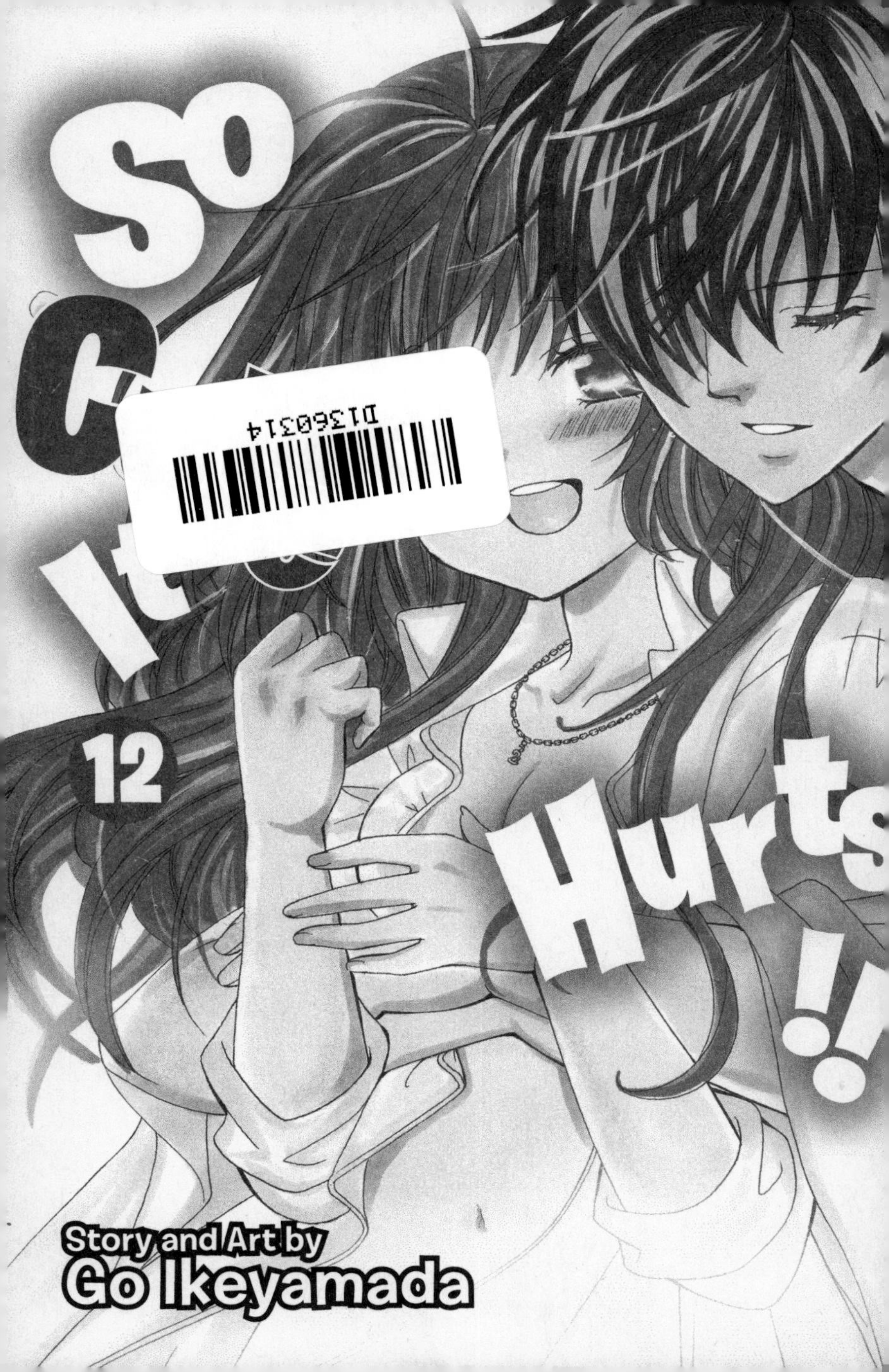
So
It
12
Hurts!!
Story and Art by
Go Ikeyamada

CHARACTERS

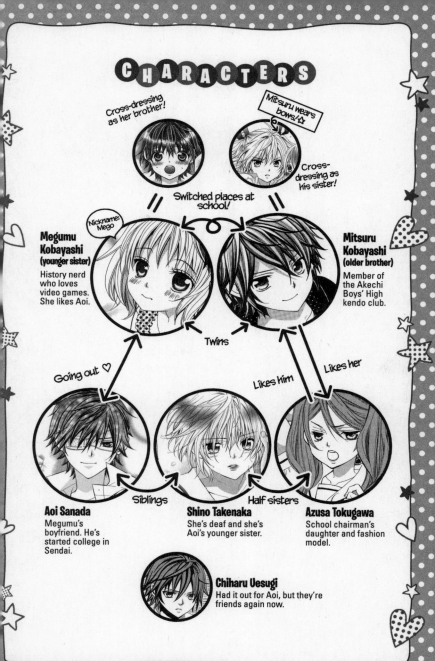

Cross-dressing as her brother!

Mitsuru wears bows!☆

Cross-dressing as his sister!

Switched places at school!

Nickname: Mego

Megumu Kobayashi (younger sister)
History nerd who loves video games. She likes Aoi.

Mitsuru Kobayashi (older brother)
Member of the Akechi Boys' High kendo club.

Twins

Going out ♡

Likes him

Likes her

Siblings

Half sisters

Aoi Sanada
Megumu's boyfriend. He's started college in Sendai.

Shino Takenaka
She's deaf and she's Aoi's younger sister.

Azusa Tokugawa
School chairman's daughter and fashion model.

Chiharu Uesugi
Had it out for Aoi, but they're friends again now.

STORY

★ Mitsuru and Megumu are twins. One day they switch places and go to each other's school for a week! That's when Megumu falls in love with Aoi. When the week is over, Megumu declares her love for Aoi, and they start dating. But Aoi is so uncomfortable around women that he passes out when he touches one.

★ One day, Aoi's eye patch falls off while he's trying to protect Megumu, exposing a scar from a burn he suffered when he was a child. Megumu's kiss on his scar heals his psychological wounds, and now they are finally able to touch each other!

★ Meanwhile, Mitsuru and Azusa are attracted to each other, but Azusa closes her heart when her parents' affairs are made public. And Shino is Azusa's half sister, born of the affair between Azusa's father and Aoi's mother! Their father has always preferred Shino, which has deeply hurt Azusa. When Mitsuru realizes how alone Azusa has been, he asks her to marry him, and she accepts. Azusa leaves Tokyo with her mother but later returns to Mitsuru. Now her father is scheming to separate the young lovers since he doesn't approve of their relationship!

CONTENTS

So Cute It Hurts!! (⁀ᴗ⁀)

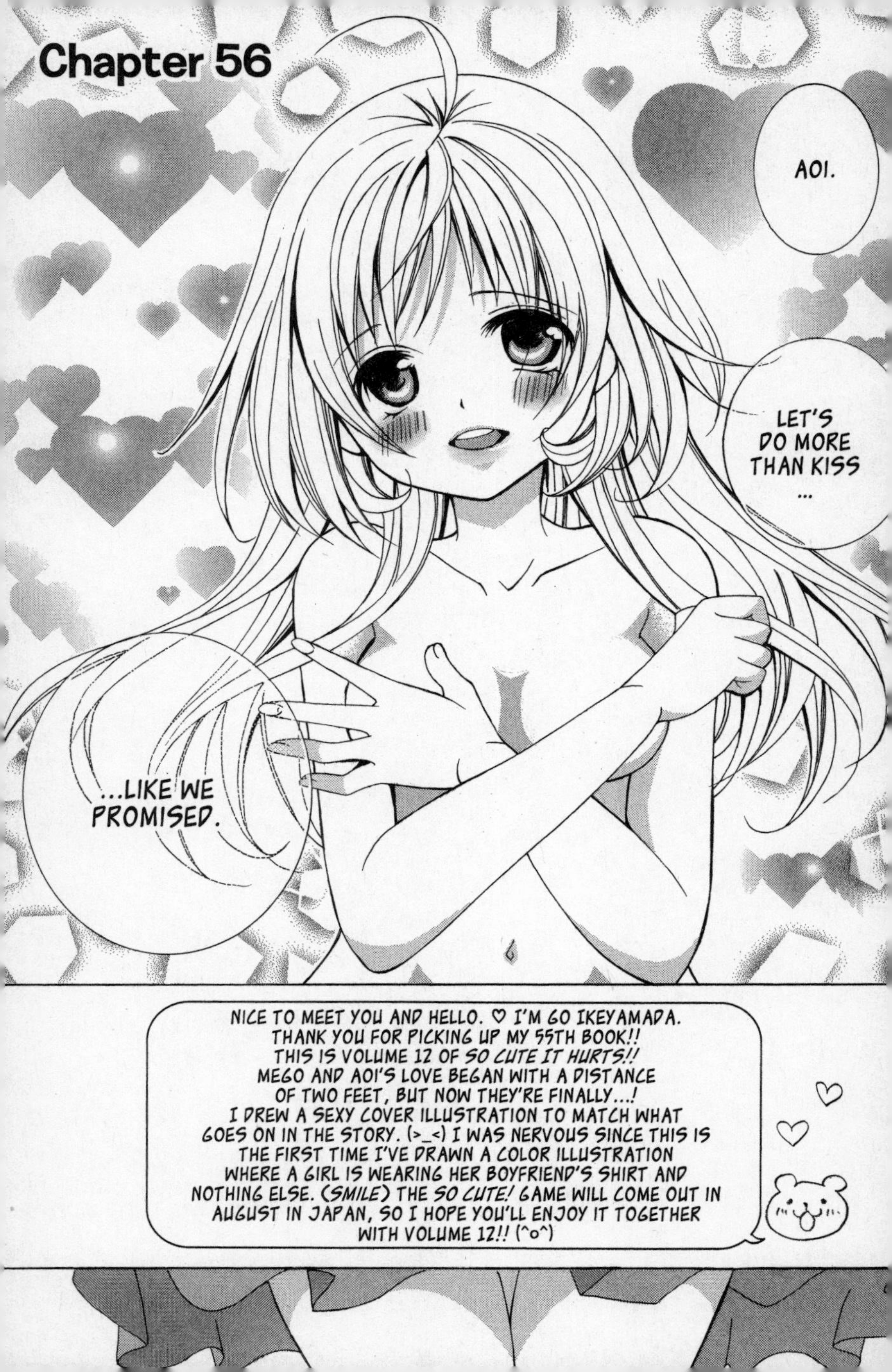
Chapter 56
AOI.
LET'S DO MORE THAN KISS ...
...LIKE WE PROMISED.
NICE TO MEET YOU AND HELLO. ♡ I'M GO IKEYAMADA. THANK YOU FOR PICKING UP MY 55TH BOOK!! THIS IS VOLUME 12 OF *SO CUTE IT HURTS!!* MEGO AND AOI'S LOVE BEGAN WITH A DISTANCE OF TWO FEET, BUT NOW THEY'RE FINALLY....! I DREW A SEXY COVER ILLUSTRATION TO MATCH WHAT GOES ON IN THE STORY. (>_<) I WAS NERVOUS SINCE THIS IS THE FIRST TIME I'VE DRAWN A COLOR ILLUSTRATION WHERE A GIRL IS WEARING HER BOYFRIEND'S SHIRT AND NOTHING ELSE. (*SMILE*) THE *SO CUTE!* GAME WILL COME OUT IN AUGUST IN JAPAN, SO I HOPE YOU'LL ENJOY IT TOGETHER WITH VOLUME 12!! (^o^)

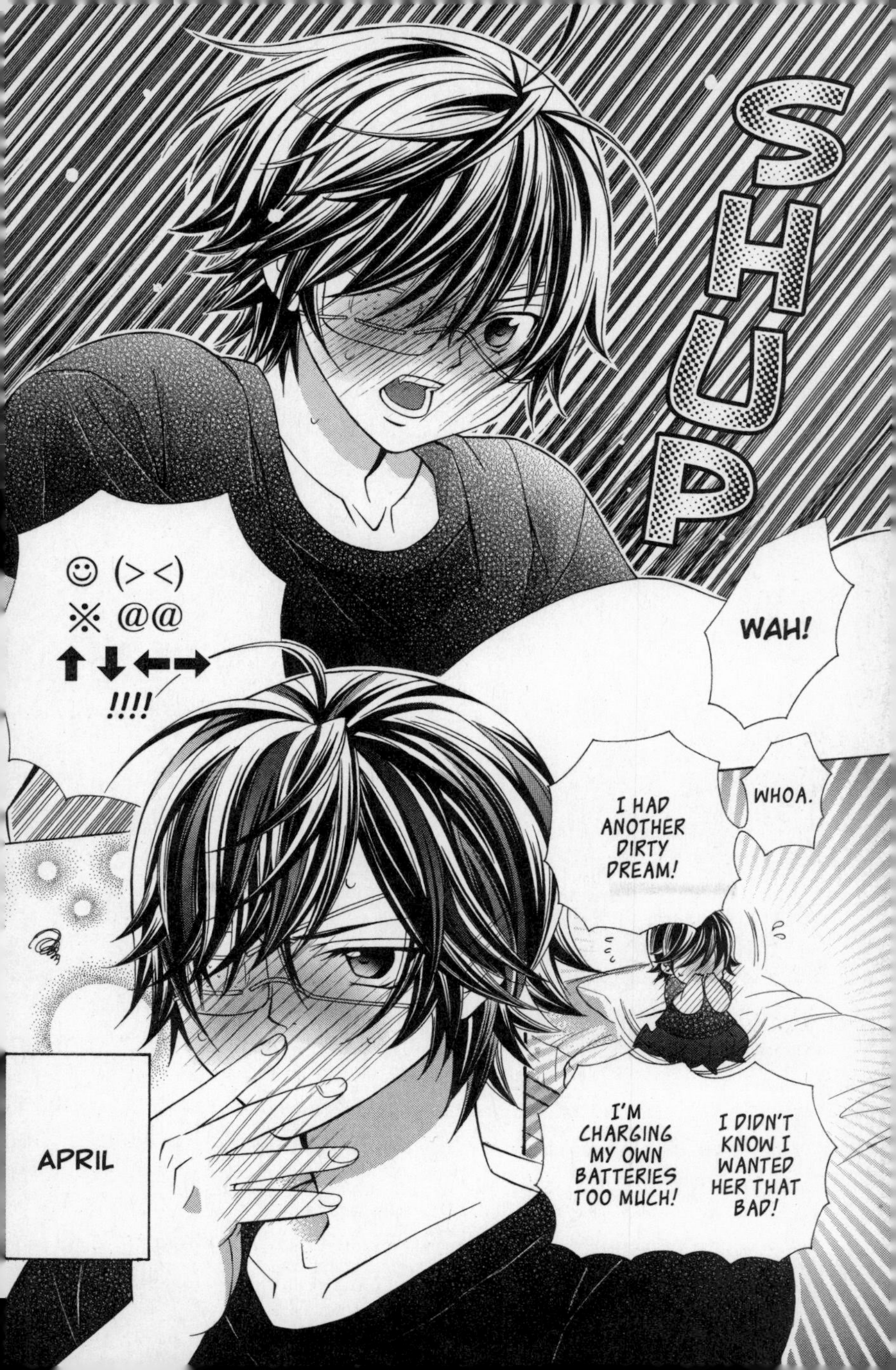
SHUP
WAH!
☺ (><)
※ @@
↑↓←→
!!!!
WHOA.
I HAD ANOTHER DIRTY DREAM!
I DIDN'T KNOW I WANTED HER THAT BAD!
I'M CHARGING MY OWN BATTERIES TOO MUCH!
APRIL

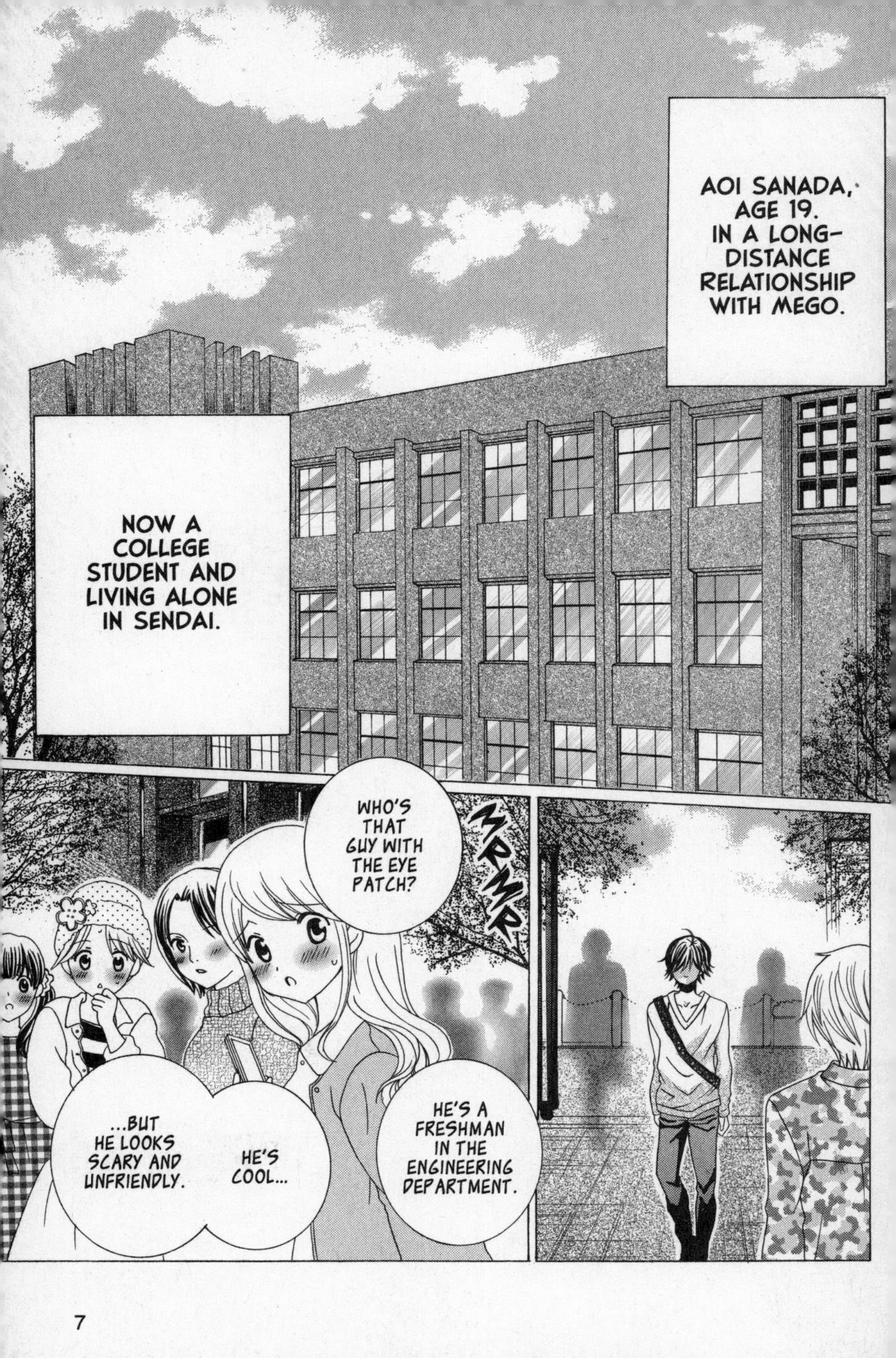
AOI SANADA, AGE 19. IN A LONG-DISTANCE RELATIONSHIP WITH MEGO.
NOW A COLLEGE STUDENT AND LIVING ALONE IN SENDAI.
MRMR
WHO'S THAT GUY WITH THE EYE PATCH?
HE'S A FRESHMAN IN THE ENGINEERING DEPARTMENT.
HE'S COOL...
...BUT HE LOOKS SCARY AND UNFRIENDLY.

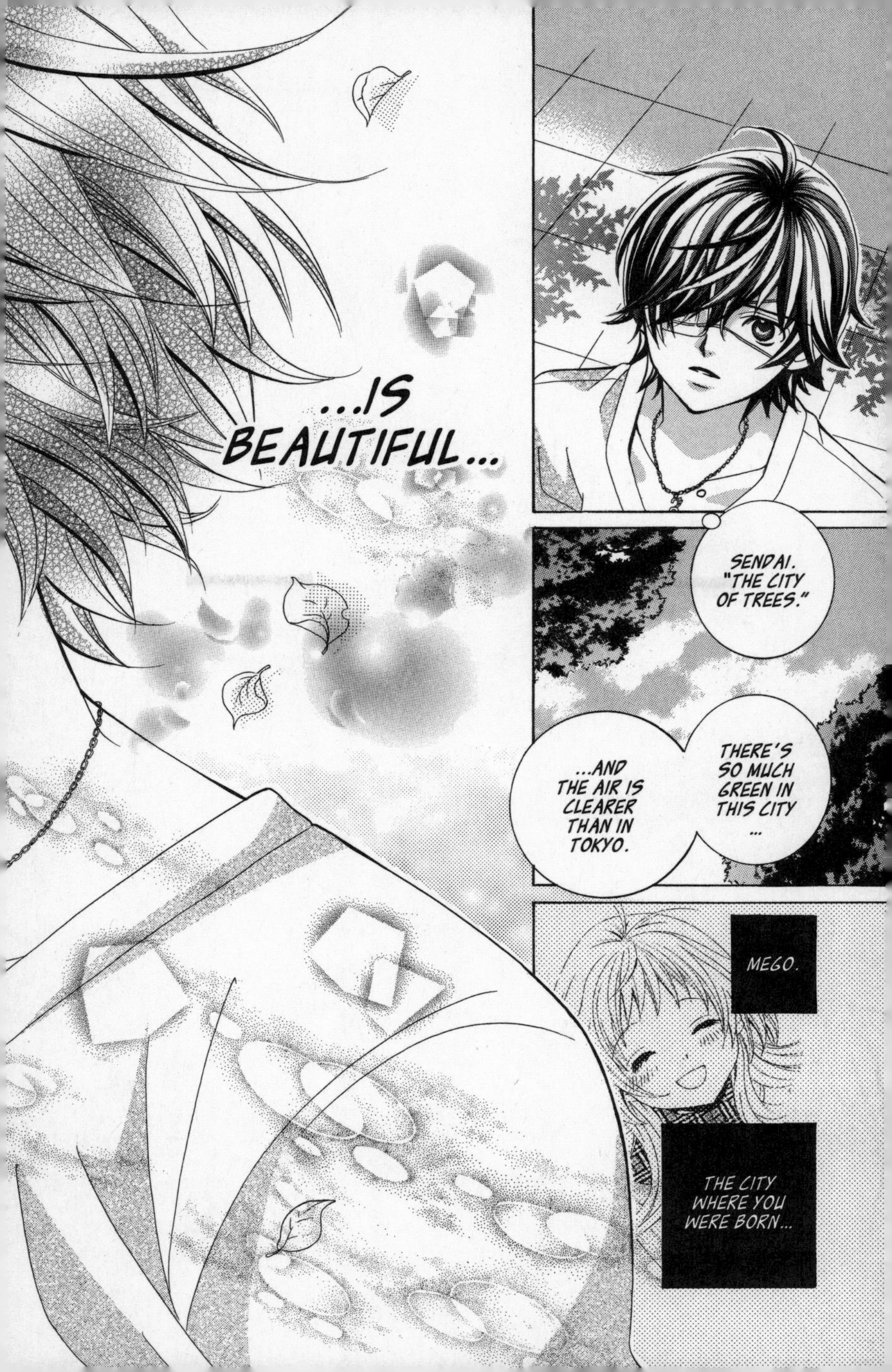
SENDAI. "THE CITY OF TREES."
THERE'S SO MUCH GREEN IN THIS CITY ...
...AND THE AIR IS CLEARER THAN IN TOKYO.
MEGO.
THE CITY WHERE YOU WERE BORN...
...IS BEAUTIFUL...

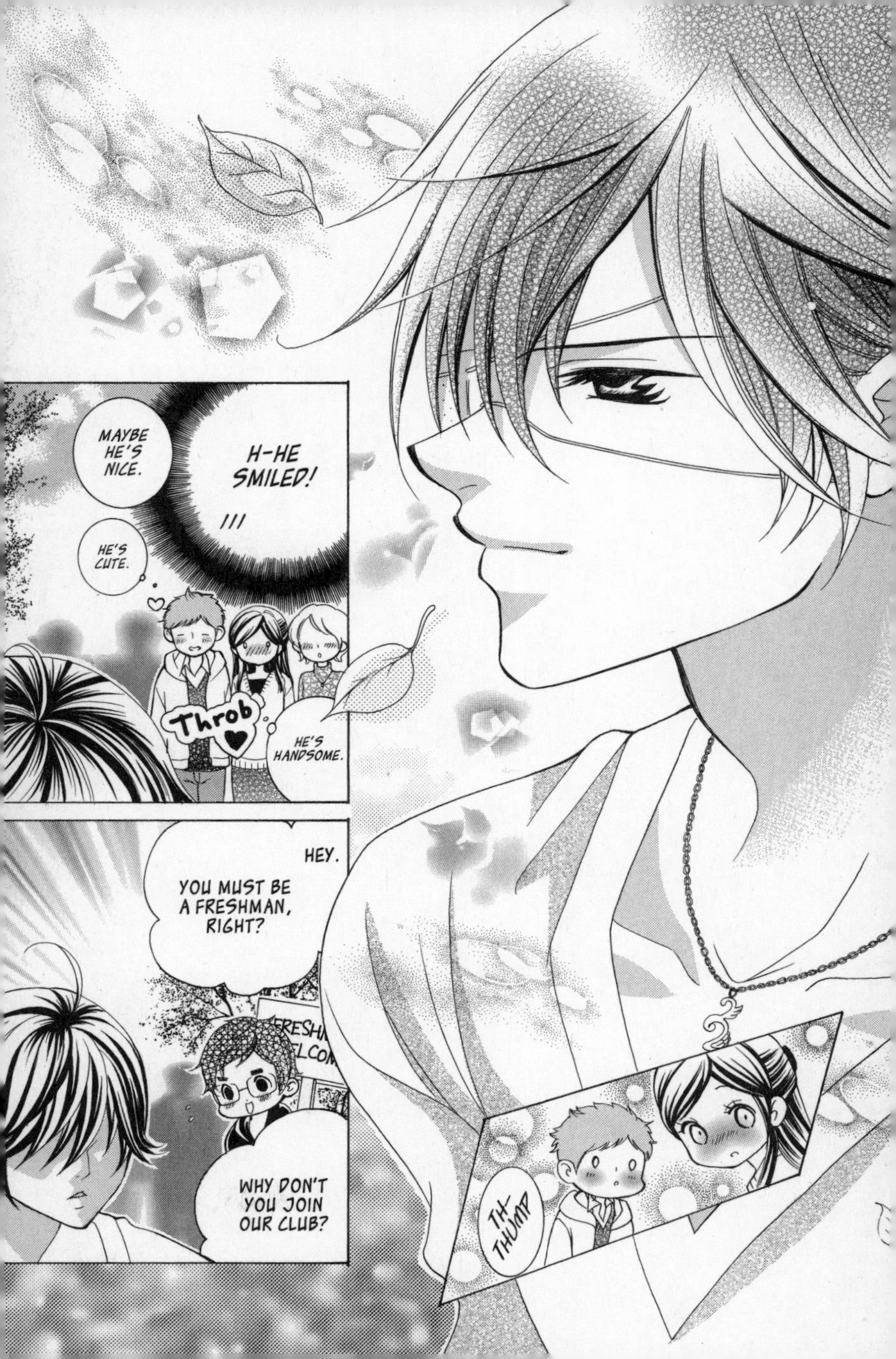

TH-THUMP
H-HE SMILED!
///
MAYBE HE'S NICE.
HE'S CUTE.
HE'S HANDSOME.
Throb
HEY.
YOU MUST BE A FRESHMAN, RIGHT?
WHY DON'T YOU JOIN OUR CLUB?

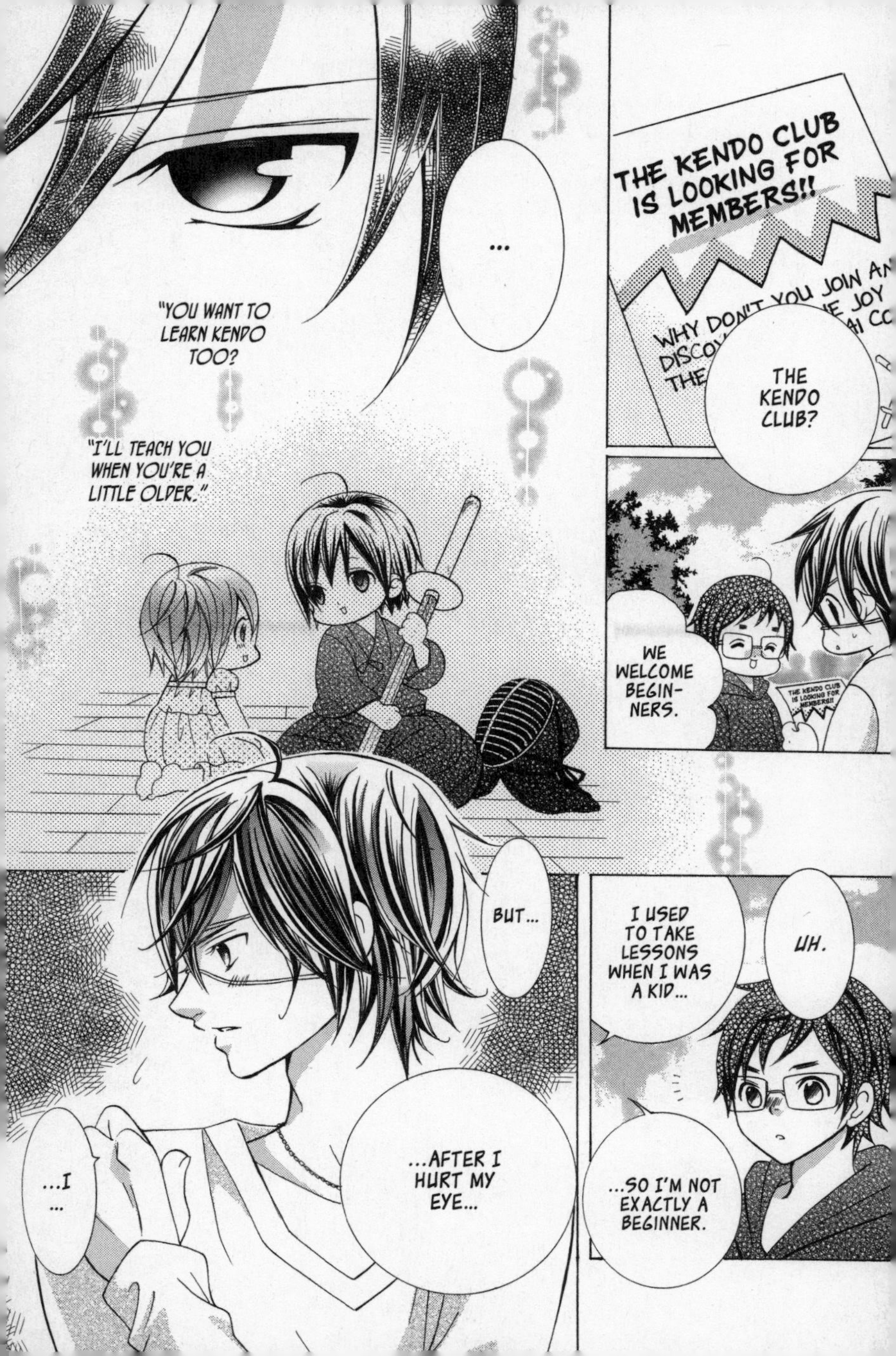
THE KENDO CLUB IS LOOKING FOR MEMBERS!!
THE KENDO CLUB?
WE WELCOME BEGINNERS.
...
"YOU WANT TO LEARN KENDO TOO?
"I'LL TEACH YOU WHEN YOU'RE A LITTLE OLDER."
UH.
I USED TO TAKE LESSONS WHEN I WAS A KID...
...SO I'M NOT EXACTLY A BEGINNER.
BUT...
...AFTER I HURT MY EYE...
...I ...

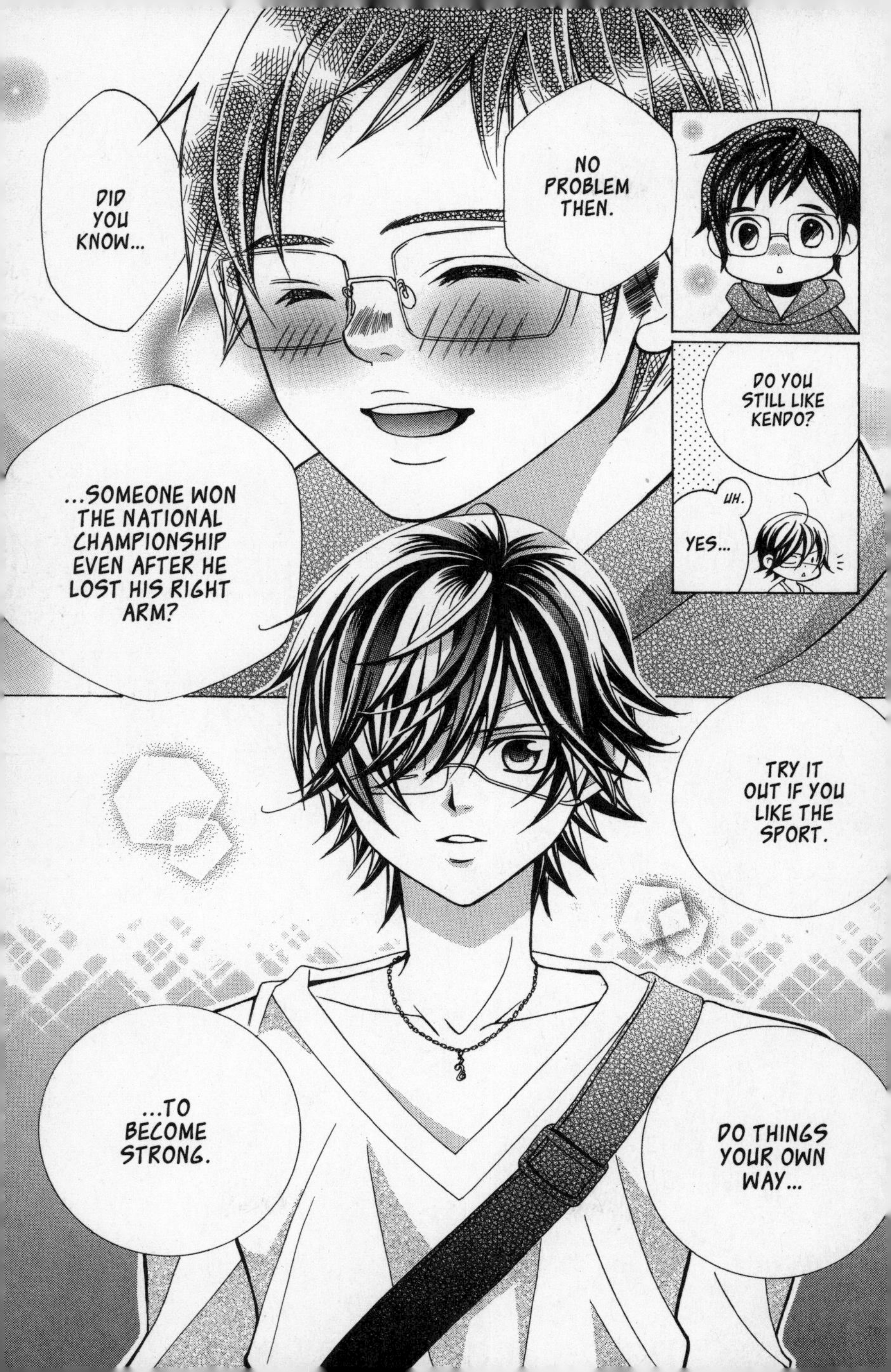
DO YOU STILL LIKE KENDO?
UH.
YES...
NO PROBLEM THEN.
DID YOU KNOW...
...SOMEONE WON THE NATIONAL CHAMPIONSHIP EVEN AFTER HE LOST HIS RIGHT ARM?
TRY IT OUT IF YOU LIKE THE SPORT.
DO THINGS YOUR OWN WAY...
...TO BECOME STRONG.

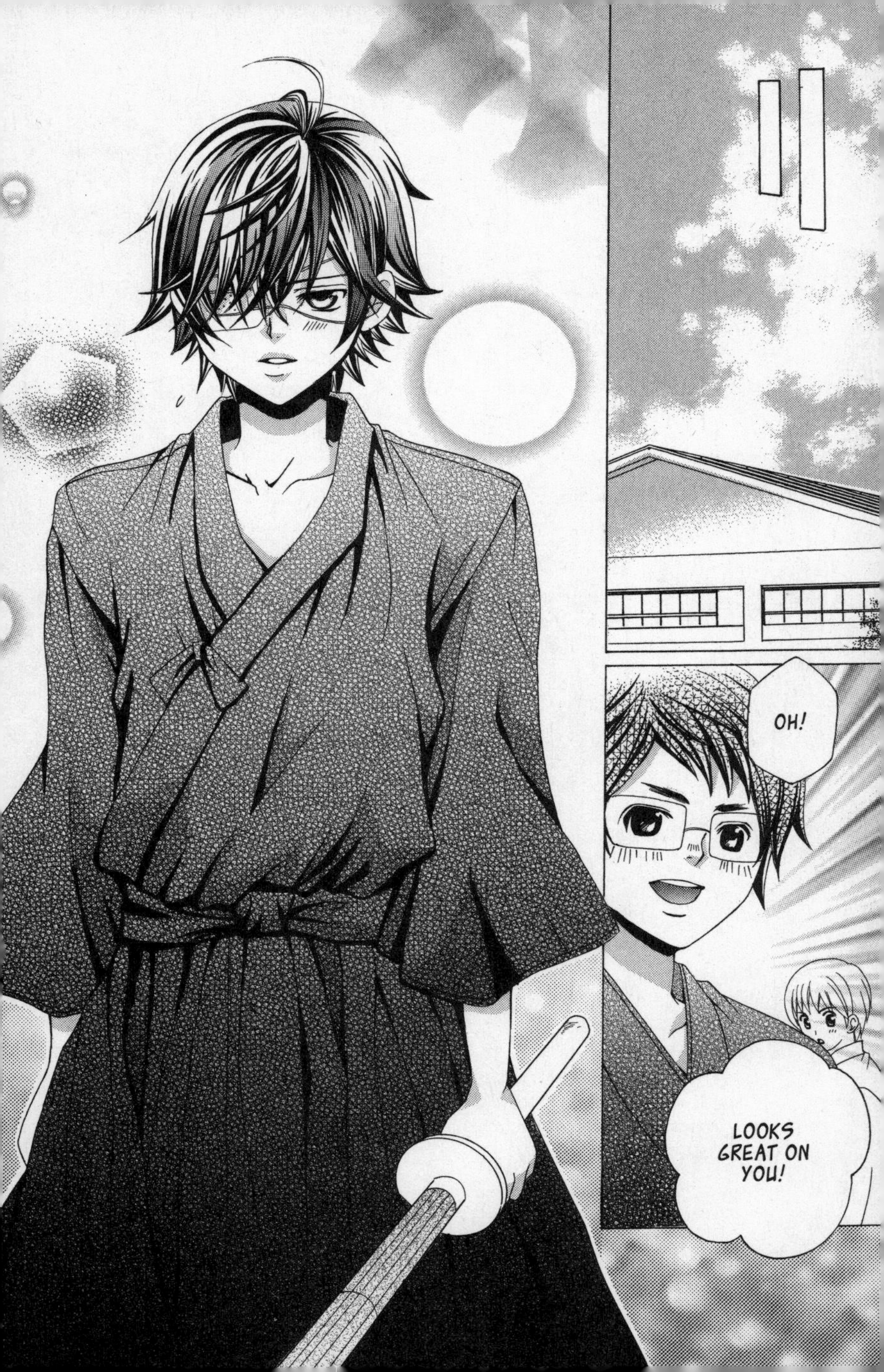
OH!
LOOKS GREAT ON YOU!

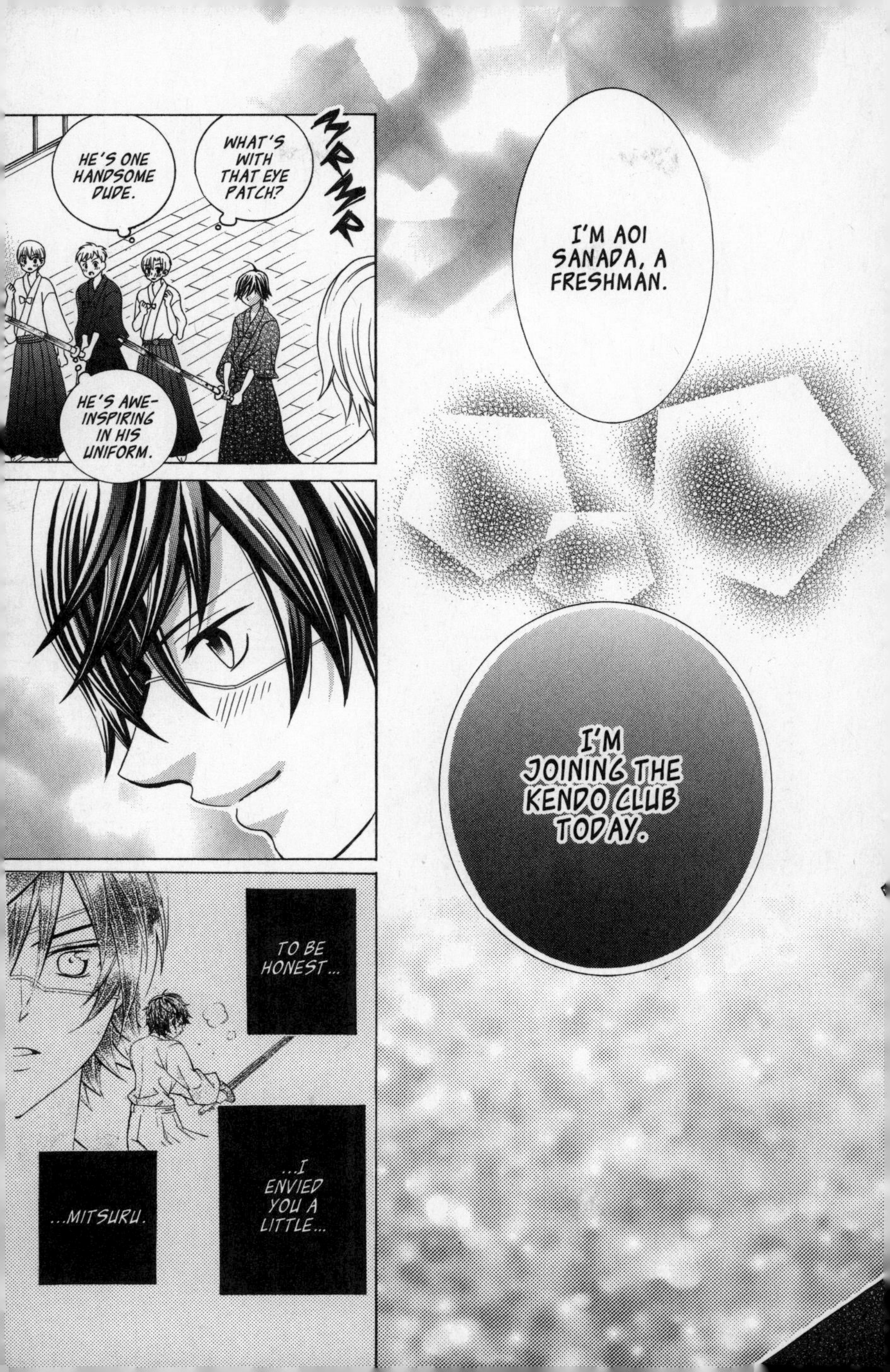
I'M AOI SANADA, A FRESHMAN.
I'M JOINING THE KENDO CLUB TODAY.
MRMR
WHAT'S WITH THAT EYE PATCH?
HE'S ONE HANDSOME DUDE.
HE'S AWE-INSPIRING IN HIS UNIFORM.
TO BE HONEST...
...I ENVIED YOU A LITTLE...
...MITSURU.

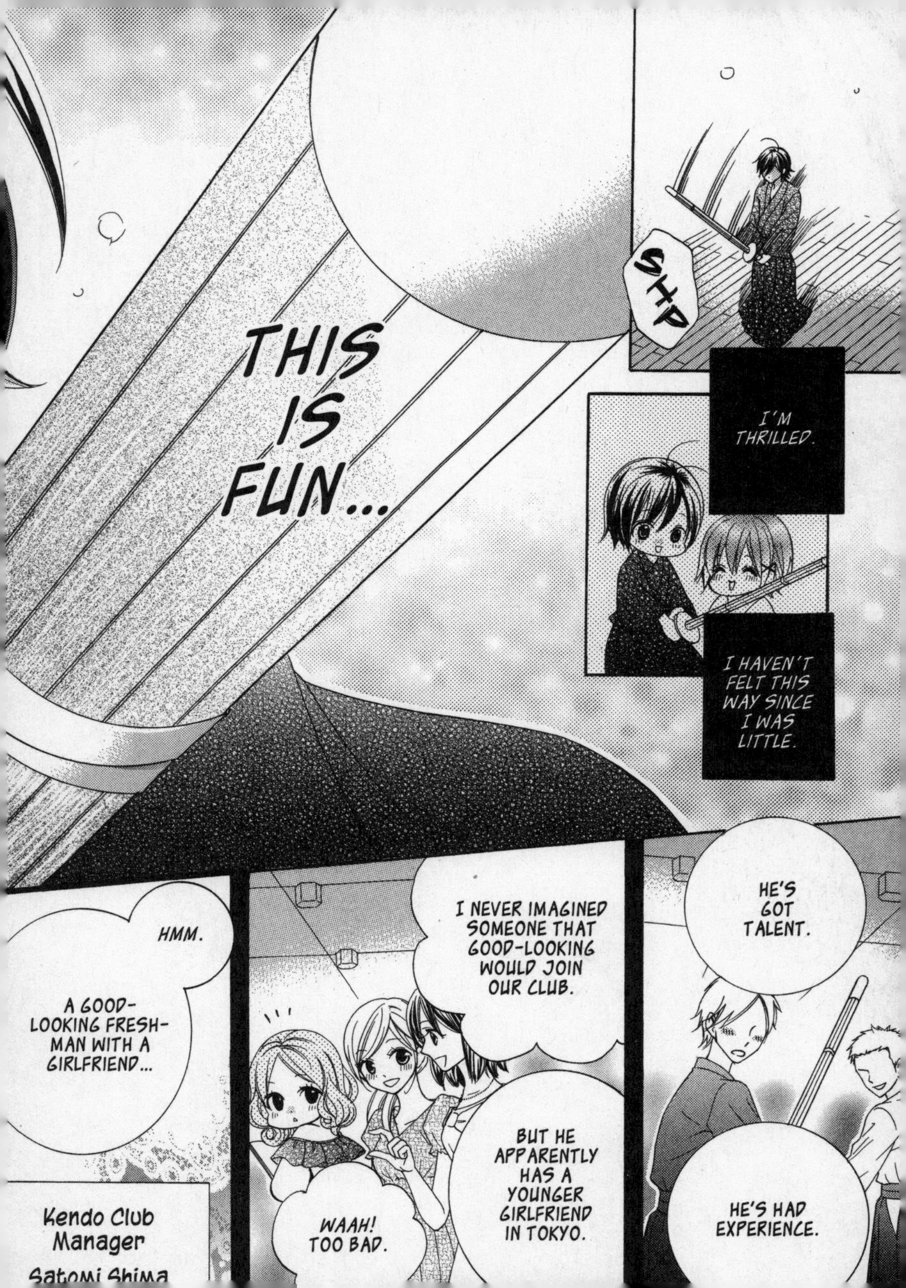
SHP
I'M THRILLED.
I HAVEN'T FELT THIS WAY SINCE I WAS LITTLE.
THIS IS FUN...
HE'S GOT TALENT.
HE'S HAD EXPERIENCE.
I NEVER IMAGINED SOMEONE THAT GOOD-LOOKING WOULD JOIN OUR CLUB.
BUT HE APPARENTLY HAS A YOUNGER GIRLFRIEND IN TOKYO.
WAAH! TOO BAD.
HMM.
A GOOD-LOOKING FRESHMAN WITH A GIRLFRIEND...
Kendo Club Manager
Satomi Shima

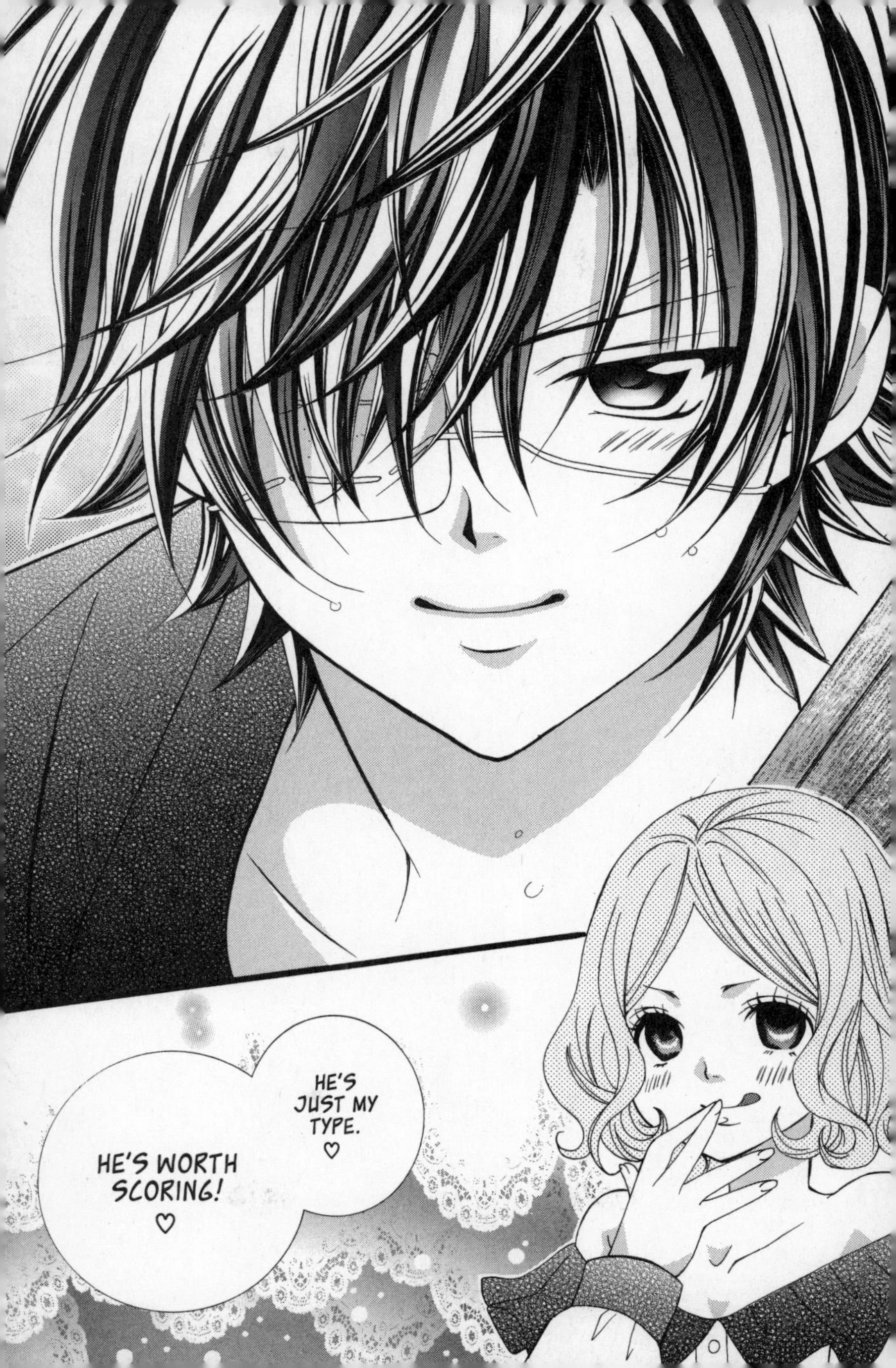
HE'S JUST MY TYPE. ♡
HE'S WORTH SCORING! ♡

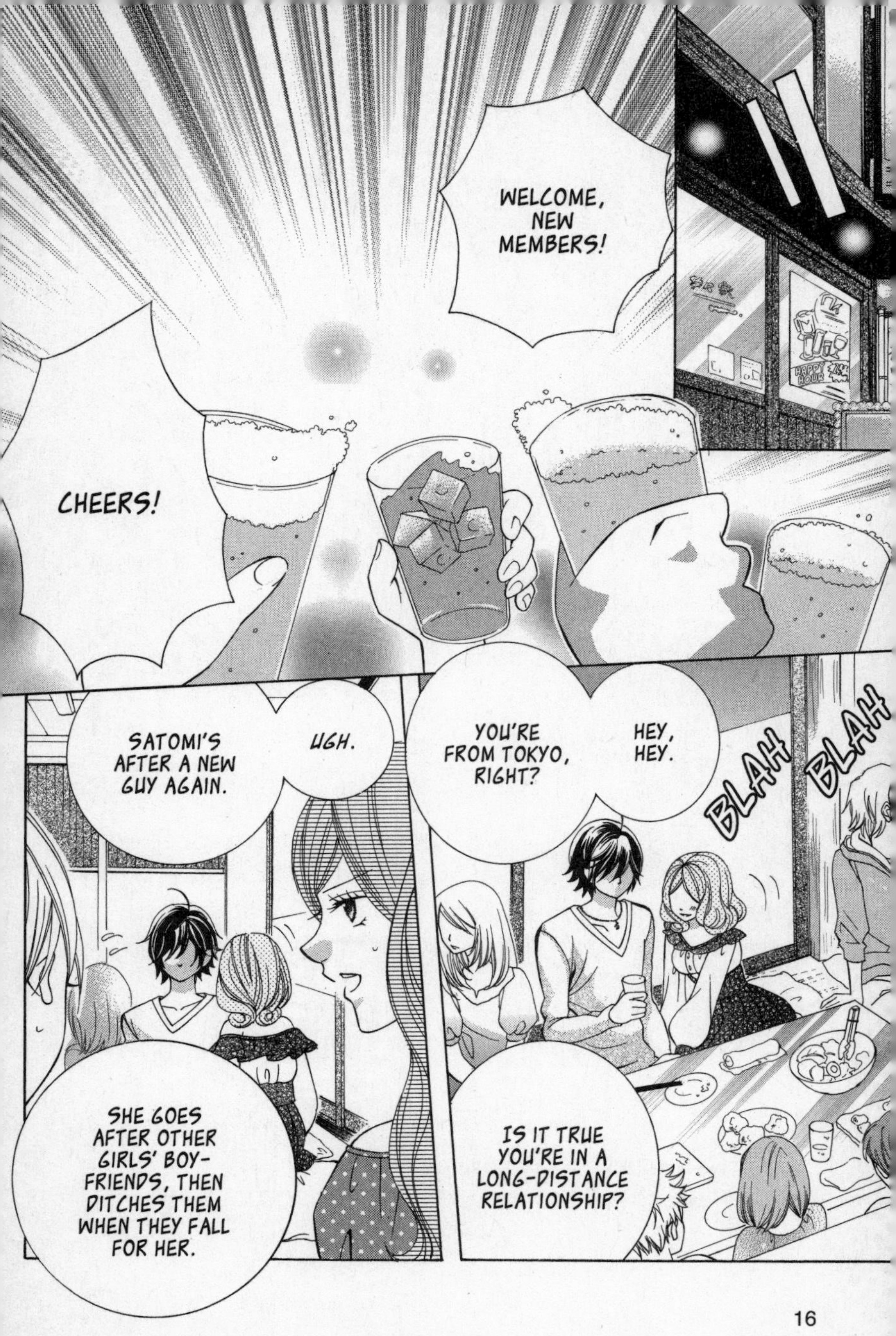
WELCOME, NEW MEMBERS!
HAPPY HOUR
CHEERS!
HEY, HEY.
YOU'RE FROM TOKYO, RIGHT?
BLAH BLAH
IS IT TRUE YOU'RE IN A LONG-DISTANCE RELATIONSHIP?
UGH.
SATOMI'S AFTER A NEW GUY AGAIN.
SHE GOES AFTER OTHER GIRLS' BOY-FRIENDS, THEN DITCHES THEM WHEN THEY FALL FOR HER.

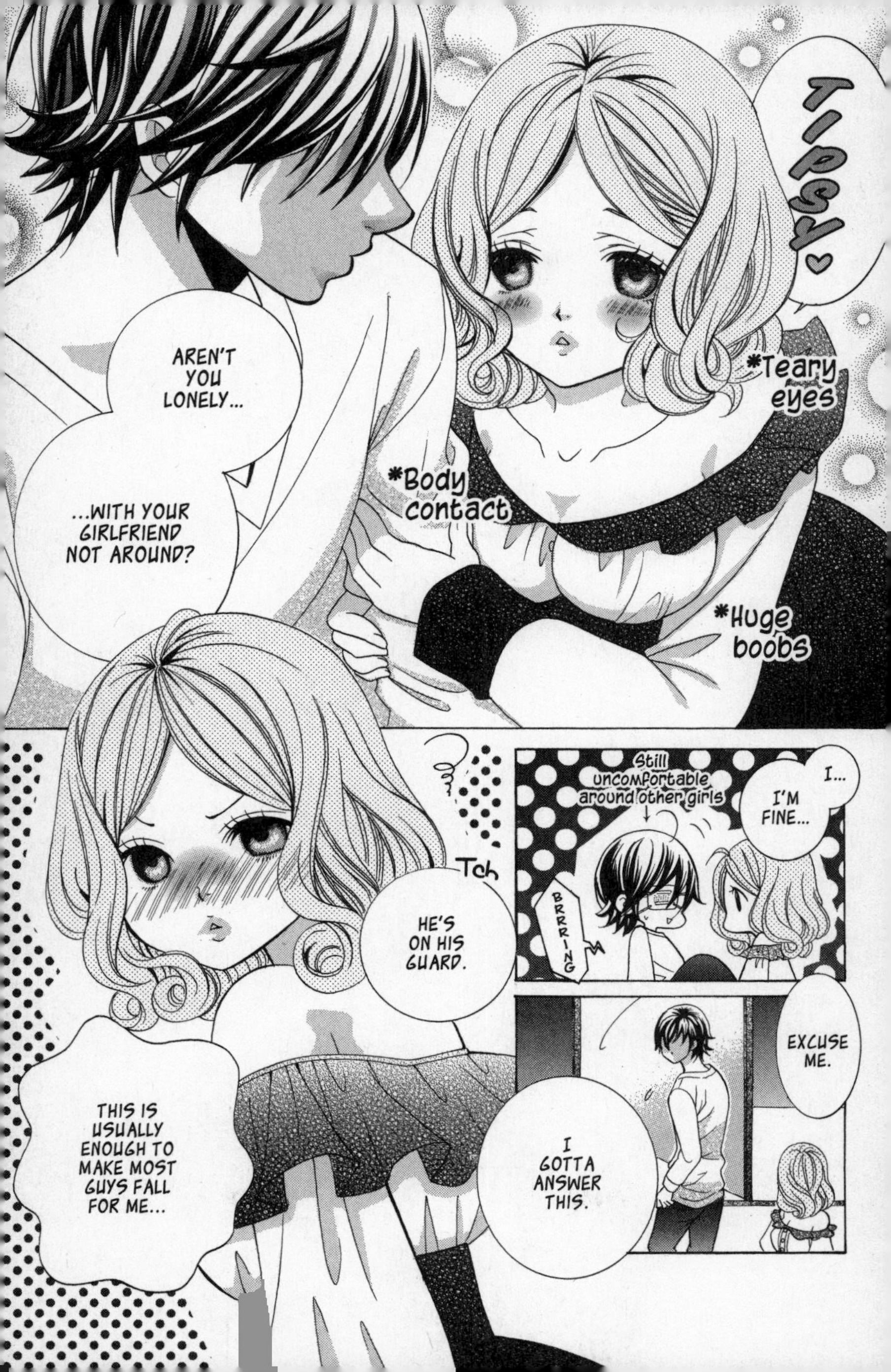
TIPSY♥
*Teary eyes
*Body contact
*Huge boobs
AREN'T YOU LONELY...
...WITH YOUR GIRLFRIEND NOT AROUND?
I...
I'M FINE...
Still uncomfortable around other girls
BRRRING
EXCUSE ME.
I GOTTA ANSWER THIS.
Tch
HE'S ON HIS GUARD.
THIS IS USUALLY ENOUGH TO MAKE MOST GUYS FALL FOR ME...

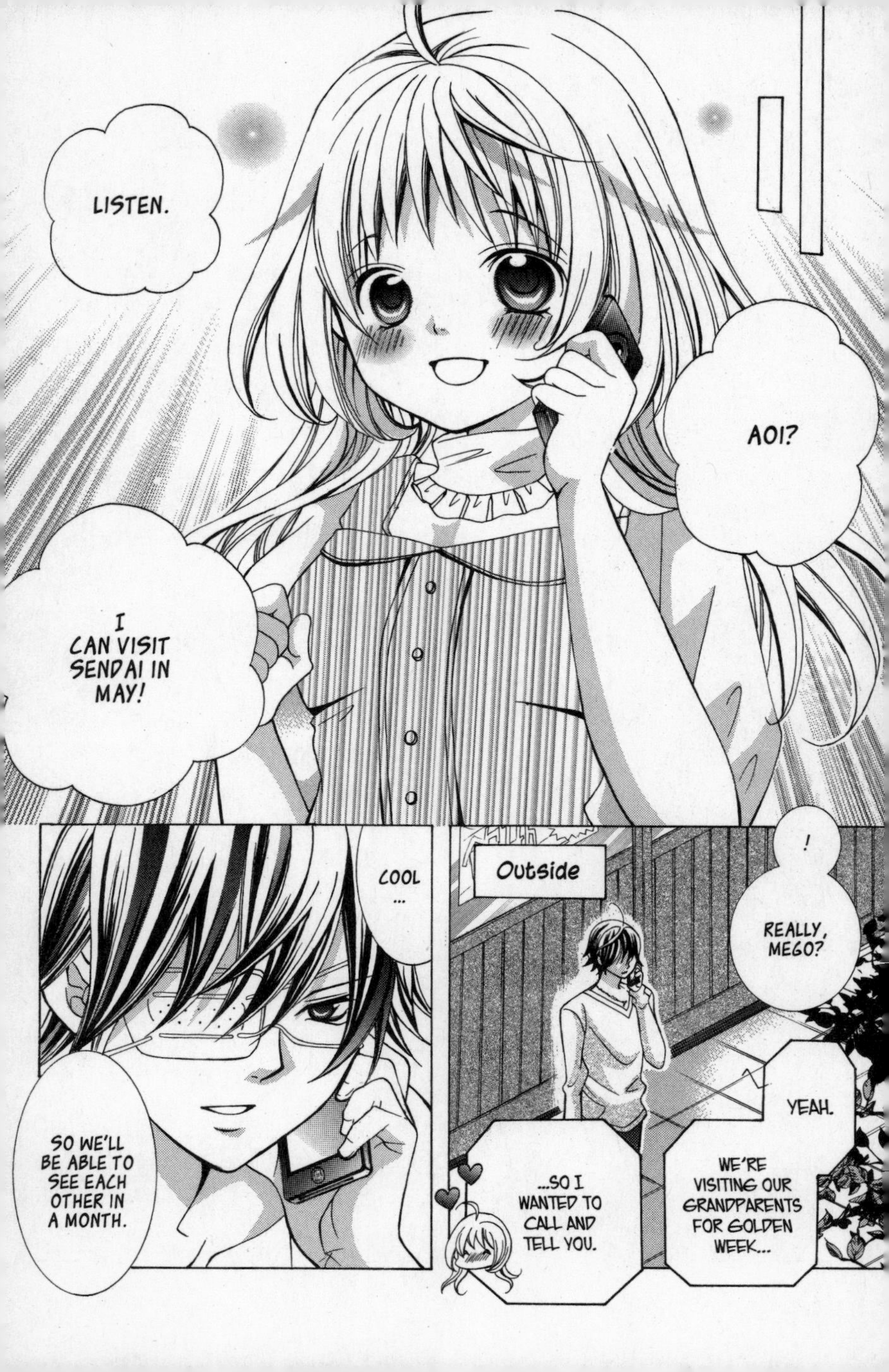
AOI?
LISTEN.
I CAN VISIT SENDAI IN MAY!
Outside
!
REALLY, MEGO?
YEAH.
WE'RE VISITING OUR GRANDPARENTS FOR GOLDEN WEEK...
...SO I WANTED TO CALL AND TELL YOU.
COOL...
SO WE'LL BE ABLE TO SEE EACH OTHER IN A MONTH.

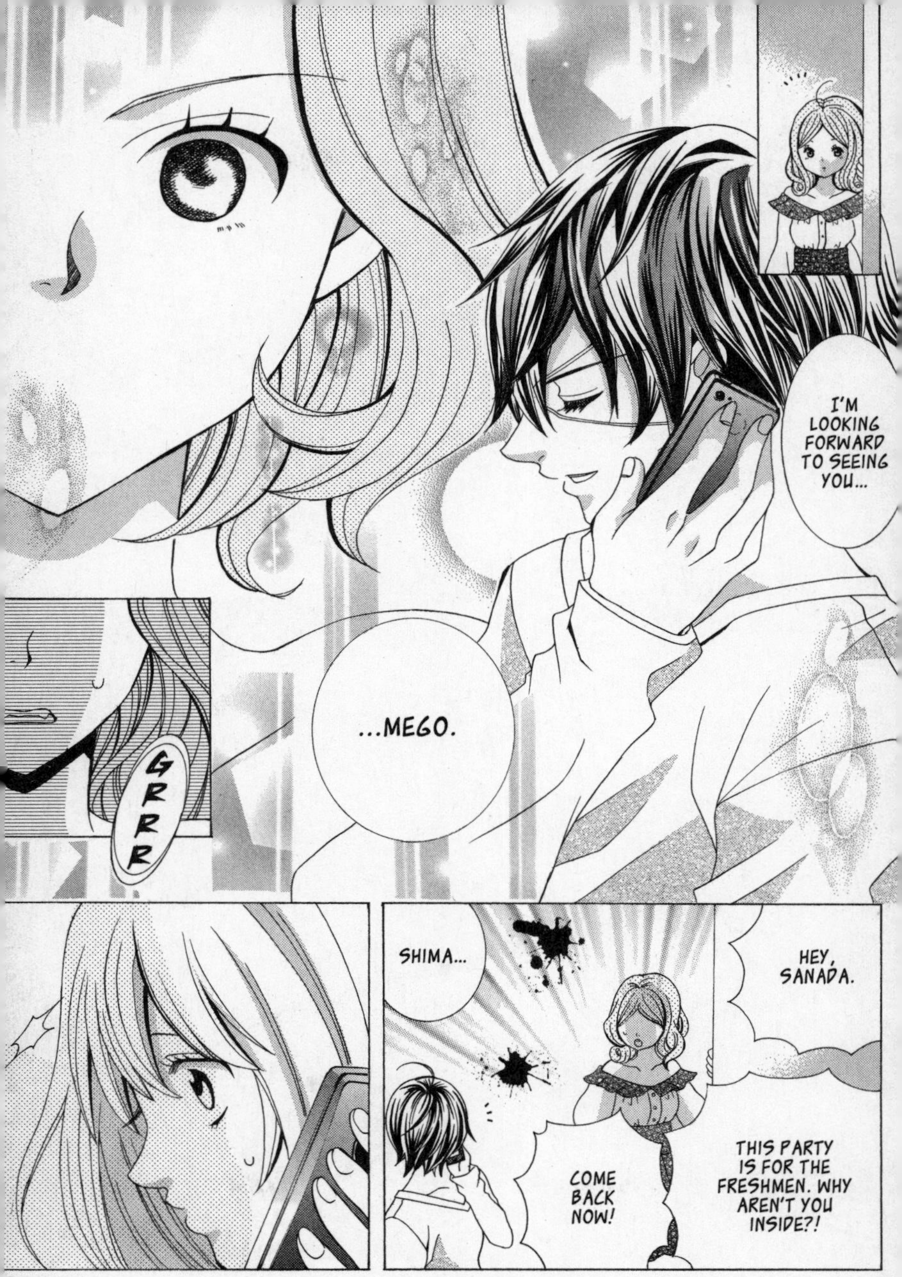
I'M LOOKING FORWARD TO SEEING YOU...
...MEGO.
GRRR
HEY, SANADA.
SHIMA...
THIS PARTY IS FOR THE FRESHMEN. WHY AREN'T YOU INSIDE?!
COME BACK NOW!

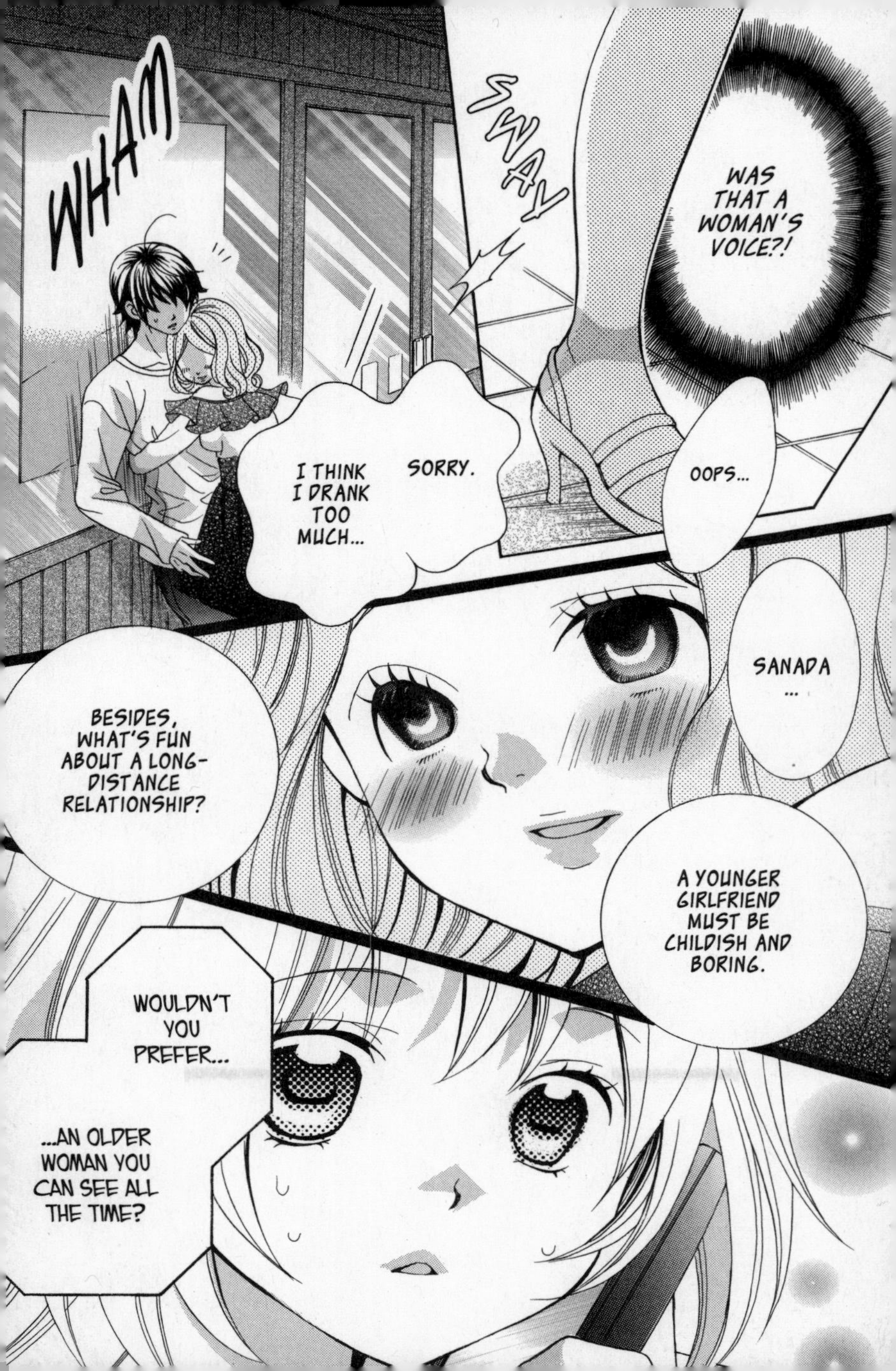
SWAY
WAS THAT A WOMAN'S VOICE?!
OOPS...
WHAM
SORRY.
I THINK I DRANK TOO MUCH...
SANADA ...
BESIDES, WHAT'S FUN ABOUT A LONG-DISTANCE RELATIONSHIP?
A YOUNGER GIRLFRIEND MUST BE CHILDISH AND BORING.
WOULDN'T YOU PREFER...
...AN OLDER WOMAN YOU CAN SEE ALL THE TIME?

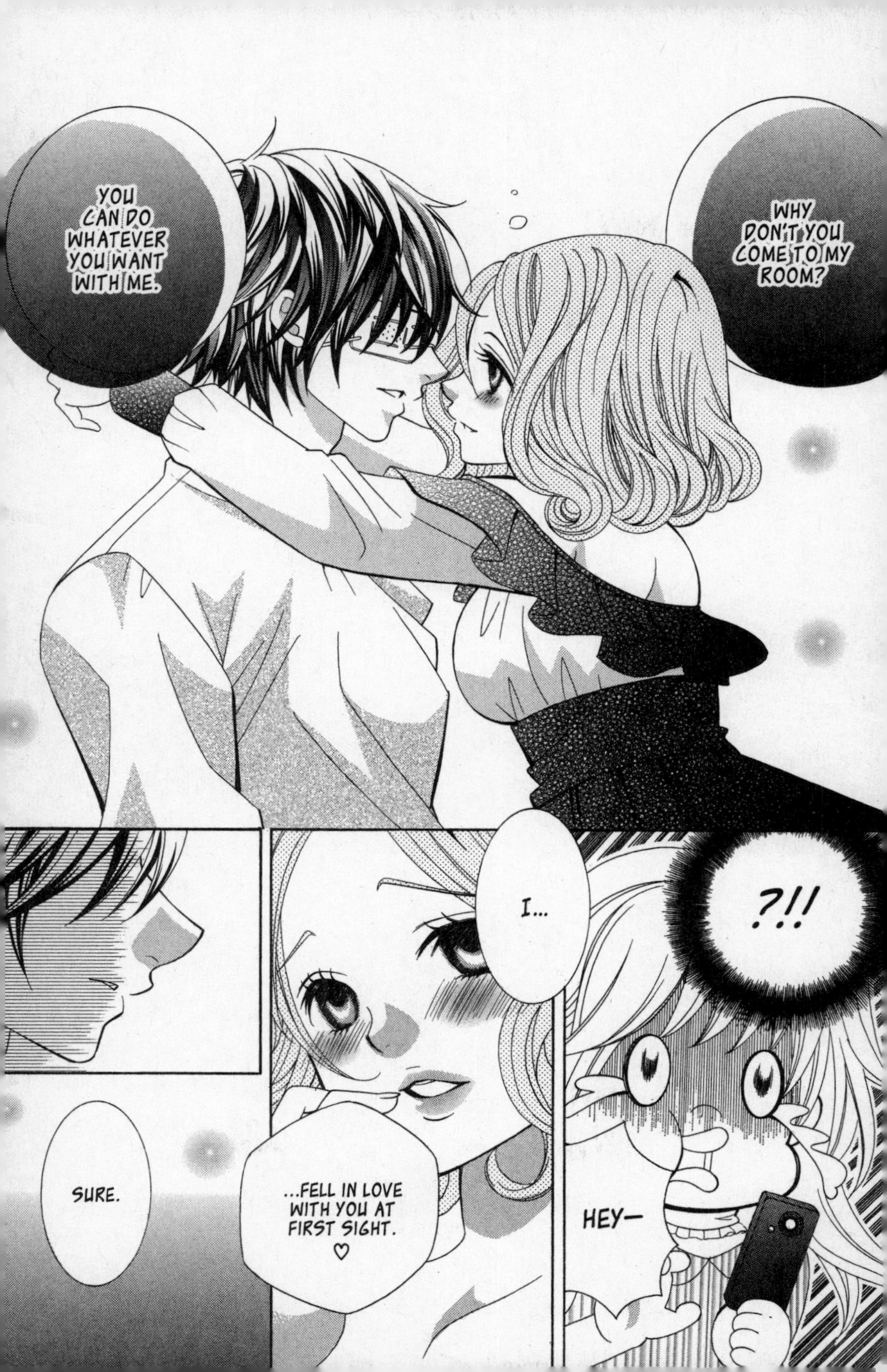
WHY DON'T YOU COME TO MY ROOM?
YOU CAN DO WHATEVER YOU WANT WITH ME.
?!!
HEY—
I...
...FELL IN LOVE WITH YOU AT FIRST SIGHT. ♡
SURE.

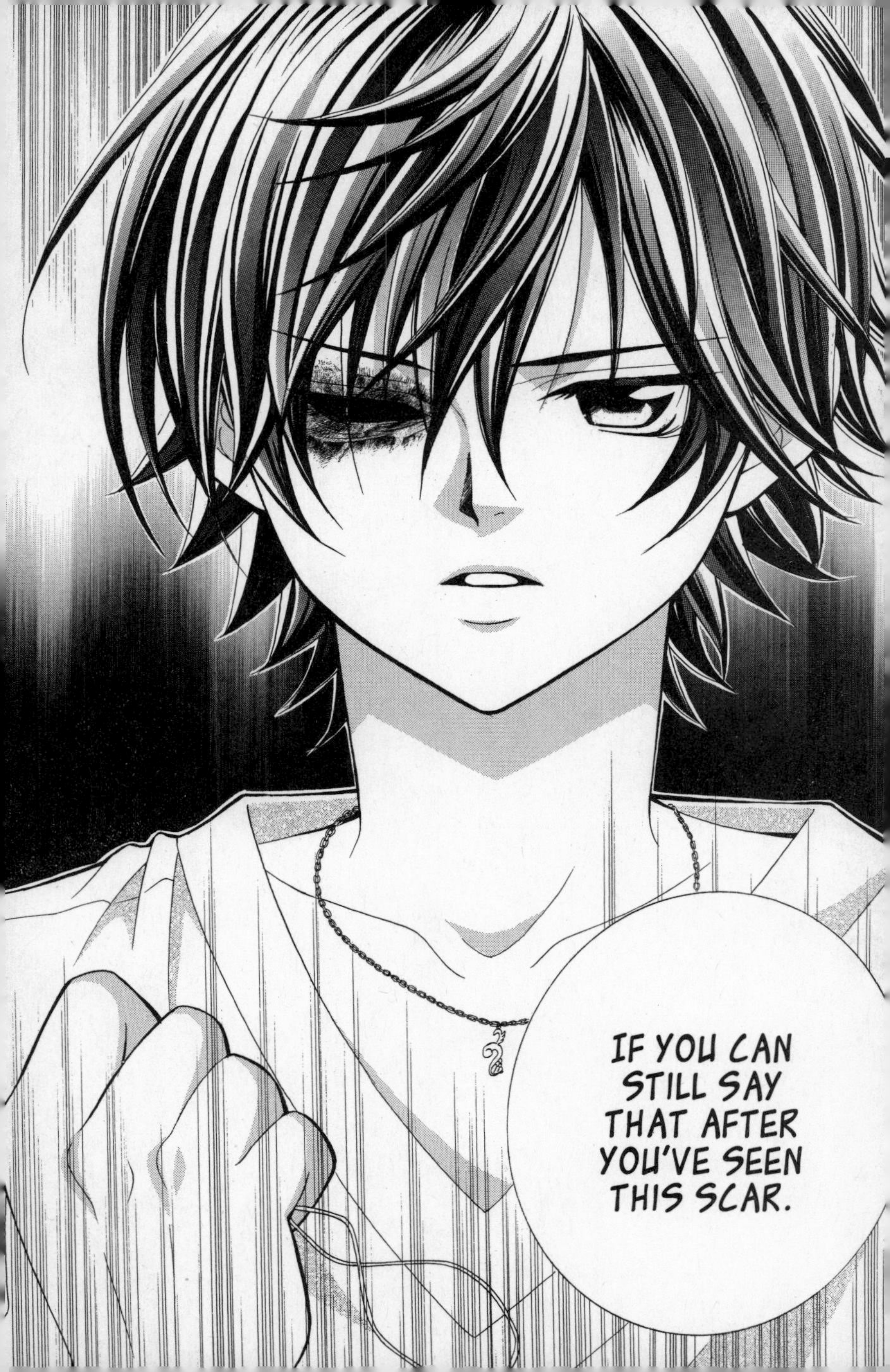
IF YOU CAN STILL SAY THAT AFTER YOU'VE SEEN THIS SCAR.

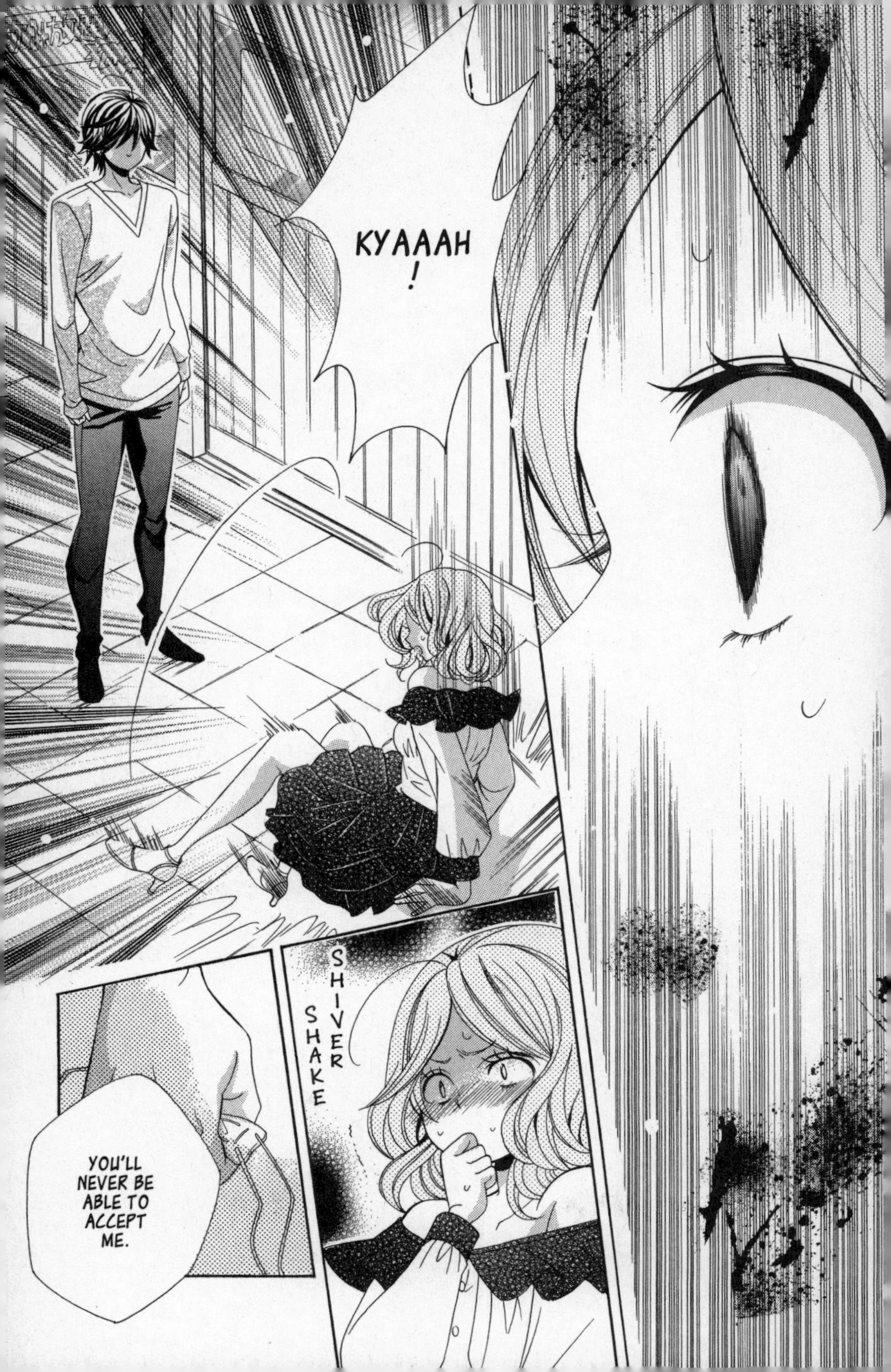
KYAAAH!
SHIVER
SHAKE
YOU'LL NEVER BE ABLE TO ACCEPT ME.

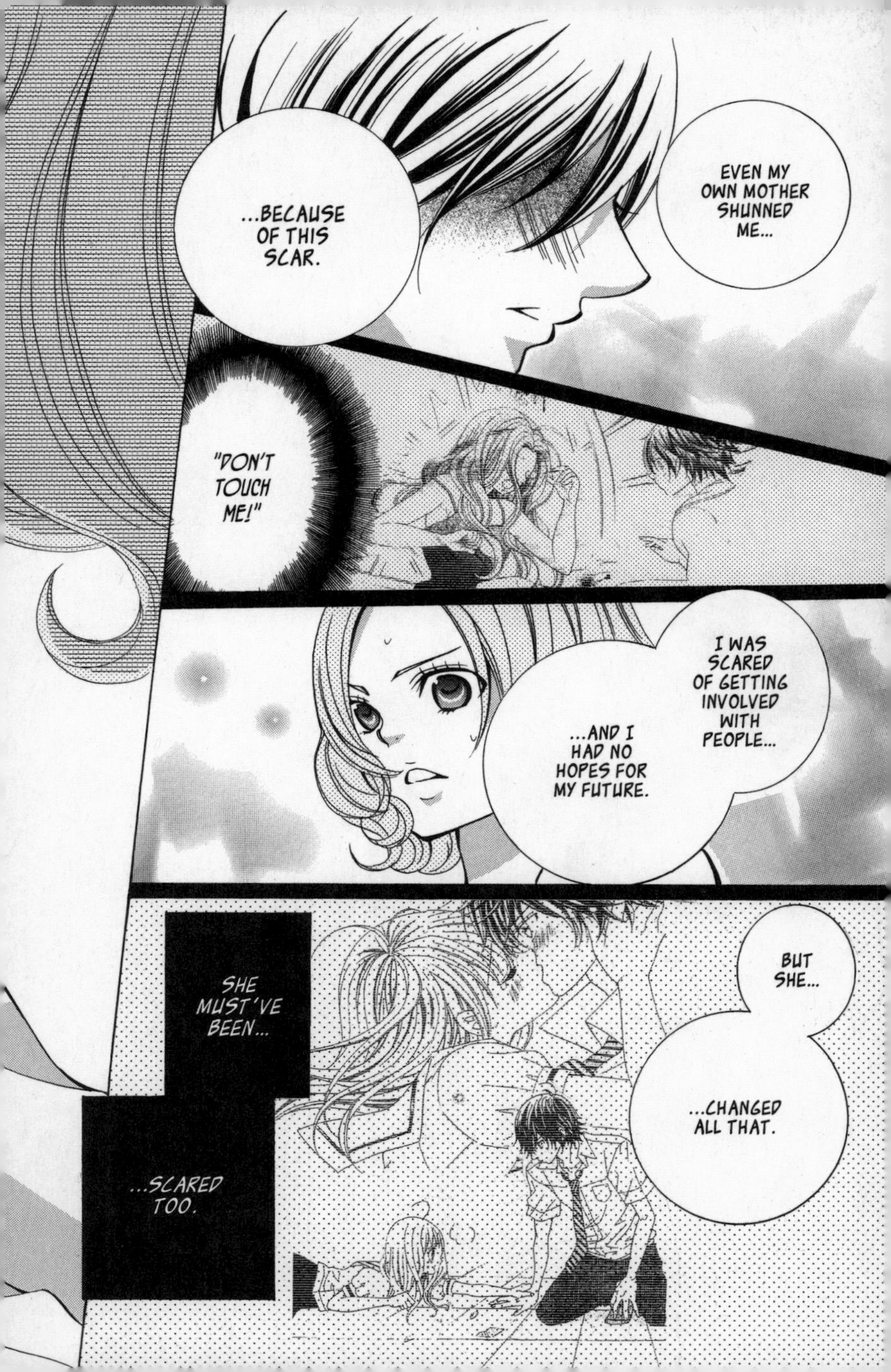
EVEN MY OWN MOTHER SHUNNED ME...
...BECAUSE OF THIS SCAR.
"DON'T TOUCH ME!"
I WAS SCARED OF GETTING INVOLVED WITH PEOPLE...
...AND I HAD NO HOPES FOR MY FUTURE.
BUT SHE...
...CHANGED ALL THAT.
SHE MUST'VE BEEN...
...SCARED TOO.

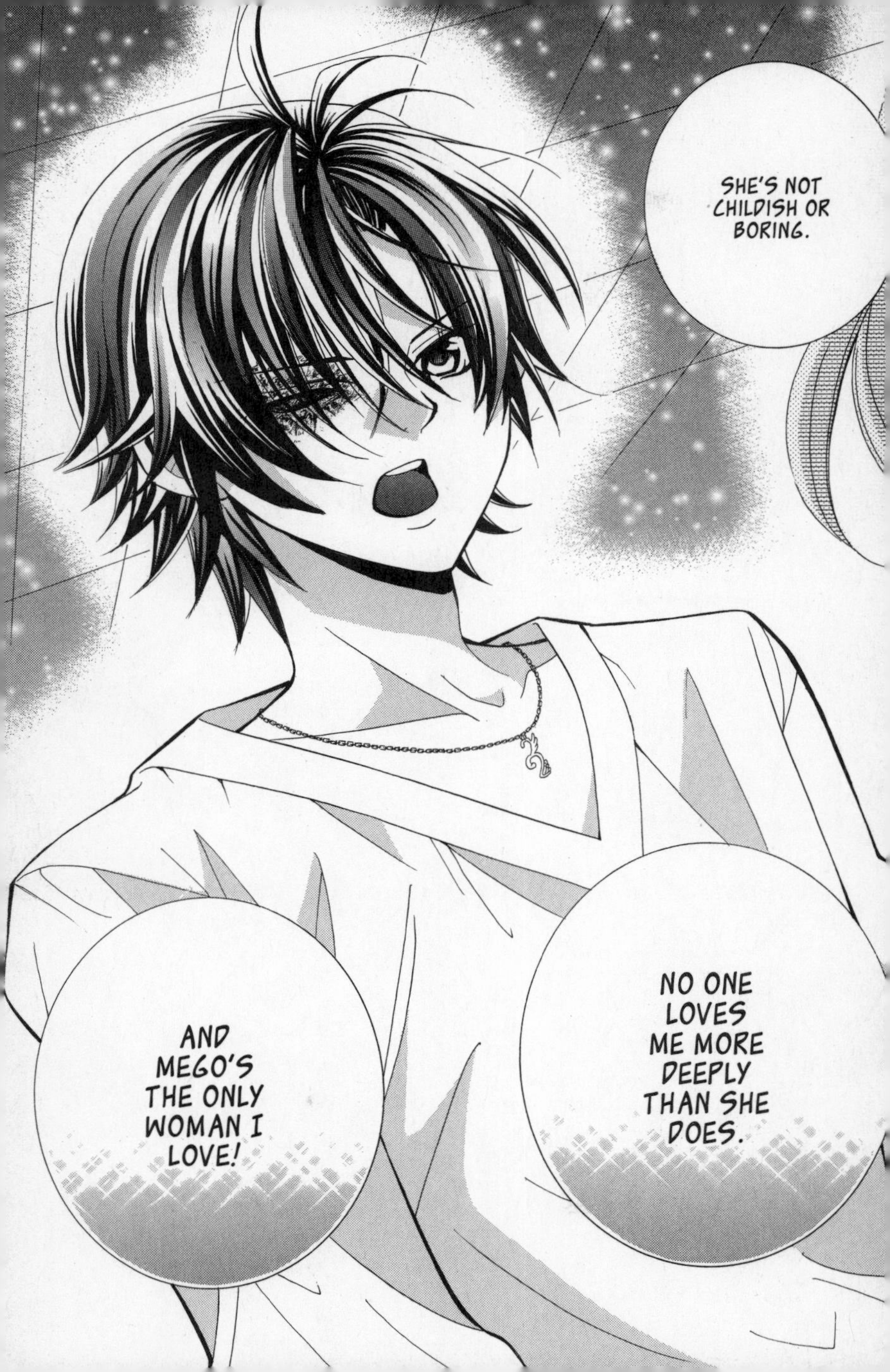
SHE'S NOT CHILDISH OR BORING.
NO ONE LOVES ME MORE DEEPLY THAN SHE DOES.
AND MEGO'S THE ONLY WOMAN I LOVE!

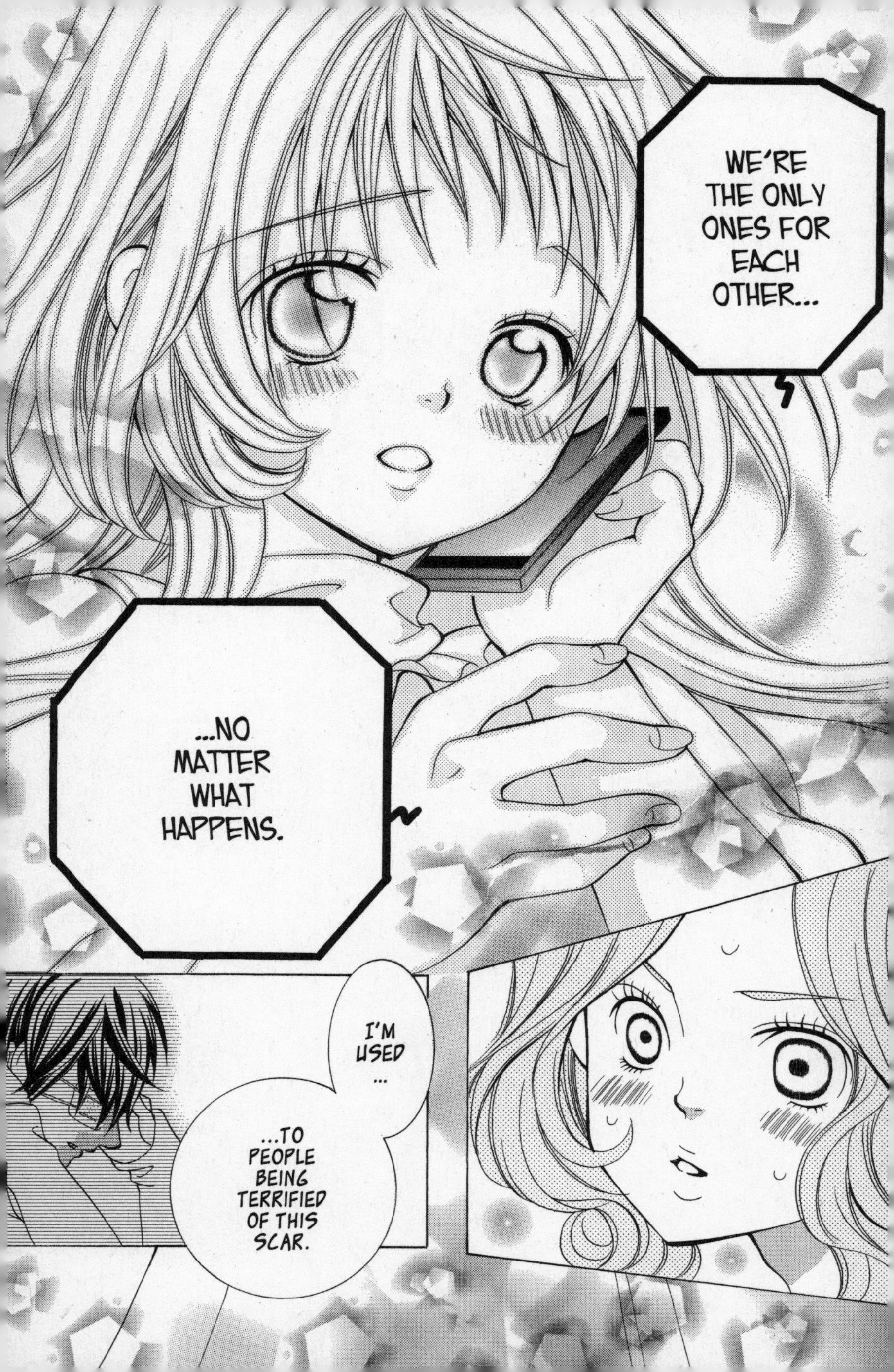
WE'RE THE ONLY ONES FOR EACH OTHER...
...NO MATTER WHAT HAPPENS.
I'M USED ...
...TO PEOPLE BEING TERRIFIED OF THIS SCAR.

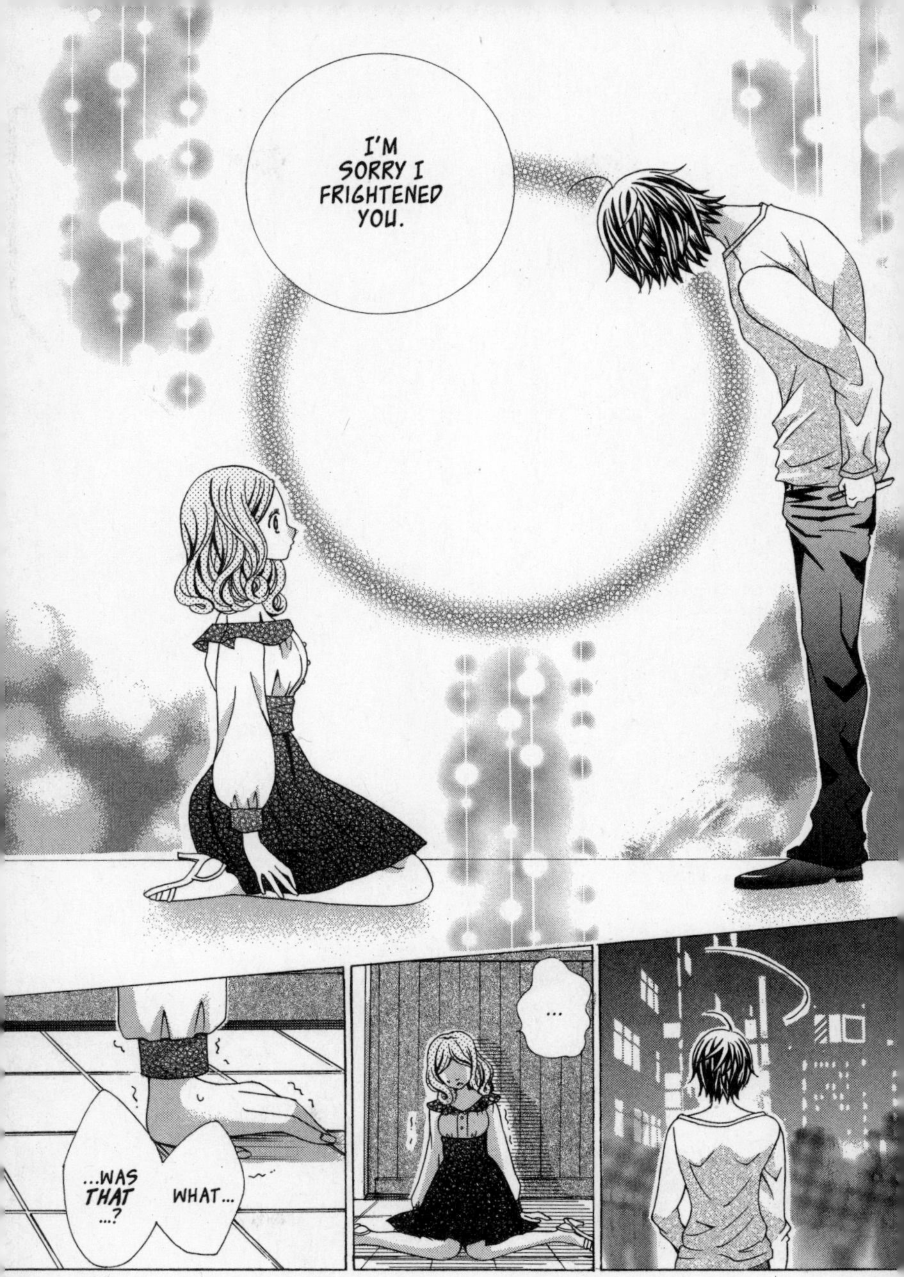
I'M SORRY I FRIGHTENED YOU.
...
WHAT...
...WAS *THAT* ...?

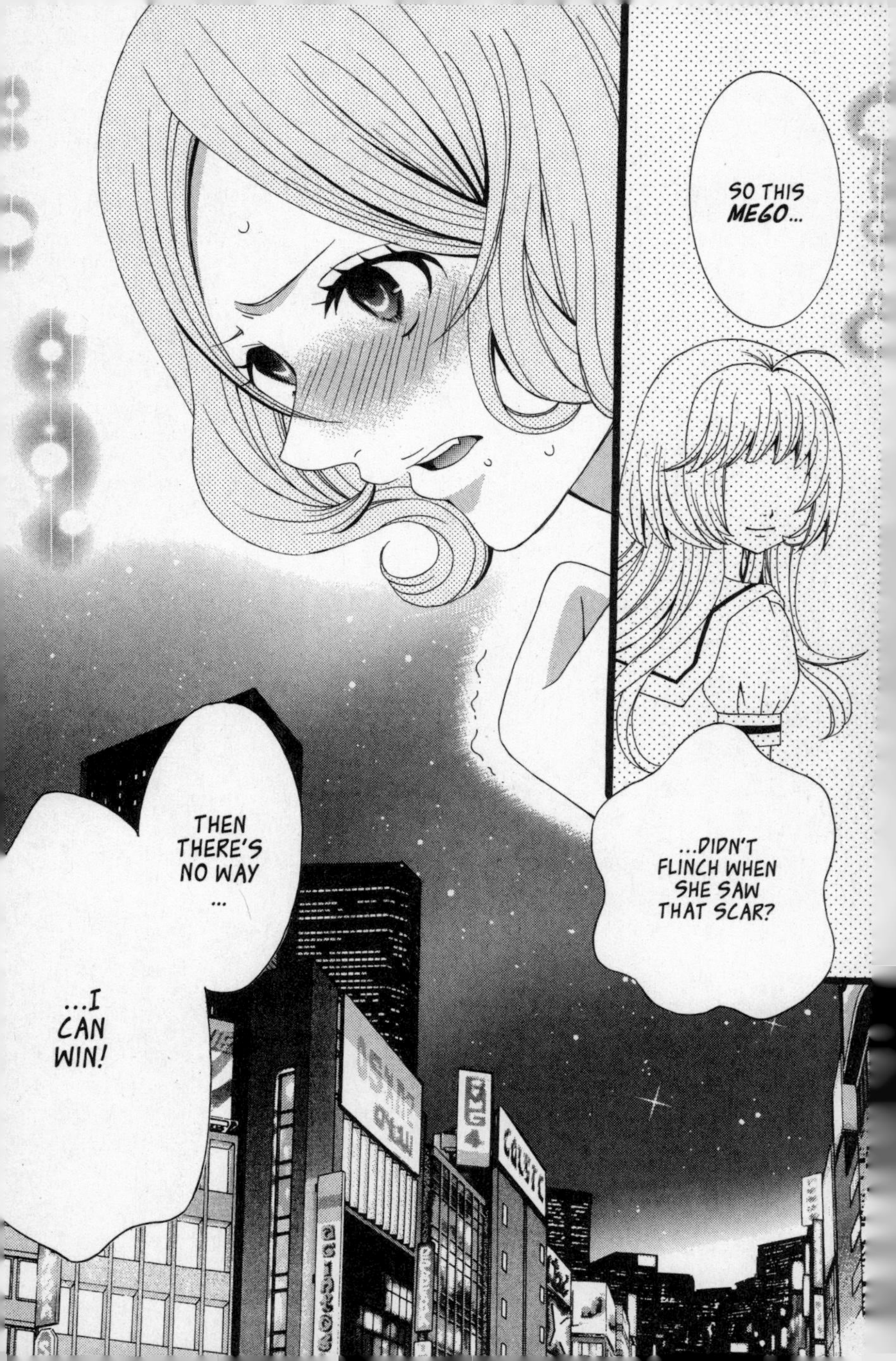
SO THIS MEGO...
...DIDN'T FLINCH WHEN SHE SAW THAT SCAR?
THEN THERE'S NO WAY ...
...I CAN WIN!

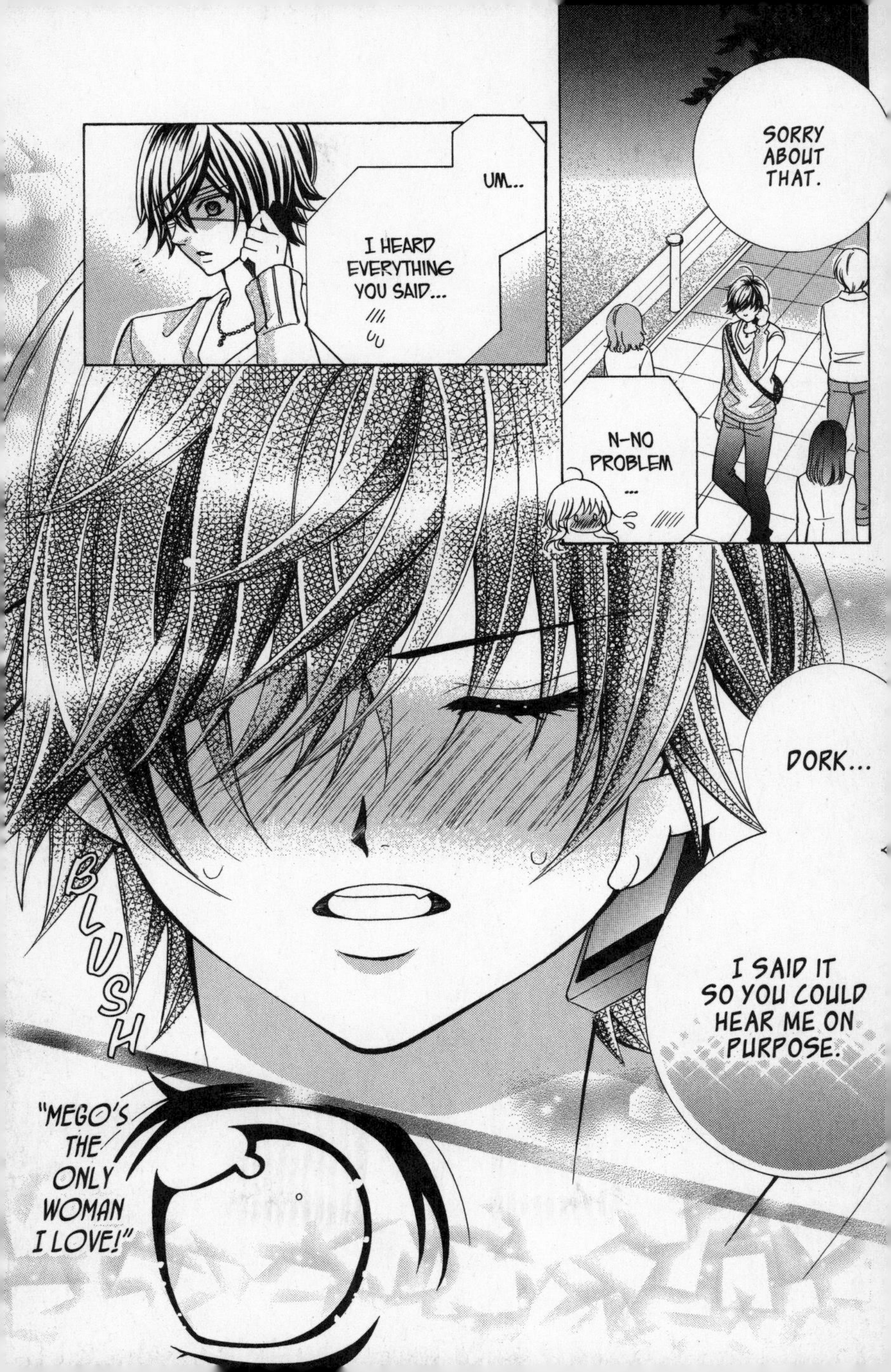
SORRY ABOUT THAT.
N-NO PROBLEM...
UM...
I HEARD EVERYTHING YOU SAID...
DORK...
I SAID IT SO YOU COULD HEAR ME ON PURPOSE.
BLUSH
"MEGO'S THE ONLY WOMAN I LOVE!"

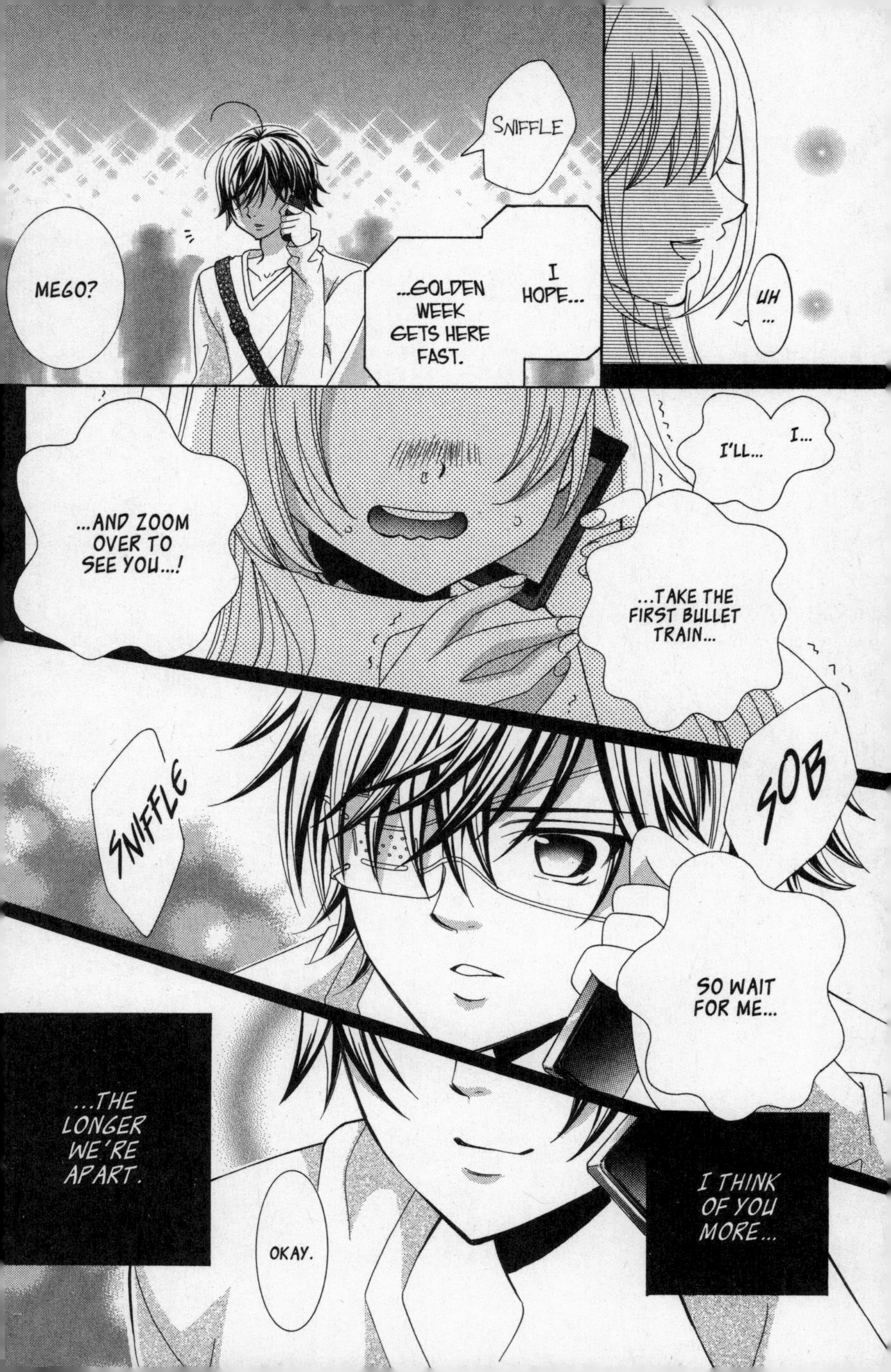
UH ...
SNIFFLE
I HOPE...
...GOLDEN WEEK GETS HERE FAST.
MEGO?
I... I'LL...
...TAKE THE FIRST BULLET TRAIN...
...AND ZOOM OVER TO SEE YOU...!
SOB
SNIFFLE
SO WAIT FOR ME...
I THINK OF YOU MORE...
OKAY.
...THE LONGER WE'RE APART.

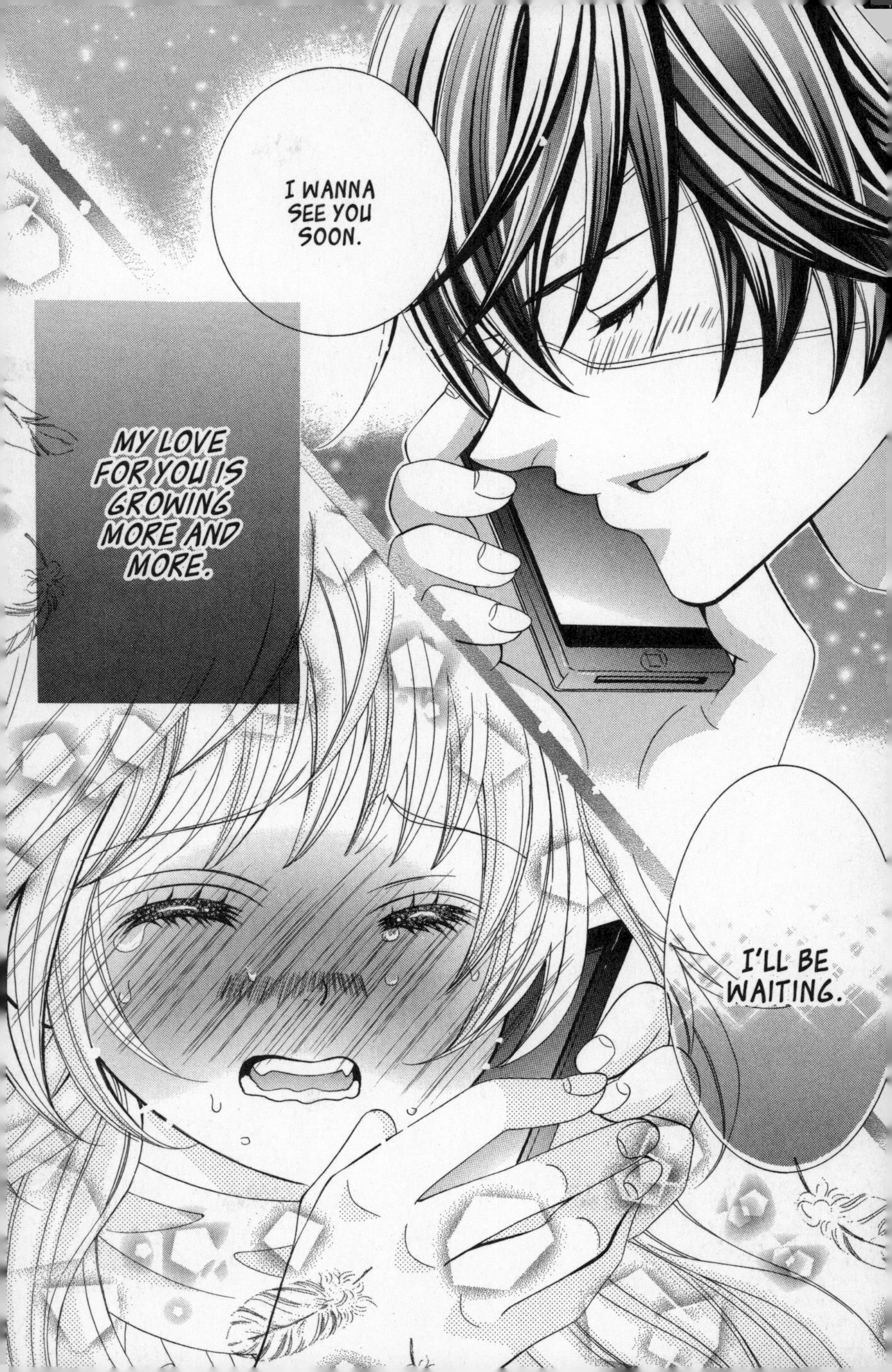
I WANNA SEE YOU SOON.
MY LOVE FOR YOU IS GROWING MORE AND MORE.
I'LL BE WAITING.

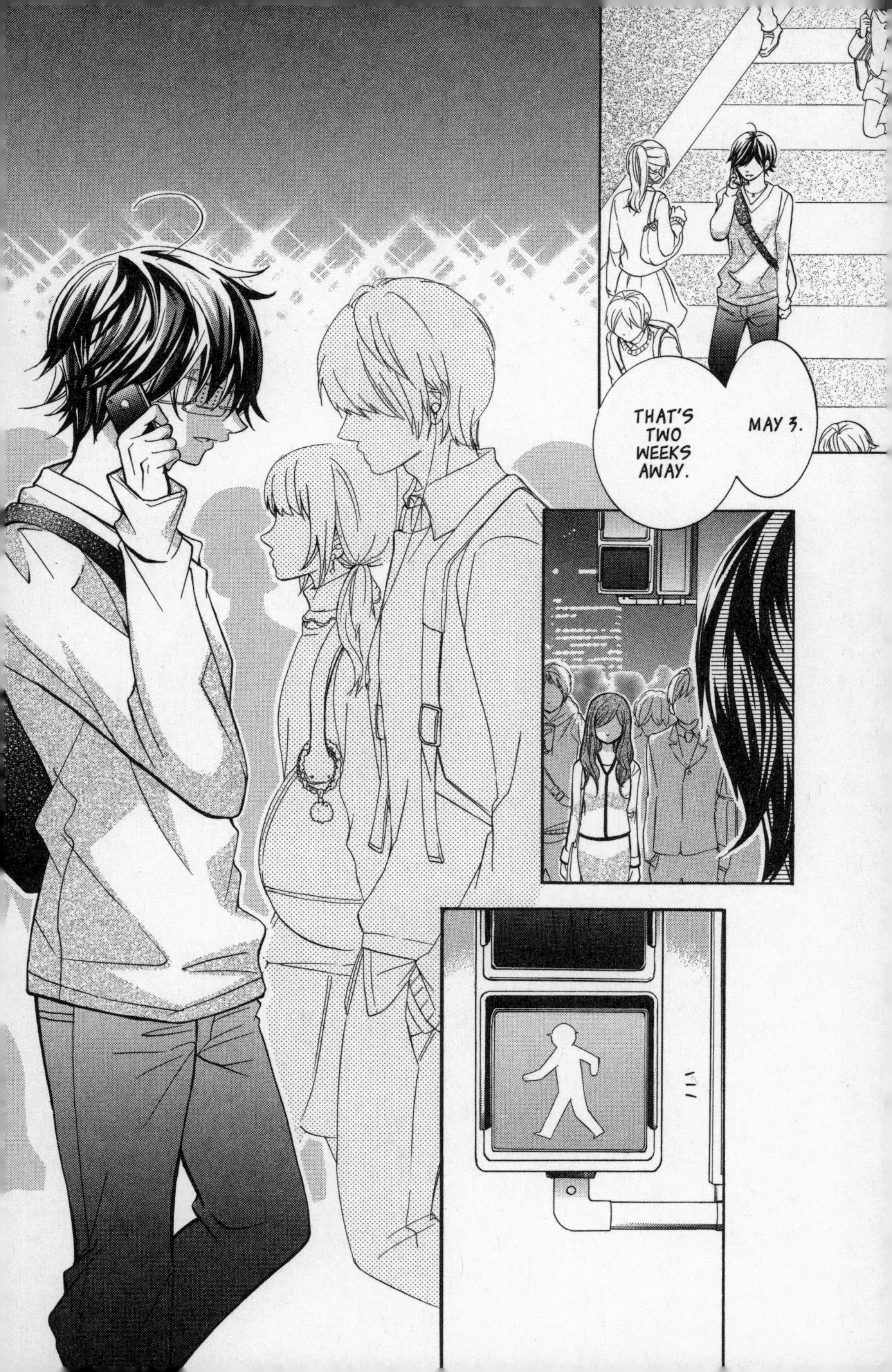
MAY 3.
THAT'S TWO WEEKS AWAY.

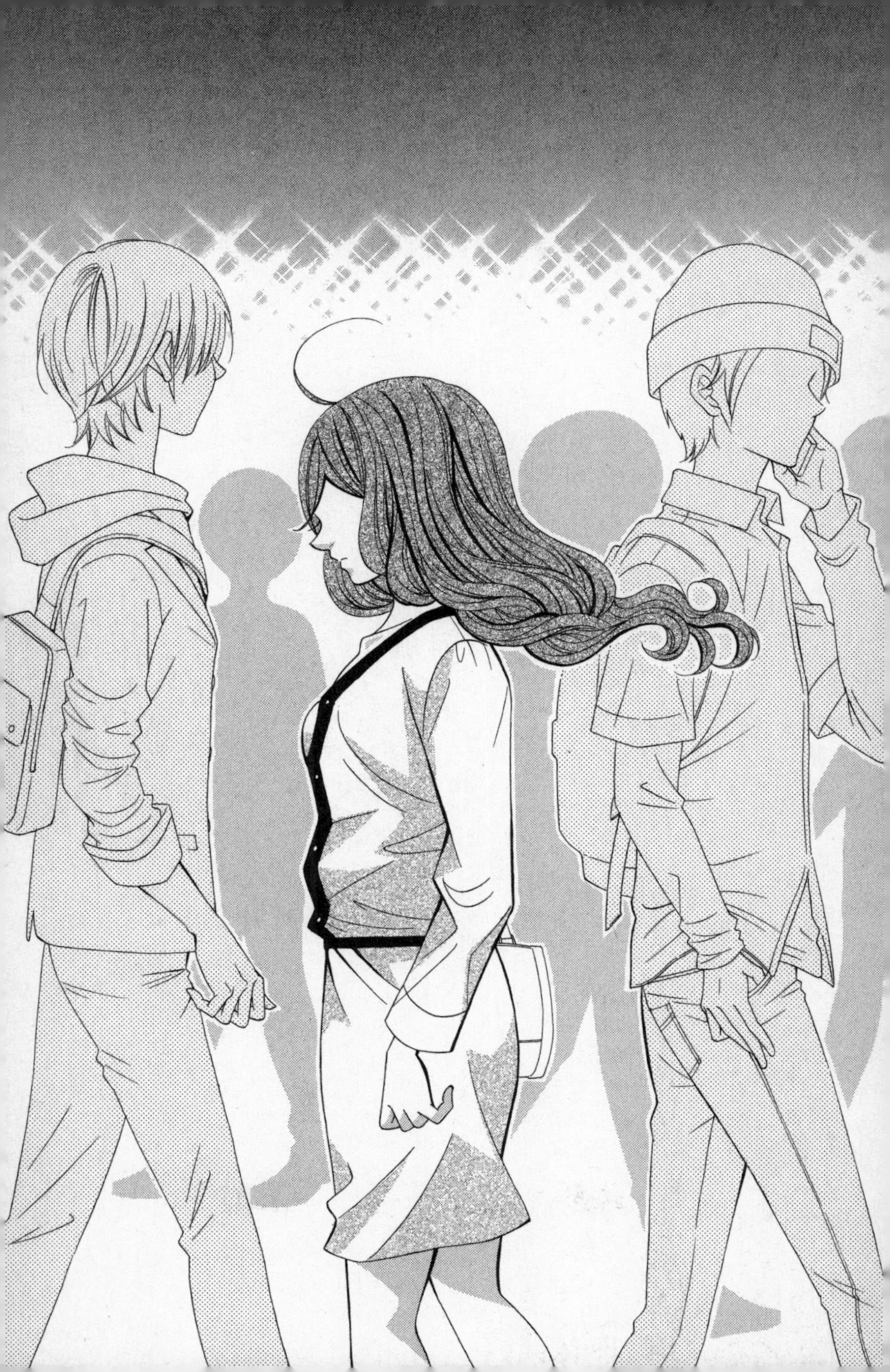

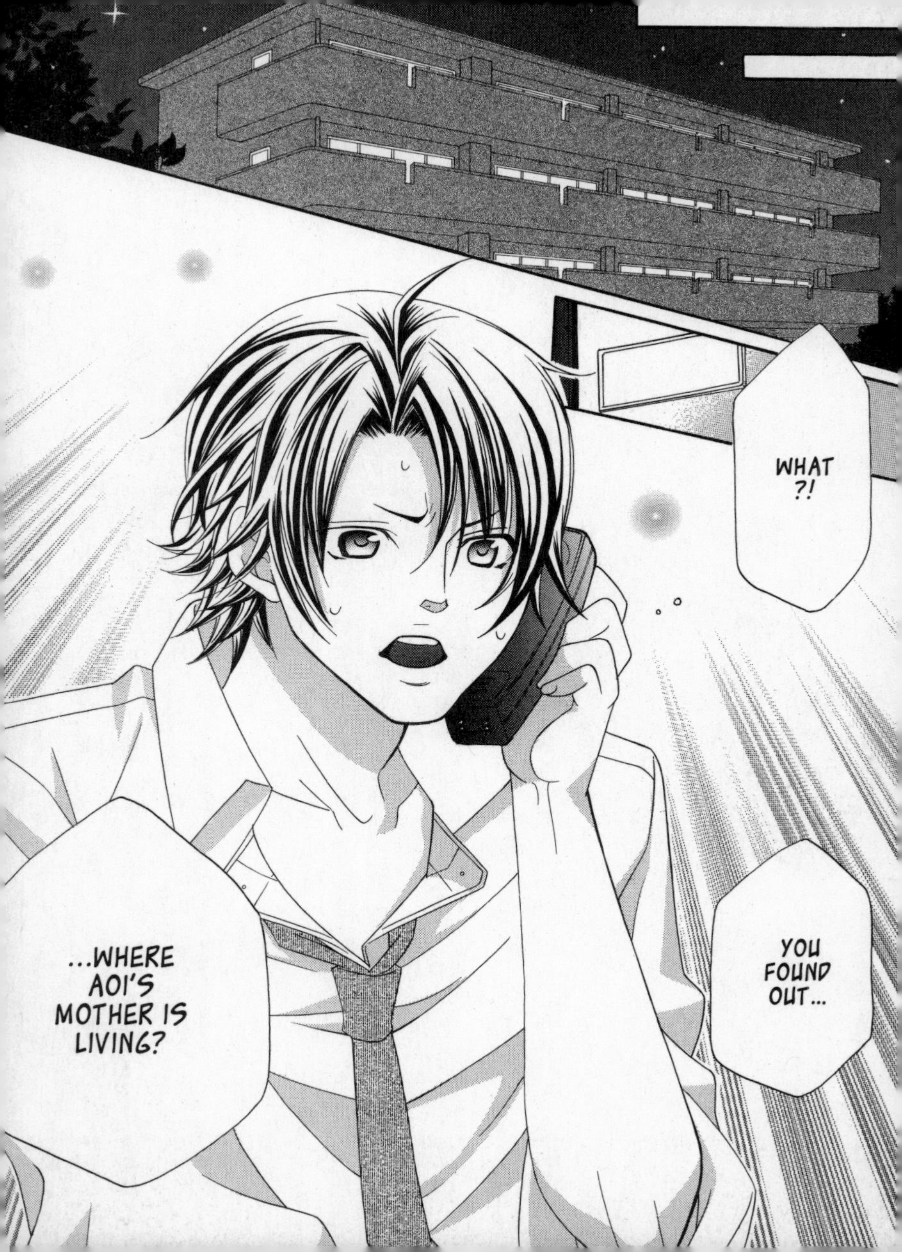
WHAT?!
YOU FOUND OUT...
...WHERE AOI'S MOTHER IS LIVING?

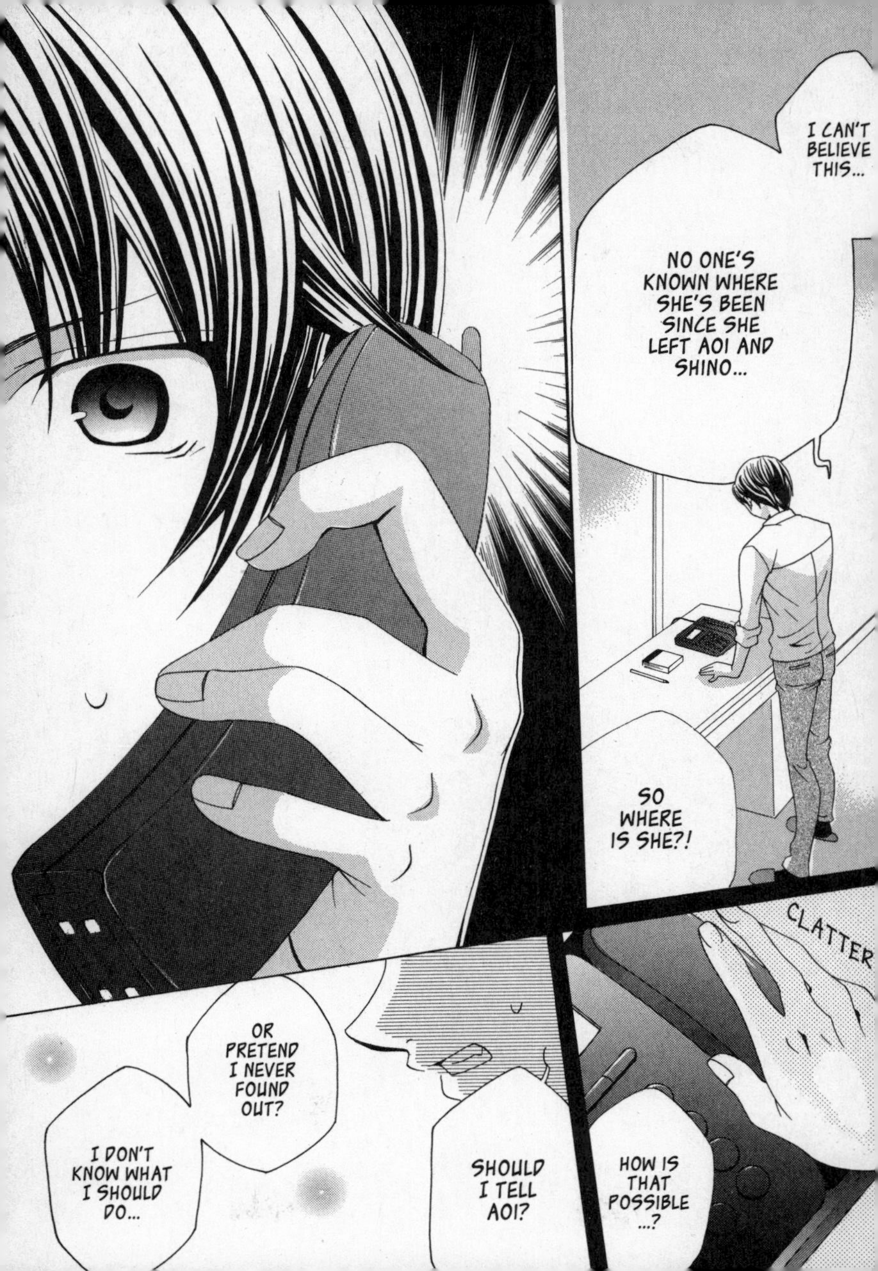
I CAN'T BELIEVE THIS...
NO ONE'S KNOWN WHERE SHE'S BEEN SINCE SHE LEFT AOI AND SHINO...
SO WHERE IS SHE?!
CLATTER
HOW IS THAT POSSIBLE ...?
SHOULD I TELL AOI?
OR PRETEND I NEVER FOUND OUT?
I DON'T KNOW WHAT I SHOULD DO...

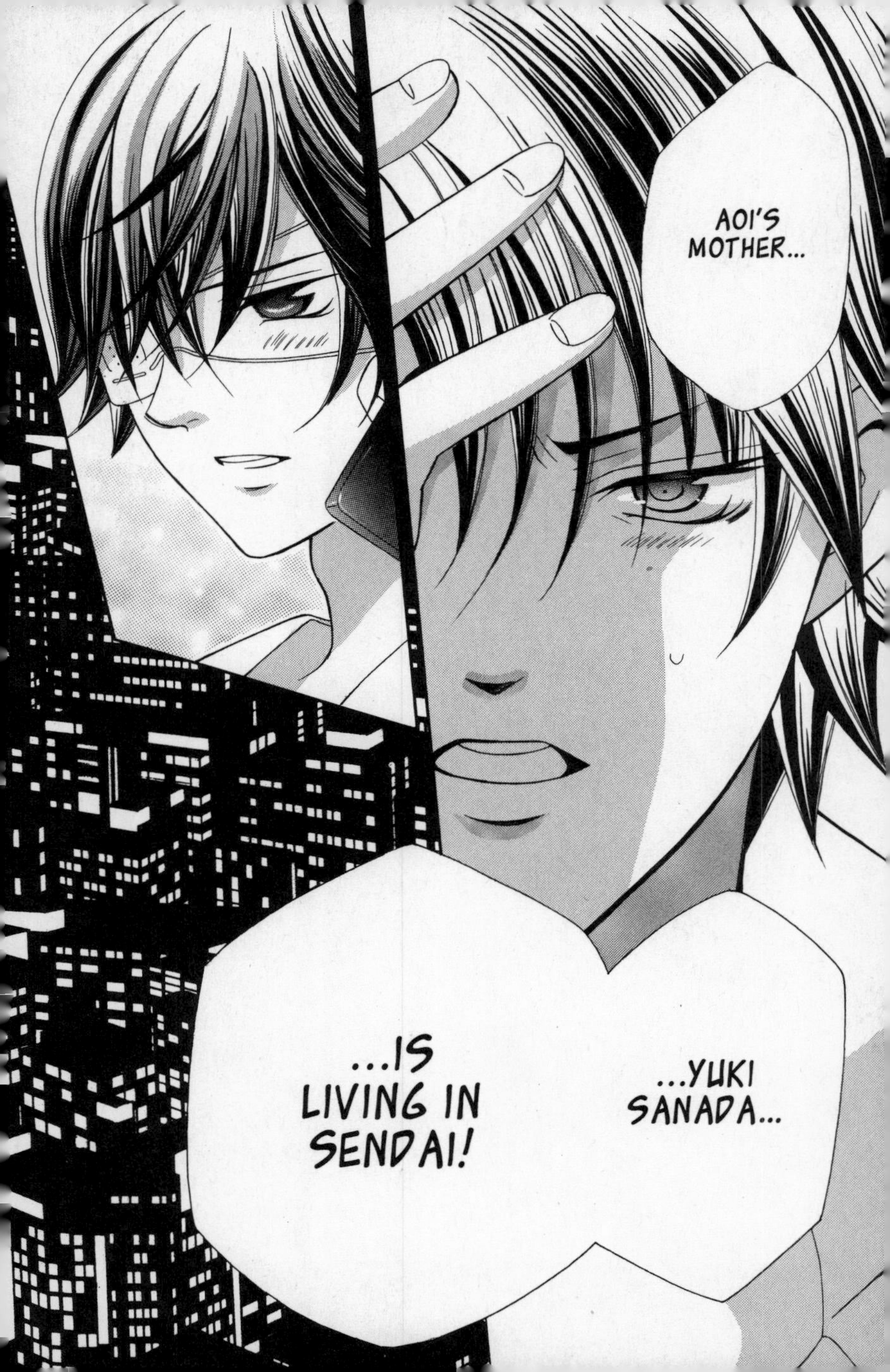
AOI'S MOTHER...
...YUKI SANADA...
...IS LIVING IN SENDAI!

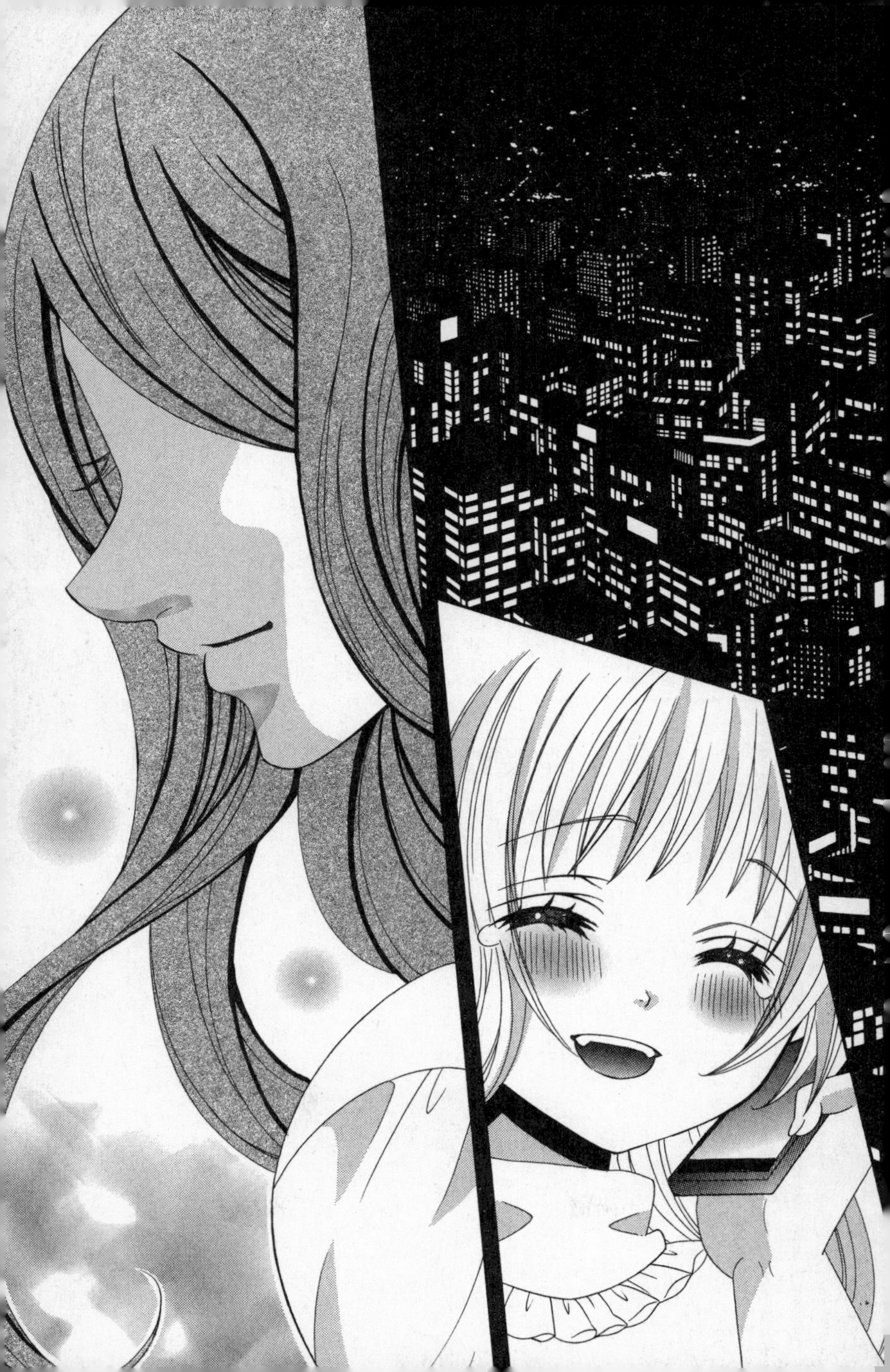

So Cute! Fan Art Feature ♥

EVERYONE'S DRAWINGS ARE SO CUTE, THEY HURT!!

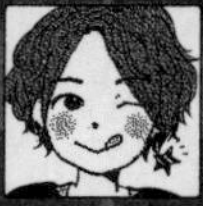

Shoji

Editor Shoji has commented on each one this time!!

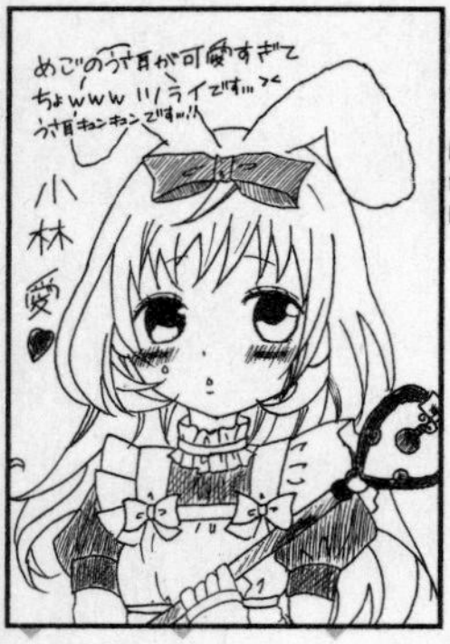

めごのうさ耳が可愛すぎて
ちょwww ツライです…><
うさ耳キュンキュンですっ!!
小林愛

Kazuki Yamauchi (Kumamoto) ←
Ed.: I wanna touch those rabbit ears!!

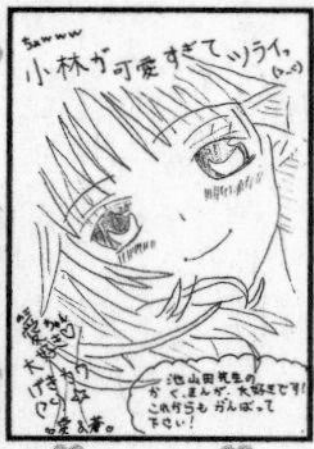

小林ガ可愛すぎてツライっ

Nao Tamura (Hyogo) →
Ed.: Yeah, totally cute!!

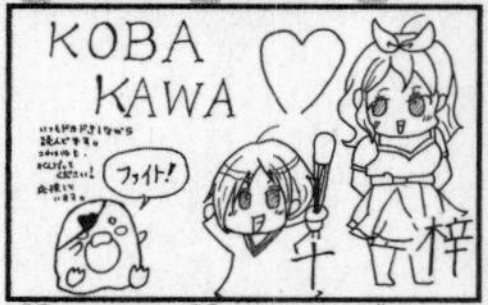

KOBA KAWA
ファイト!
梓

Misa Piyopiyo (Gifu) ↑
Ed.: I'm rooting for their love too!

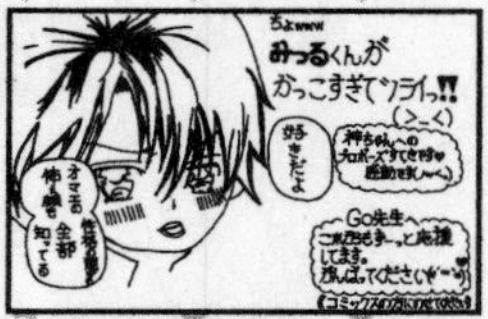

ちょwww みつるくんが かっこすぎてツライっ!!

Yui (Kanagawa) ↑
Ed.: Mitsuru is really manly!

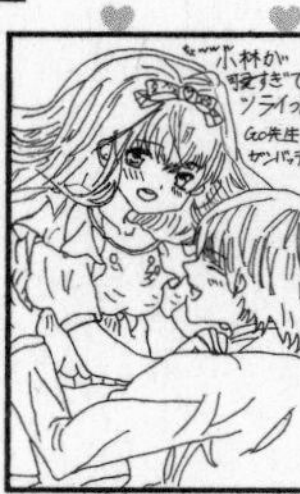

小林が可愛すぎてツライっ!!

Y♡N (Kochi) ←
Ed.: A happy couple! Daddy's happy for you...

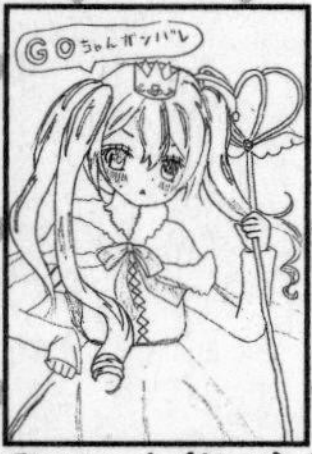

GOちゃんガンバレ

Flower * (Aichi) ↑
Ed.: Oh-ho! The queen is here!!

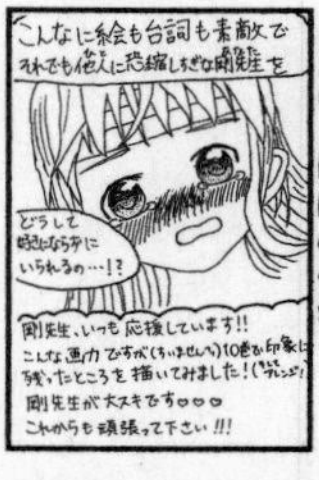

剛先生、いつも応援しています!!
これからも頑張って下さい!!!

Ayumi Momose (Kanagawa) ←
Ed.: I'd die from cuteness overload if someone said this to me.♥

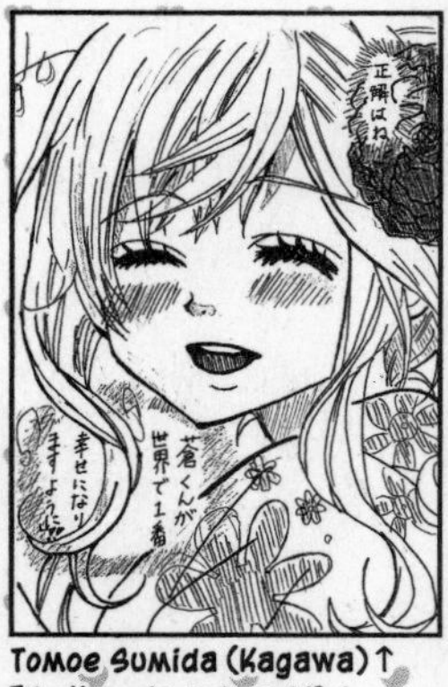

蒼くんが世界で1番

Tomoe Sumida (Kagawa) ↑
Ed.: Mego is so beautiful it hurts...

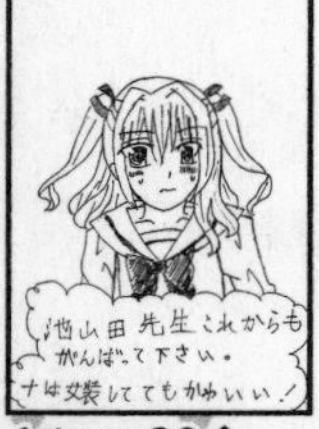

池山田先生これからもがんばって下さい。

SakuranBO (Miyagi) ↑
Ed.: My heart flutters at the cross-dressed Mitsuru!!

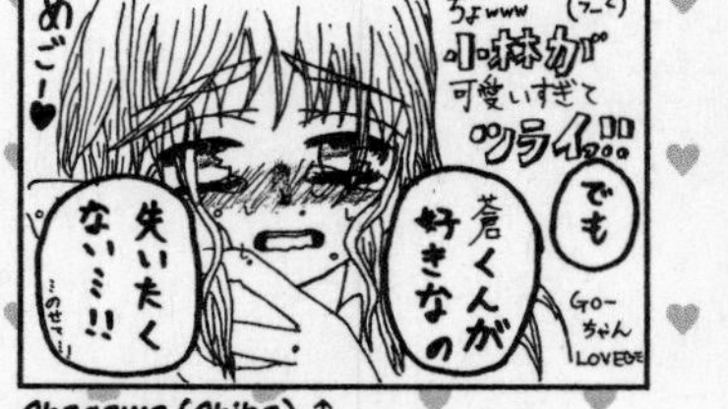

めご…♥
ちょwww 小林が可愛いすぎてツライ…
でも 蒼くんが好きなの
失いたくない…!!
Go-ちゃん LOVE

Chagawa (Chiba) ↑
Ed.: I'm in tears seeing Mego's tears...

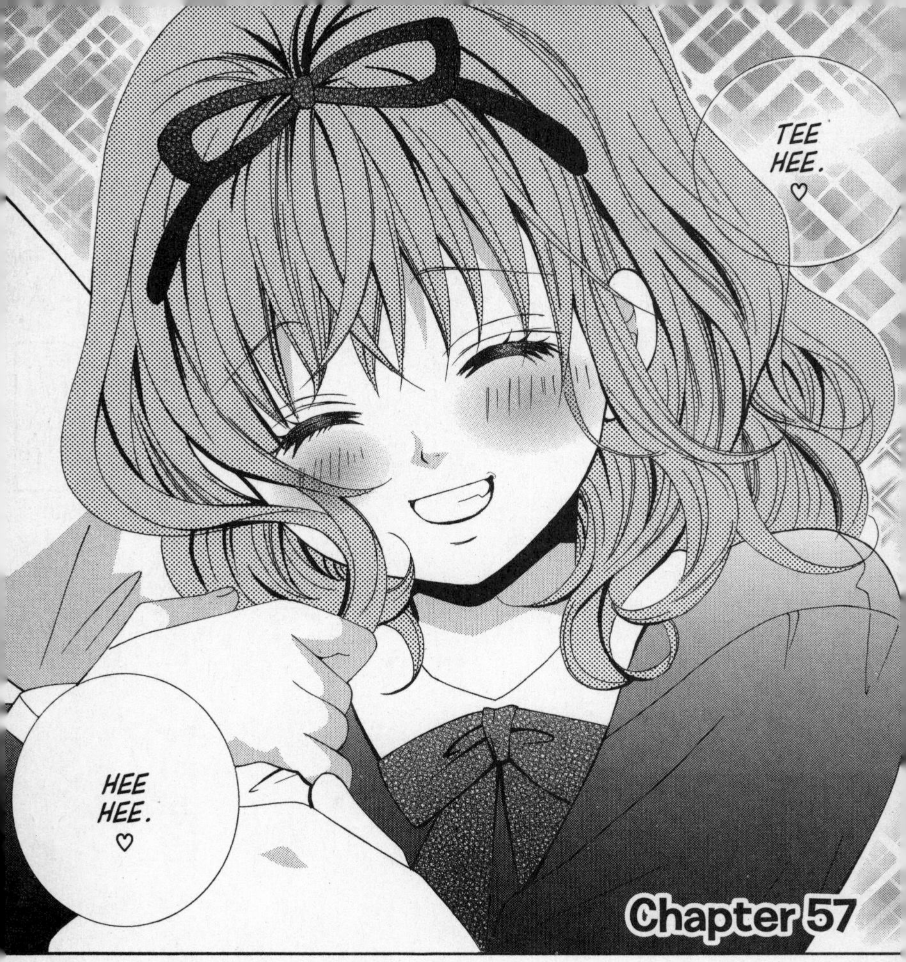
TEE HEE. ♡
HEE HEE. ♡
Chapter 57

THANK YOU FOR ALWAYS SENDING ME LOVELY LETTERS AND DRAWINGS. ♡ THANK YOU TO MY READERS WHO SENT ME GIFTS FOR MY BIRTHDAY IN MAY!! I'M VERY GRATEFUL FOR YOUR THOUGHTS!! (ToT)

PLEASE SEND YOUR THOUGHTS AND ANY REQUESTS REGARDING THE SERIES AFTER READING VOLUME 12. ♡

GO IKEYAMADA
C/O SHOJO BEAT
VIZ MEDIA, LLC
P.O. BOX 77010
SAN FRANCISCO, CA
94107 (^o^)

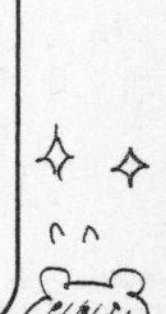

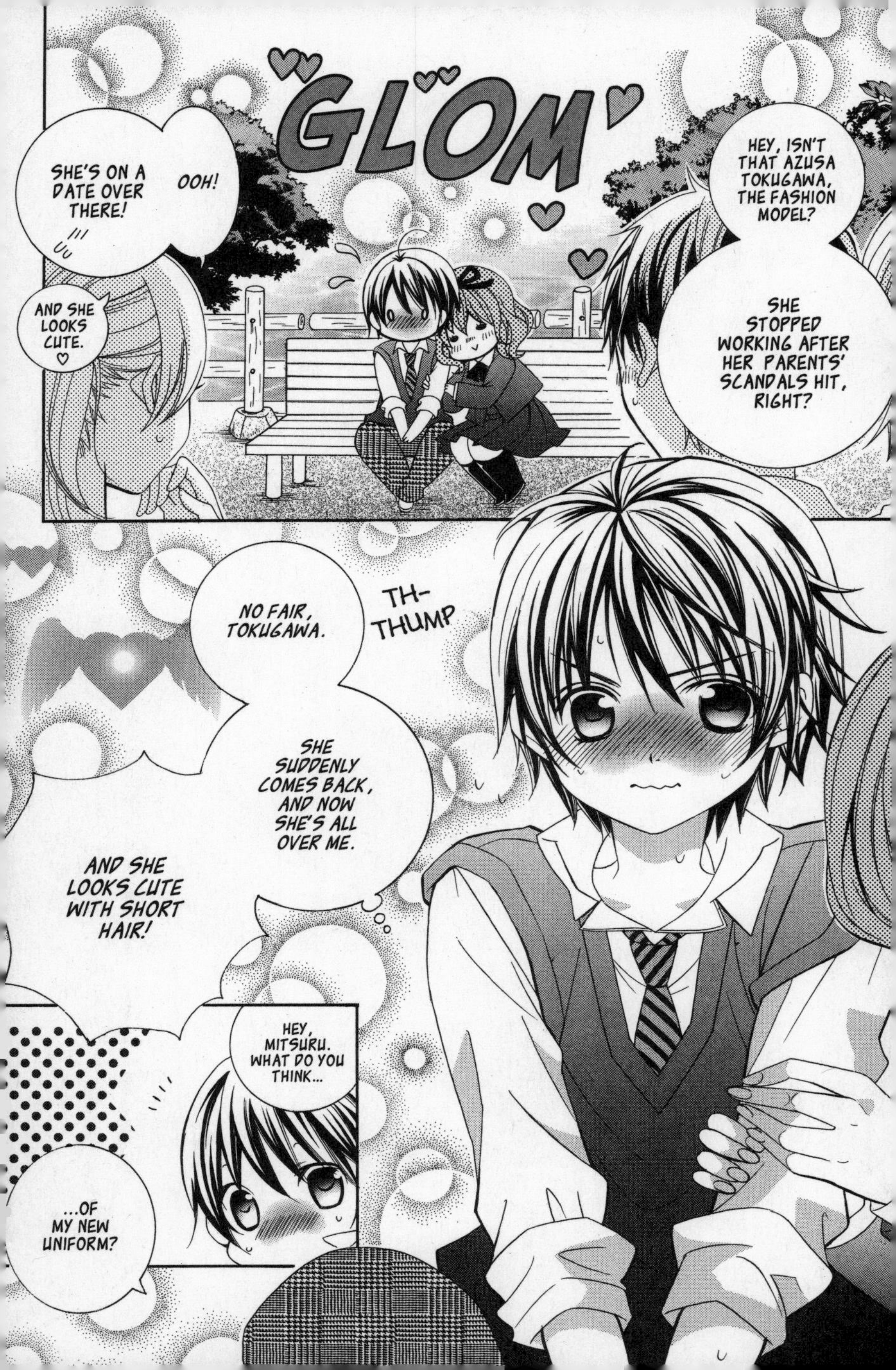
HEY, ISN'T THAT AZUSA TOKUGAWA, THE FASHION MODEL?
SHE STOPPED WORKING AFTER HER PARENTS' SCANDALS HIT, RIGHT?
GLOM
SHE'S ON A DATE OVER THERE!
OOH!
AND SHE LOOKS CUTE. ♡
NO FAIR, TOKUGAWA.
TH-THUMP
SHE SUDDENLY COMES BACK, AND NOW SHE'S ALL OVER ME.
AND SHE LOOKS CUTE WITH SHORT HAIR!
HEY, MITSURU. WHAT DO YOU THINK...
...OF MY NEW UNIFORM?

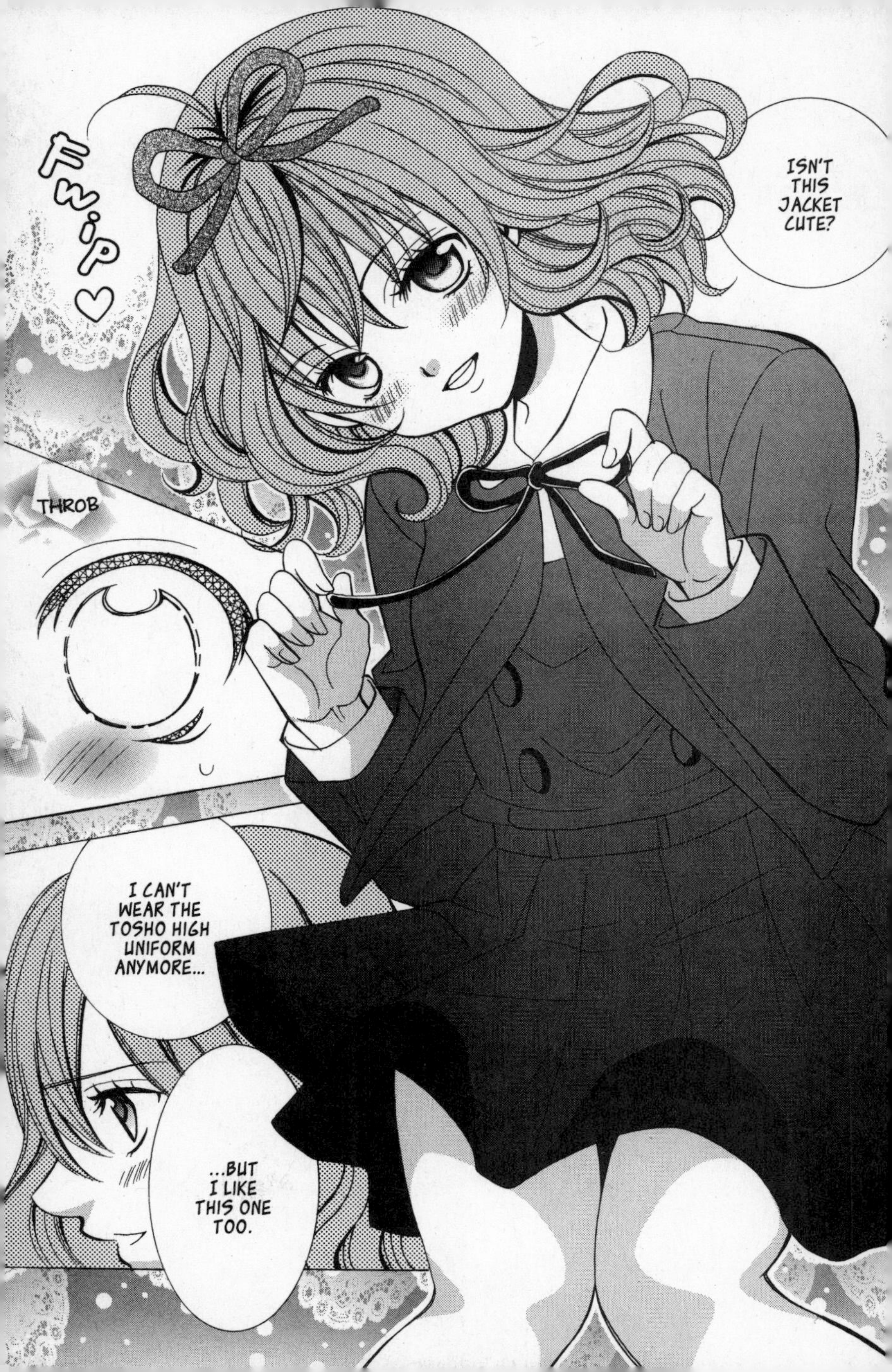
ISN'T THIS JACKET CUTE?
Fwip♥
THROB
I CAN'T WEAR THE TOSHO HIGH UNIFORM ANYMORE...
...BUT I LIKE THIS ONE TOO.

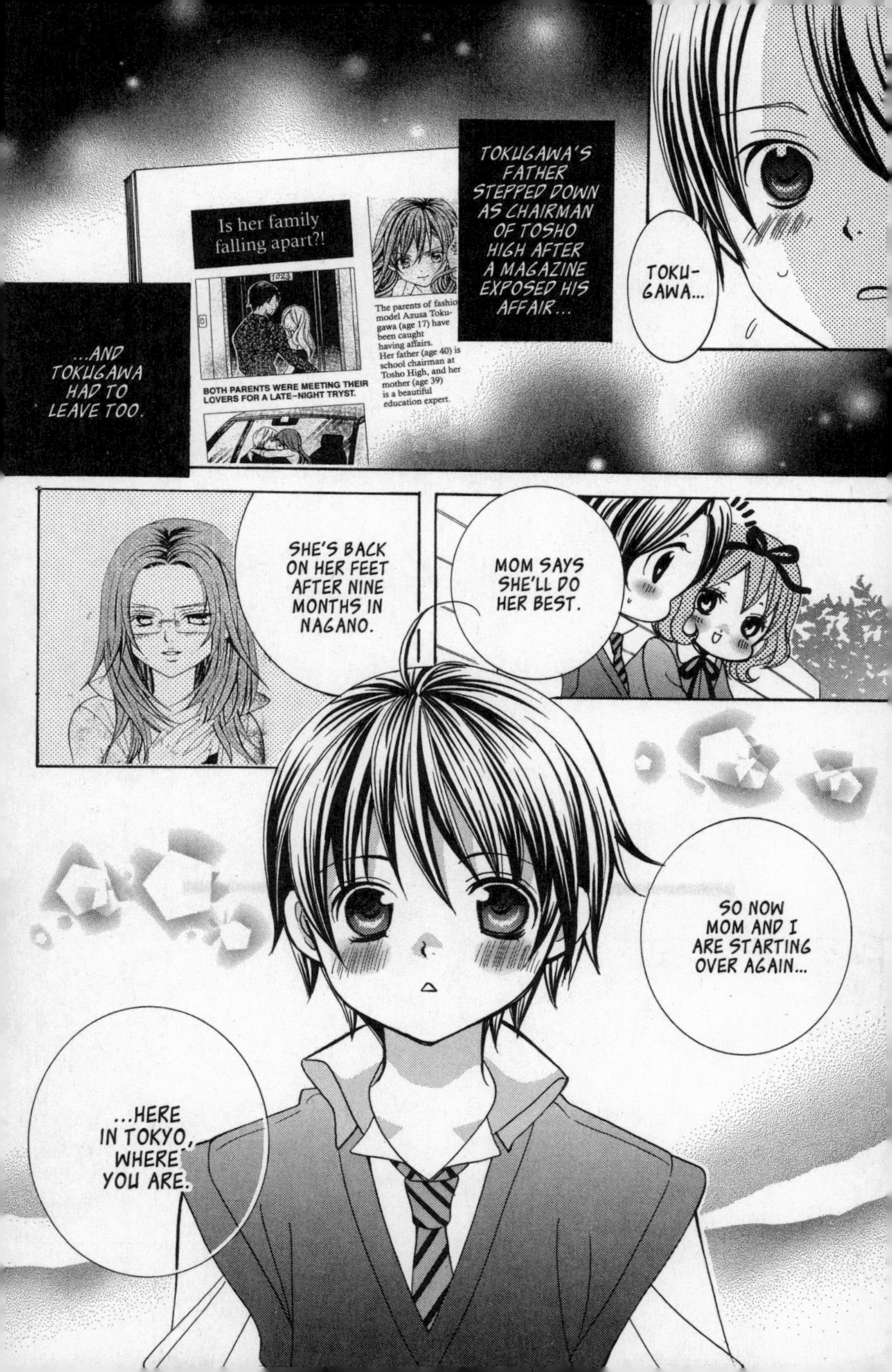
TOKU-GAWA...
TOKUGAWA'S FATHER STEPPED DOWN AS CHAIRMAN OF TOSHO HIGH AFTER A MAGAZINE EXPOSED HIS AFFAIR...
Is her family falling apart?!
The parents of fashio model Azusa Toku-gawa (age 17) have been caught having affairs. Her father (age 40) is school chairman at Tosho High, and her mother (age 39) is a beautiful education expert.
BOTH PARENTS WERE MEETING THEIR LOVERS FOR A LATE-NIGHT TRYST.
...AND TOKUGAWA HAD TO LEAVE TOO.
MOM SAYS SHE'LL DO HER BEST.
SHE'S BACK ON HER FEET AFTER NINE MONTHS IN NAGANO.
SO NOW MOM AND I ARE STARTING OVER AGAIN...
...HERE IN TOKYO, WHERE YOU ARE.

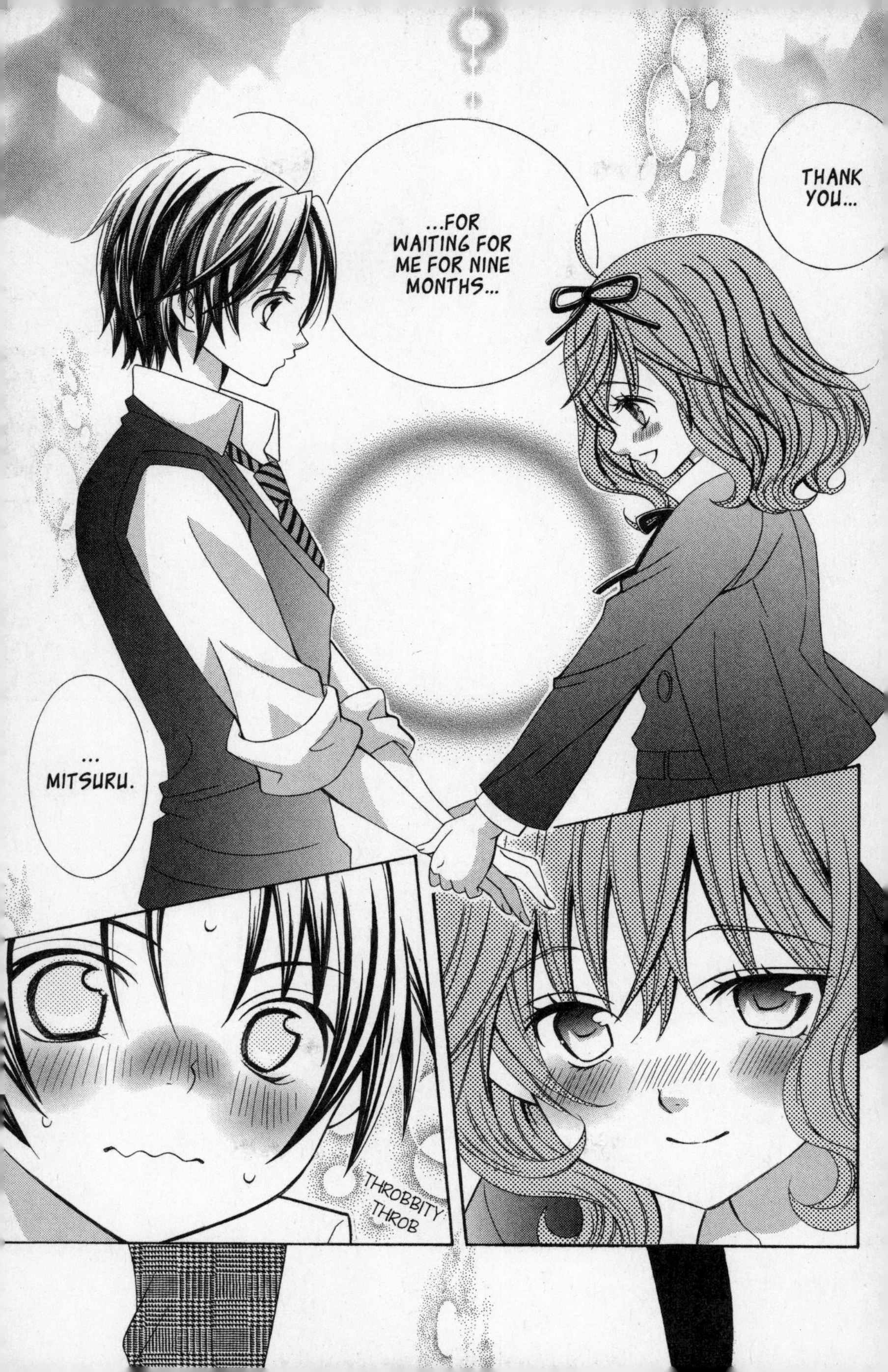
THANK YOU...
...FOR WAITING FOR ME FOR NINE MONTHS...
... MITSURU.
THROBBITY THROB

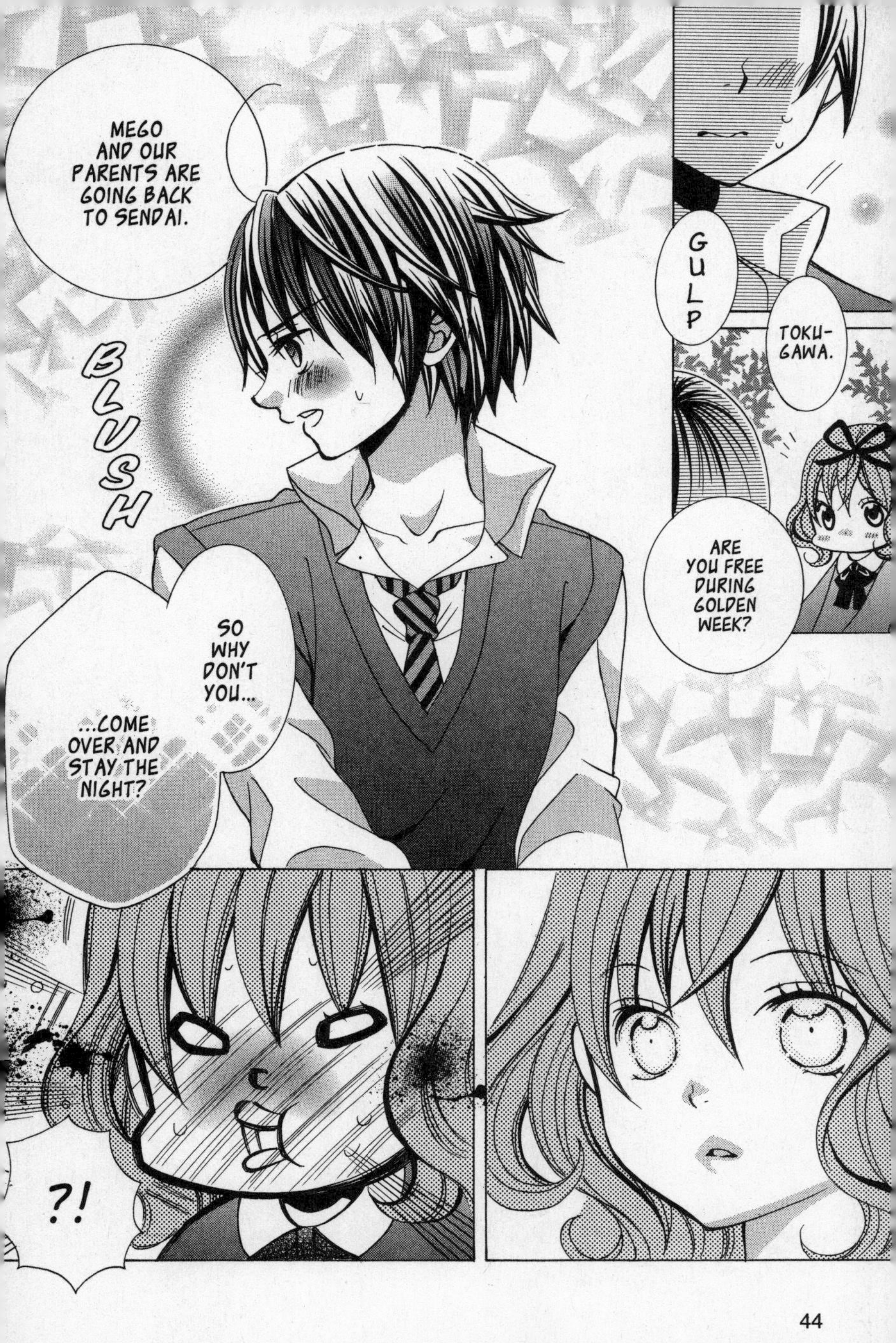
GULP
TOKU-GAWA.
ARE YOU FREE DURING GOLDEN WEEK?
MEGO AND OUR PARENTS ARE GOING BACK TO SENDAI.
BLUSH
SO WHY DON'T YOU...
...COME OVER AND STAY THE NIGHT?
?!

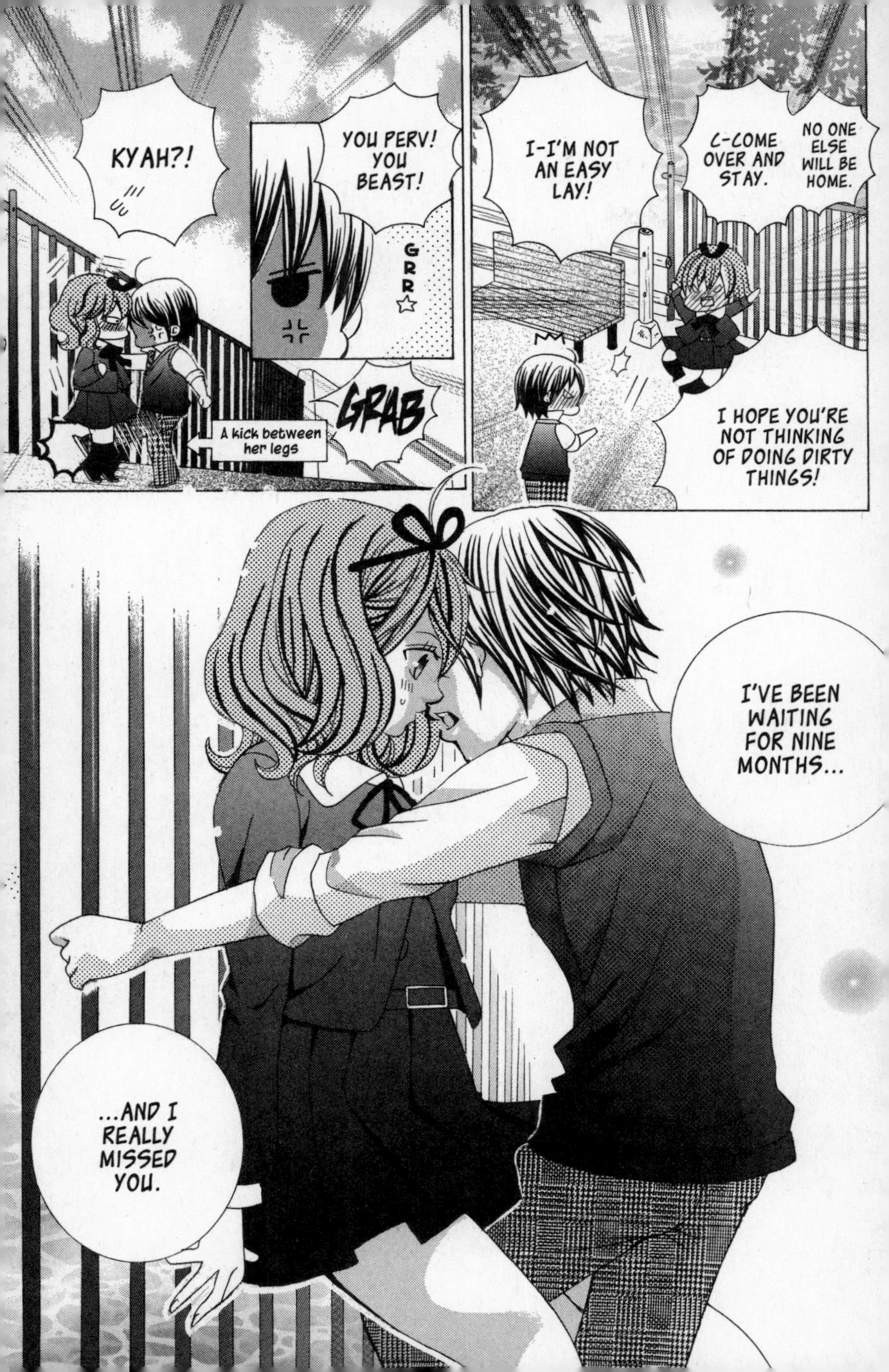
NO ONE ELSE WILL BE HOME.
C-COME OVER AND STAY.
I-I'M NOT AN EASY LAY!
I HOPE YOU'RE NOT THINKING OF DOING DIRTY THINGS!
YOU PERV! YOU BEAST!
GRR☆
GRAB
KYAH?!
A kick between her legs
I'VE BEEN WAITING FOR NINE MONTHS...
...AND I REALLY MISSED YOU.

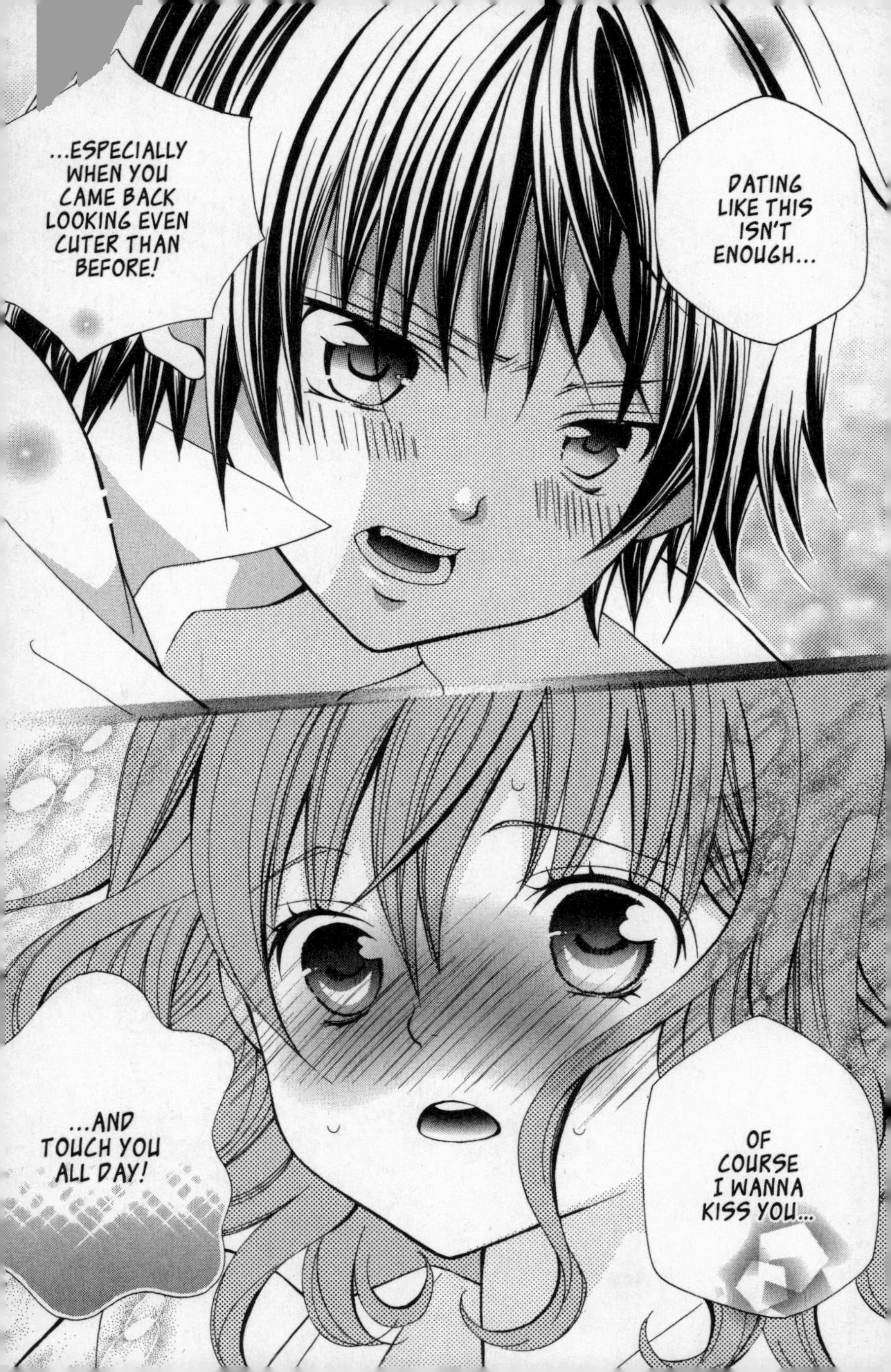
DATING LIKE THIS ISN'T ENOUGH...
...ESPECIALLY WHEN YOU CAME BACK LOOKING EVEN CUTER THAN BEFORE!
OF COURSE I WANNA KISS YOU...
...AND TOUCH YOU ALL DAY!

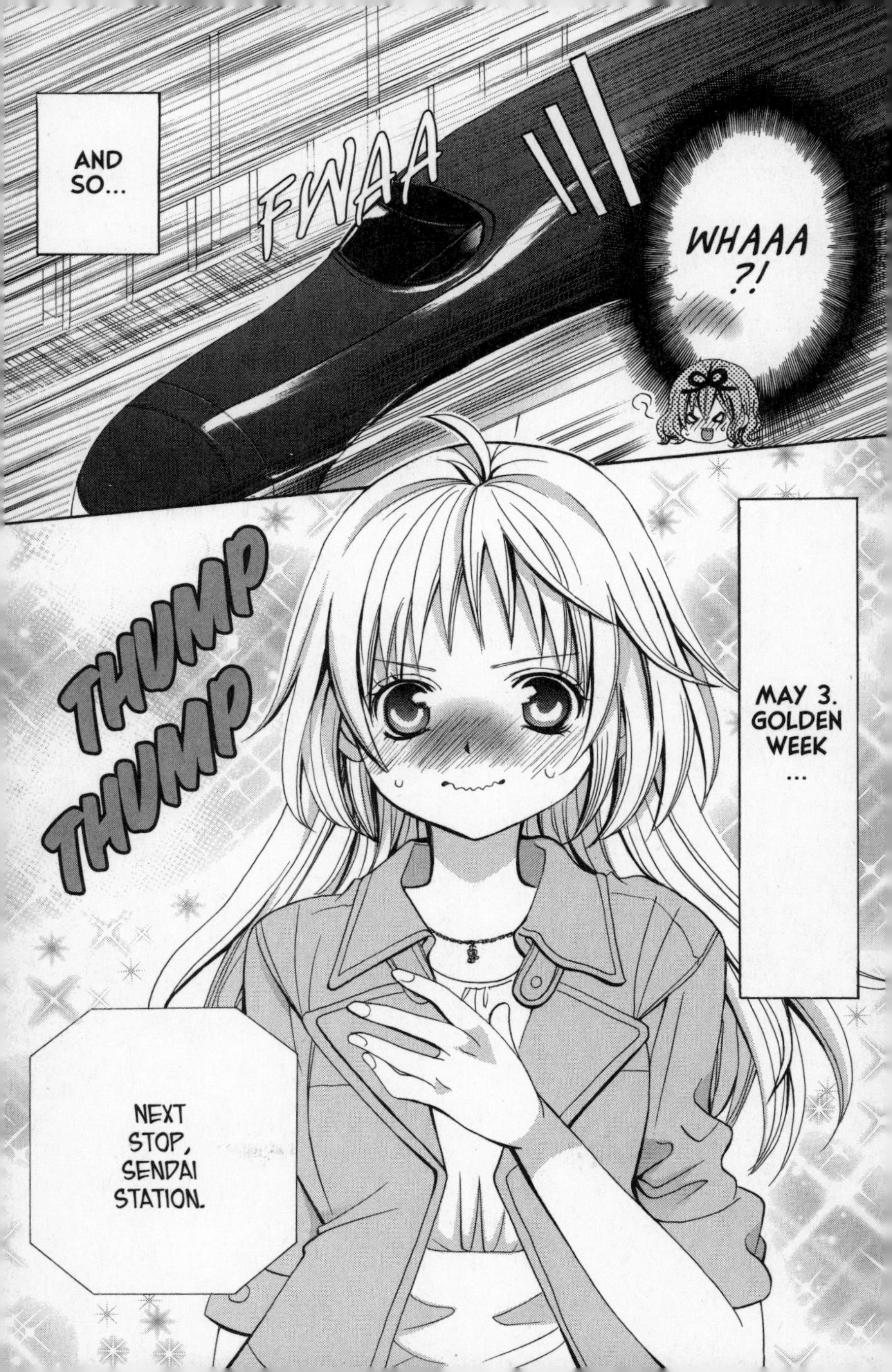
AND SO...
FWAA
WHAAA ?!
MAY 3. GOLDEN WEEK ...
THUMP THUMP
NEXT STOP, SENDAI STATION.

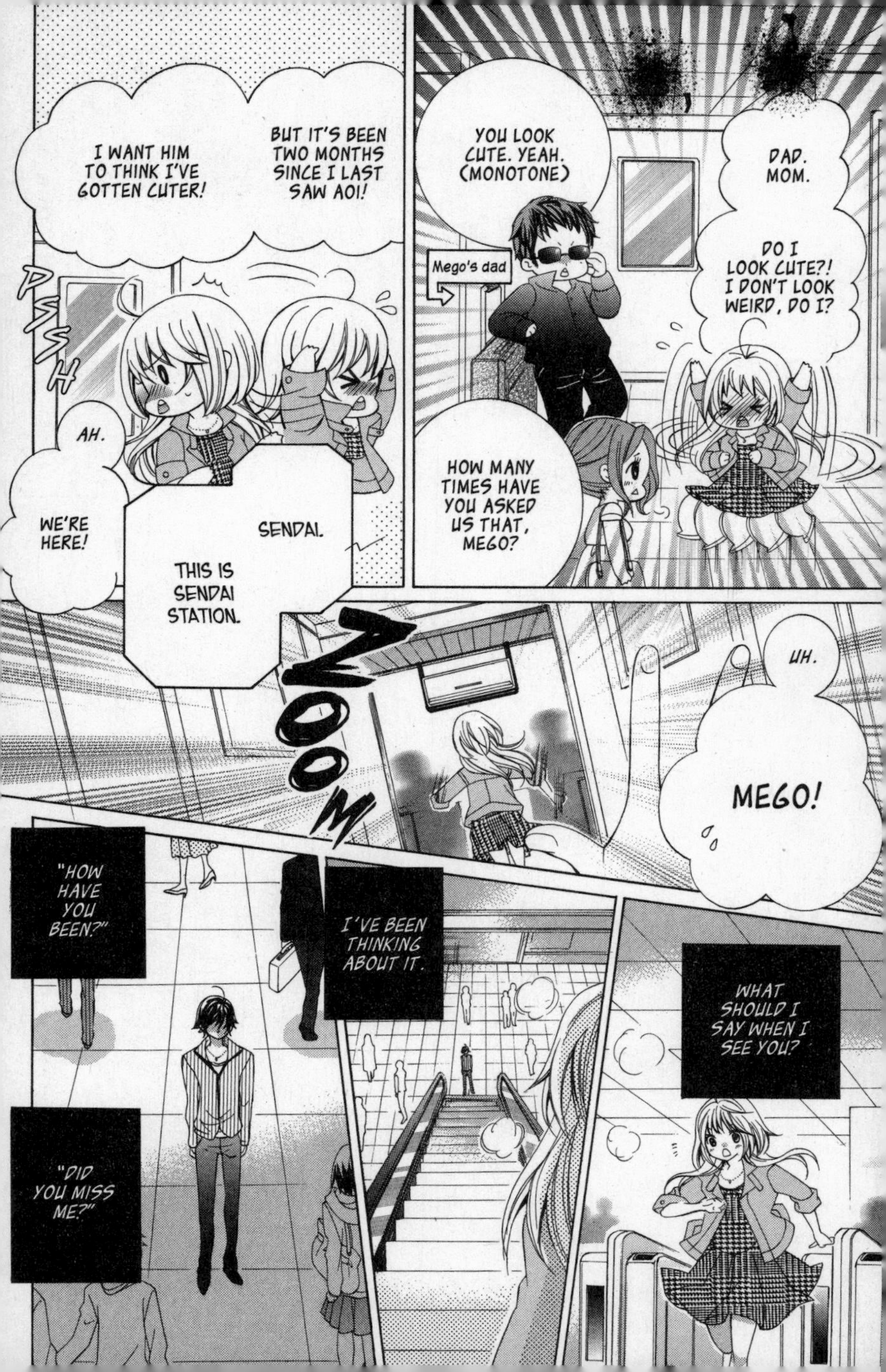
DAD. MOM.
DO I LOOK CUTE?! I DON'T LOOK WEIRD, DO I?
YOU LOOK CUTE. YEAH. (MONOTONE)
Mego's dad
HOW MANY TIMES HAVE YOU ASKED US THAT, MEGO?
BUT IT'S BEEN TWO MONTHS SINCE I LAST SAW AOI!
I WANT HIM TO THINK I'VE GOTTEN CUTER!
PSSH
SENDAI.
THIS IS SENDAI STATION.
AH.
WE'RE HERE!
UH.
MEGO!
ZOOOM
WHAT SHOULD I SAY WHEN I SEE YOU?
I'VE BEEN THINKING ABOUT IT.
"HOW HAVE YOU BEEN?"
"DID YOU MISS ME?"

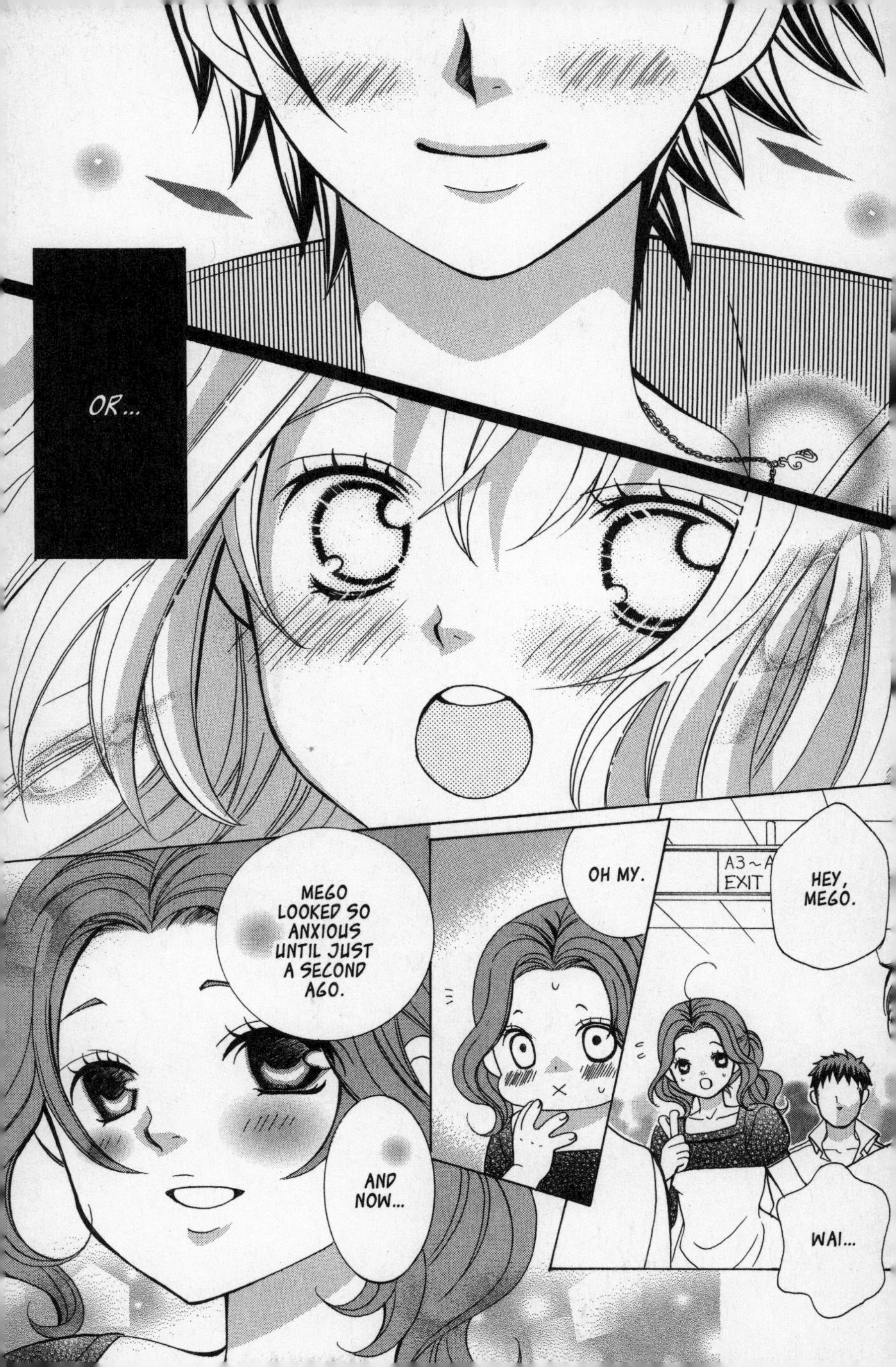
OR...
HEY, MEGO.
A3~A
EXIT
WAI...
OH MY.
MEGO LOOKED SO ANXIOUS UNTIL JUST A SECOND AGO.
AND NOW...

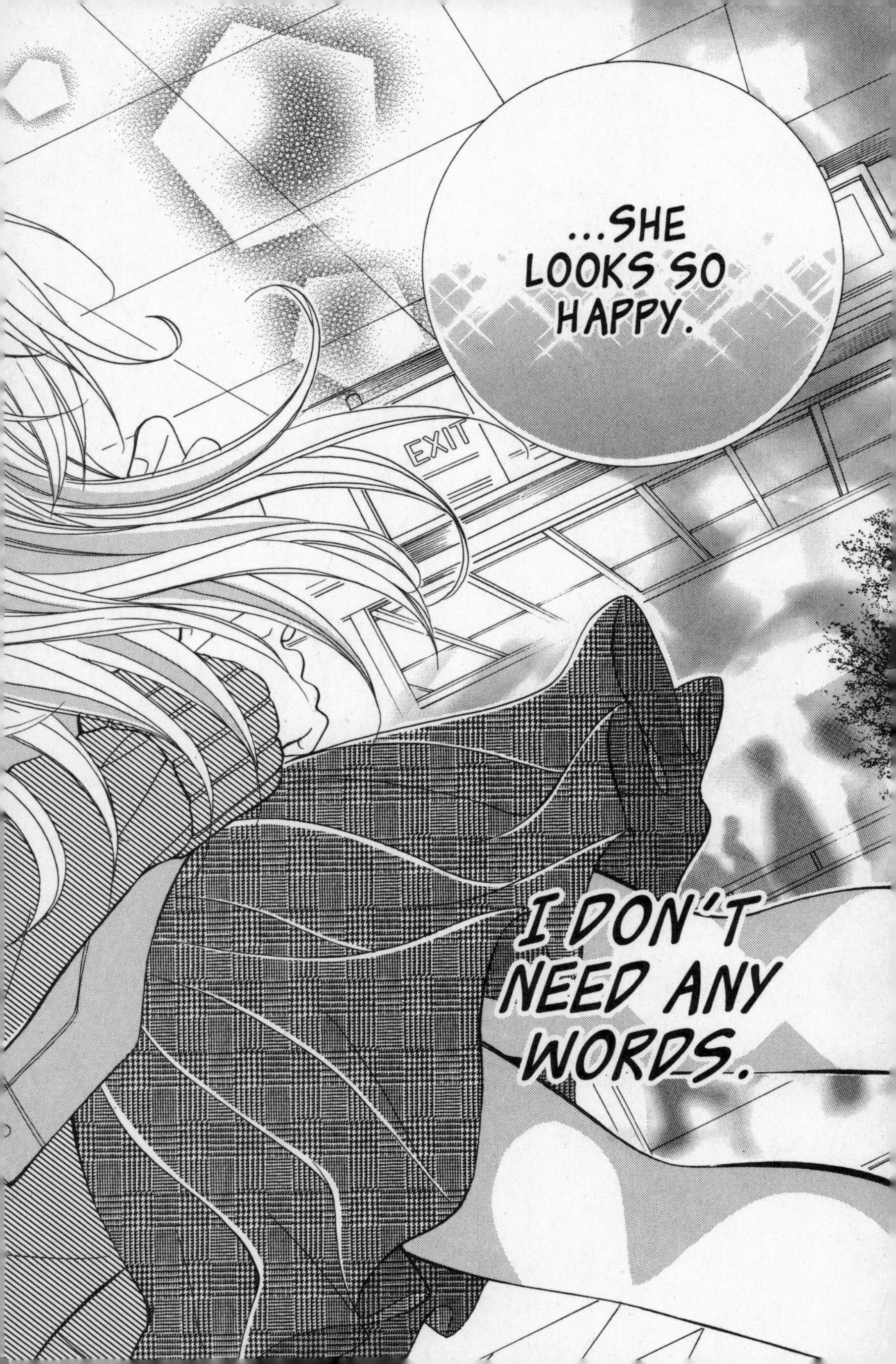
...SHE LOOKS SO HAPPY.
EXIT
I DON'T NEED ANY WORDS.

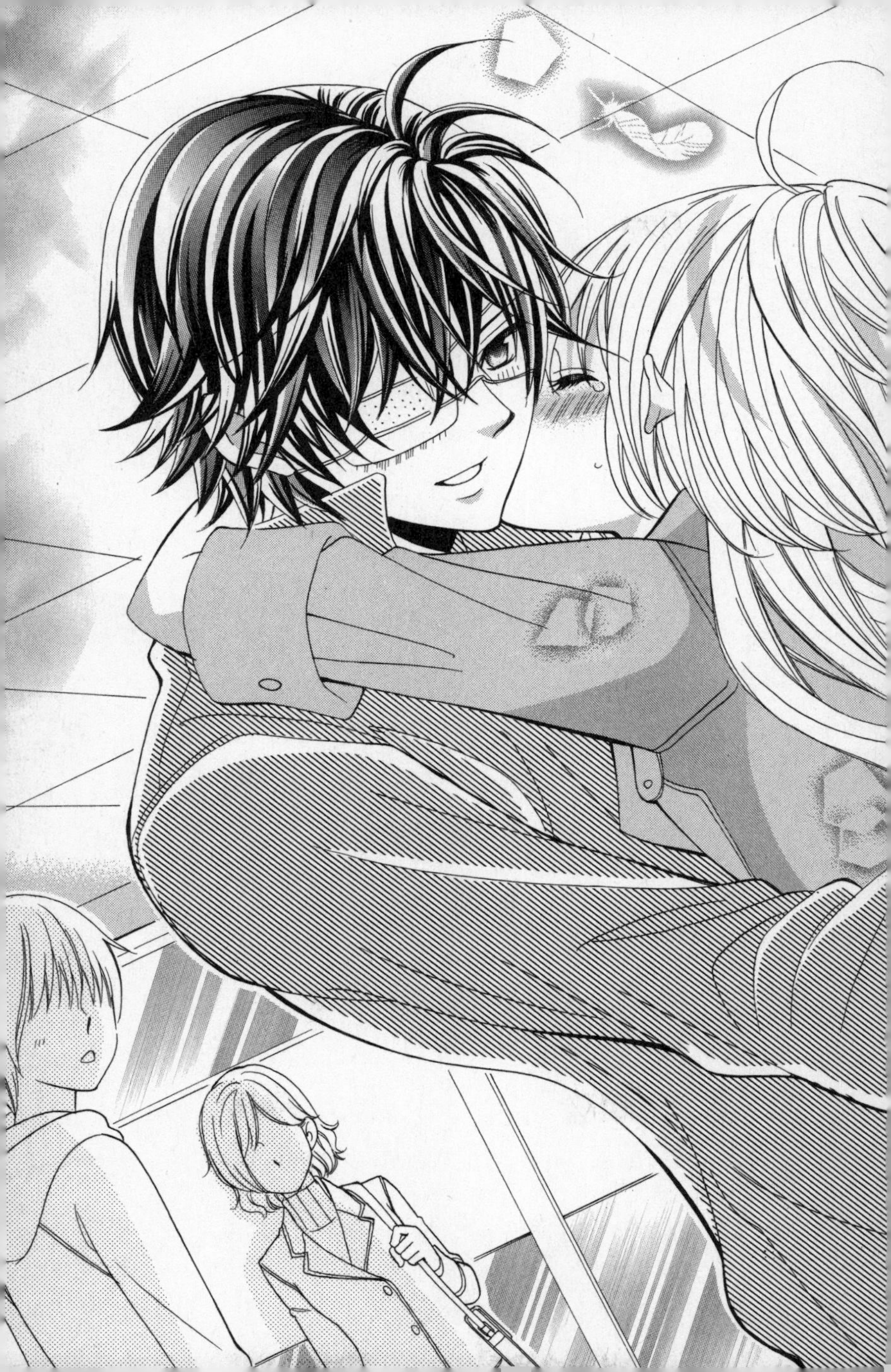

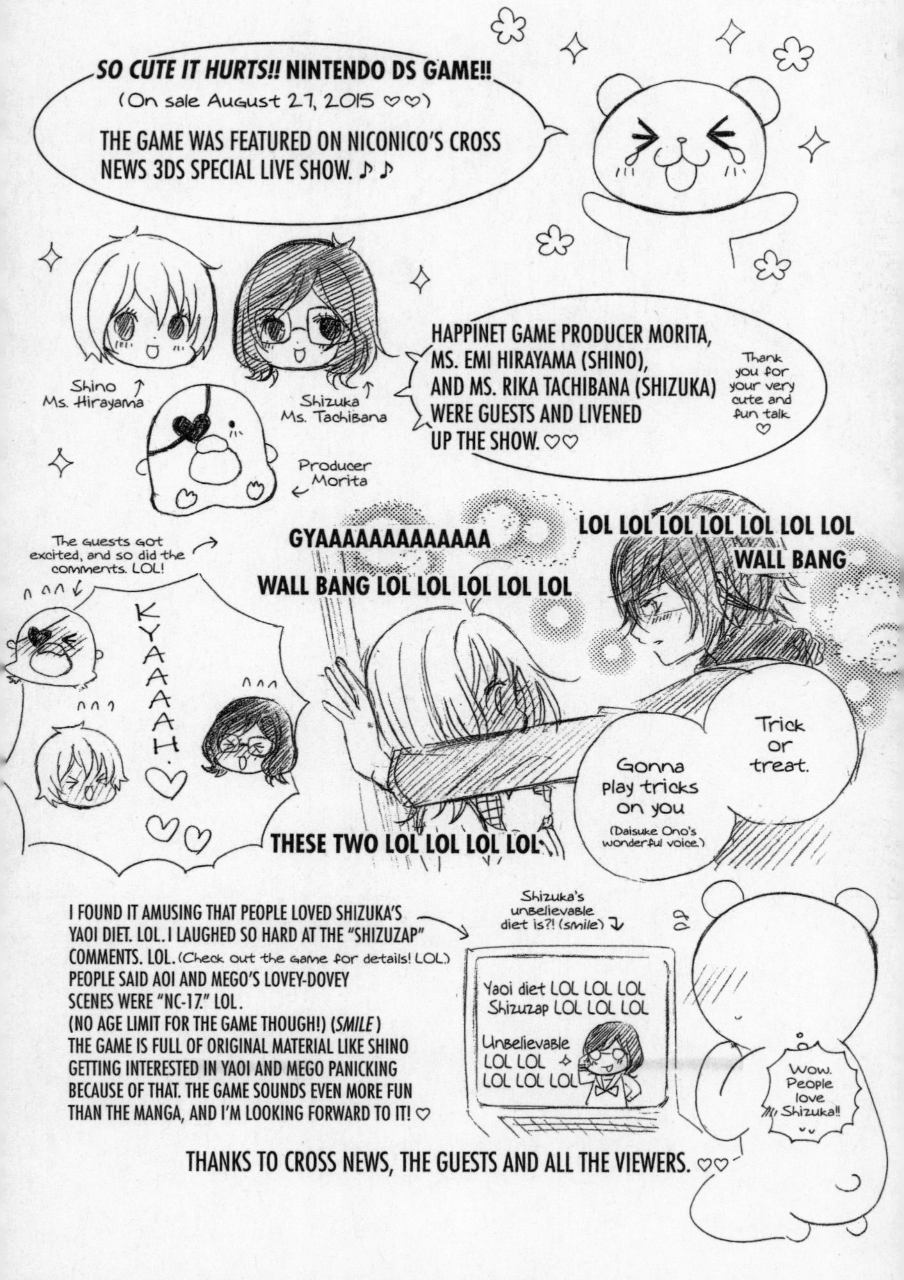
SO CUTE IT HURTS!! NINTENDO DS GAME!!
(On sale August 27, 2015 ♡♡)
THE GAME WAS FEATURED ON NICONICO'S CROSS NEWS 3DS SPECIAL LIVE SHOW. ♪♪
HAPPINET GAME PRODUCER MORITA, MS. EMI HIRAYAMA (SHINO), AND MS. RIKA TACHIBANA (SHIZUKA) WERE GUESTS AND LIVENED UP THE SHOW. ♡♡
Thank you for your very cute and fun talk ♡
Shizuka Ms. Tachibana
Shino Ms. Hirayama
Producer Morita
LOL LOL LOL LOL LOL LOL LOL
WALL BANG
GYAAAAAAAAAAAAA
WALL BANG LOL LOL LOL LOL LOL
The guests got excited, and so did the comments. LOL!
KYAAAAH.♡
Trick or treat.
Gonna play tricks on you
(Daisuke Ono's wonderful voice.)
THESE TWO LOL LOL LOL LOL
I FOUND IT AMUSING THAT PEOPLE LOVED SHIZUKA'S YAOI DIET. LOL. I LAUGHED SO HARD AT THE "SHIZUZAP" COMMENTS. LOL. (Check out the game for details! LOL.) PEOPLE SAID AOI AND MEGO'S LOVEY-DOVEY SCENES WERE "NC-17." LOL. (NO AGE LIMIT FOR THE GAME THOUGH!) (SMILE) THE GAME IS FULL OF ORIGINAL MATERIAL LIKE SHINO GETTING INTERESTED IN YAOI AND MEGO PANICKING BECAUSE OF THAT. THE GAME SOUNDS EVEN MORE FUN THAN THE MANGA, AND I'M LOOKING FORWARD TO IT! ♡
Shizuka's unbelievable diet is?! (smile)
Yaoi diet LOL LOL LOL
Shizuzap LOL LOL LOL
Unbelievable LOL LOL LOL LOL LOL
Wow. People love Shizuka!!
THANKS TO CROSS NEWS, THE GUESTS AND ALL THE VIEWERS. ♡♡

Chapter 58

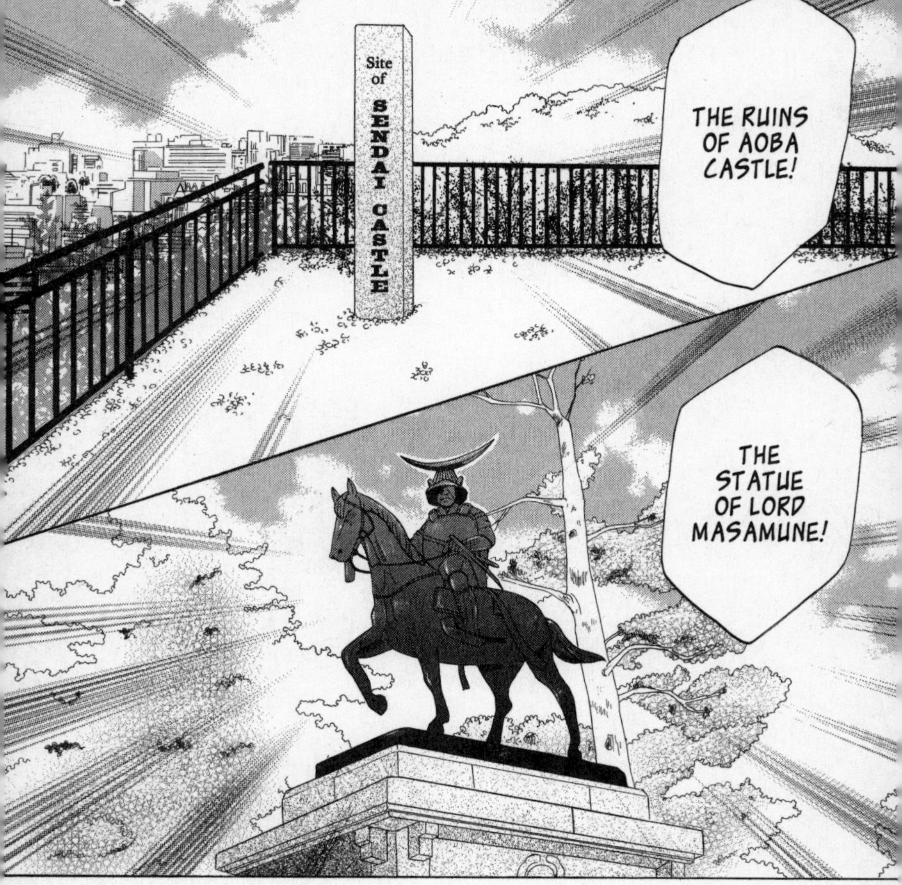
Site of
SENDAI CASTLE
THE RUINS OF AOBA CASTLE!
THE STATUE OF LORD MASAMUNE!

WHAT'S-NEW-IN-ANIME

PART THREE OF *JOJO* WAS SO GOOD! I'VE LOVED THE MANGA SINCE I WAS LITTLE, AND I CRIED AT THE VERY LAST SCENE. (>_<) I JUST LOVED KAKYOIN'S FINAL EMERALD SPLASH AND THE CRYING JOTARO'S "ORAORAORAORA!" I LOVE PART FOUR AS WELL, SO I WANT THAT TO BE MADE INTO AN ANIME TOO. ♡

I ALSO LOVED *FATE/STAY NIGHT UBW* AND *SERAPH OF THE END*! RIN AND ARCHER ARE MY FAVORITE FATE CHARACTERS. ♡ SABER IS CUTE, AND SHIRO WAS COOL AT THE END. (ToT) FERID AND MIKA ARE MY FAVORITE SERAPH CHARACTERS. ♪ I'M SO LOOKING FORWARD TO WHAT'LL HAPPEN TO YU AND MIKA!

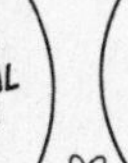

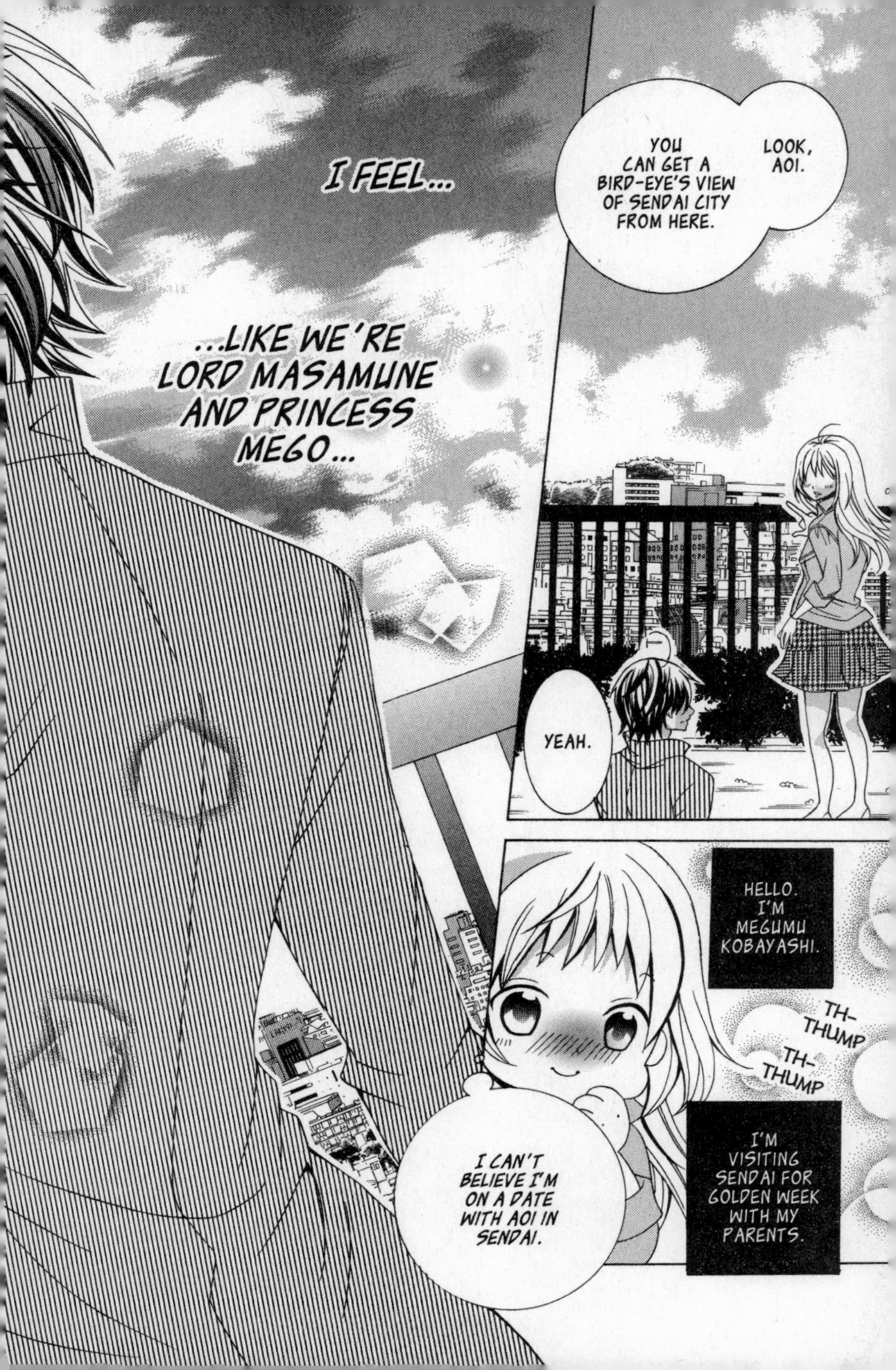
LOOK, AOI.
YOU CAN GET A BIRD-EYE'S VIEW OF SENDAI CITY FROM HERE.
YEAH.
HELLO. I'M MEGUMU KOBAYASHI.
TH-THUMP
TH-THUMP
I'M VISITING SENDAI FOR GOLDEN WEEK WITH MY PARENTS.
I CAN'T BELIEVE I'M ON A DATE WITH AOI IN SENDAI.
I FEEL...
...LIKE WE'RE LORD MASAMUNE AND PRINCESS MEGO...

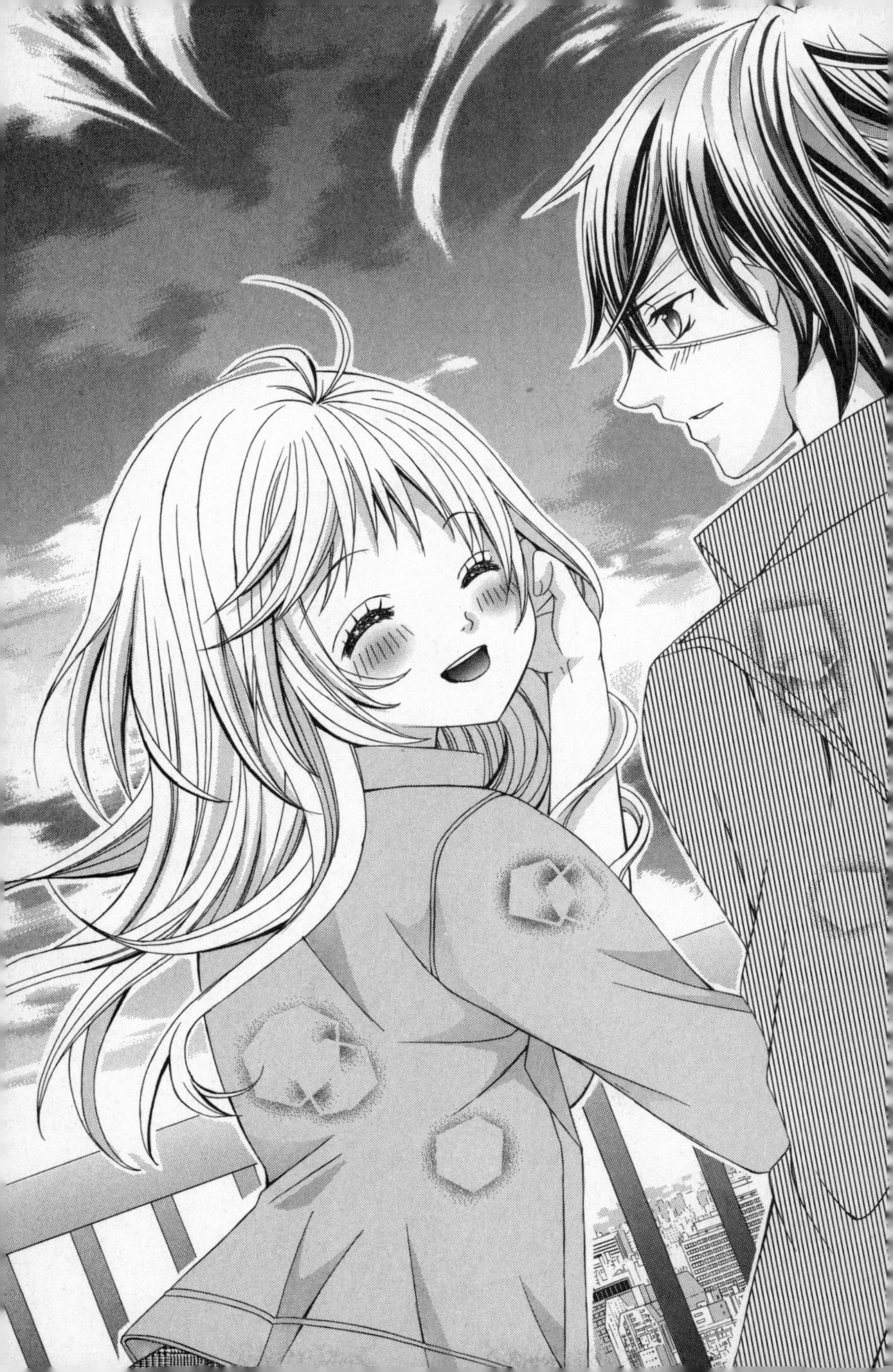

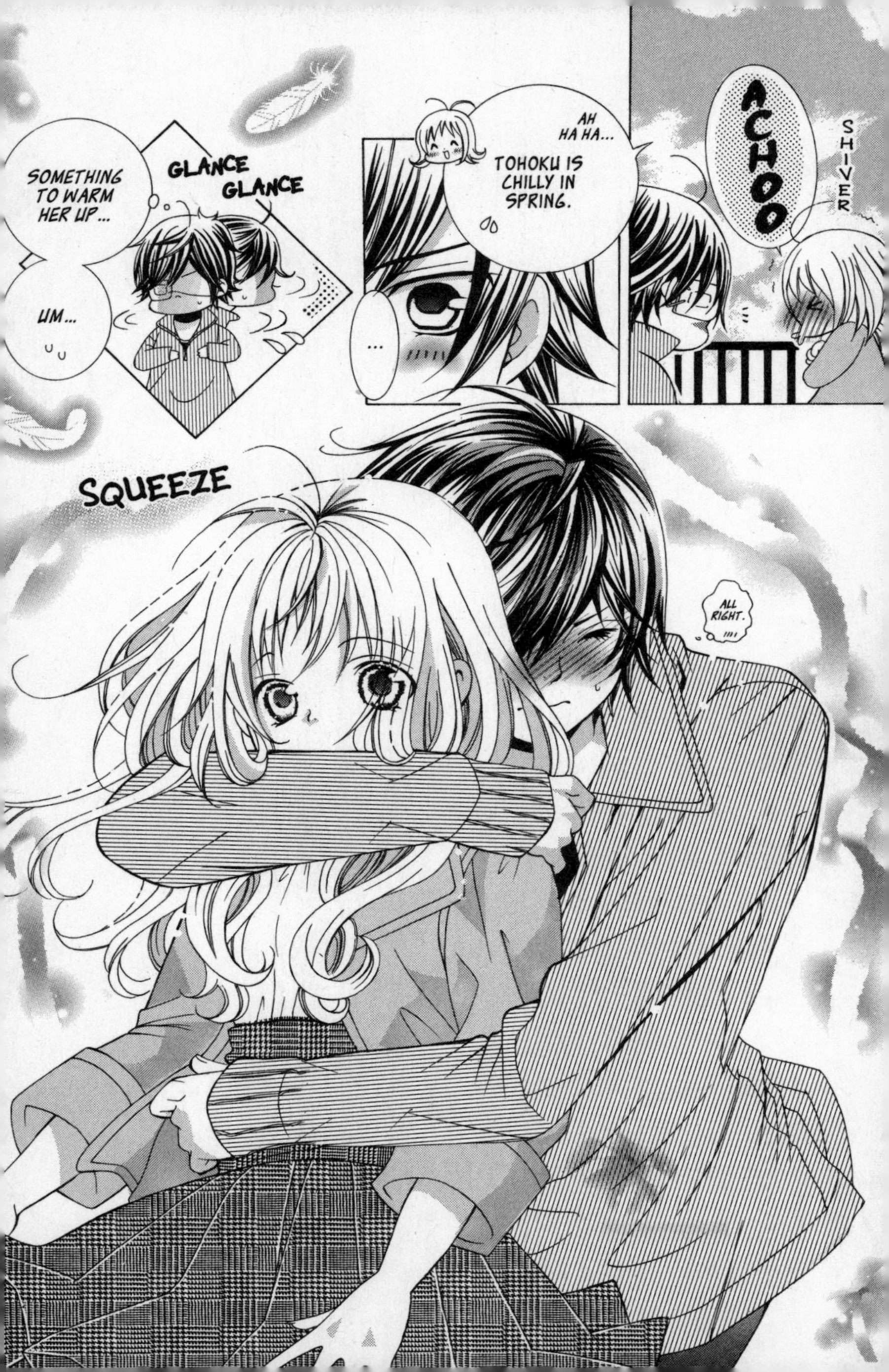
ACHOO
SHIVER
AH HA HA... TOHOKU IS CHILLY IN SPRING.
...
GLANCE GLANCE
SOMETHING TO WARM HER UP...
UM...
SQUEEZE
ALL RIGHT.

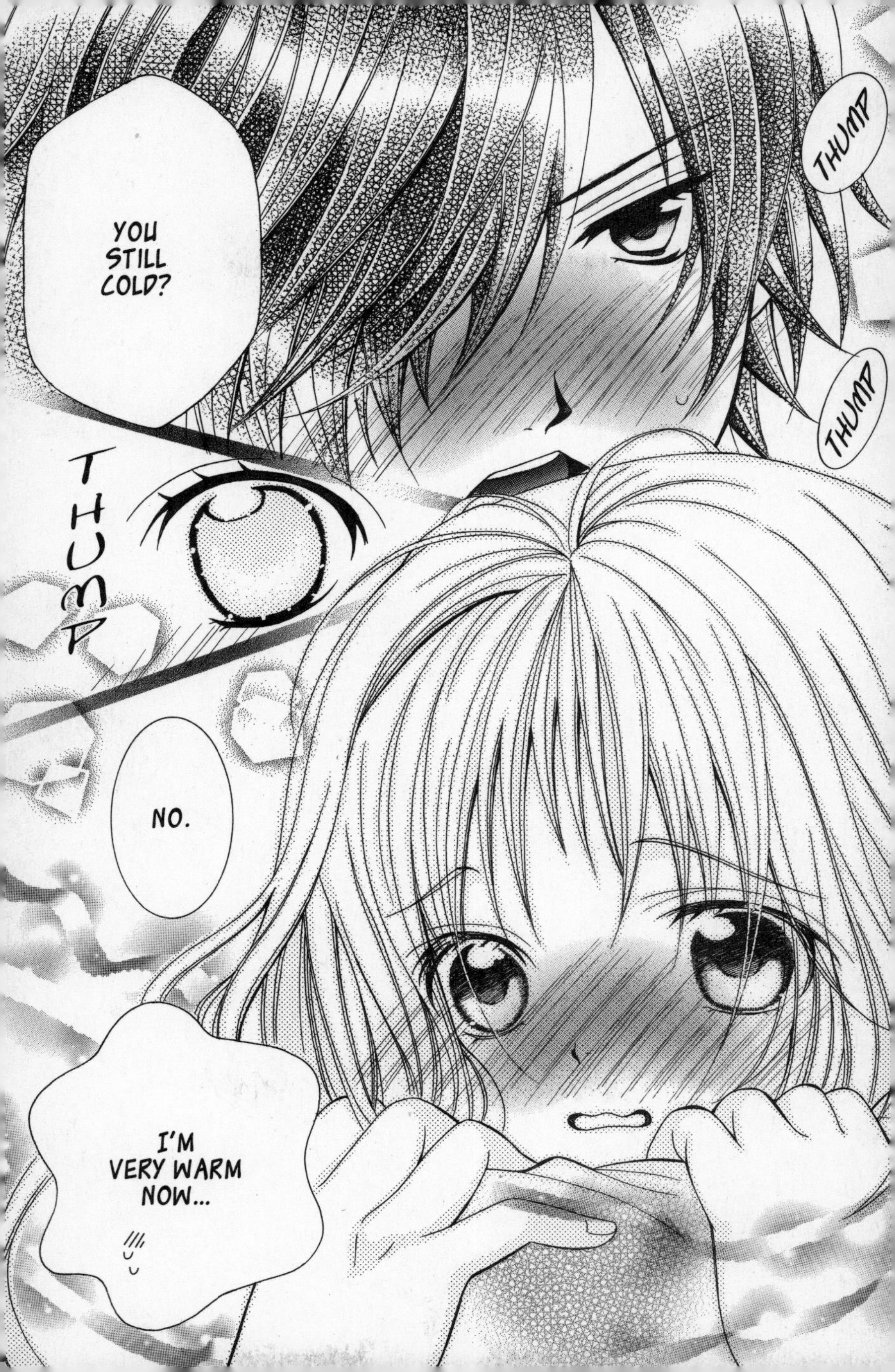
THUMP
YOU STILL COLD?
THUMP
THUMP
NO.
I'M VERY WARM NOW...

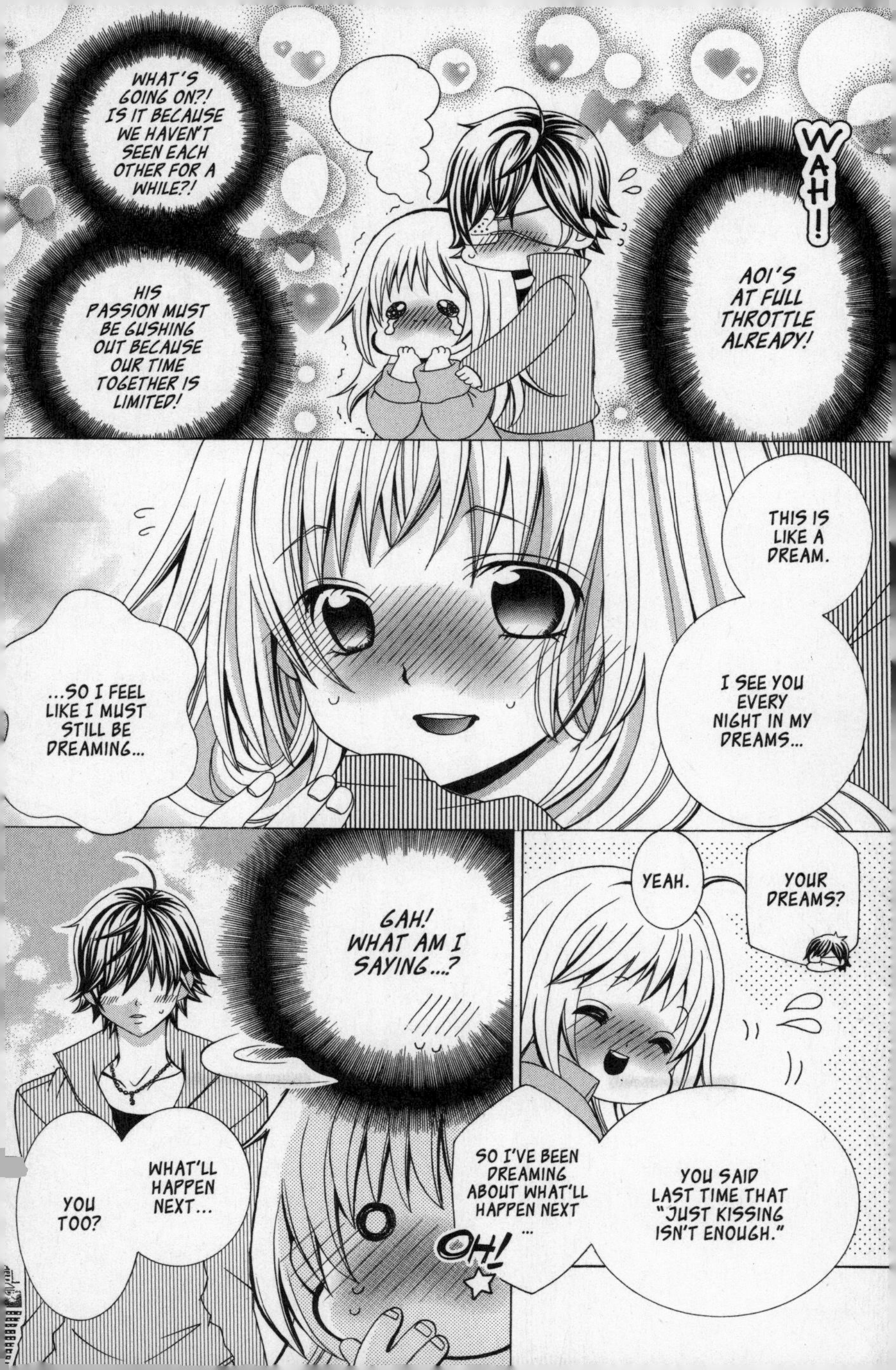
WAH!
AOI'S AT FULL THROTTLE ALREADY!
WHAT'S GOING ON?! IS IT BECAUSE WE HAVEN'T SEEN EACH OTHER FOR A WHILE?!
HIS PASSION MUST BE GUSHING OUT BECAUSE OUR TIME TOGETHER IS LIMITED!
THIS IS LIKE A DREAM.
I SEE YOU EVERY NIGHT IN MY DREAMS...
...SO I FEEL LIKE I MUST STILL BE DREAMING...
YOUR DREAMS?
YEAH.
YOU SAID LAST TIME THAT "JUST KISSING ISN'T ENOUGH."
SO I'VE BEEN DREAMING ABOUT WHAT'LL HAPPEN NEXT ...
OH!
GAH! WHAT AM I SAYING...?
WHAT'LL HAPPEN NEXT...
YOU TOO?

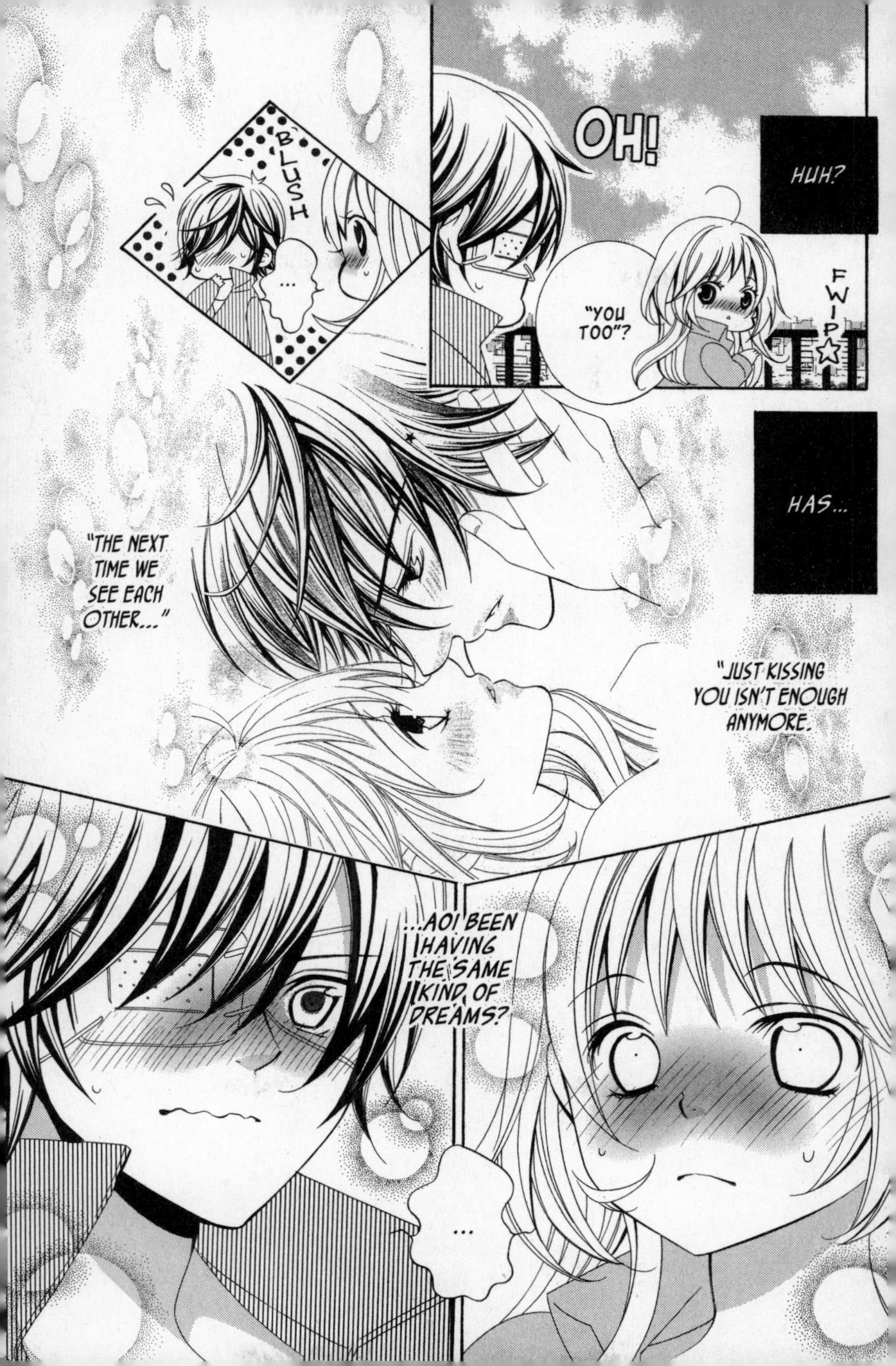
HUH?
OH!
FWIP☆
"YOU TOO"?
BLUSH
...
HAS...
"JUST KISSING YOU ISN'T ENOUGH ANYMORE.
"THE NEXT TIME WE SEE EACH OTHER..."
...AOI BEEN HAVING THE SAME KIND OF DREAMS?
...

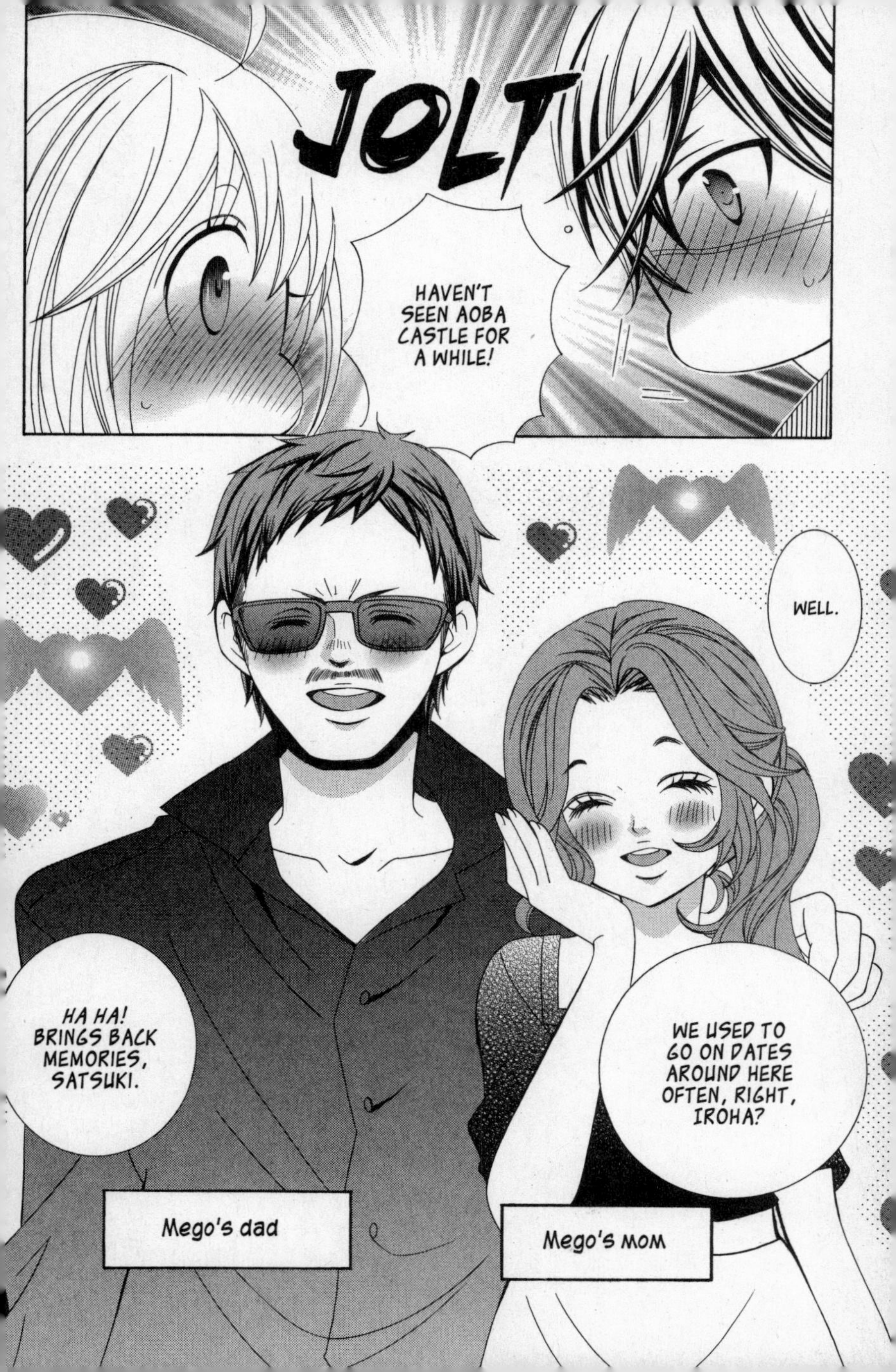
JOLT
HAVEN'T SEEN AOBA CASTLE FOR A WHILE!
WELL.
WE USED TO GO ON DATES AROUND HERE OFTEN, RIGHT, IROHA?
Mego's mom
HA HA! BRINGS BACK MEMORIES, SATSUKI.
Mego's dad

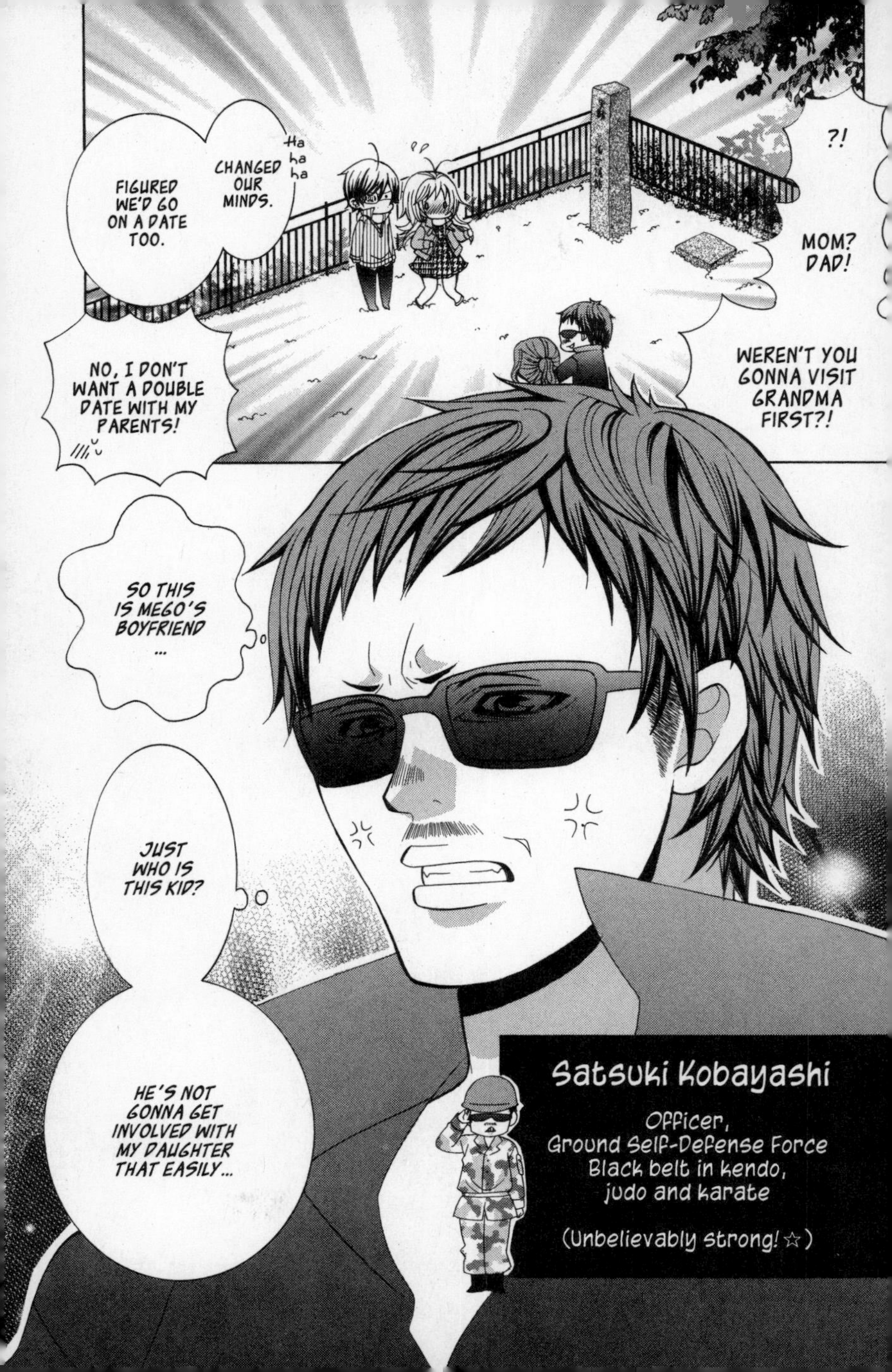
?!
MOM? DAD!
WEREN'T YOU GONNA VISIT GRANDMA FIRST?!
Ha ha ha
CHANGED OUR MINDS.
FIGURED WE'D GO ON A DATE TOO.
NO, I DON'T WANT A DOUBLE DATE WITH MY PARENTS!
SO THIS IS MEGO'S BOYFRIEND ...
JUST WHO IS THIS KID?
HE'S NOT GONNA GET INVOLVED WITH MY DAUGHTER THAT EASILY...
Satsuki Kobayashi
Officer, Ground Self-Defense Force
Black belt in kendo, judo and karate
(Unbelievably strong! ☆)

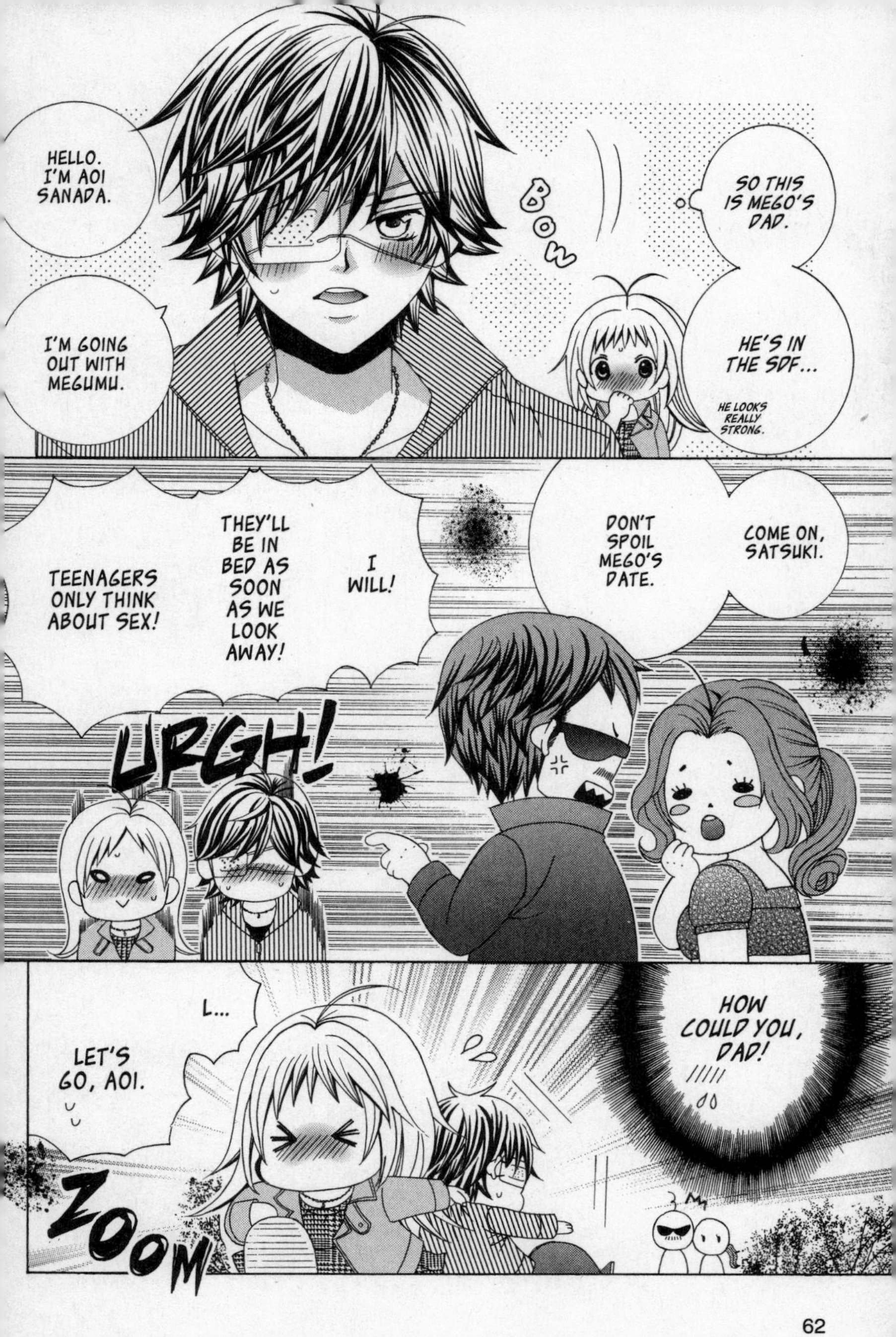
SO THIS IS MEGO'S DAD.
HE'S IN THE SDF...
HE LOOKS REALLY STRONG.
BOW
HELLO. I'M AOI SANADA.
I'M GOING OUT WITH MEGUMU.
COME ON, SATSUKI.
DON'T SPOIL MEGO'S DATE.
I WILL!
THEY'LL BE IN BED AS SOON AS WE LOOK AWAY!
TEENAGERS ONLY THINK ABOUT SEX!
URGH!
HOW COULD YOU, DAD!
L...
LET'S GO, AOI.
ZOOM

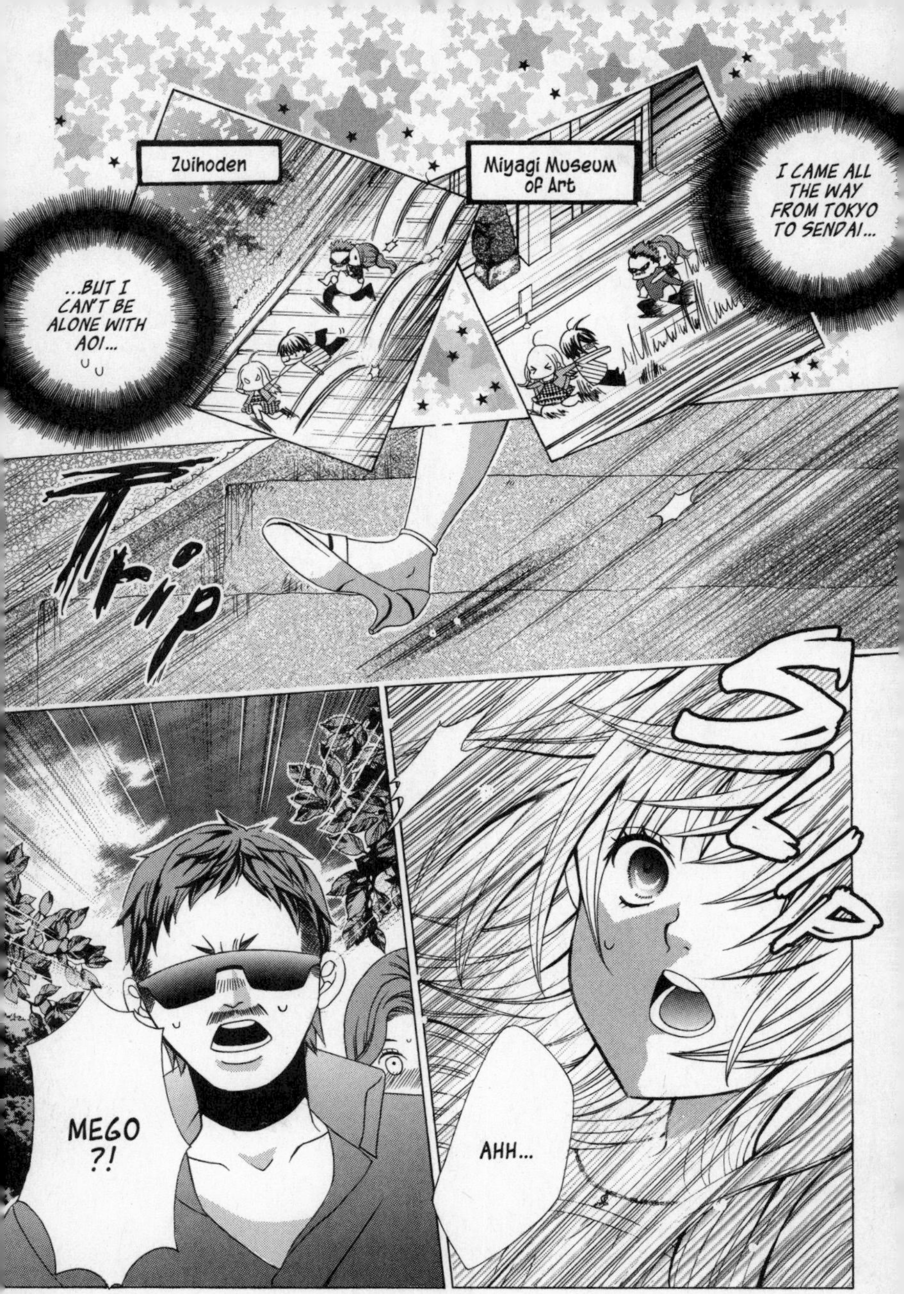
I CAME ALL THE WAY FROM TOKYO TO SENDAI...
Miyagi Museum of Art
Zuihoden
...BUT I CAN'T BE ALONE WITH AOI...
Trip
AHH...
MEGO ?!

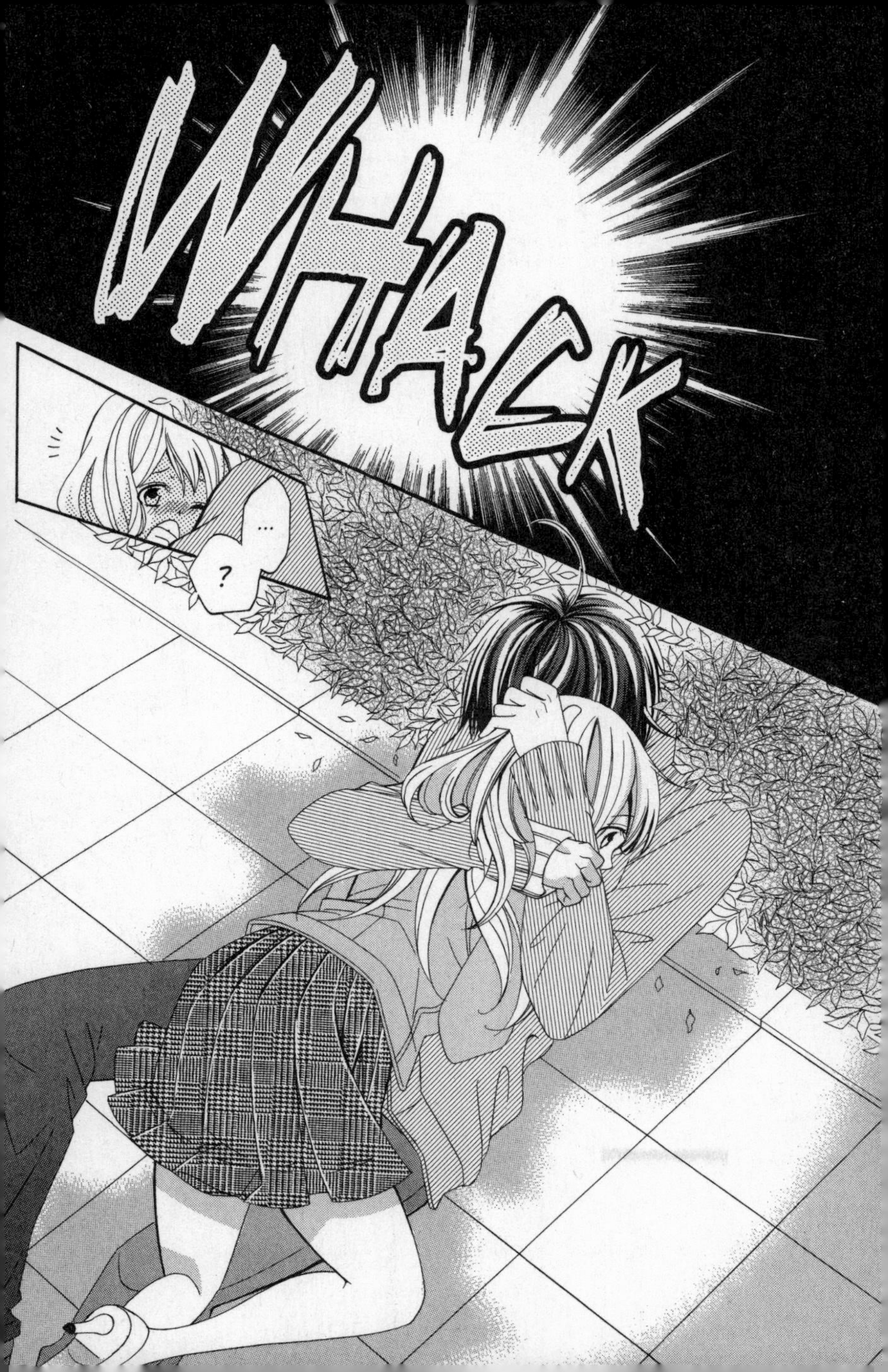
WHACK
...
?

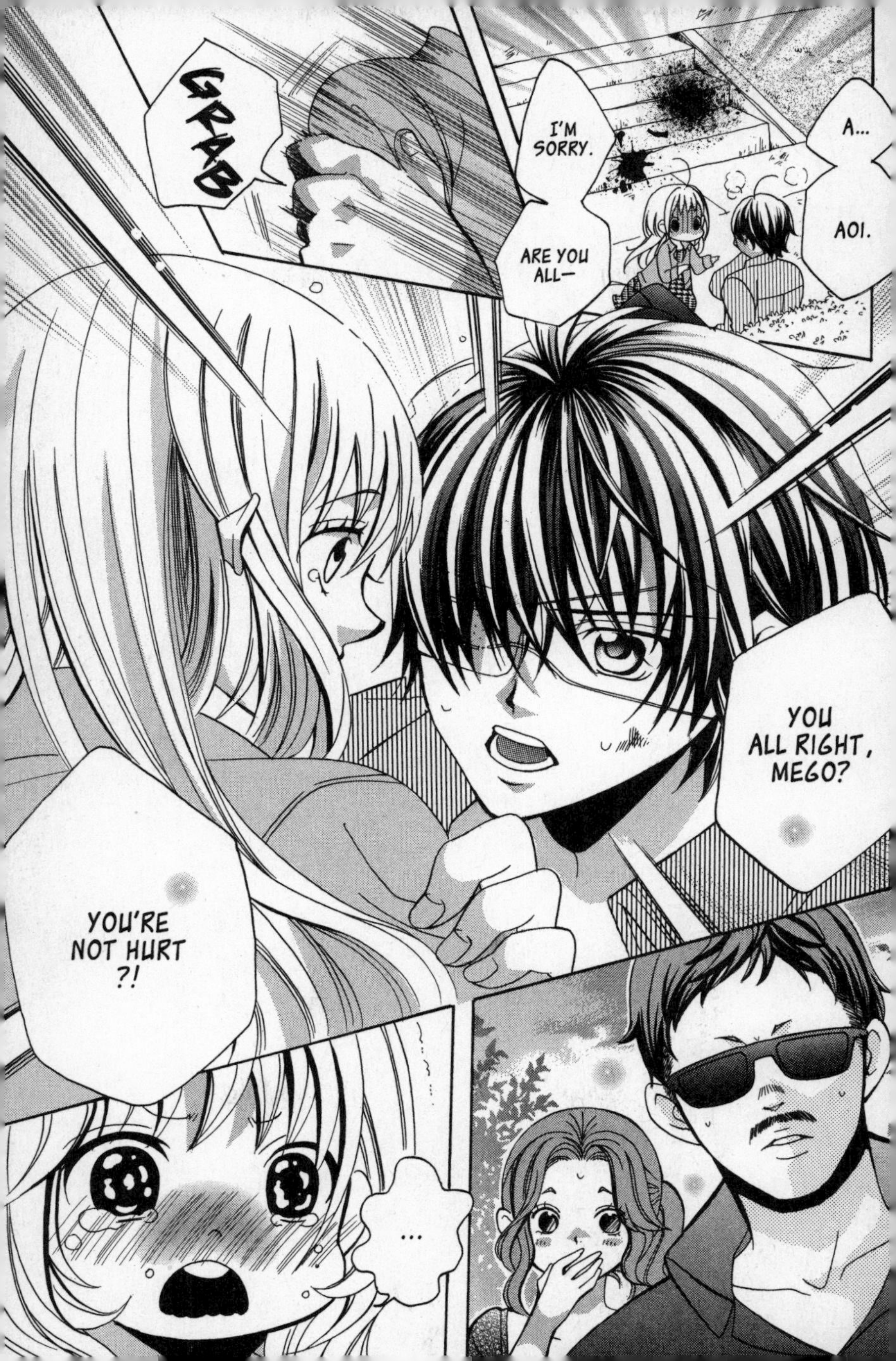
A...
AOI.
I'M SORRY.
ARE YOU ALL—
GRAB
YOU ALL RIGHT, MEGO?
YOU'RE NOT HURT ?!
...

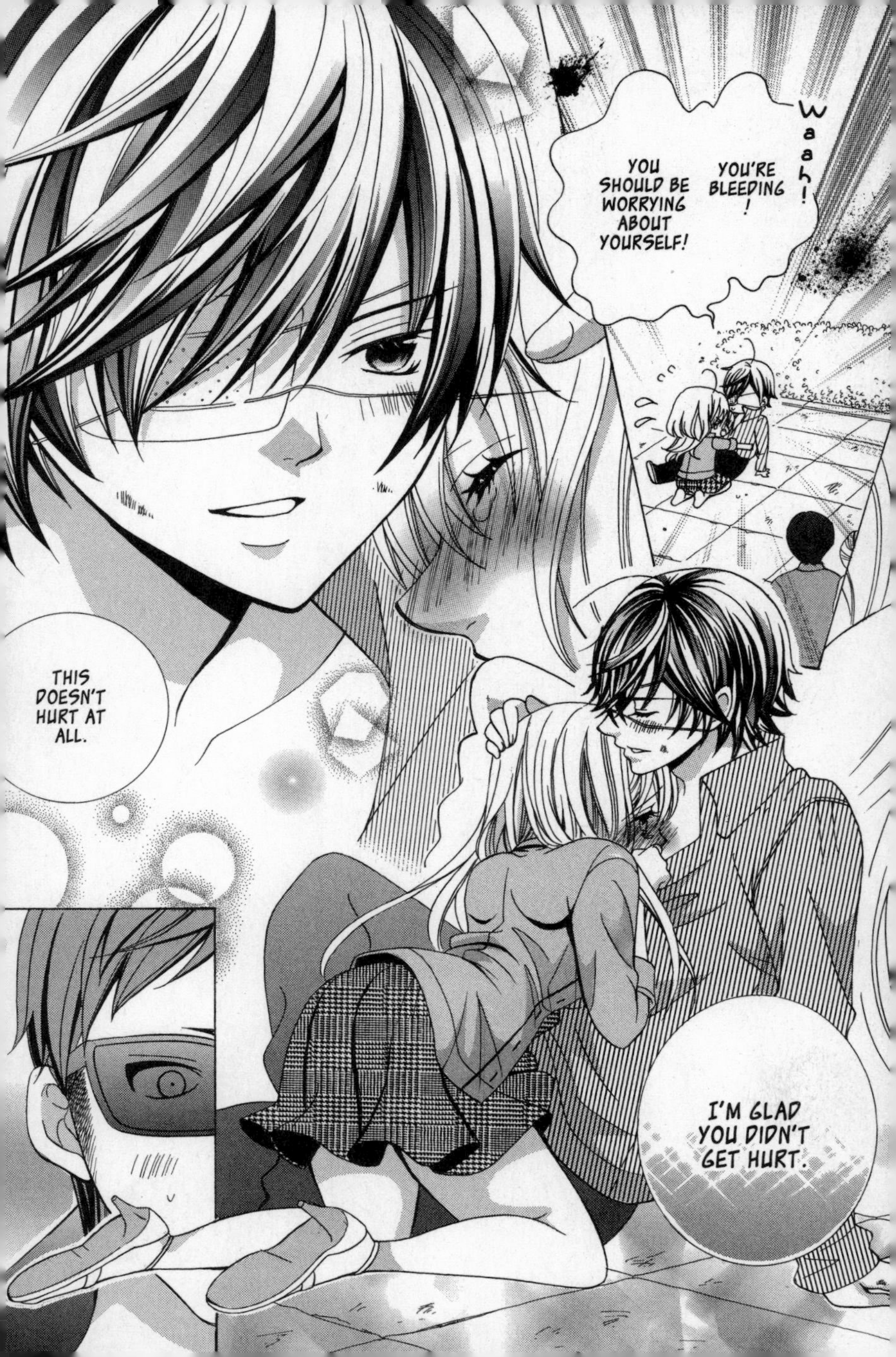
Waah!
YOU'RE BLEEDING!
YOU SHOULD BE WORRYING ABOUT YOURSELF!
THIS DOESN'T HURT AT ALL.
I'M GLAD YOU DIDN'T GET HURT.

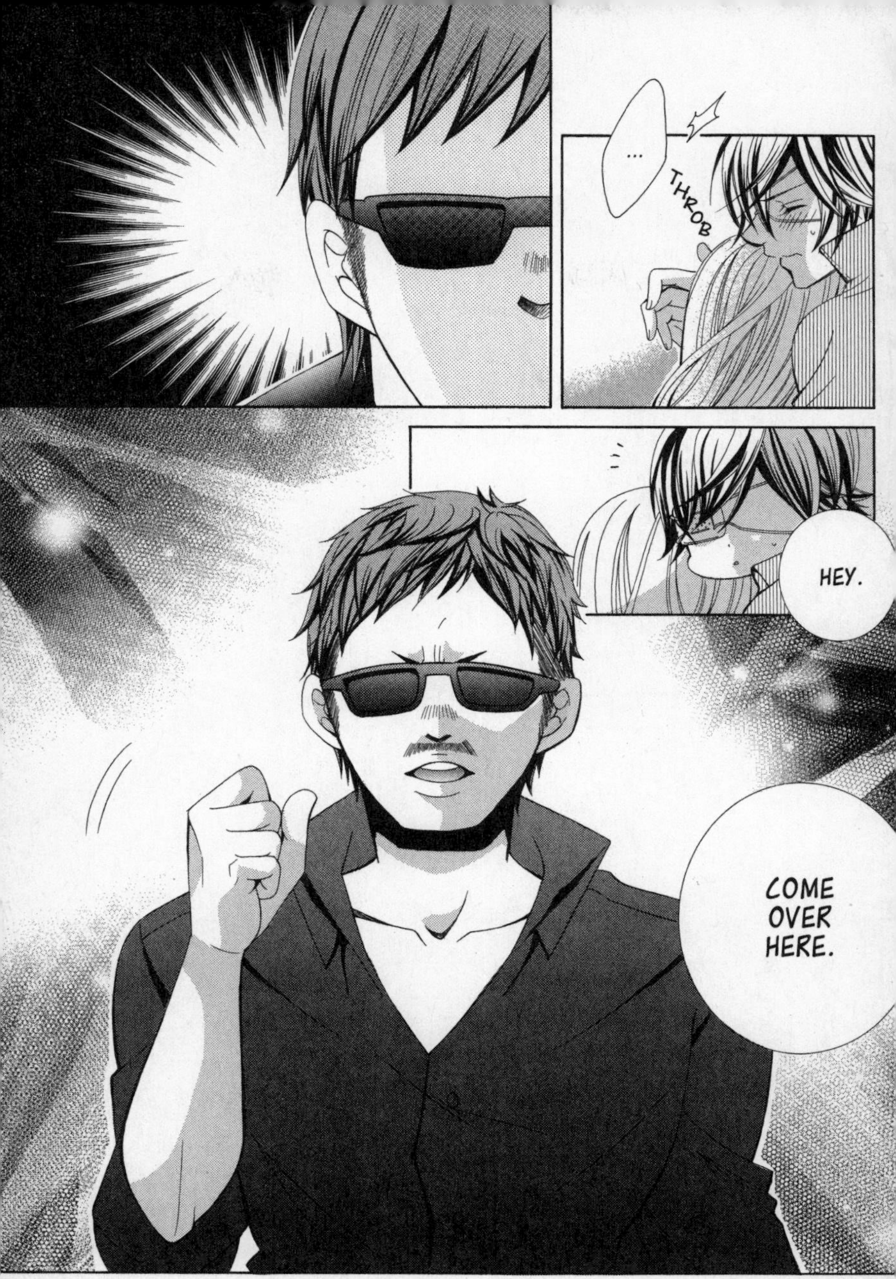
...
THROB
HEY.
COME OVER HERE.

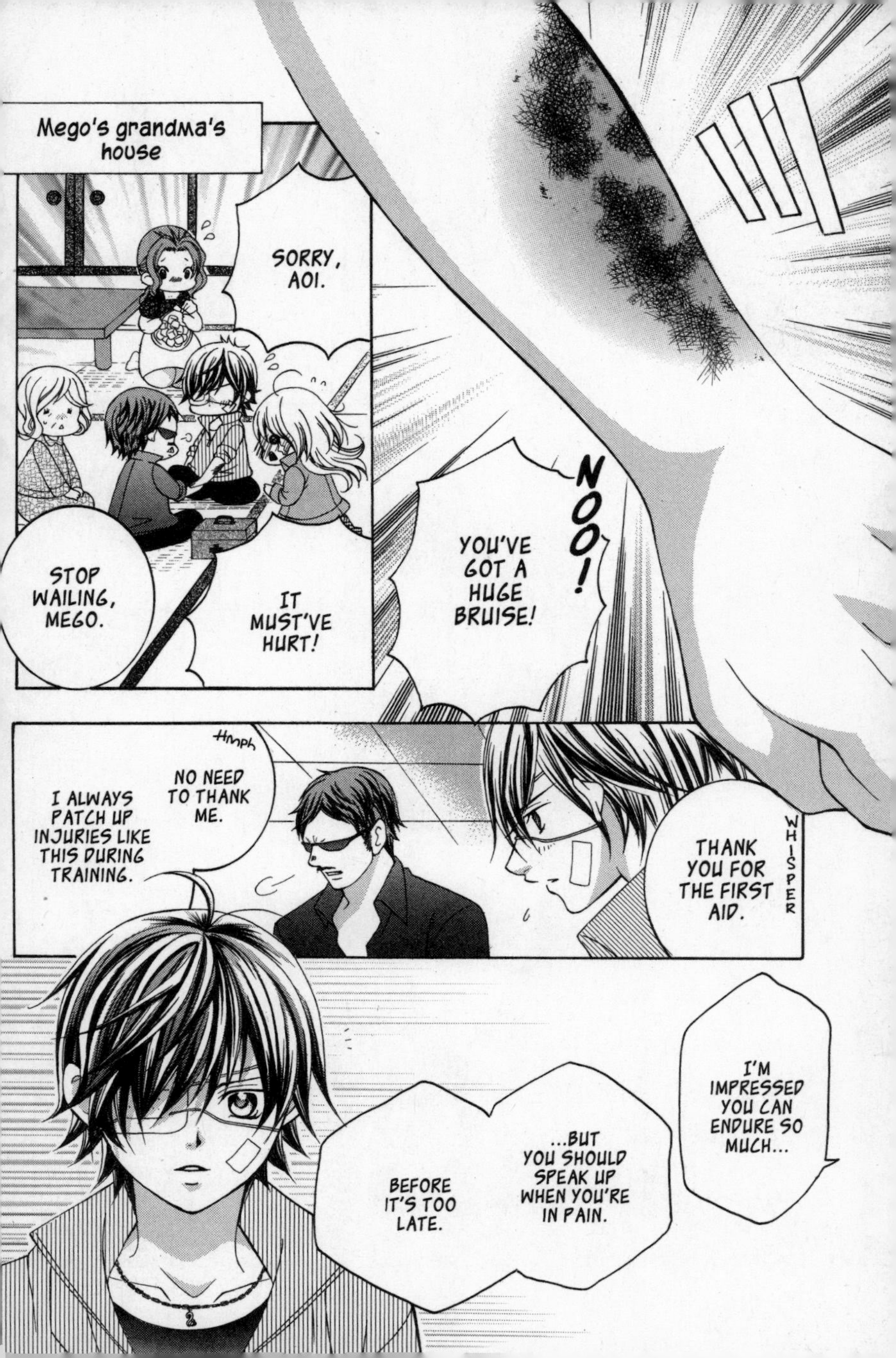
NOOO!
YOU'VE GOT A HUGE BRUISE!
Mego's grandma's house
SORRY, AOI.
IT MUST'VE HURT!
STOP WAILING, MEGO.
WHISPER
THANK YOU FOR THE FIRST AID.
Hmph
NO NEED TO THANK ME.
I ALWAYS PATCH UP INJURIES LIKE THIS DURING TRAINING.
I'M IMPRESSED YOU CAN ENDURE SO MUCH...
...BUT YOU SHOULD SPEAK UP WHEN YOU'RE IN PAIN.
BEFORE IT'S TOO LATE.

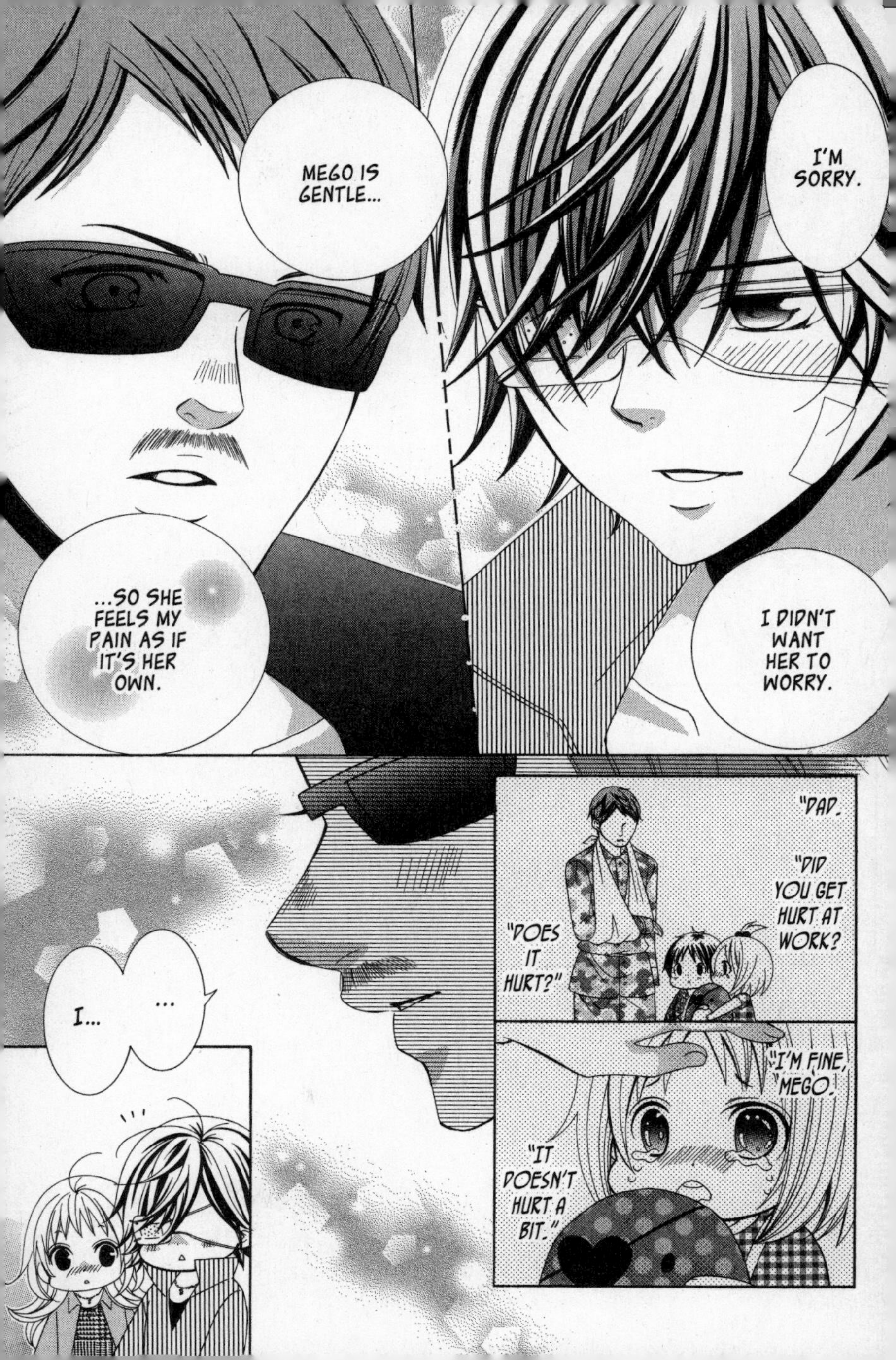

I'M SORRY.
I DIDN'T WANT HER TO WORRY.
MEGO IS GENTLE...
...SO SHE FEELS MY PAIN AS IF IT'S HER OWN.
"DAD.
"DID YOU GET HURT AT WORK?
"DOES IT HURT?"
"I'M FINE, MEGO.
"IT DOESN'T HURT A BIT."
...
I...

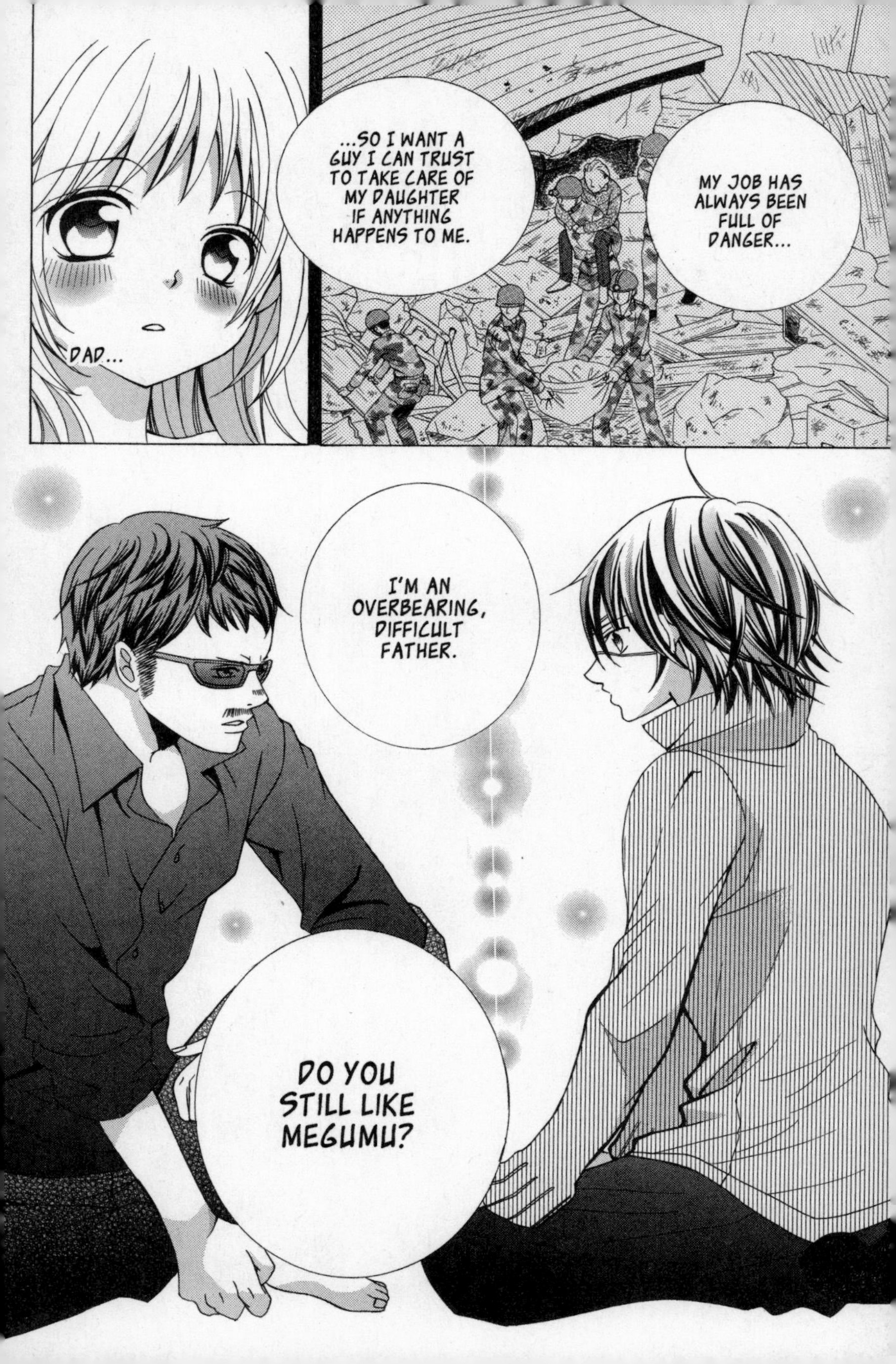
MY JOB HAS ALWAYS BEEN FULL OF DANGER...
...SO I WANT A GUY I CAN TRUST TO TAKE CARE OF MY DAUGHTER IF ANYTHING HAPPENS TO ME.
DAD...
I'M AN OVERBEARING, DIFFICULT FATHER.
DO YOU STILL LIKE MEGUMU?

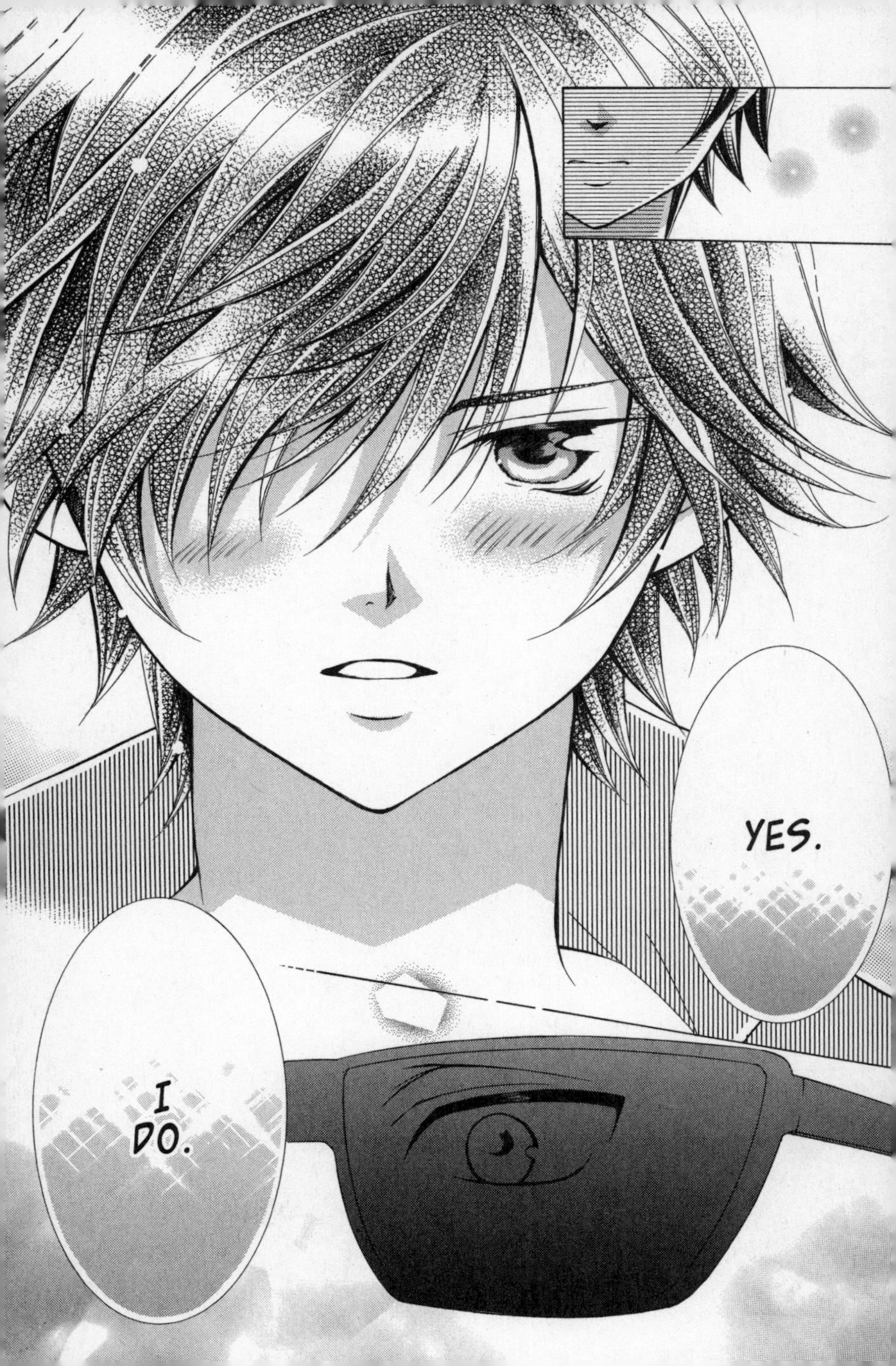
YES.
I DO.

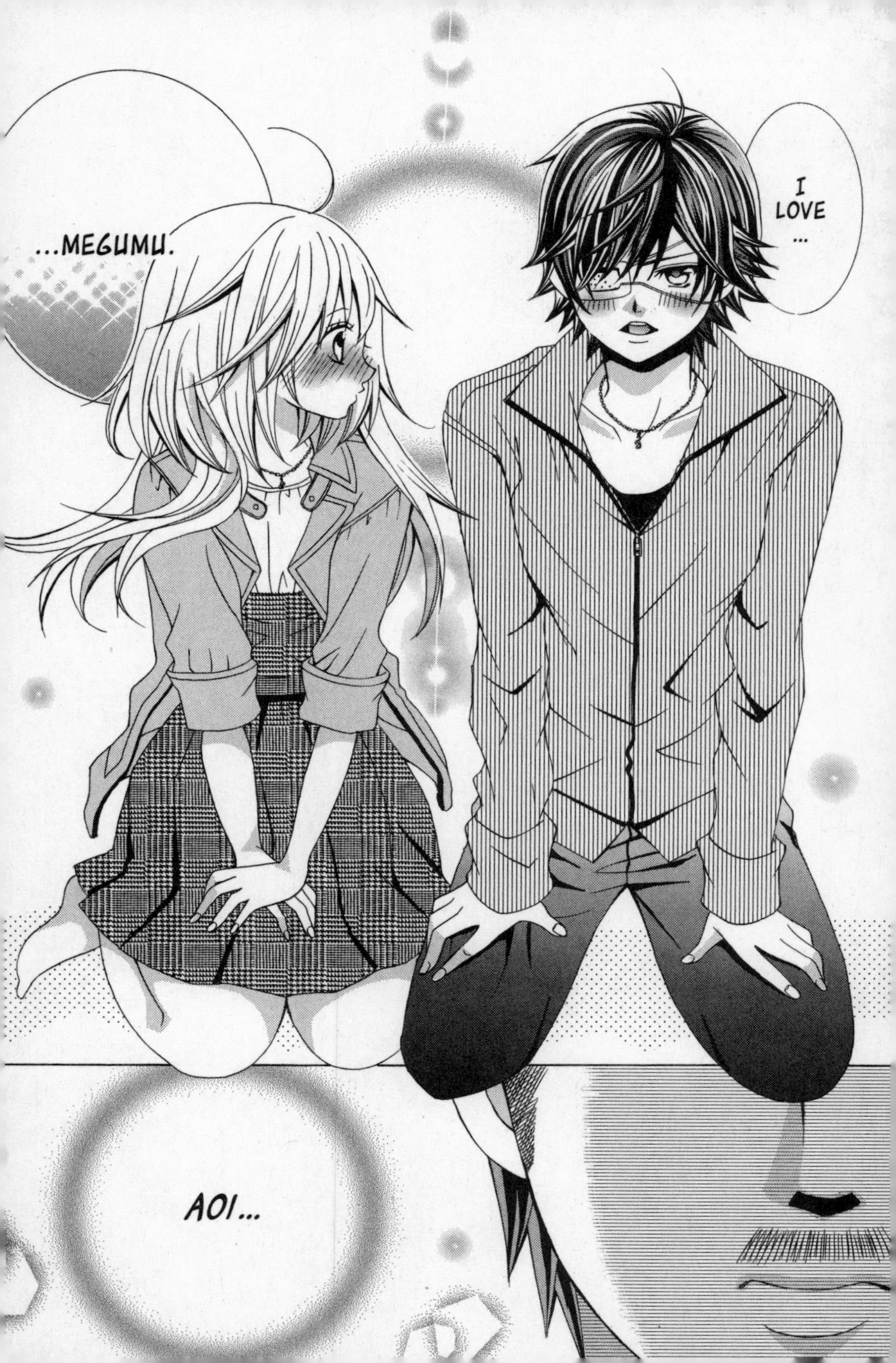
I LOVE ...
...MEGUMU.
AOI...

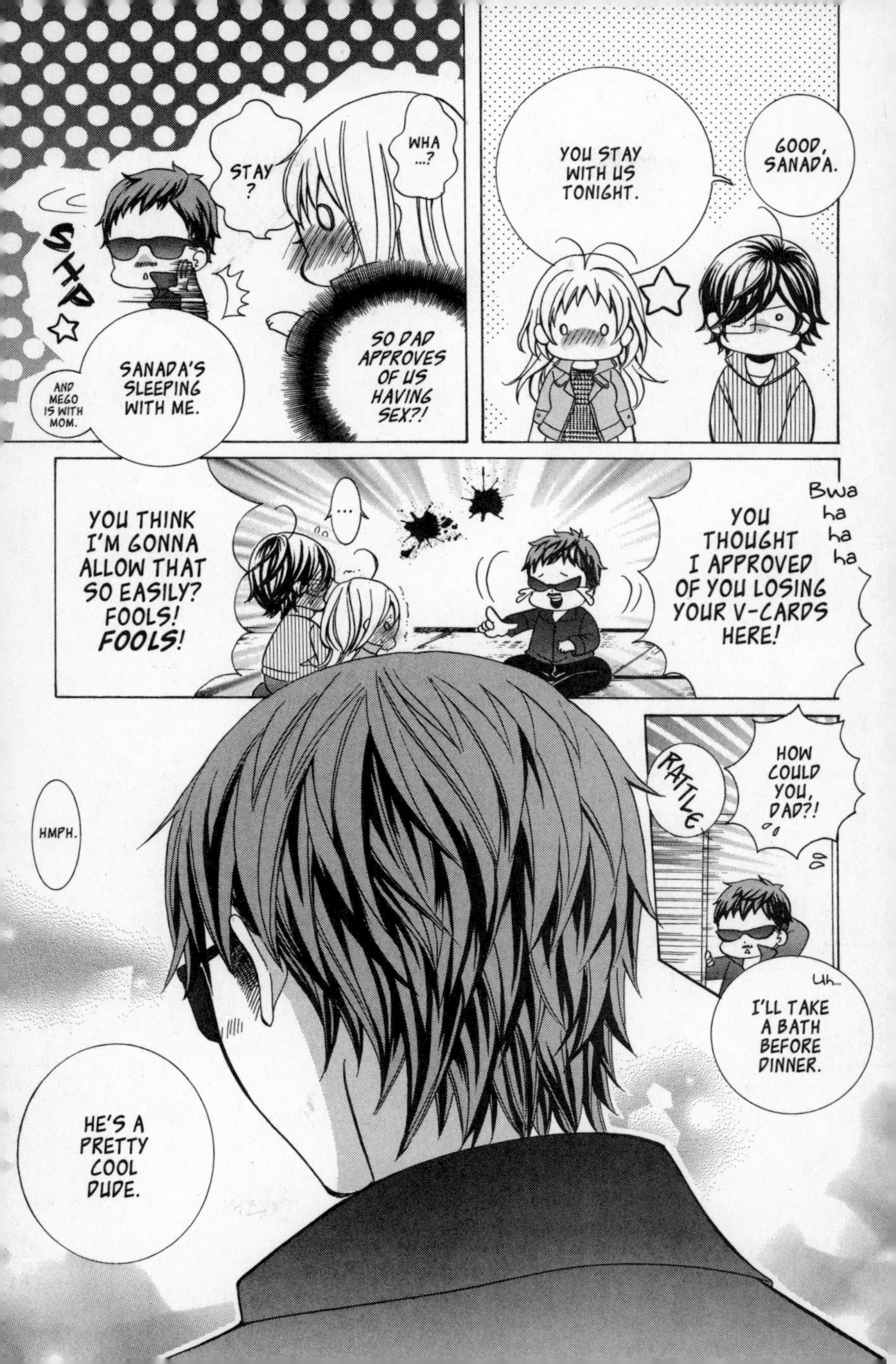
GOOD, SANADA.
YOU STAY WITH US TONIGHT.
WHA ...?
STAY?
SHP
SO DAD APPROVES OF US HAVING SEX?!
SANADA'S SLEEPING WITH ME.
AND MEGO IS WITH MOM.
Bwa ha ha ha
YOU THOUGHT I APPROVED OF YOU LOSING YOUR V-CARDS HERE!
...
YOU THINK I'M GONNA ALLOW THAT SO EASILY? FOOLS! FOOLS!
HOW COULD YOU, DAD?!
RATTLE
Uh...
I'LL TAKE A BATH BEFORE DINNER.
HMPH.
HE'S A PRETTY COOL DUDE.

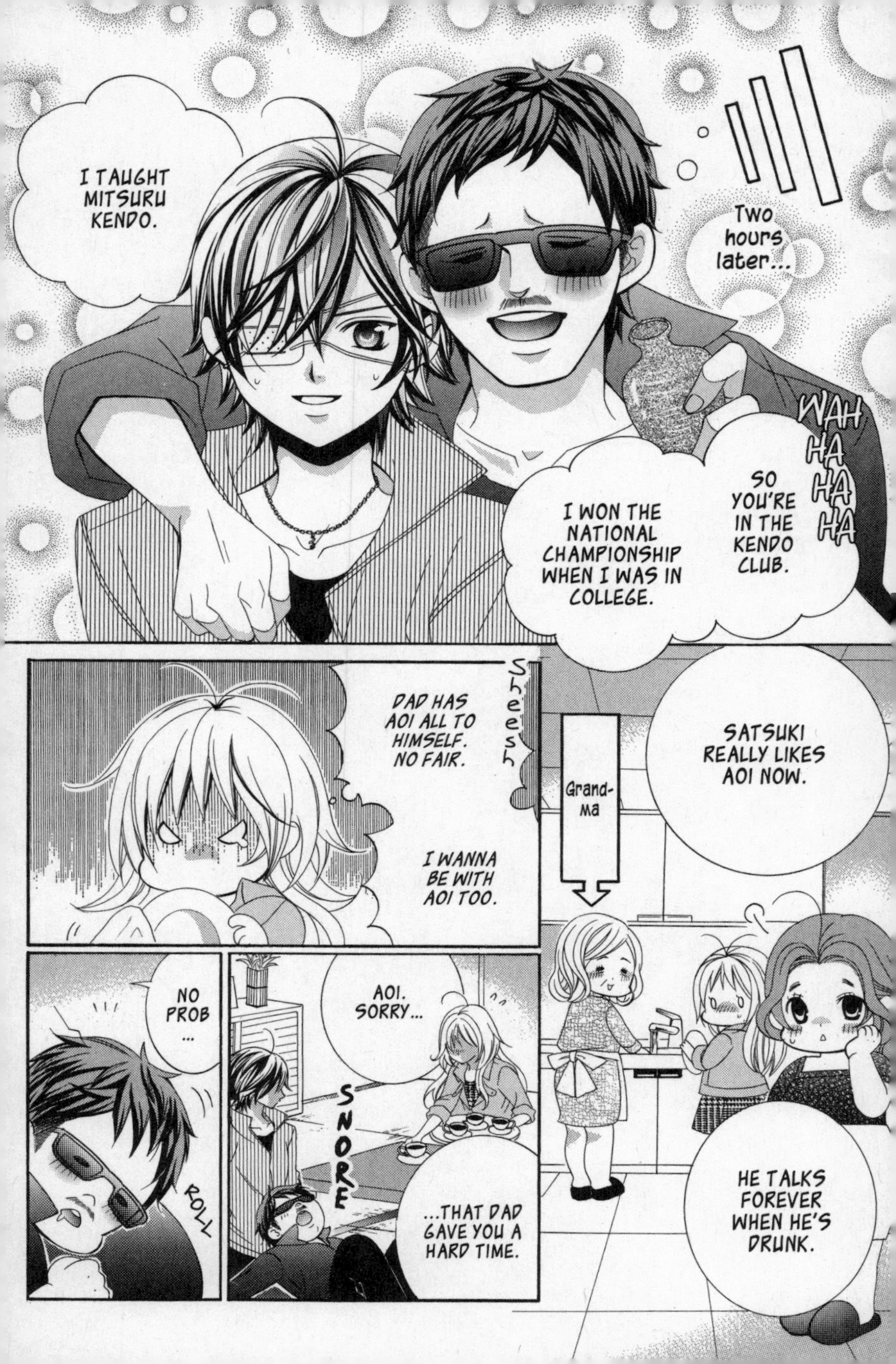
Two hours later...
SO YOU'RE IN THE KENDO CLUB.
WAH HA HA HA
I WON THE NATIONAL CHAMPIONSHIP WHEN I WAS IN COLLEGE.
I TAUGHT MITSURU KENDO.
SATSUKI REALLY LIKES AOI NOW.
Grand-ma
HE TALKS FOREVER WHEN HE'S DRUNK.
Sheesh
DAD HAS AOI ALL TO HIMSELF. NO FAIR.
I WANNA BE WITH AOI TOO.
AOI. SORRY...
SNORE
...THAT DAD GAVE YOU A HARD TIME.
NO PROB ...
ROLL

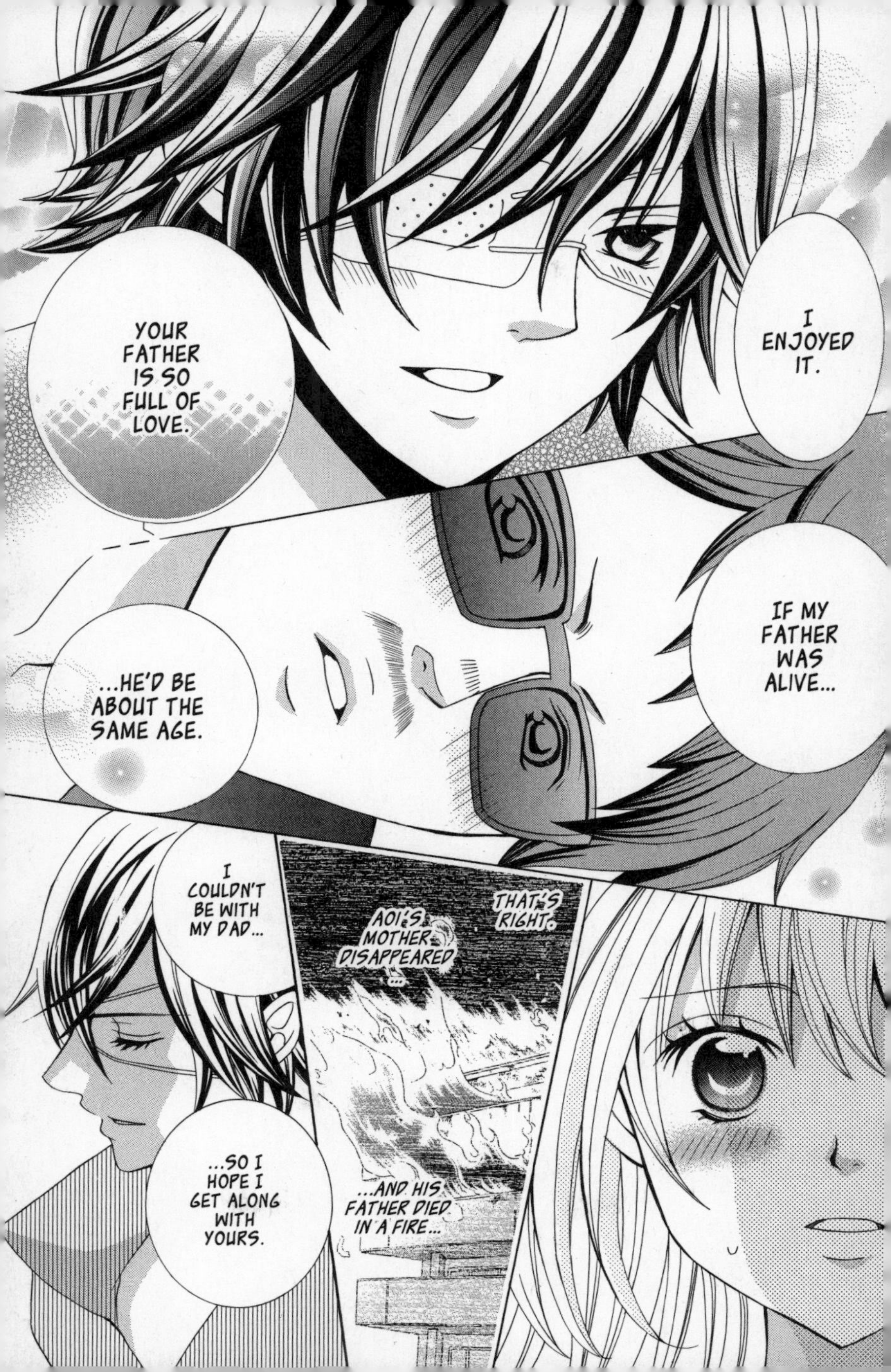
I ENJOYED IT.
YOUR FATHER IS SO FULL OF LOVE.
IF MY FATHER WAS ALIVE...
...HE'D BE ABOUT THE SAME AGE.
THAT'S RIGHT.
AOI'S MOTHER DISAPPEARED...
...AND HIS FATHER DIED IN A FIRE...
I COULDN'T BE WITH MY DAD...
...SO I HOPE I GET ALONG WITH YOURS.

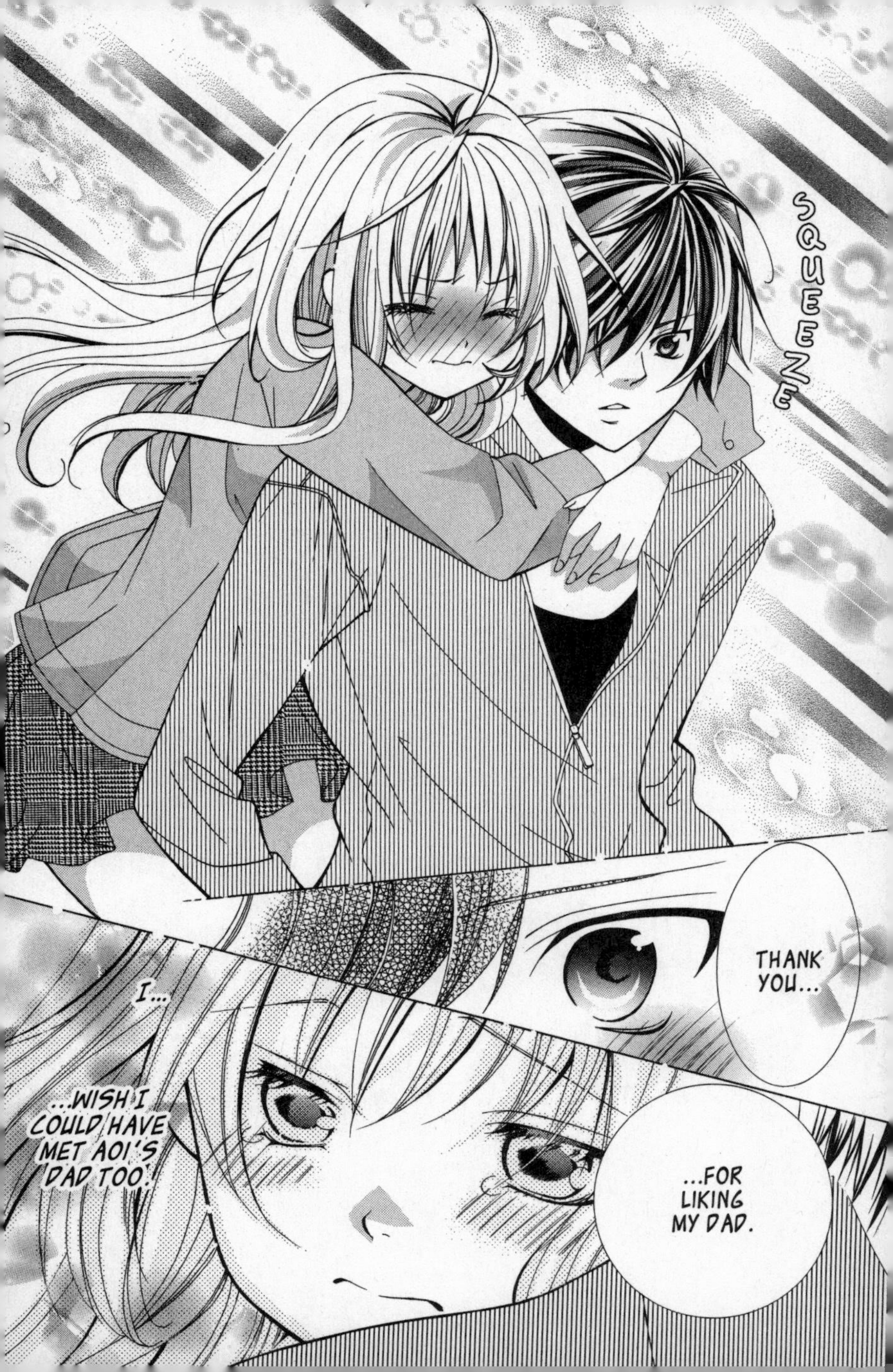
SQUEEZE
THANK YOU...
...FOR LIKING MY DAD.
I...
...WISH I COULD HAVE MET AOI'S DAD TOO.

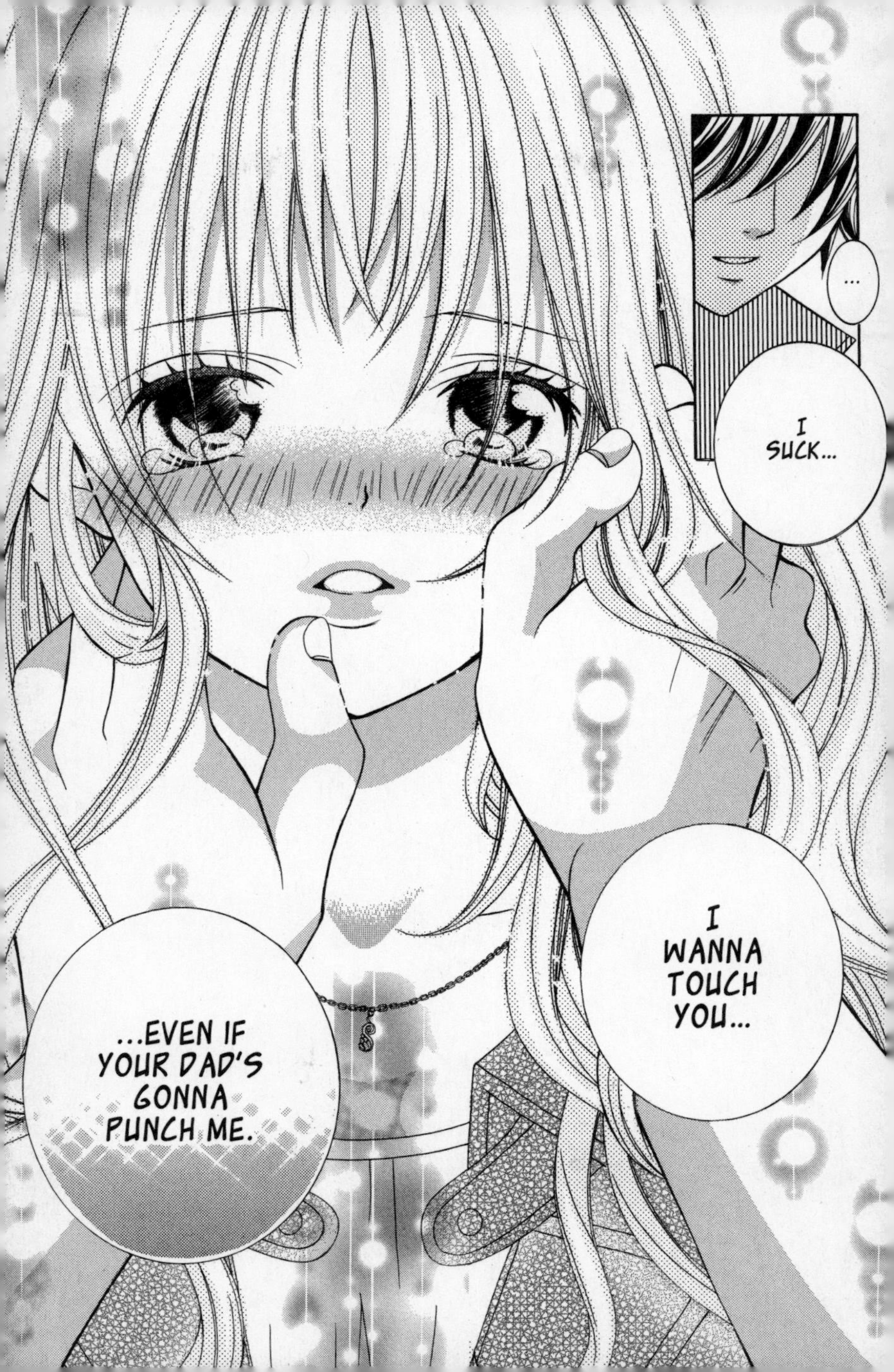
...
I SUCK...
I WANNA TOUCH YOU...
...EVEN IF YOUR DAD'S GONNA PUNCH ME.

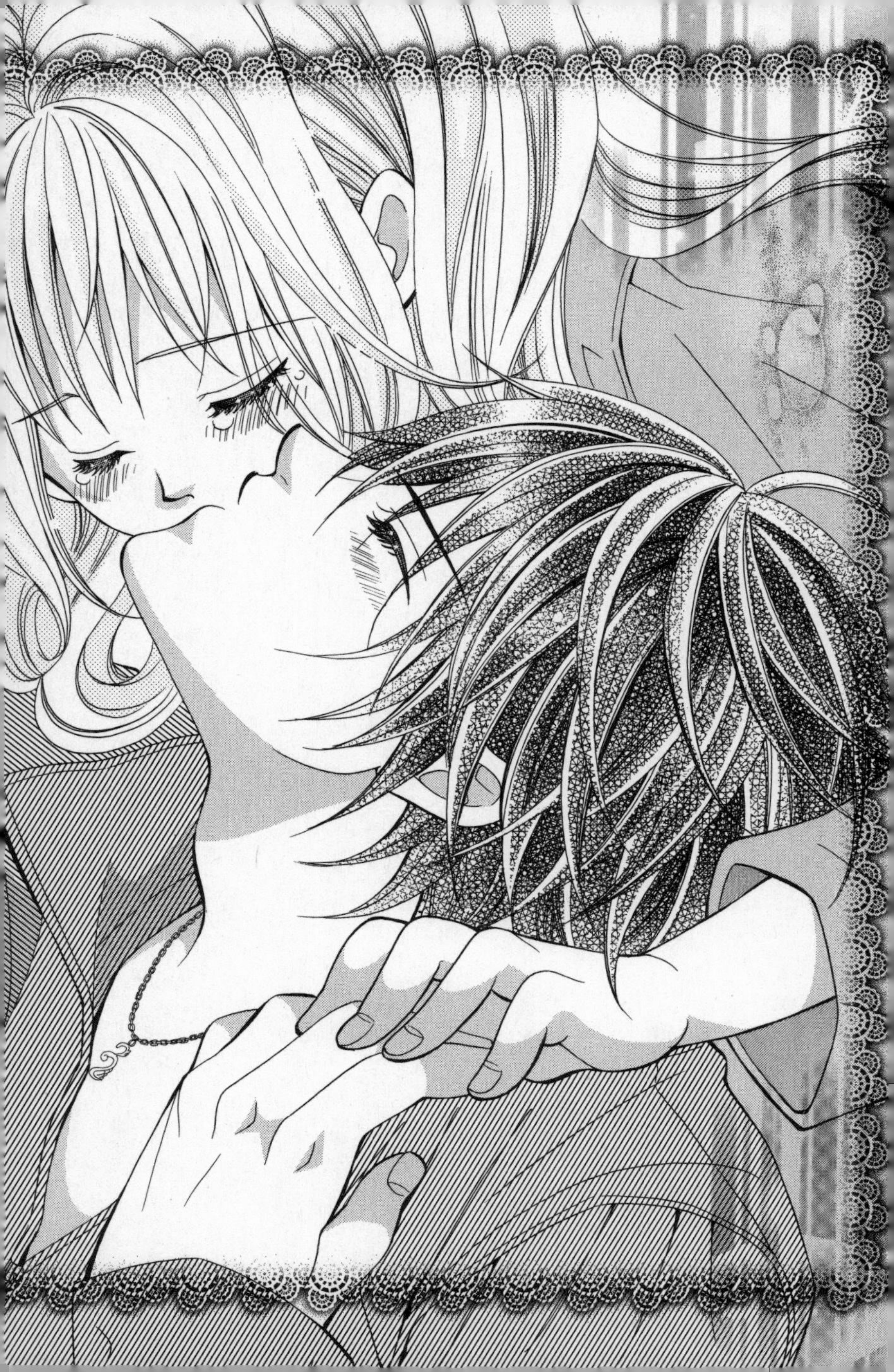

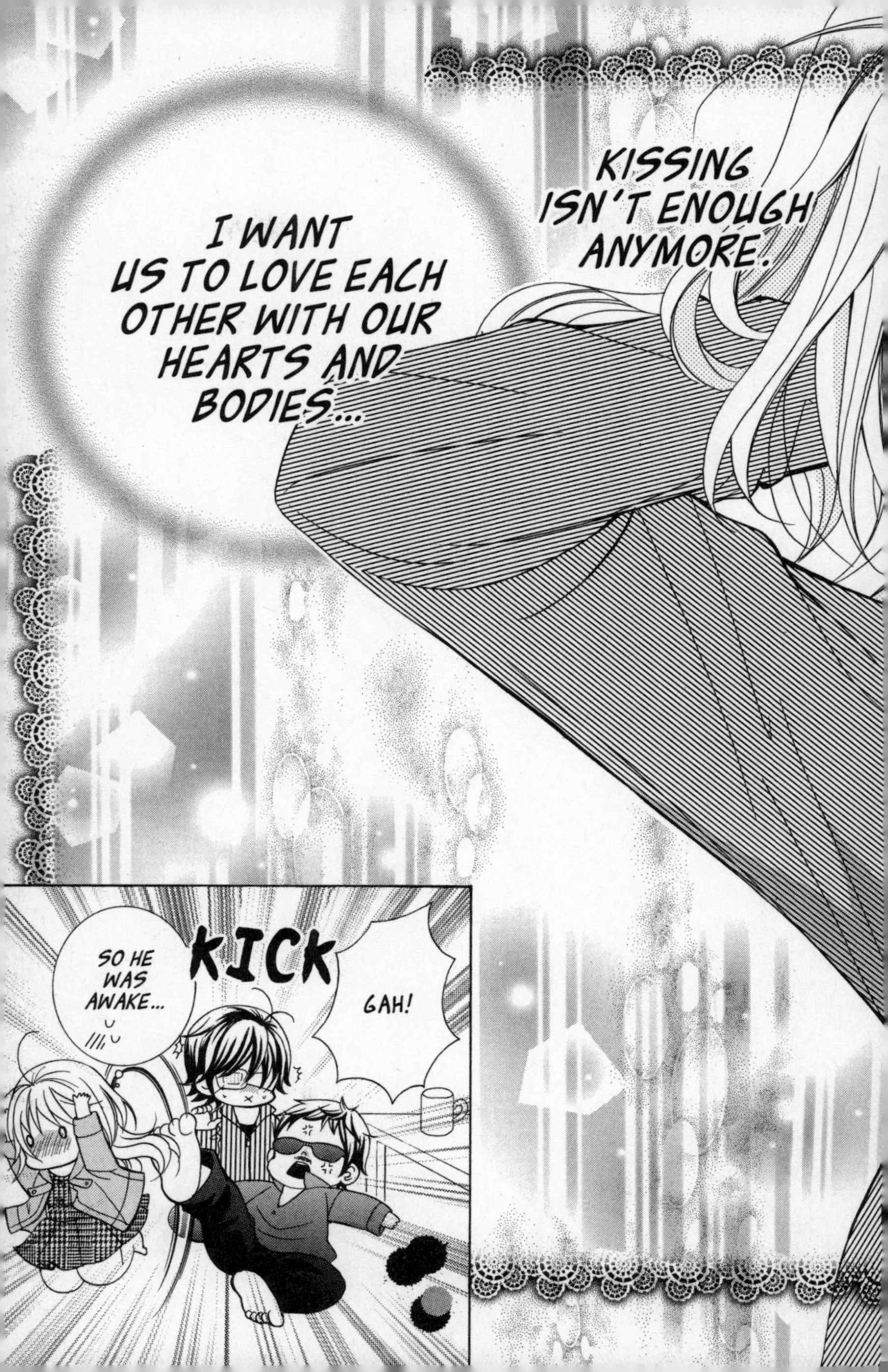
KISSING ISN'T ENOUGH ANYMORE.
I WANT US TO LOVE EACH OTHER WITH OUR HEARTS AND BODIES...
GAH!
KICK
SO HE WAS AWAKE...

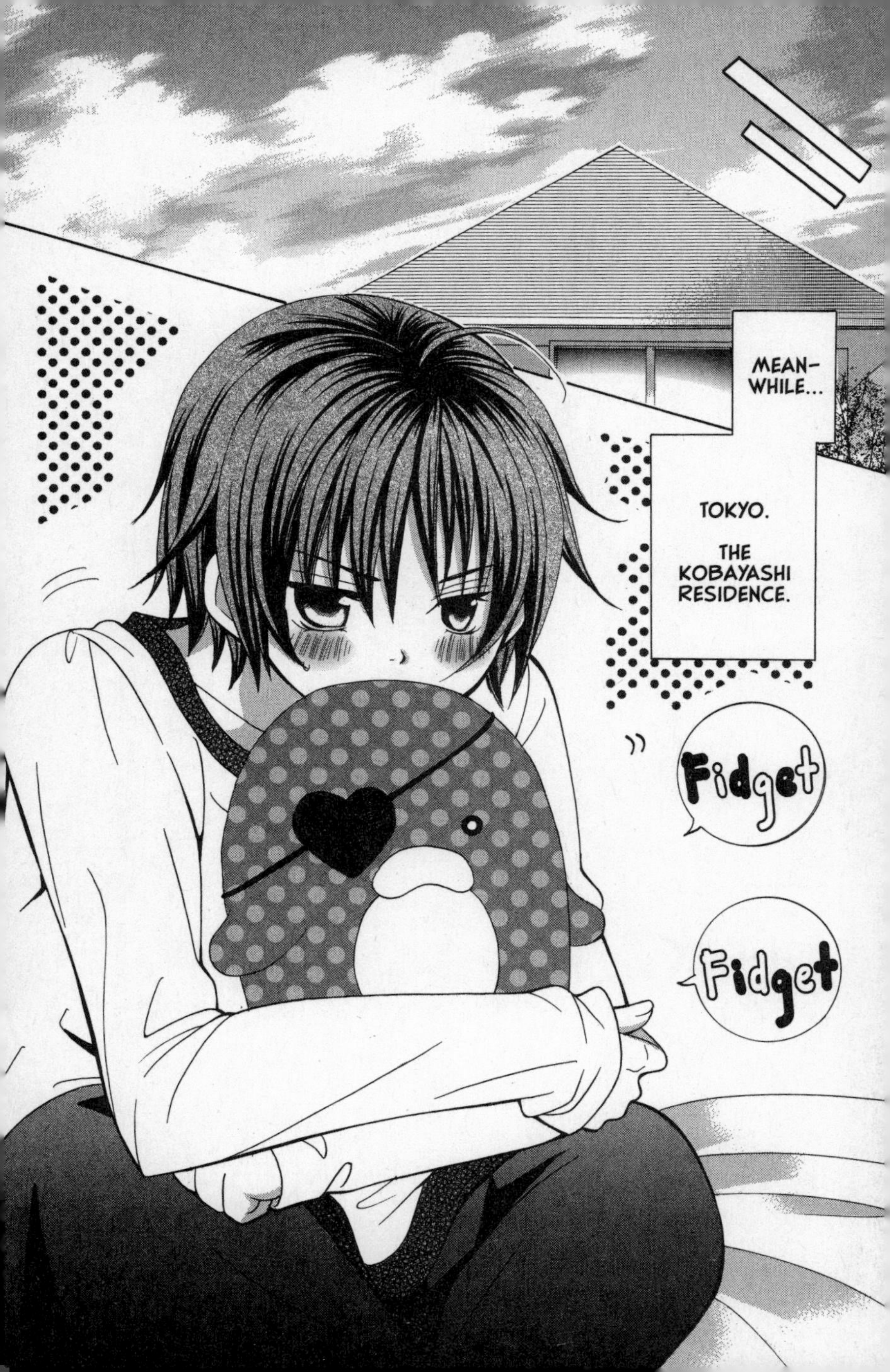
MEAN-WHILE...
TOKYO.
THE KOBAYASHI RESIDENCE.
Fidget
Fidget

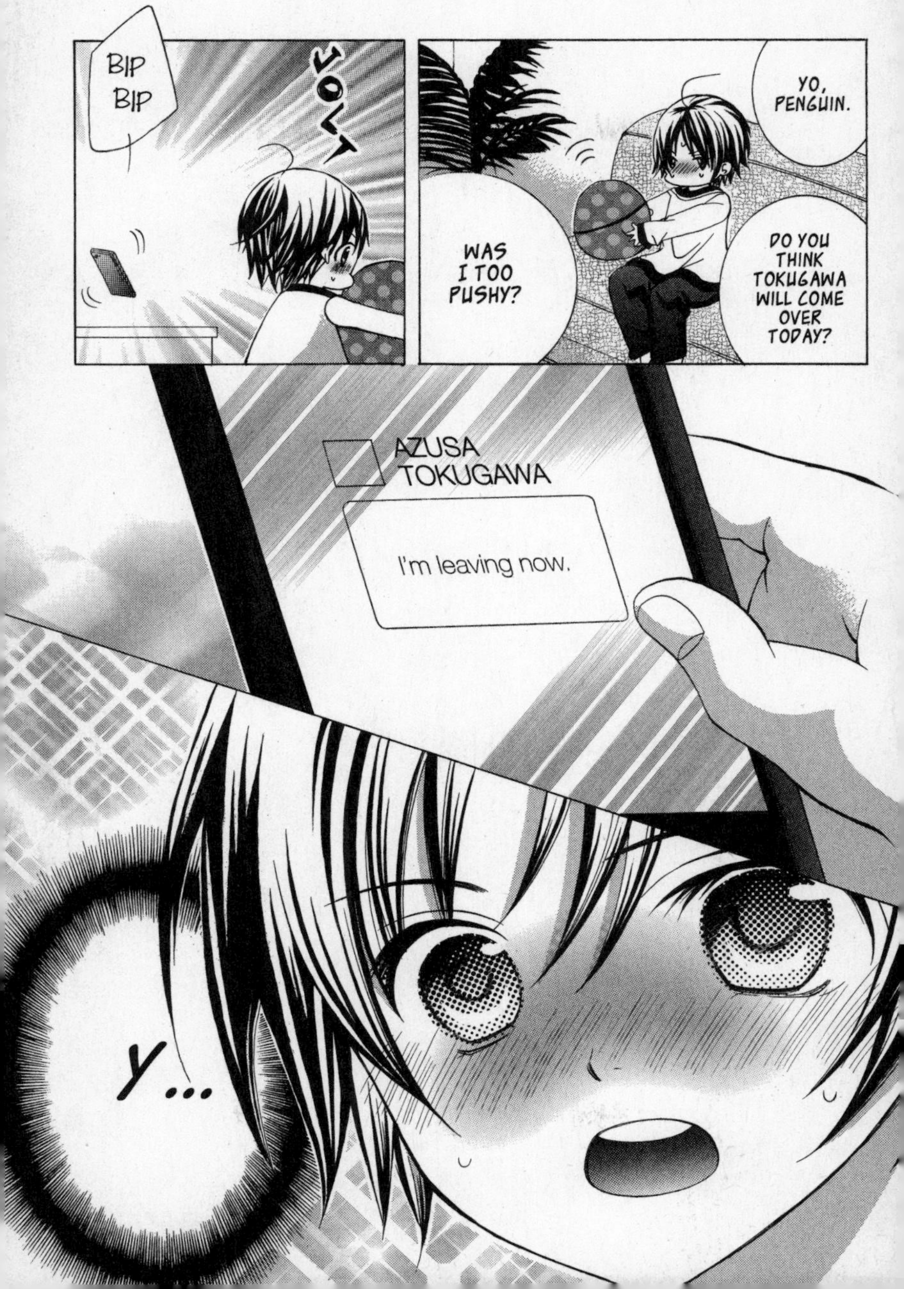
YO, PENGUIN.
DO YOU THINK TOKUGAWA WILL COME OVER TODAY?
WAS I TOO PUSHY?
BIP BIP
JOLT
AZUSA TOKUGAWA
I'm leaving now.
Y...

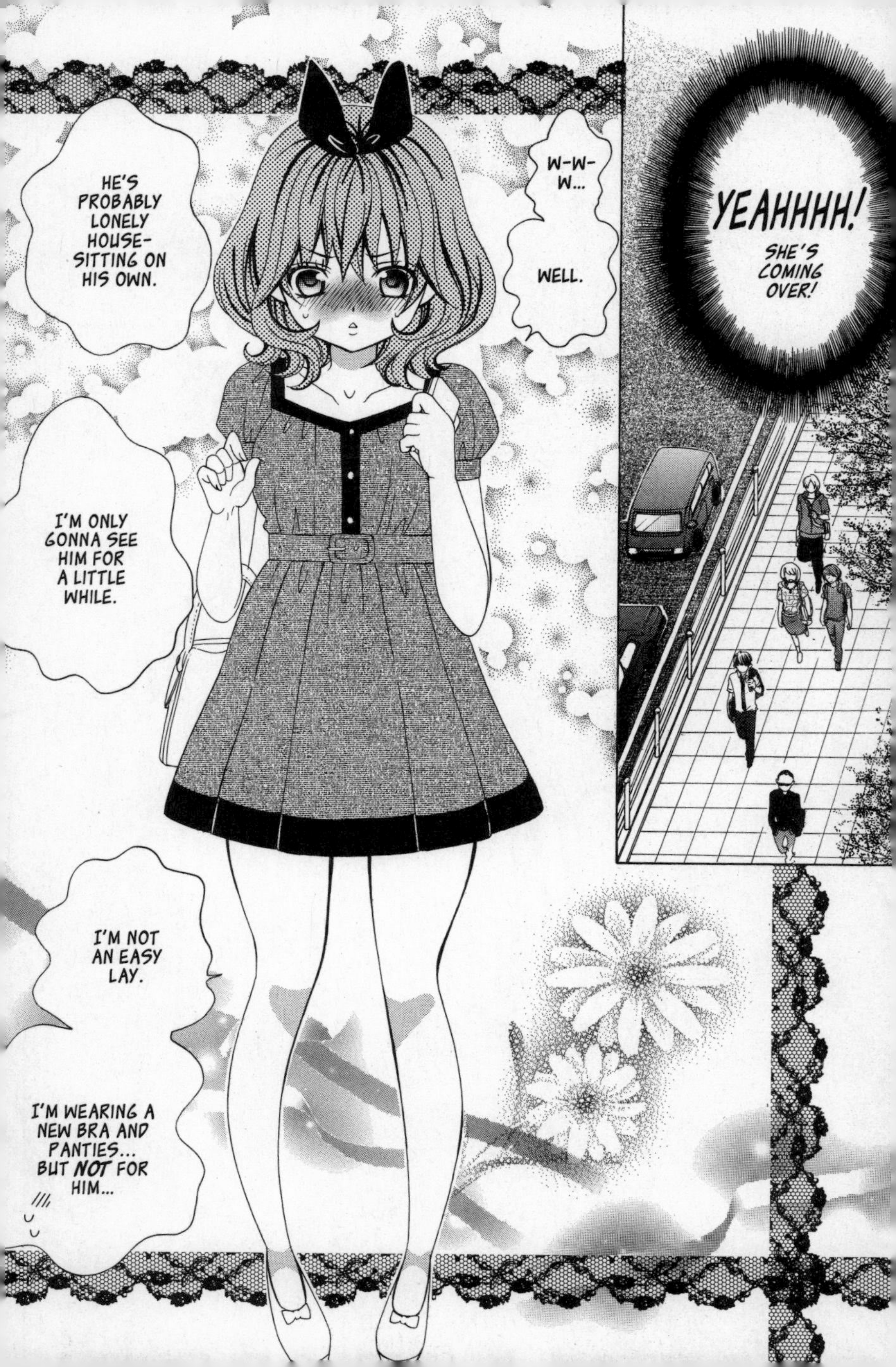
YEAHHHH!
SHE'S COMING OVER!
W-W-W... WELL.
HE'S PROBABLY LONELY HOUSE-SITTING ON HIS OWN.
I'M ONLY GONNA SEE HIM FOR A LITTLE WHILE.
I'M NOT AN EASY LAY.
I'M WEARING A NEW BRA AND PANTIES... BUT *NOT* FOR HIM...

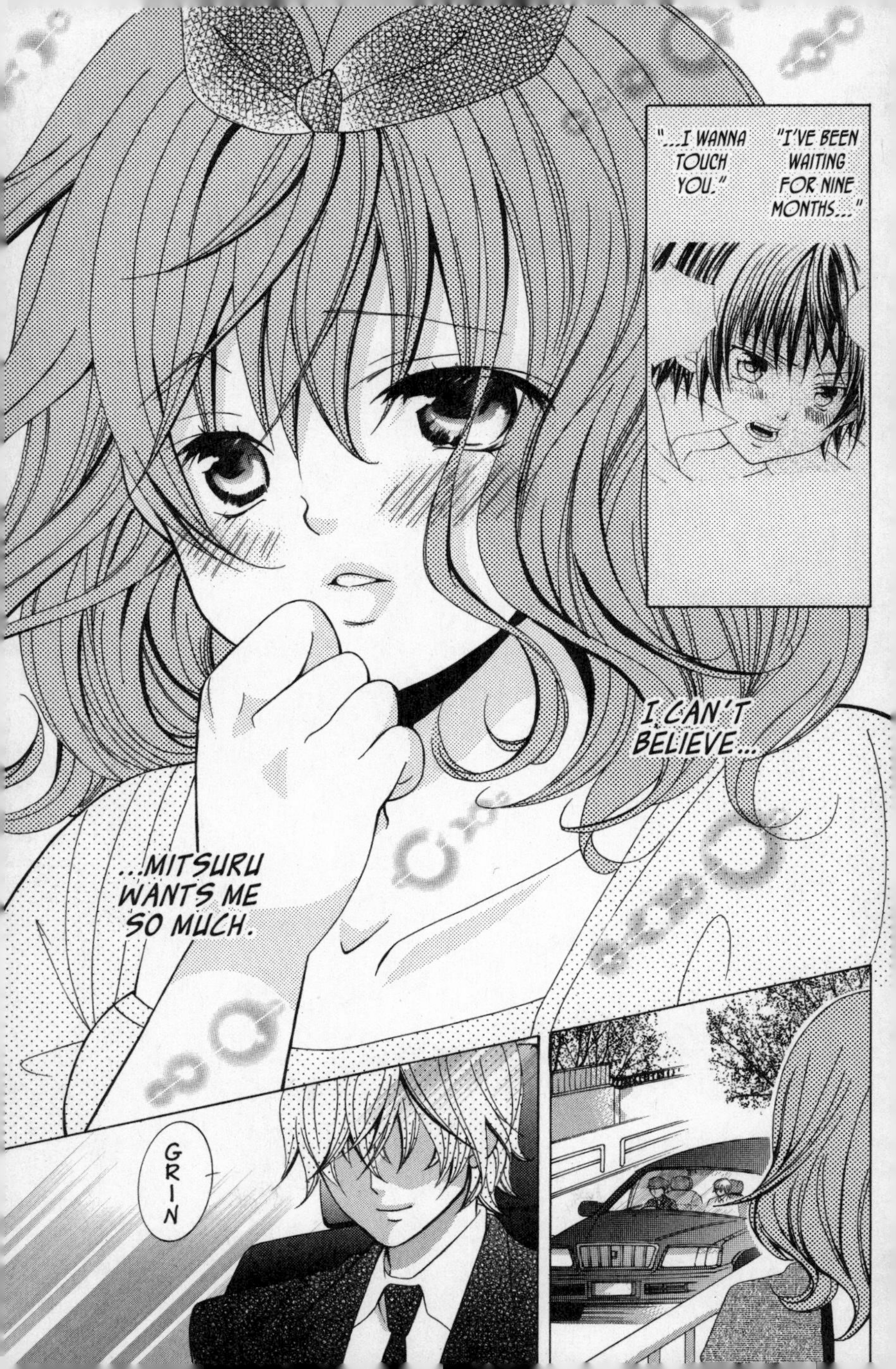
"I'VE BEEN WAITING FOR NINE MONTHS..."
"...I WANNA TOUCH YOU."
I CAN'T BELIEVE...
...MITSURU WANTS ME SO MUCH.
GRIN

CHAK
HEY.
YOU'RE DRESSED UP NICE.
ARE YOU GOING ON A DATE?
HELLO ...
WHAT THE HECK?
IS HE TRYING TO PICK ME UP?
...
I AM.
I CAN'T ALLOW YOU TO BE UNFAITHFUL LIKE THAT...
...SINCE YOU'RE MY FUTURE WIFE.

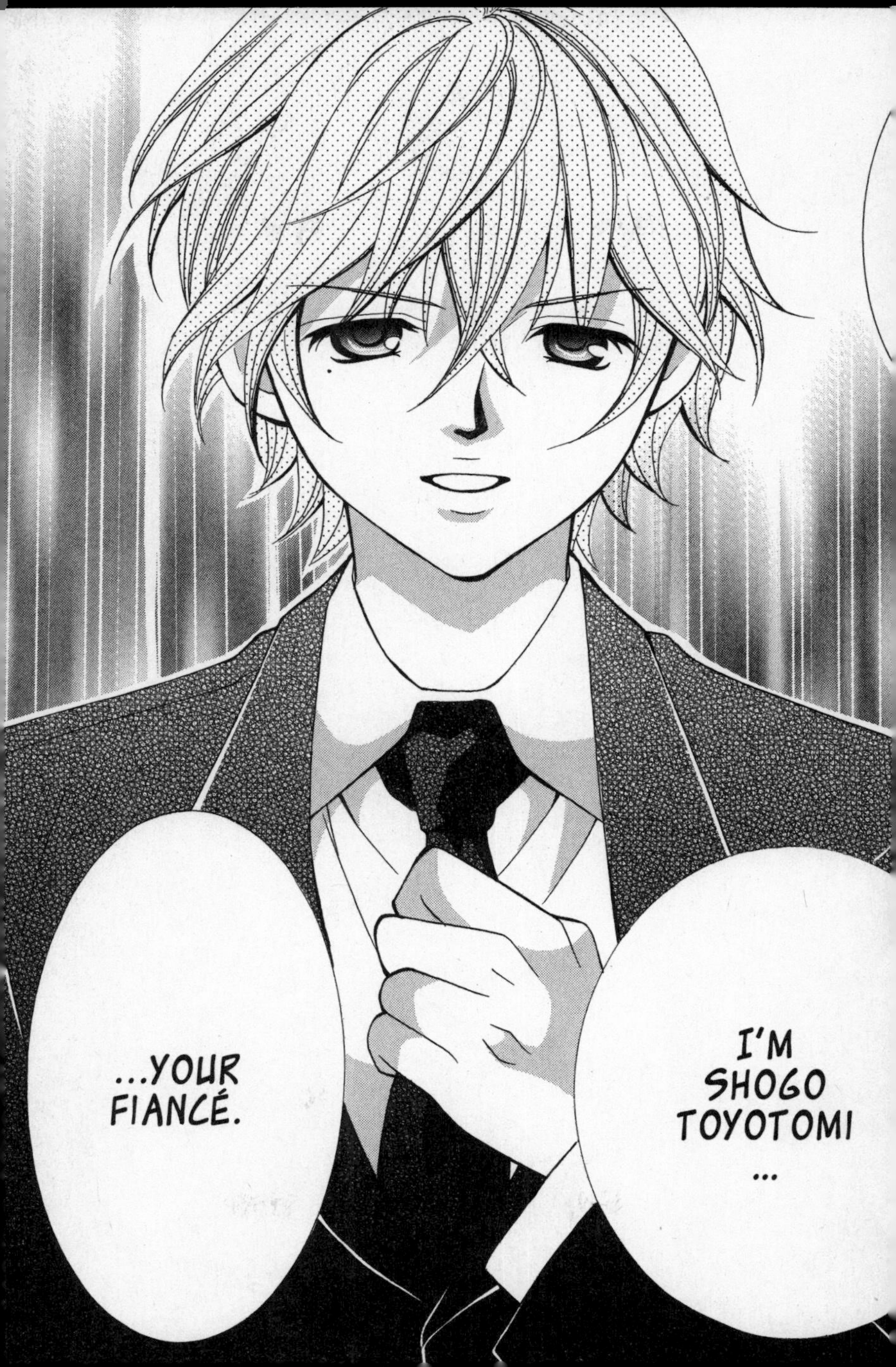
I'M SHOGO TOYOTOMI ...
...YOUR FIANCÉ.

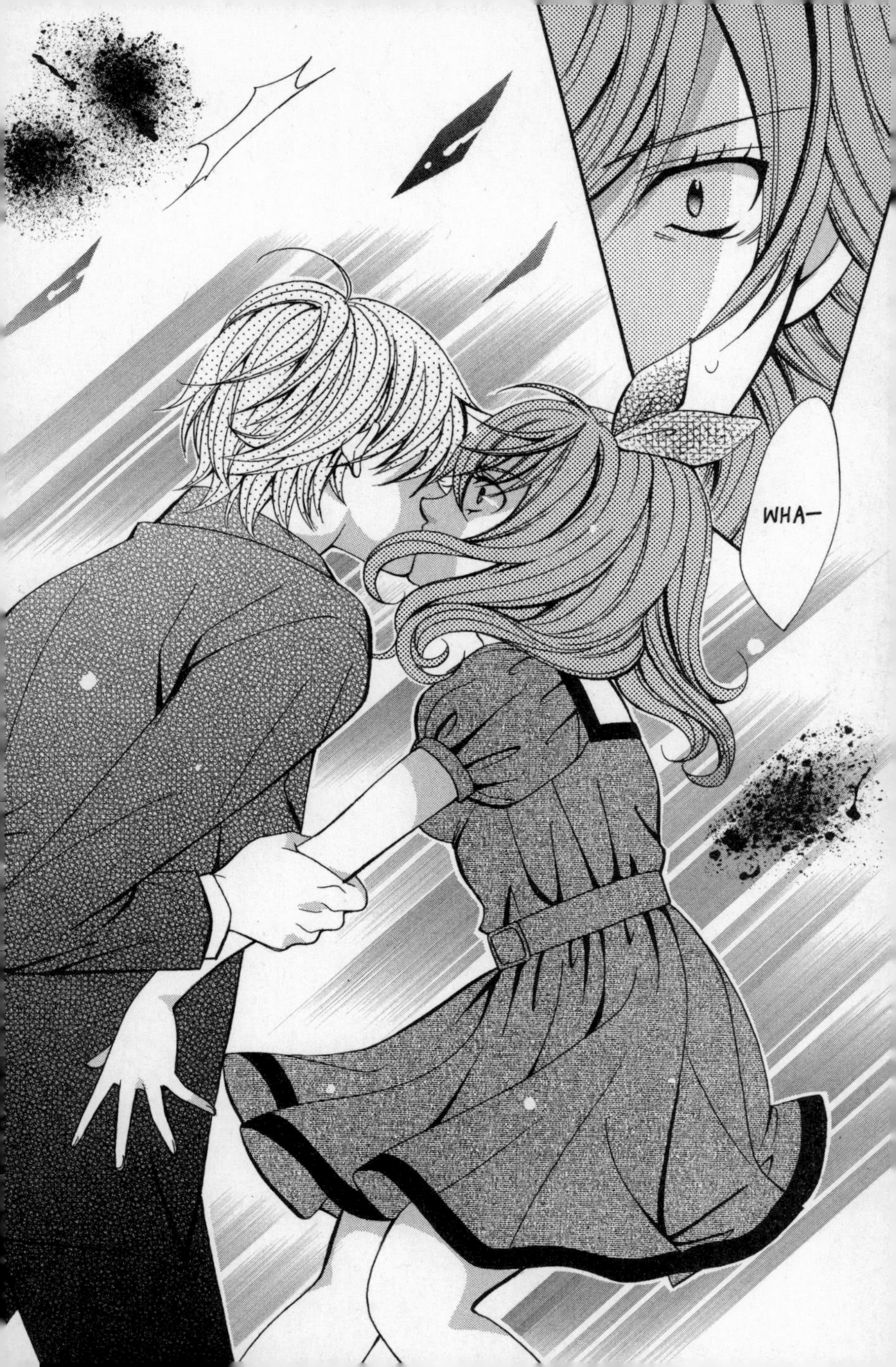
WHA—

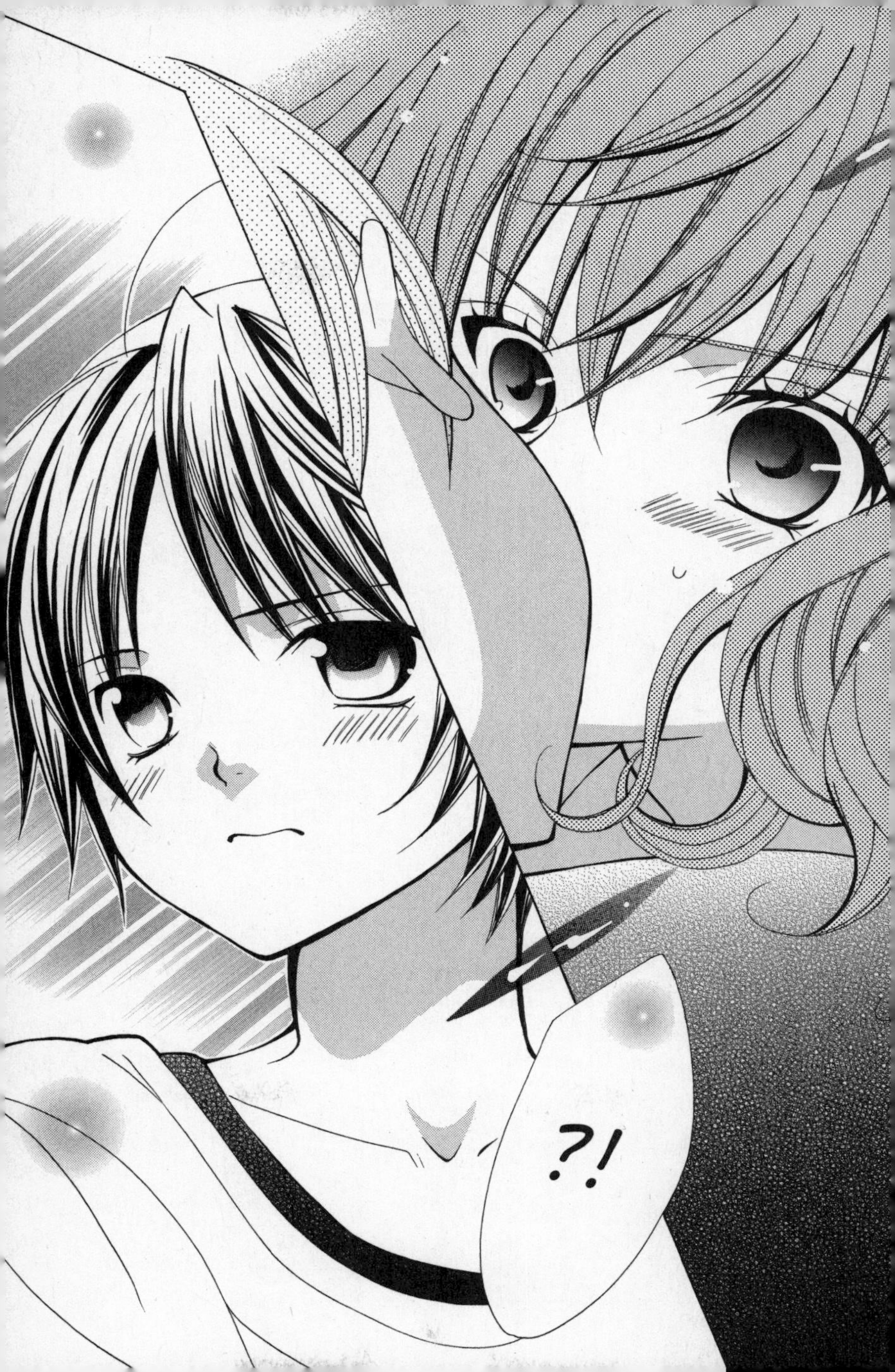
?!

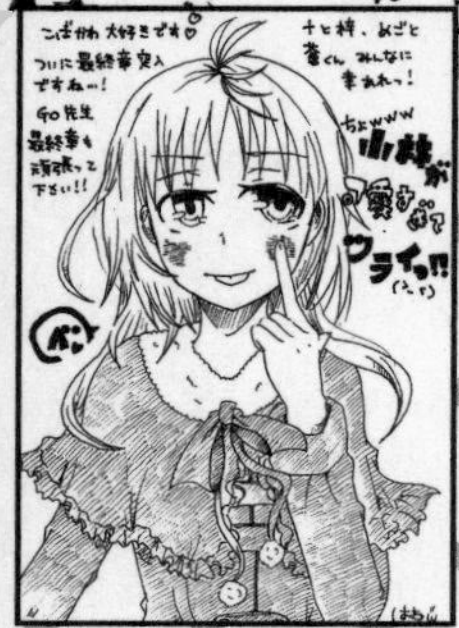
こばかわ大好きです♡
ついに最終章突入ですねー!
GO先生最終章も頑張って下さい!!
ツライっ!!

Hacchin (Hokkaido) ←
Ed.: Her "bleh" is super cute!

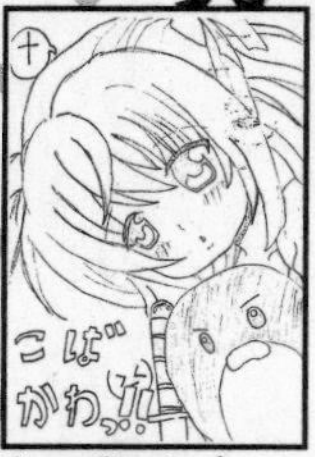
こばかわっ!!

Runa Ikeda ↑ (Okinawa)
Ed.: Both Mego and Penguin are so very cute!!

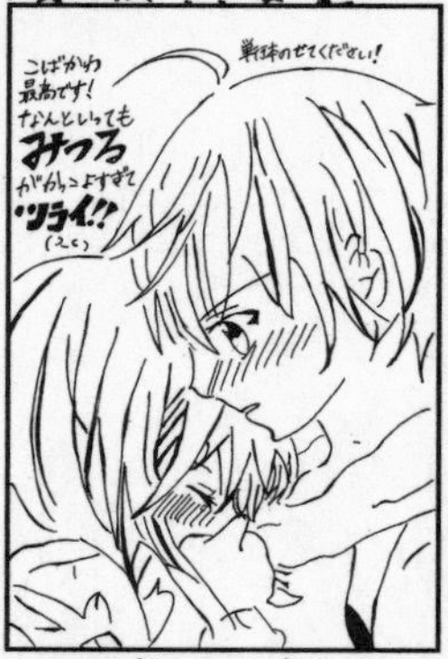
こばかわ最高です!
なんといってもみつるがかっこよすぎてツライ!!

Kajiyuki (Ishikawa) ↑
Ed.: I'm jealous cuz Mitsuru's becoming more and more cool!

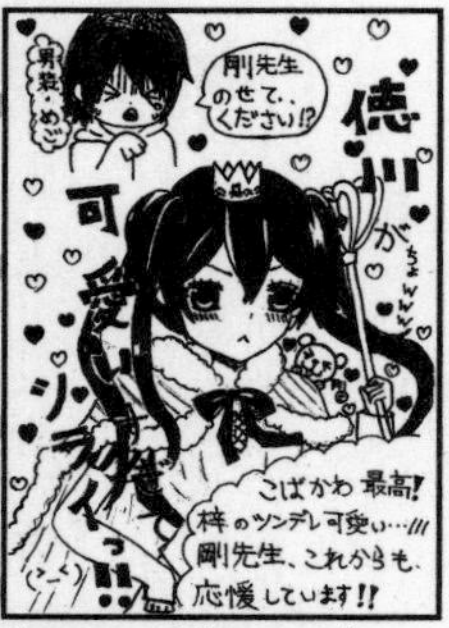
剛先生のせてください!?
こばかわ最高!
梓のツンデレ可愛い…!!!
剛先生、これからも応援しています!!

Masayoshi Ikegami ↑ (Kanagawa)
Ed.: I love both the cross-dressed Mego and the tsundere Azusa.♥

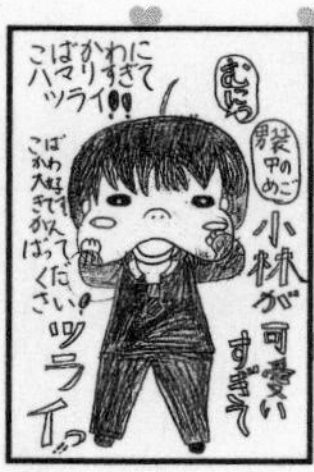
こばかわにハマりすぎてツライ!!
小林が可愛すぎてツライっ

Akari Osawa (Saitama) ←
Ed.: Mego's cheeks are really stretchy!

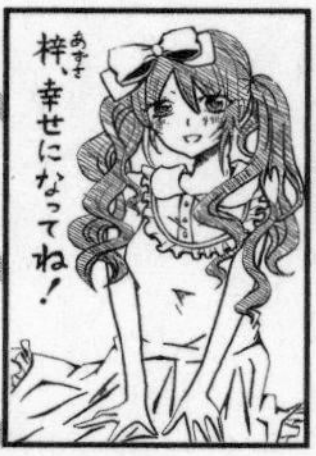
梓、幸せになってね!

Oto M (Aichi) ←
Ed.: "I'll make her happy for sure!" -Mitsuru

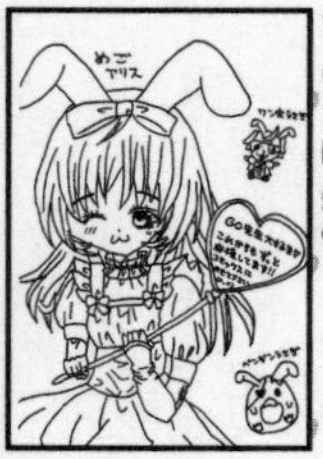

Tomoyu (Aichi) ←
Ed.: Everyone's got rabbit ears!!

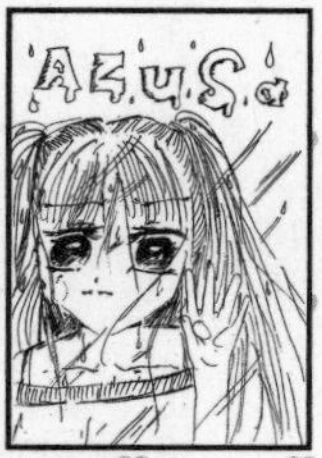
AZUSA

Koyupan ↑ (Hokkaido)
Ed.: Azusa looks beautiful even through a window!

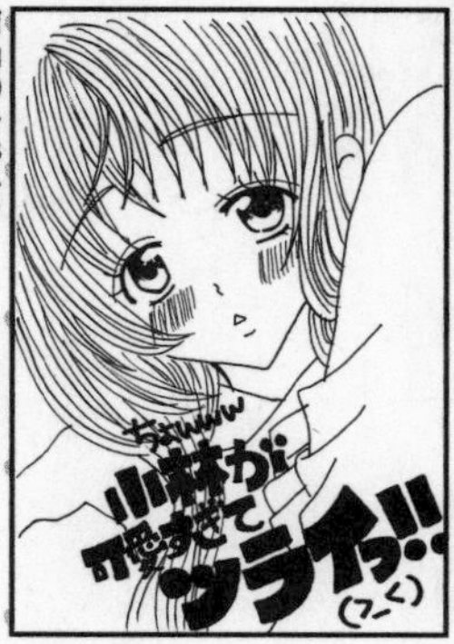
ちょwww
小林が可愛すぎてツライっ!!

Natsuki Uchida (Tokyo) →
Ed.: Here's a super-pure girl.♥

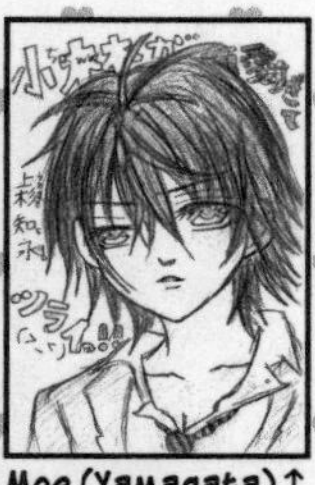

Moe (Yamagata) ↑
Ed.: Heeeeere's a quiet-looking Uesugi!!

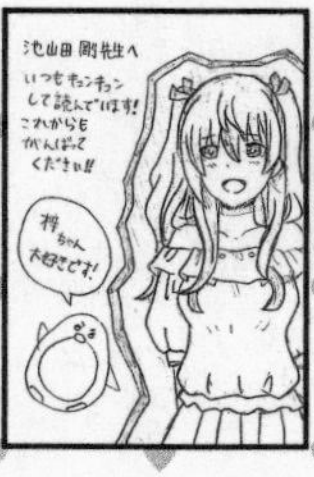
池山田剛先生へ
いつもキュンキュンして読んでます!
これからもがんばってください!!

Kurobuchi Megane (Aichi) ←
Ed.: Squee! to the super-cute Azusa!!

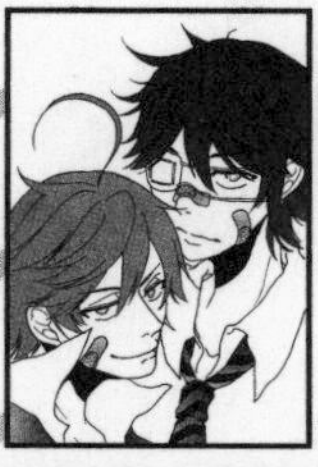

Edao (Chiba) ←
Ed.: A super cool pair, Satchan and Uesugi!!

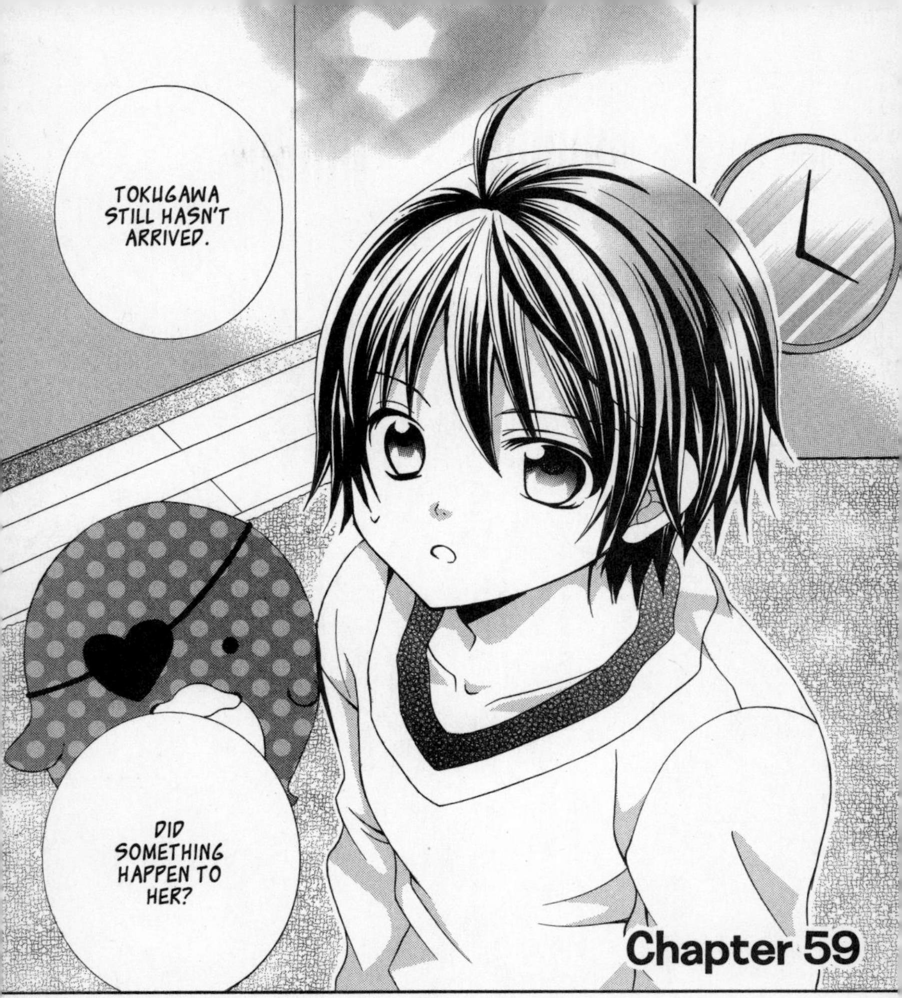
TOKUGAWA STILL HASN'T ARRIVED.
DID SOMETHING HAPPEN TO HER?

Chapter 59

ABOUT THE CHARACTERS. (^o^)
THE NEW CHARACTER SHOGO TOYOTOMI IS A RARE CHARACTER WITH DROOPING EYES, AND I ENJOY DRAWING HIM. ♪
A LOT OF MIDDLE-AGED MEN APPEAR IN *SO CUTE!*, SUCH AS AZUSA'S DAD, MEGO AND MITSURU'S DAD AND AOI'S GUARDIAN KAGETSUNA. THEY ALL LOOK LIKE THEY DON'T BELONG IN A SHOJO MANGA, SO DRAWING THEM IS A VERY NEW EXPERIENCE. (*SMILE*) I USED TO FIND IT DIFFICULT TO DRAW MIDDLE-AGED MEN WHEN I WAS YOUNGER, BUT I'VE GROWN TO LOVE THEM AS I'VE CONTINUED DRAWING THEM, AND NOW I ENJOY DRAWING THEM. LOL! MEGO AND MITSURU'S DAD WAS ORIGINALLY SUPPOSED TO APPEAR IN CHAPTER 1, FIGHTING MITSURU AND TRAINING HIM, BUT I HAD TO DELETE THE SCENE BECAUSE OF PAGE CONSTRAINTS, AND IT TOOK THREE YEARS FOR HIM TO APPEAR. LOL! ROOT FOR HIM, SINCE HE'LL BE PLAYING AN ACTIVE ROLE FROM NOW ON! ♡♡ (^o^)

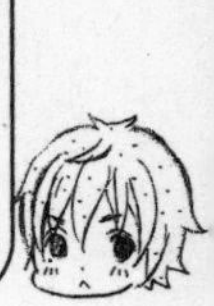

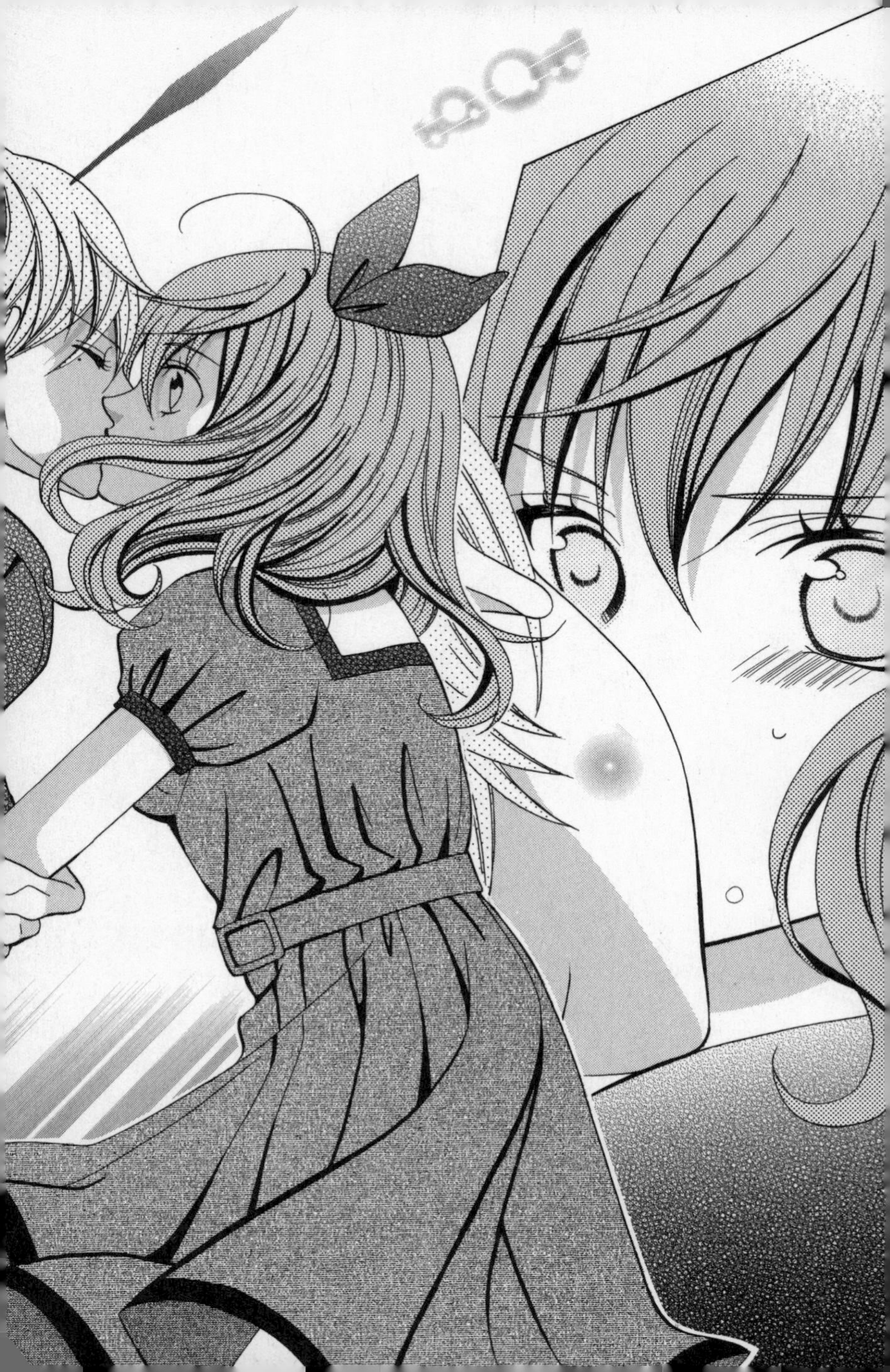

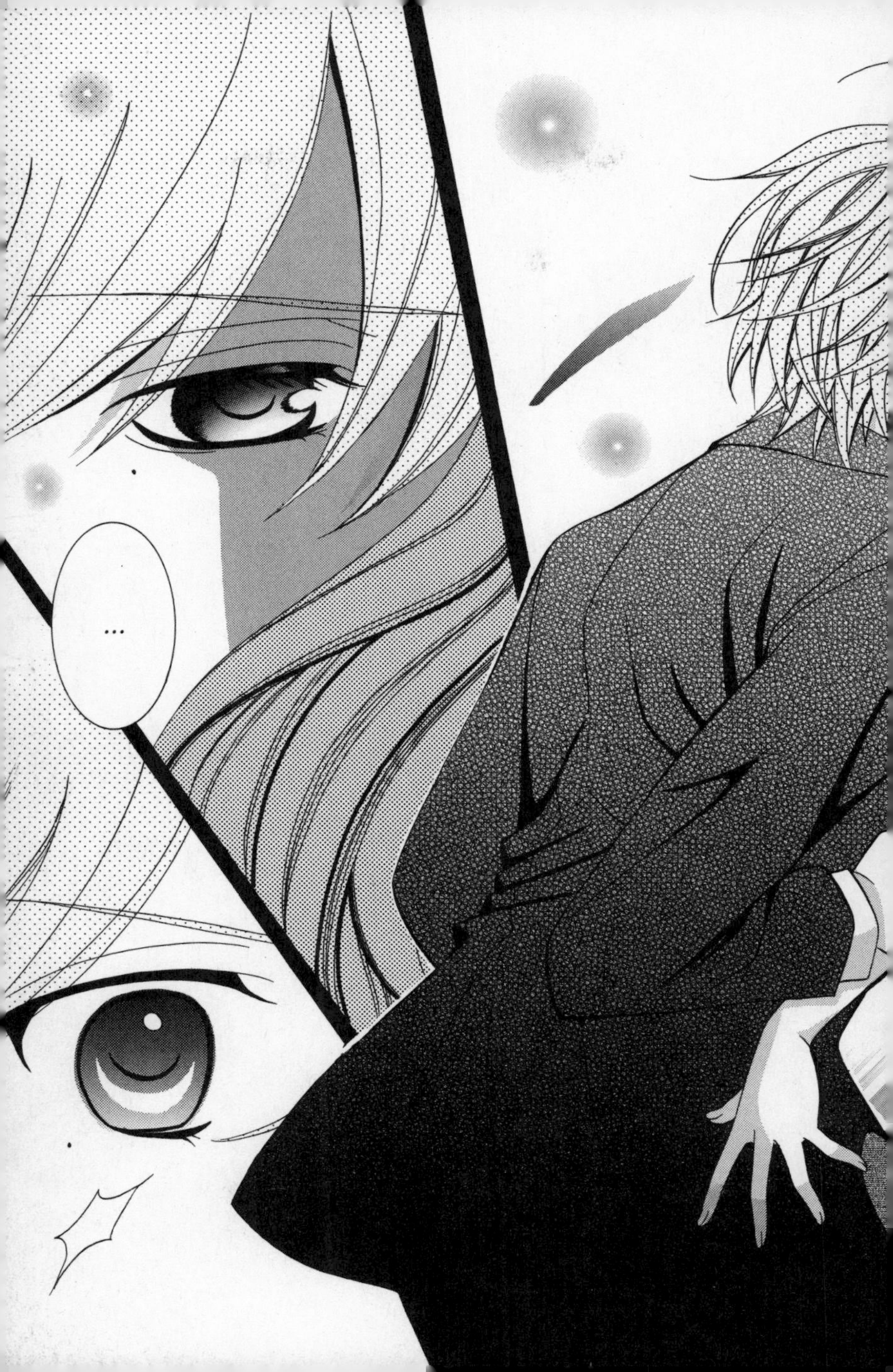
...

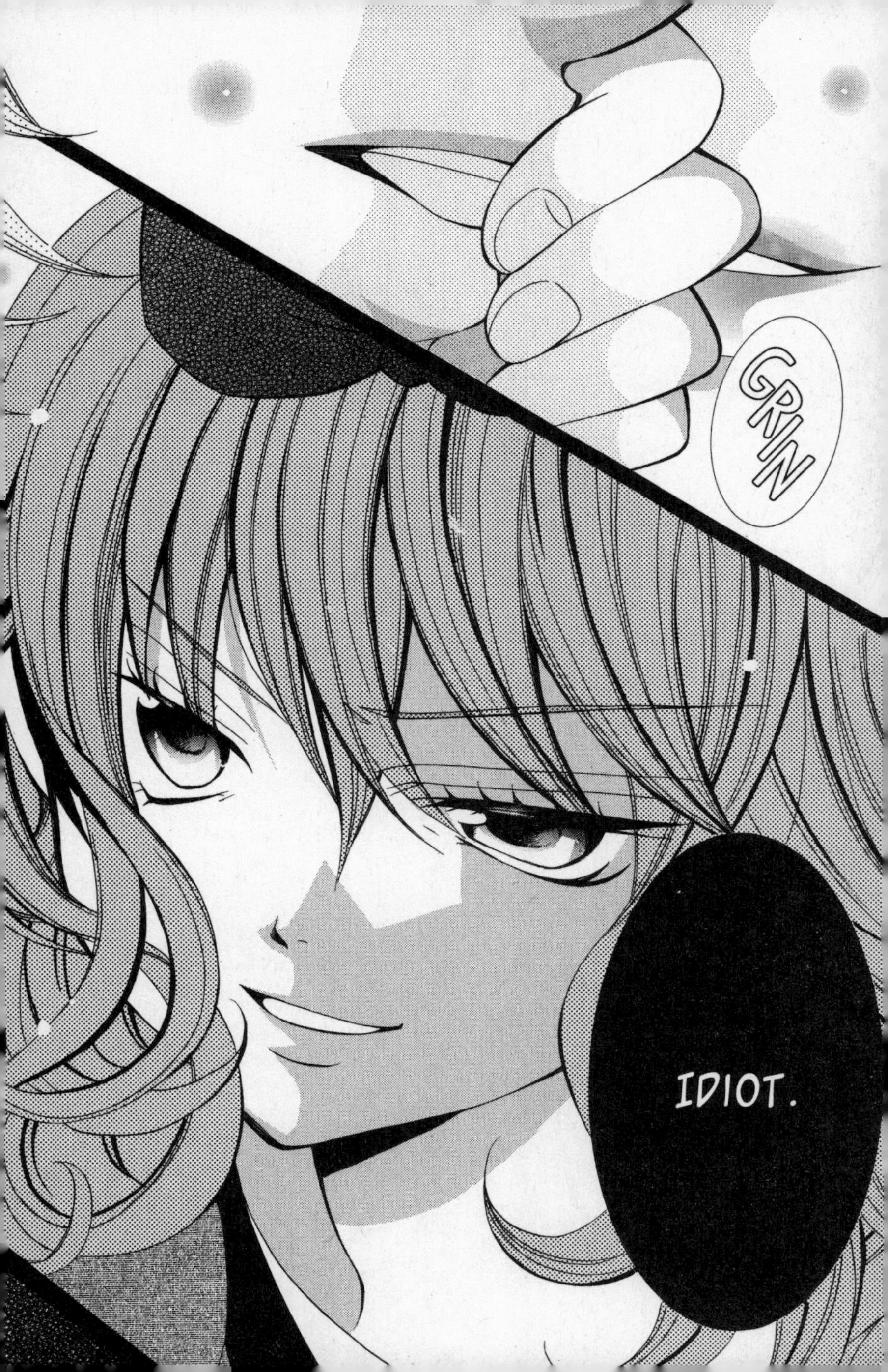
GRIN
IDIOT.

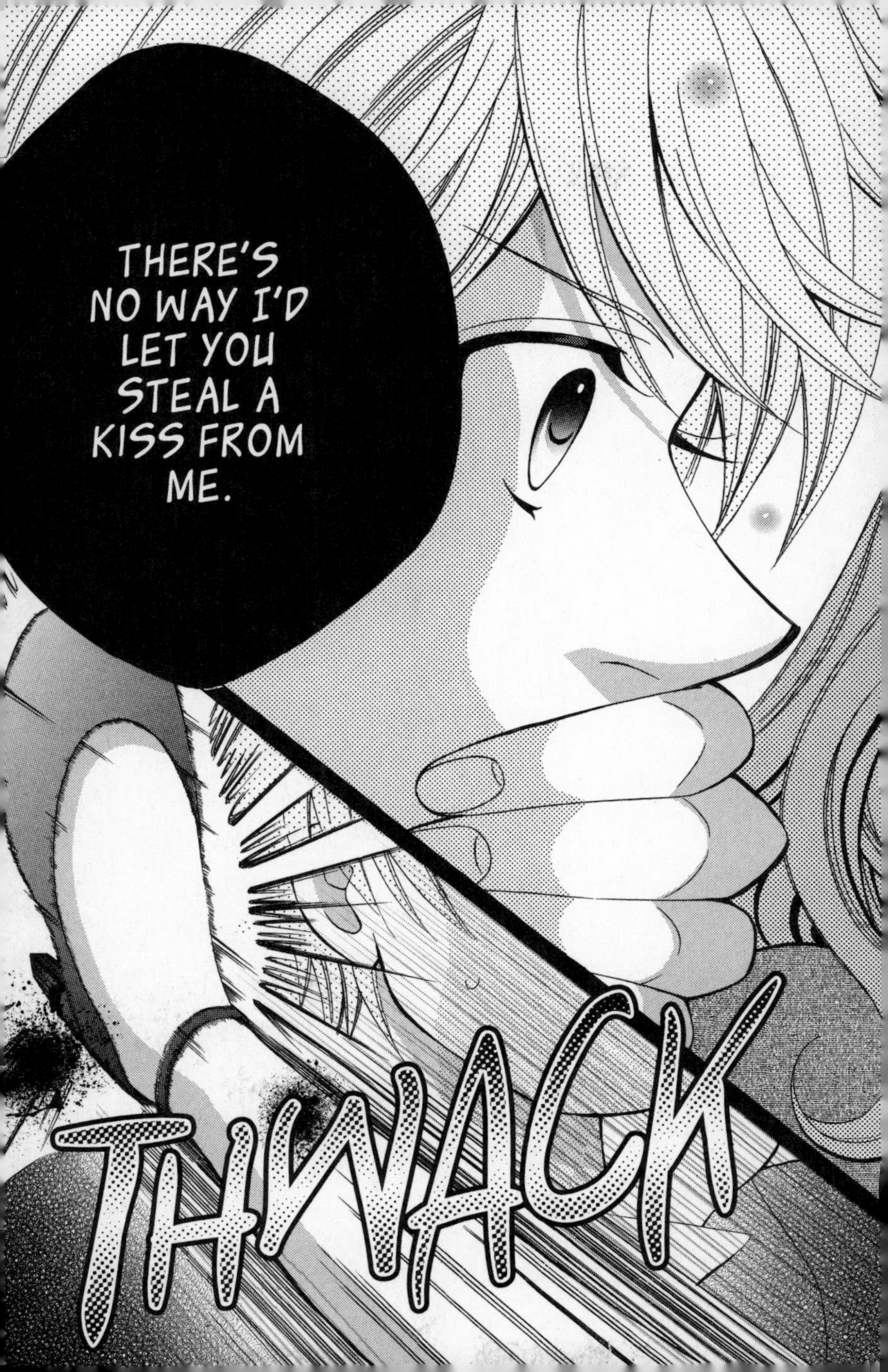
THERE'S NO WAY I'D LET YOU STEAL A KISS FROM ME.
THWACK

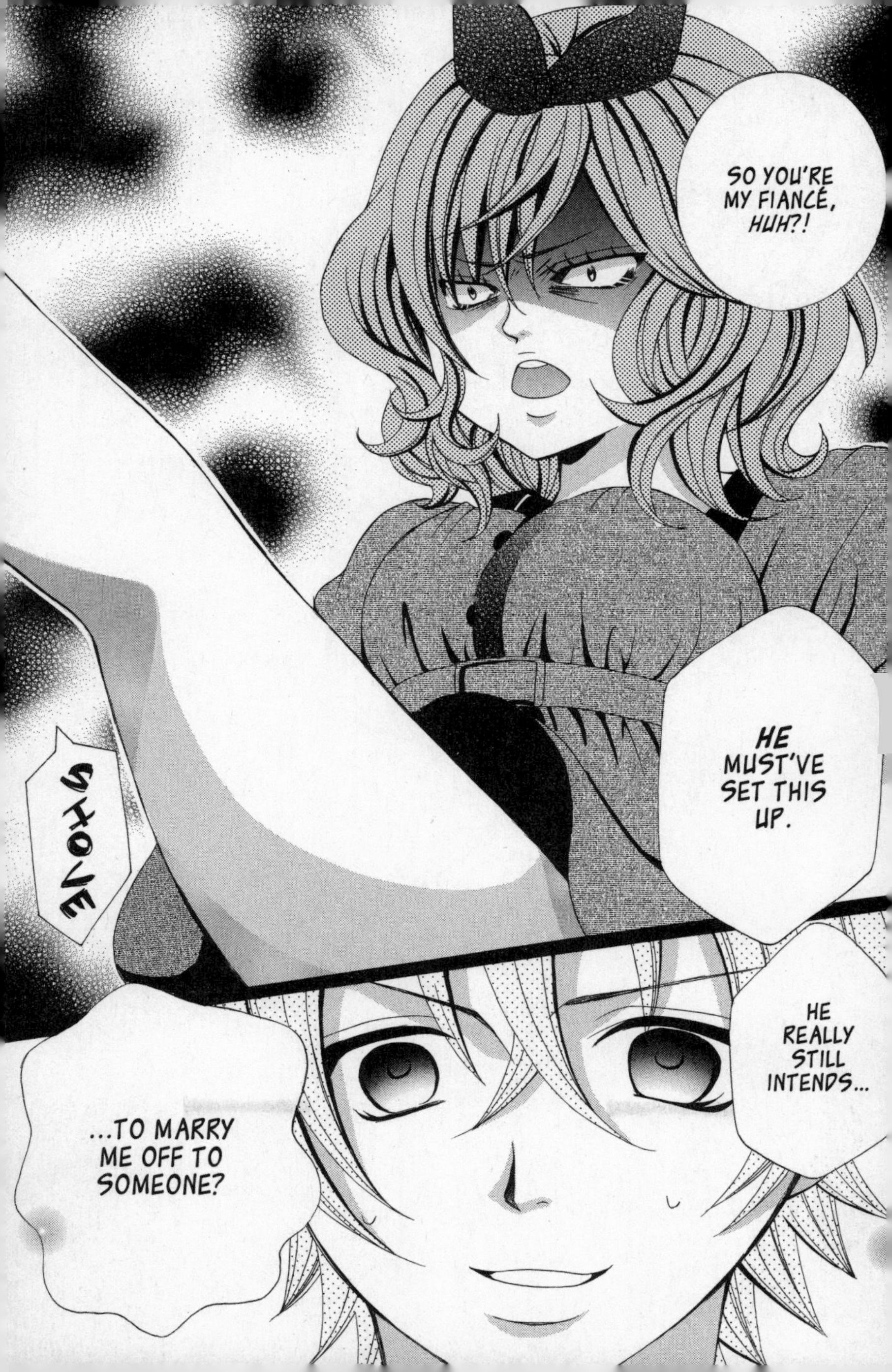
SO YOU'RE MY FIANCÉ, HUH?!
HE MUST'VE SET THIS UP.
SHOVE
HE REALLY STILL INTENDS...
...TO MARRY ME OFF TO SOMEONE?

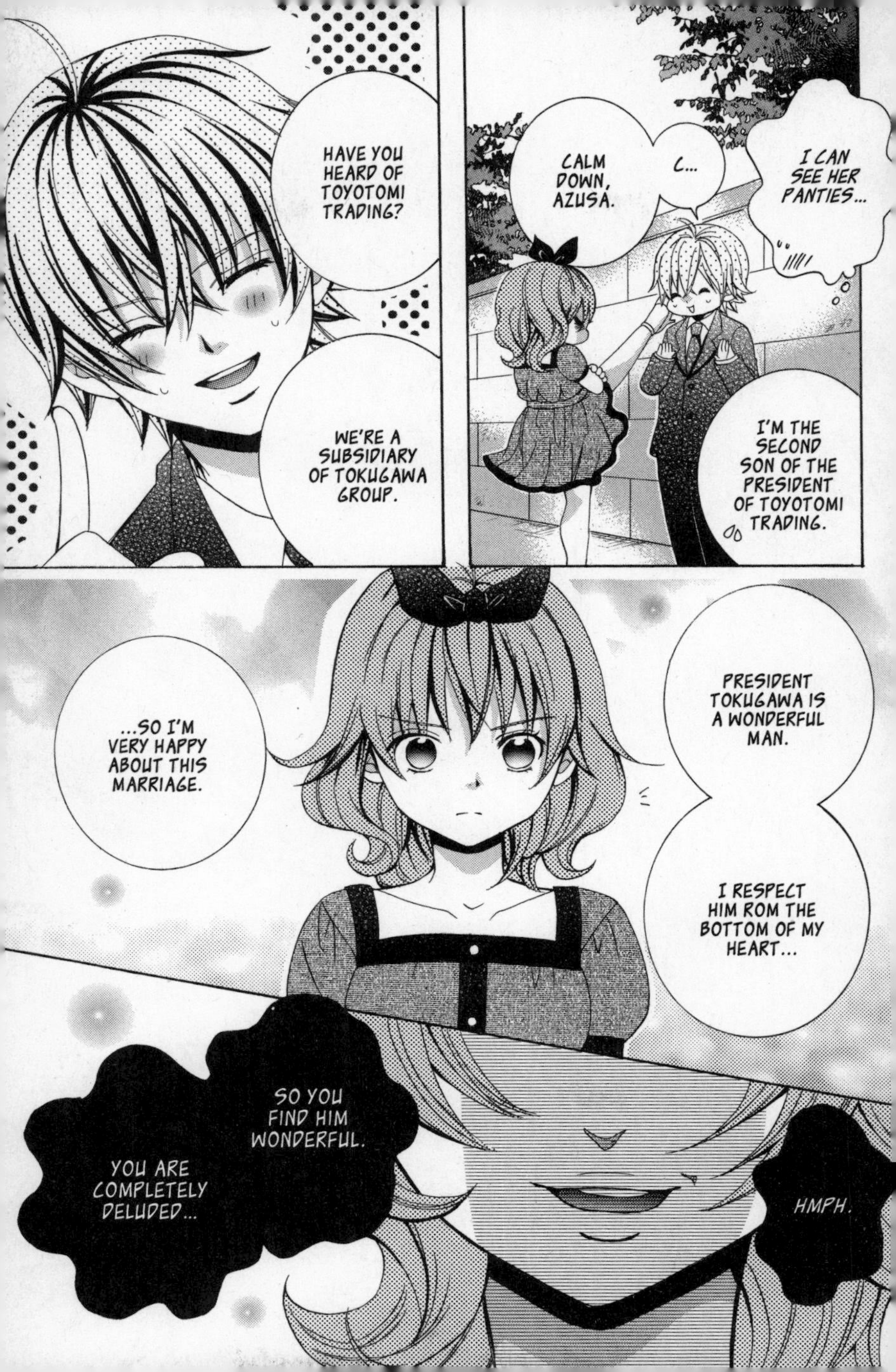
I CAN SEE HER PANTIES...
C...
CALM DOWN, AZUSA.
I'M THE SECOND SON OF THE PRESIDENT OF TOYOTOMI TRADING.
HAVE YOU HEARD OF TOYOTOMI TRADING?
WE'RE A SUBSIDIARY OF TOKUGAWA GROUP.
PRESIDENT TOKUGAWA IS A WONDERFUL MAN.
I RESPECT HIM ROM THE BOTTOM OF MY HEART...
...SO I'M VERY HAPPY ABOUT THIS MARRIAGE.
HMPH.
SO YOU FIND HIM WONDERFUL.
YOU ARE COMPLETELY DELUDED...

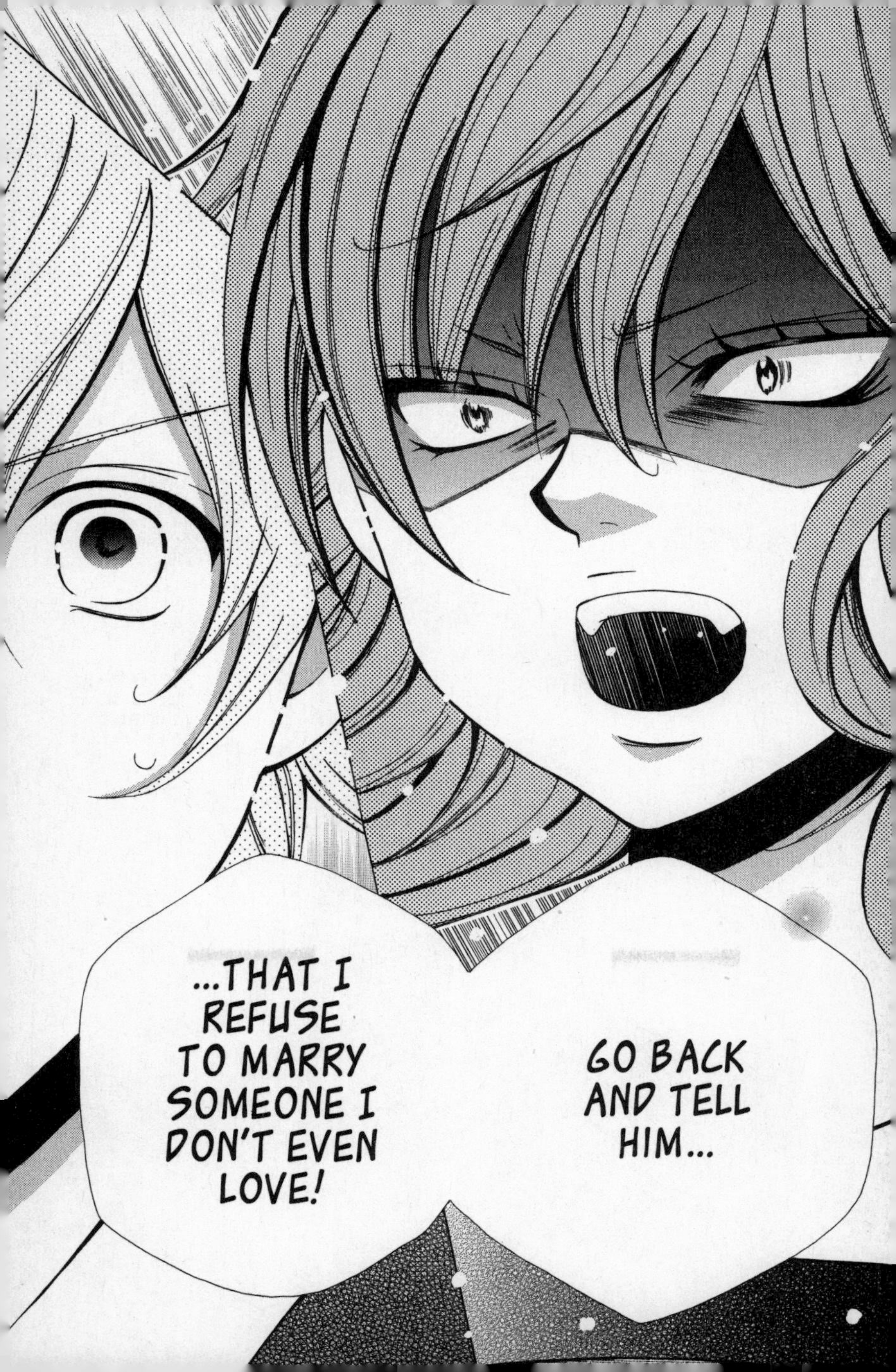
GO BACK AND TELL HIM...
...THAT I REFUSE TO MARRY SOMEONE I DON'T EVEN LOVE!

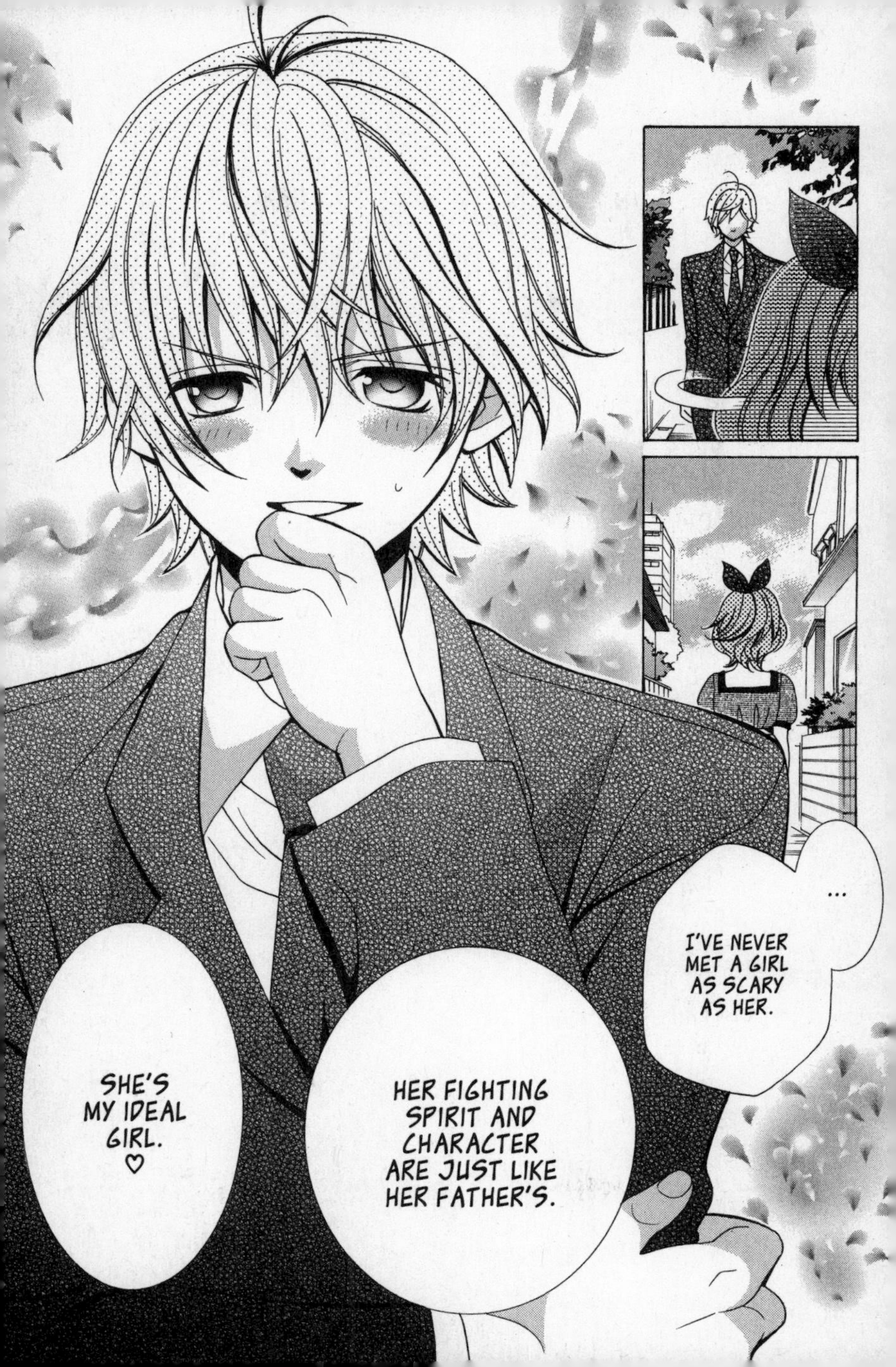
...
I'VE NEVER MET A GIRL AS SCARY AS HER.
HER FIGHTING SPIRIT AND CHARACTER ARE JUST LIKE HER FATHER'S.
SHE'S MY IDEAL GIRL. ♡

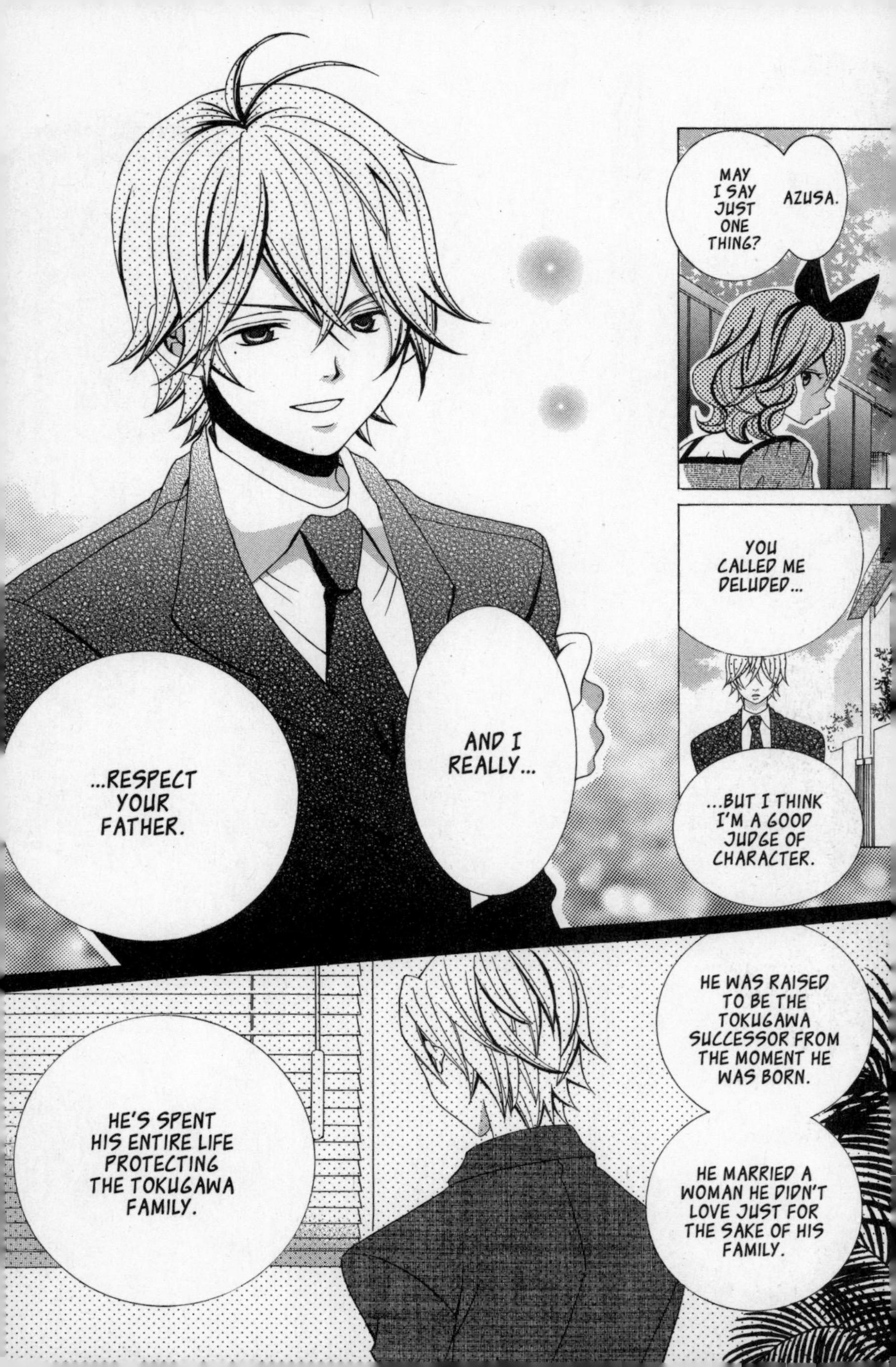
AZUSA.
MAY I SAY JUST ONE THING?
YOU CALLED ME DELUDED...
...BUT I THINK I'M A GOOD JUDGE OF CHARACTER.
AND I REALLY...
...RESPECT YOUR FATHER.
HE WAS RAISED TO BE THE TOKUGAWA SUCCESSOR FROM THE MOMENT HE WAS BORN.
HE MARRIED A WOMAN HE DIDN'T LOVE JUST FOR THE SAKE OF HIS FAMILY.
HE'S SPENT HIS ENTIRE LIFE PROTECTING THE TOKUGAWA FAMILY.

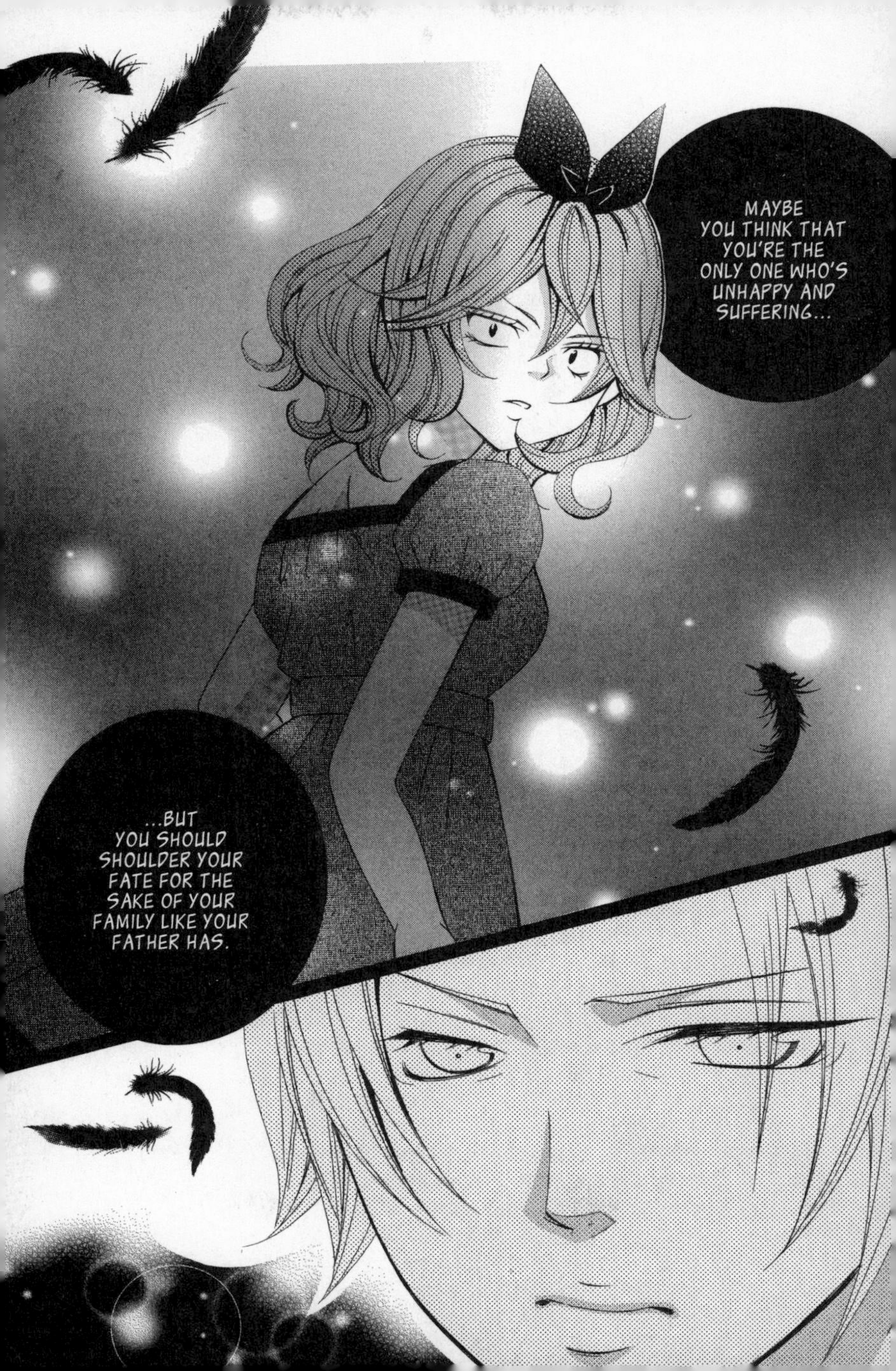
MAYBE YOU THINK THAT YOU'RE THE ONLY ONE WHO'S UNHAPPY AND SUFFERING...
...BUT YOU SHOULD SHOULDER YOUR FATE FOR THE SAKE OF YOUR FAMILY LIKE YOUR FATHER HAS.

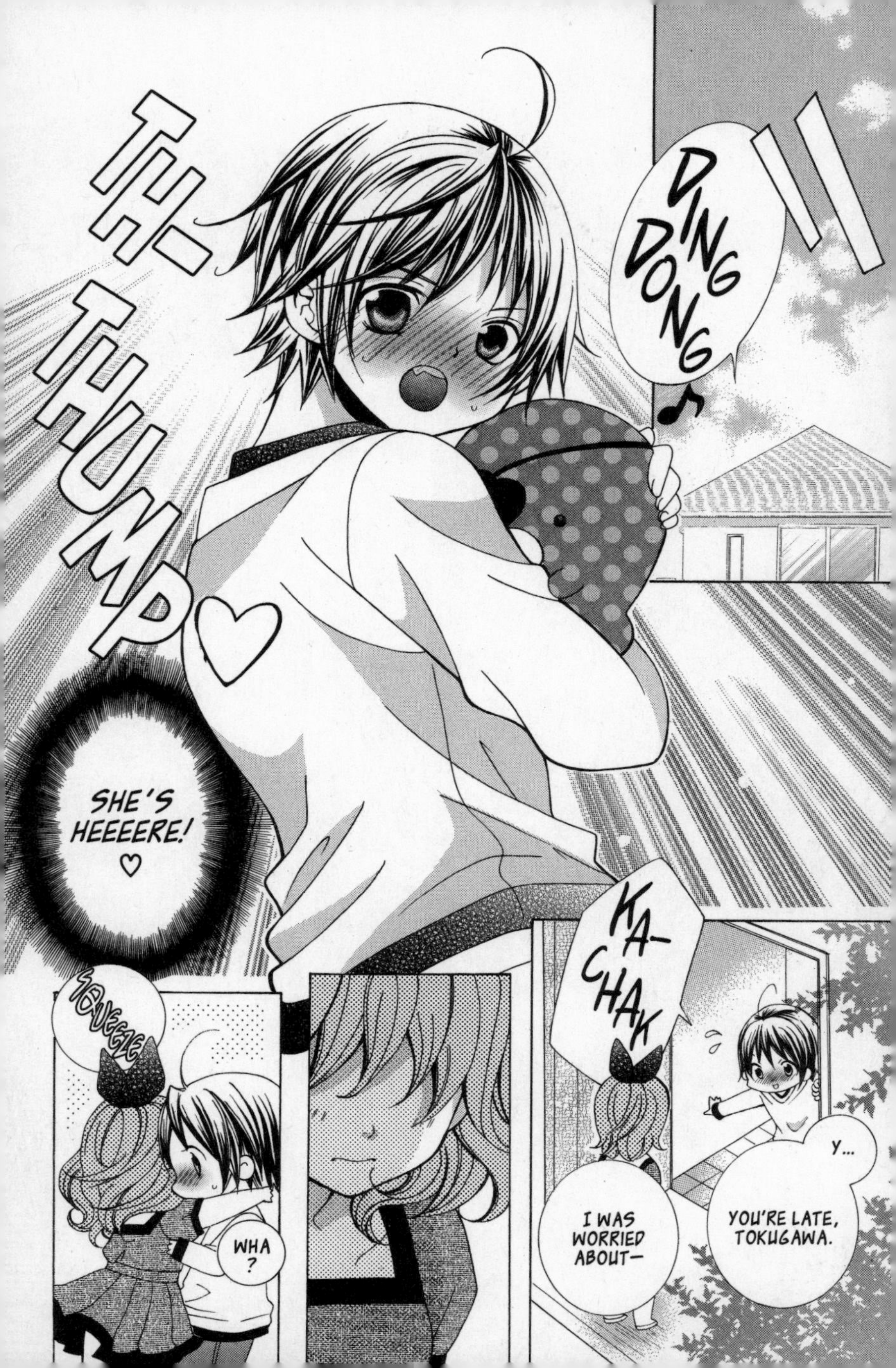
DING DONG ♪
TH-THUMP ♡
SHE'S HEEEEERE! ♡
KA-CHAK
Y...
YOU'RE LATE, TOKUGAWA.
I WAS WORRIED ABOUT—
SQUEEZE
WHA?

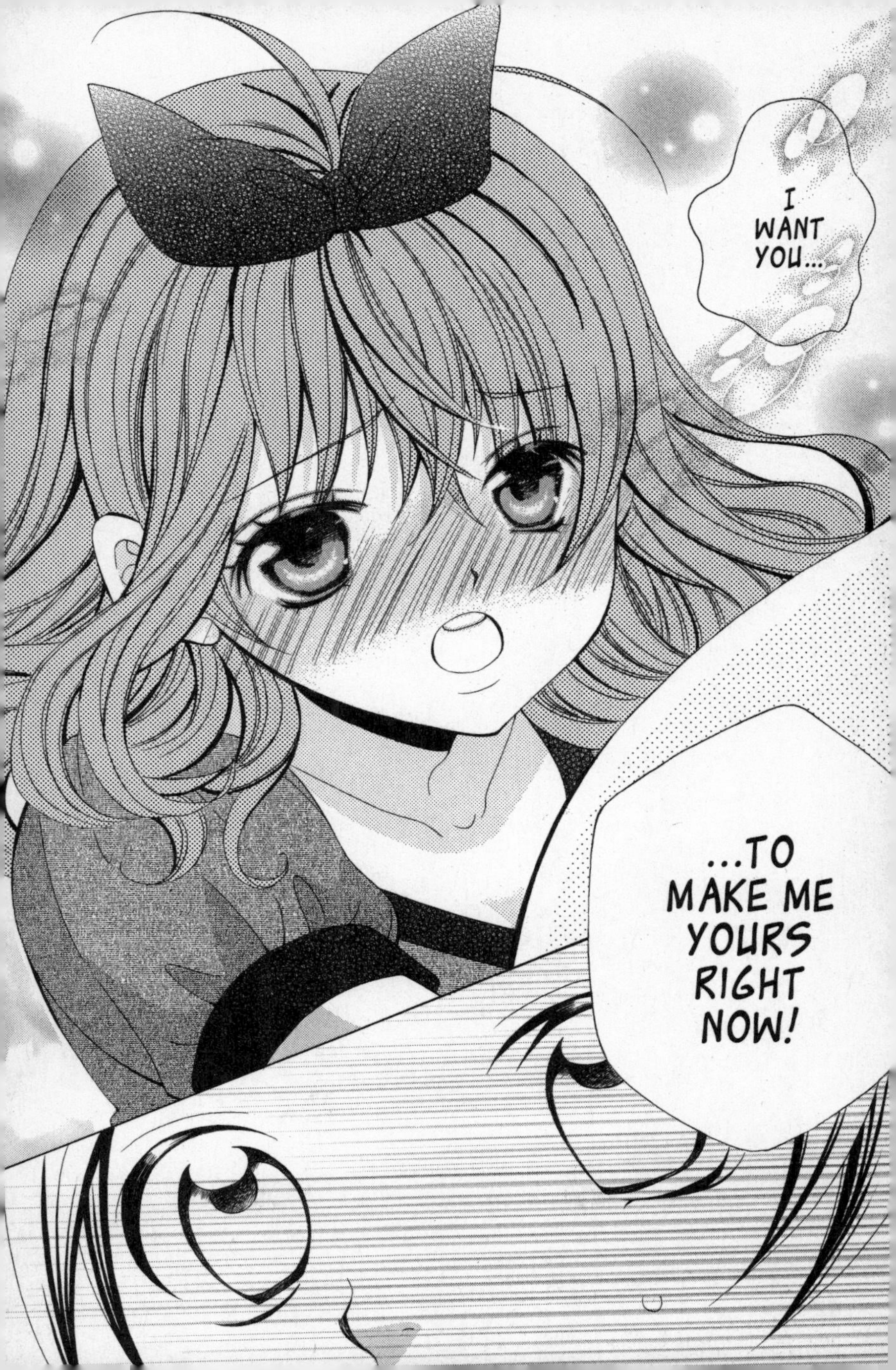
I WANT YOU...
...TO MAKE ME YOURS RIGHT NOW!

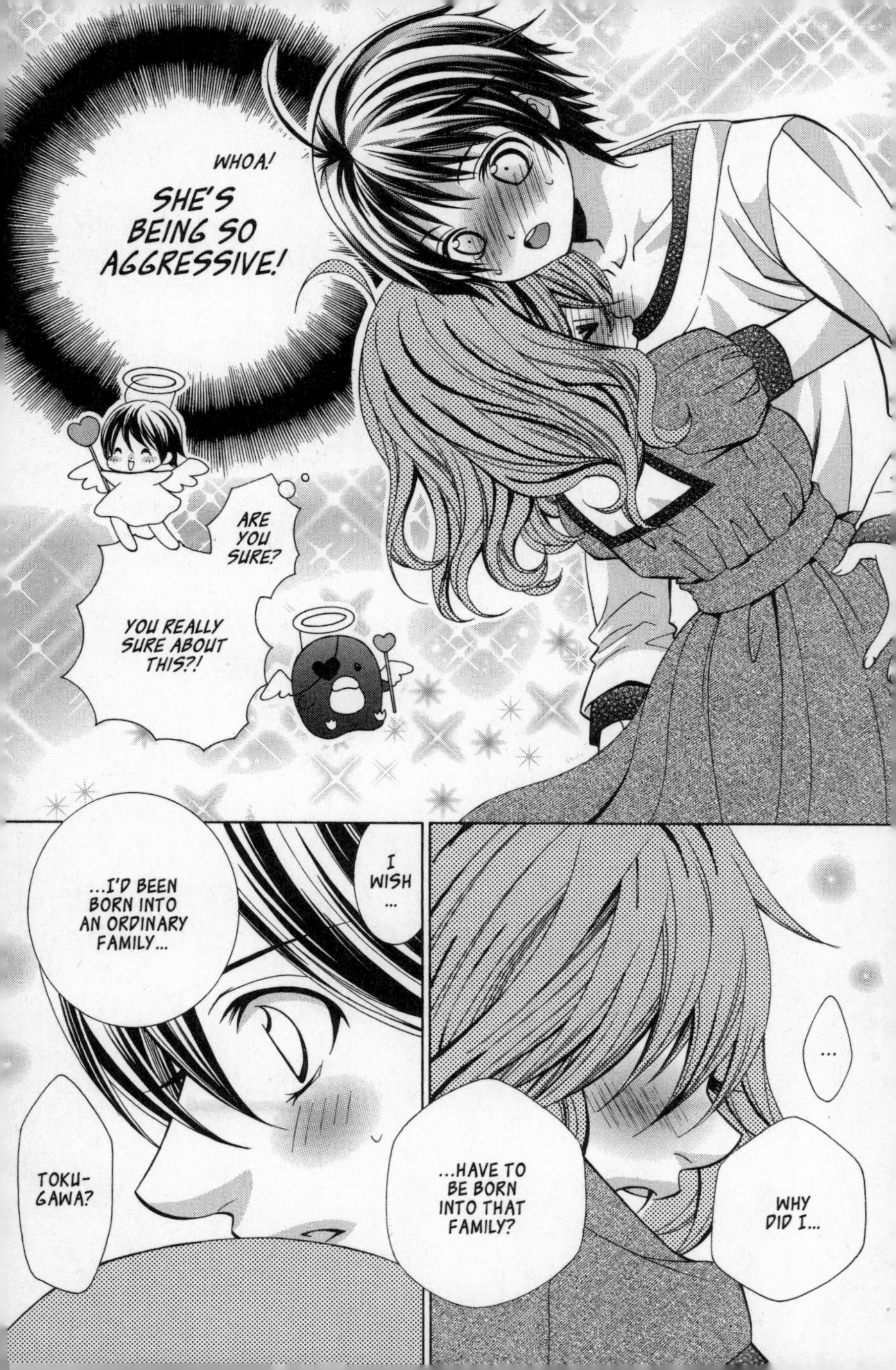
WHOA!
SHE'S BEING SO AGGRESSIVE!
ARE YOU SURE?
YOU REALLY SURE ABOUT THIS?!
...
WHY DID I...
...HAVE TO BE BORN INTO THAT FAMILY?
I WISH...
...I'D BEEN BORN INTO AN ORDINARY FAMILY...
TOKU-GAWA?

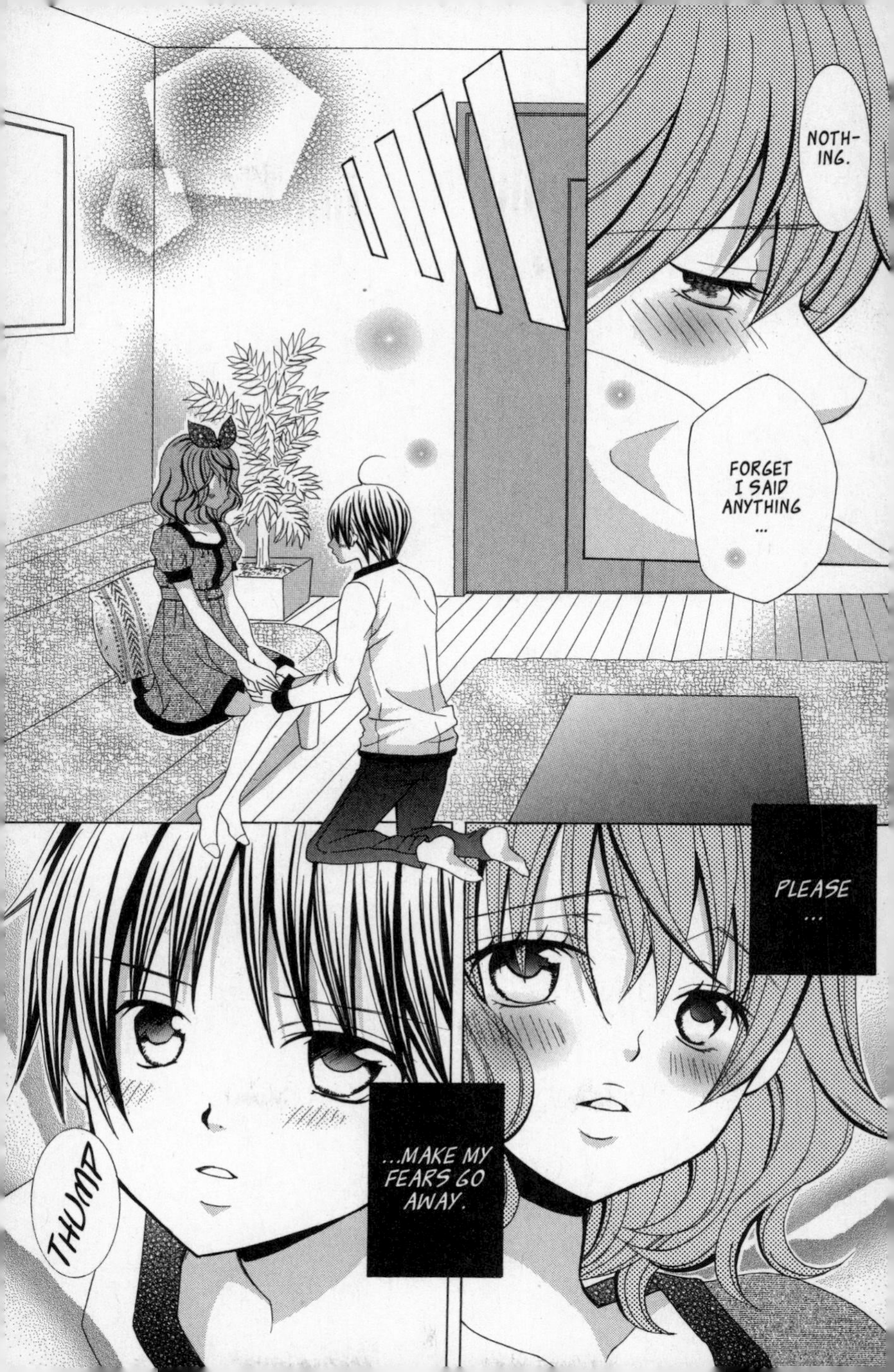
NOTH-ING.
FORGET I SAID ANYTHING ...
PLEASE ...
...MAKE MY FEARS GO AWAY.
THUMP

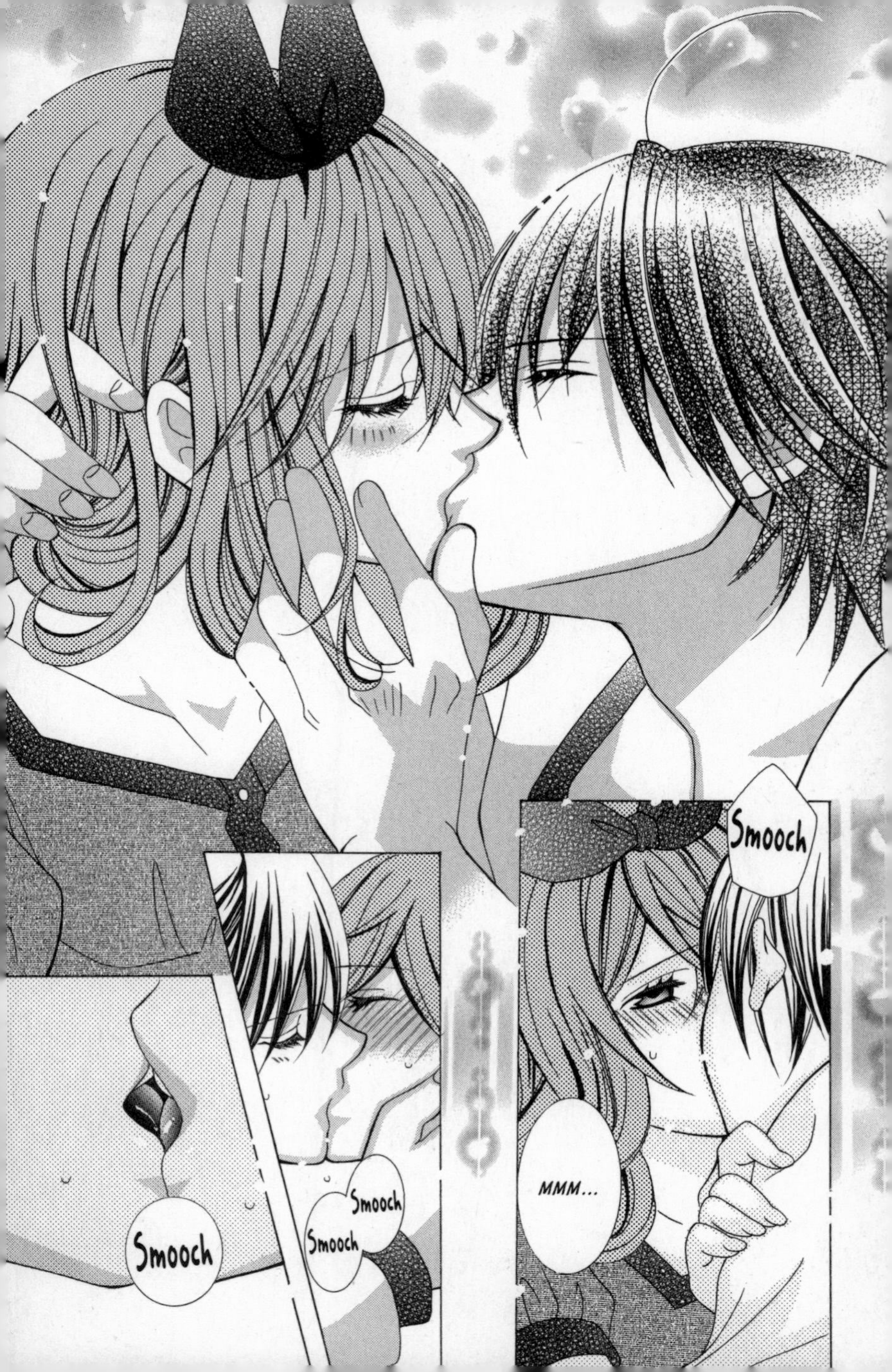
Smooch
MMM...
Smooch
Smooch
Smooch

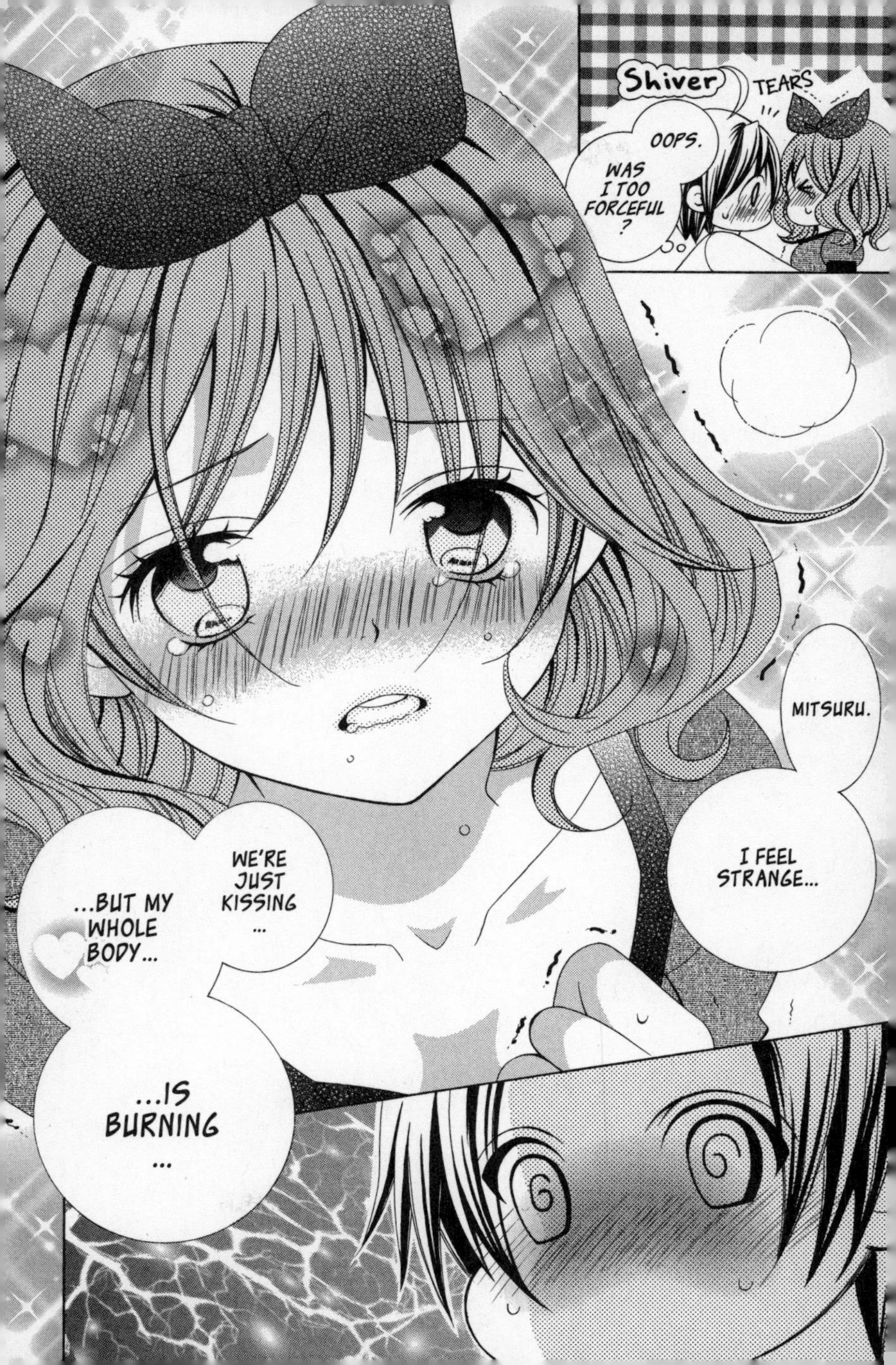
Shiver
TEARS
OOPS.
WAS I TOO FORCEFUL?
MITSURU.
I FEEL STRANGE...
WE'RE JUST KISSING...
...BUT MY WHOLE BODY...
...IS BURNING...

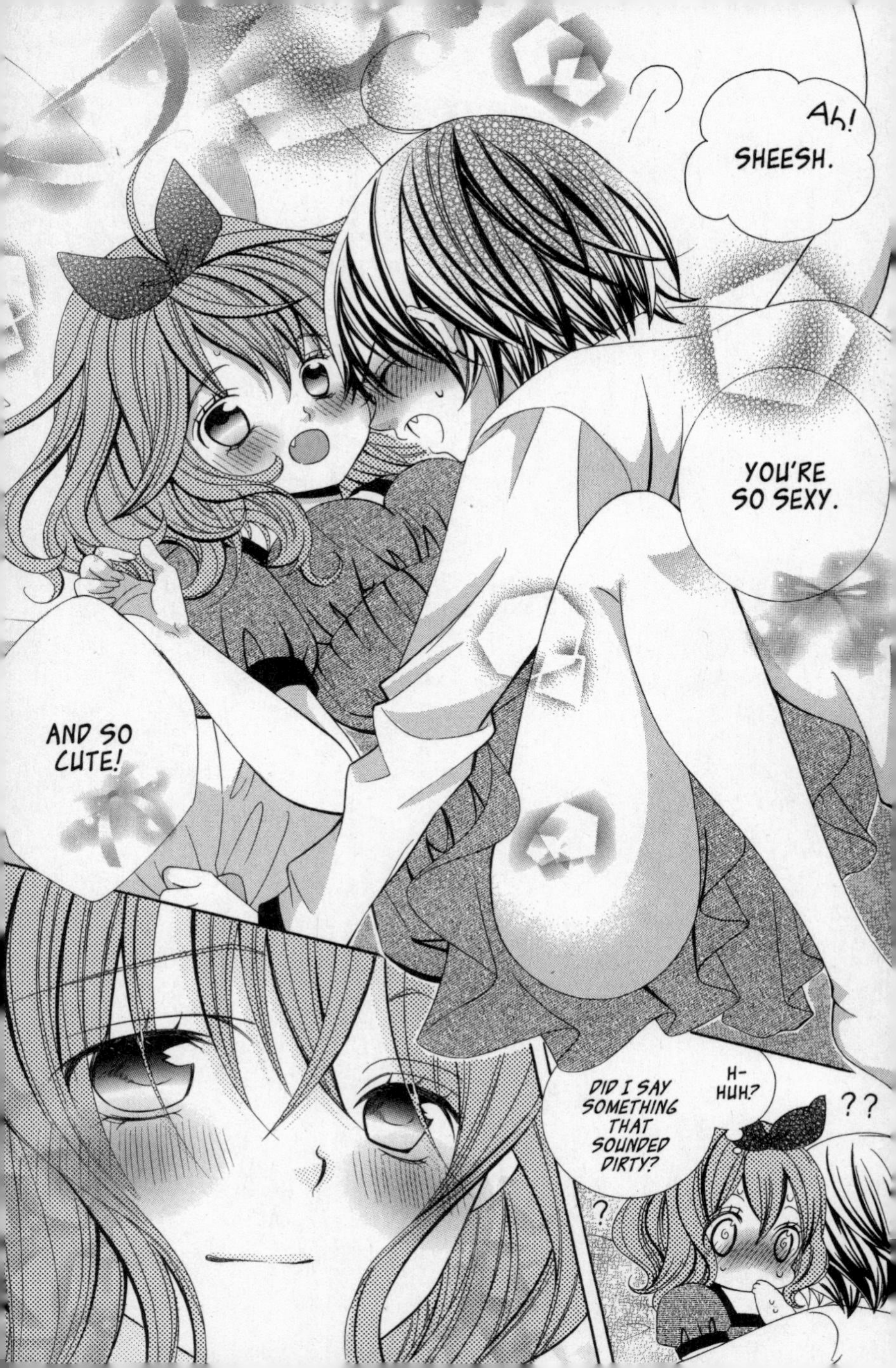
Ah! SHEESH.
YOU'RE SO SEXY.
AND SO CUTE!
H-HUH?
??
DID I SAY SOMETHING THAT SOUNDED DIRTY?

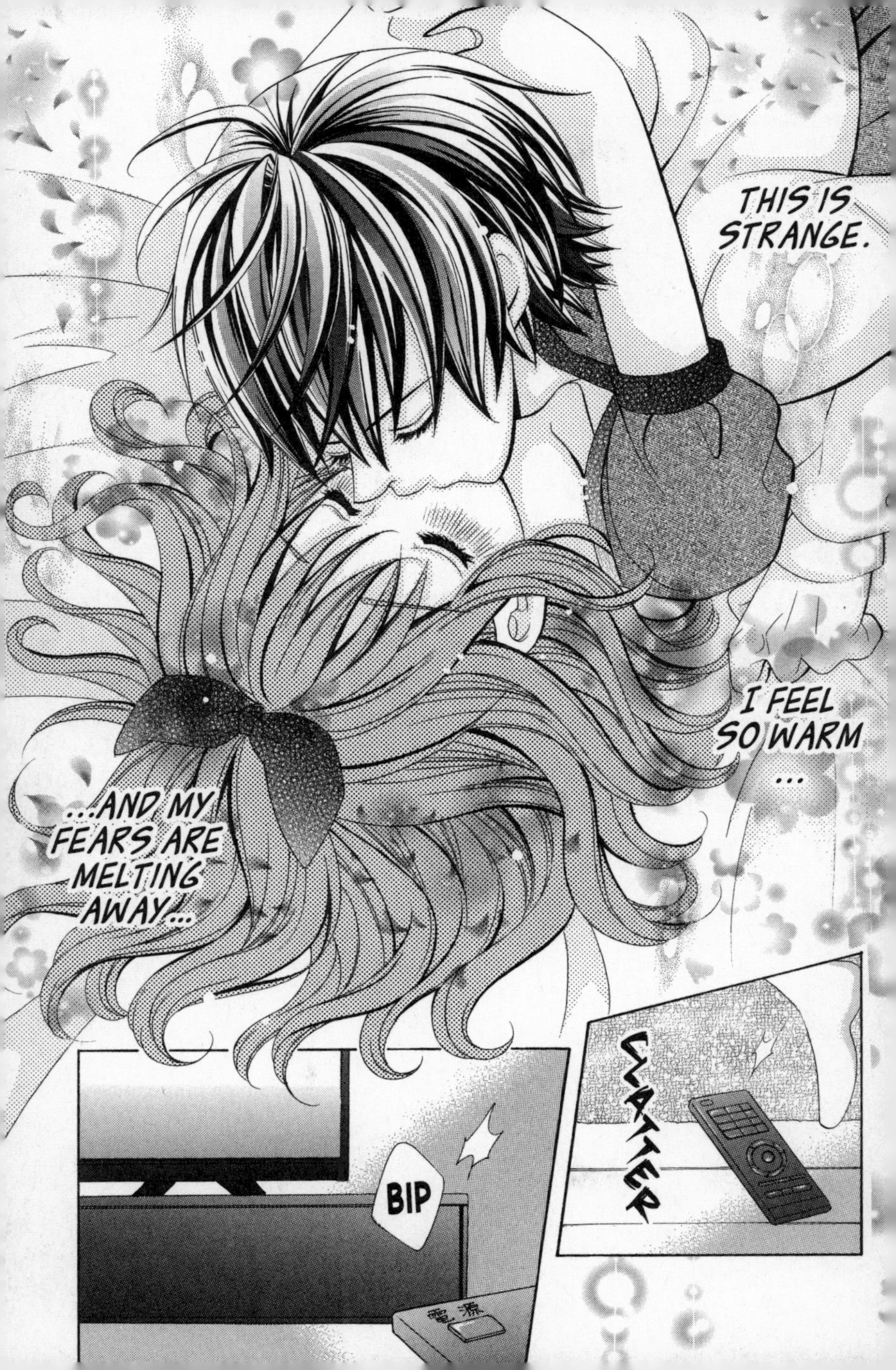
THIS IS STRANGE.
I FEEL SO WARM ...
...AND MY FEARS ARE MELTING AWAY...
CLATTER
BIP
電源

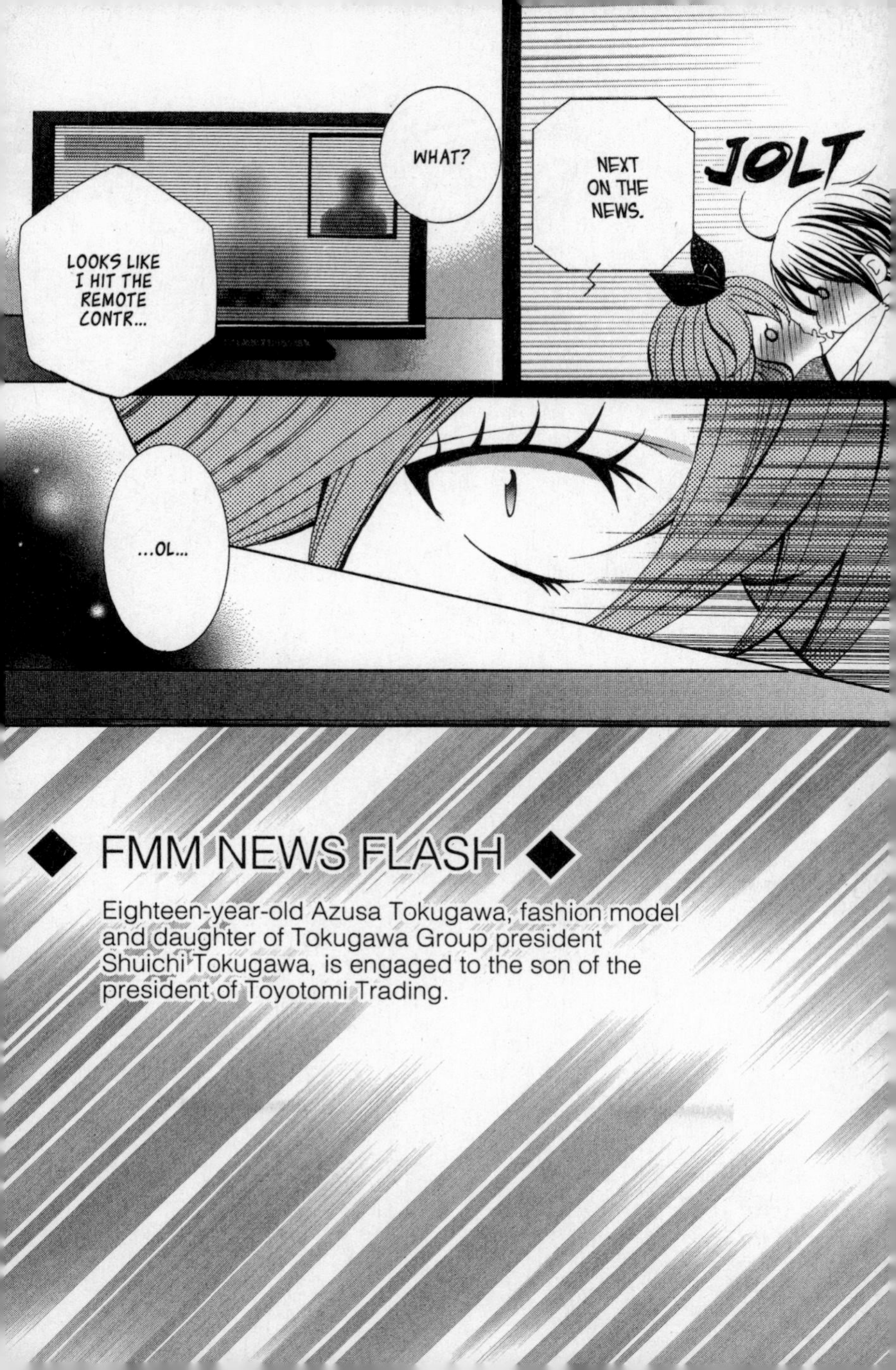
NEXT ON THE NEWS.
JOLT
WHAT?
LOOKS LIKE I HIT THE REMOTE CONTR...
...OL...
◆ FMM NEWS FLASH ◆
Eighteen-year-old Azusa Tokugawa, fashion model and daughter of Tokugawa Group president Shuichi Tokugawa, is engaged to the son of the president of Toyotomi Trading.

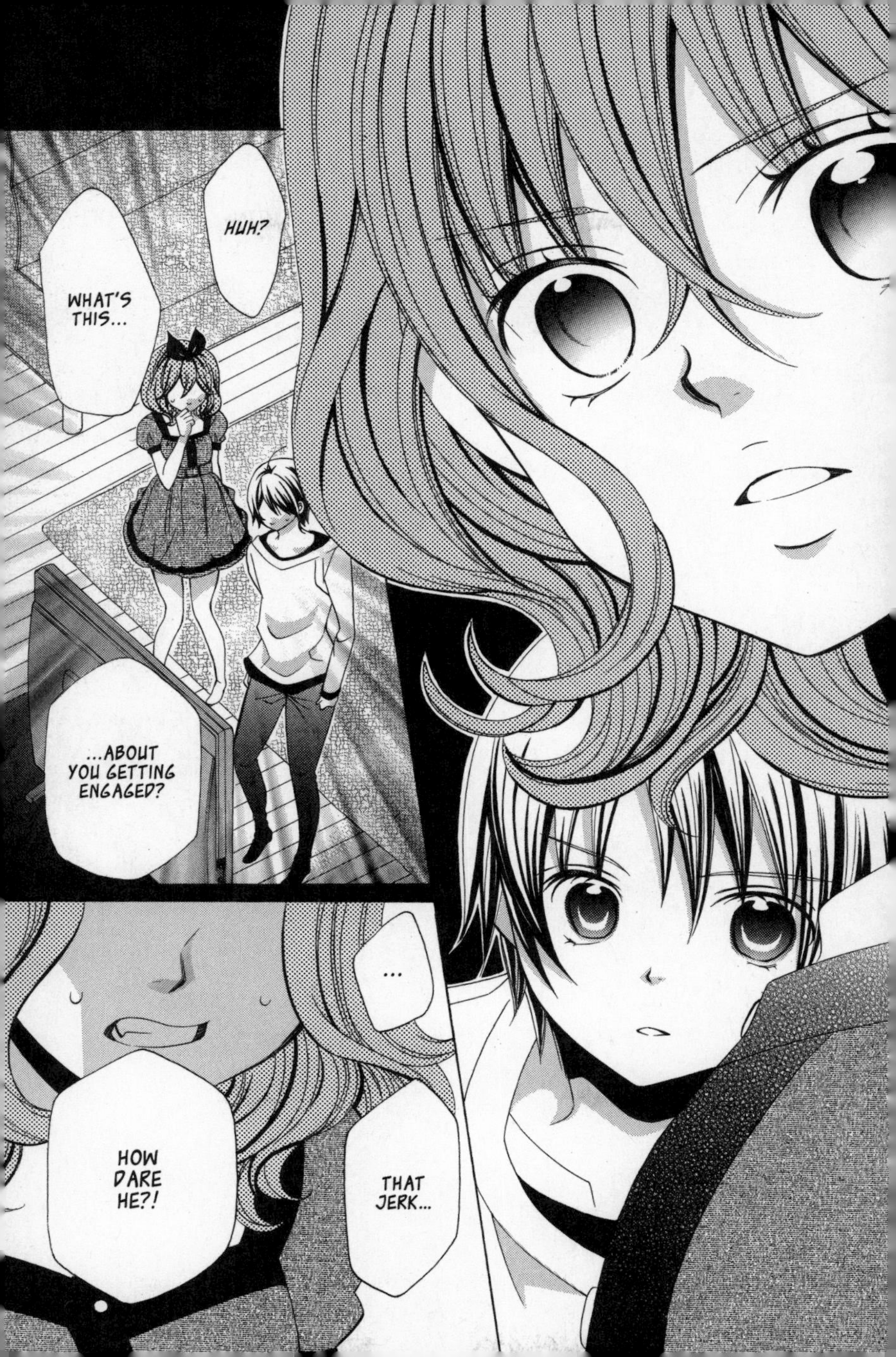
HUH?
WHAT'S THIS...
...ABOUT YOU GETTING ENGAGED?
...
THAT JERK...
HOW DARE HE?!

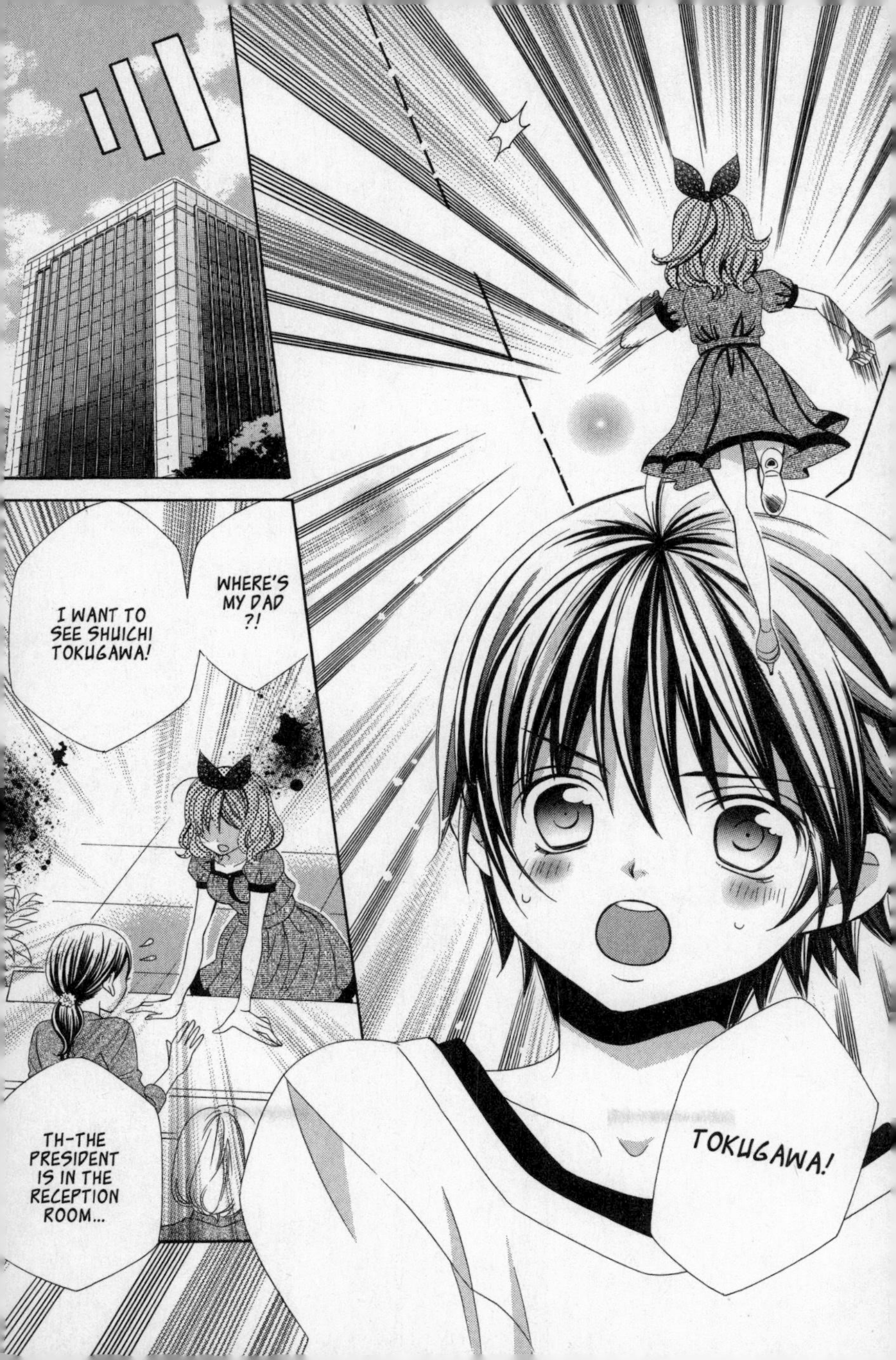
TOKUGAWA!
WHERE'S MY DAD ?!
I WANT TO SEE SHUICHI TOKUGAWA!
TH-THE PRESIDENT IS IN THE RECEPTION ROOM...

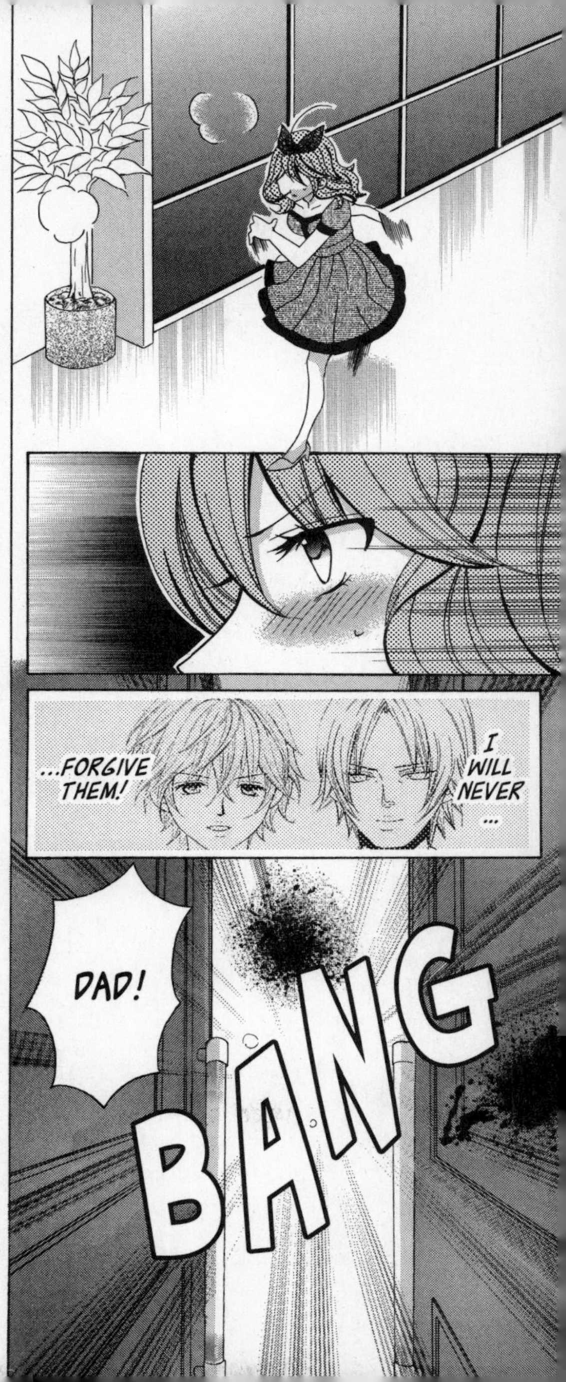
I WILL NEVER ...
...FORGIVE THEM!
BANG
DAD!

SPECIAL THANKS

Yuka Ito-sama,
Rieko Hirai-sama,
Kayoko Takahashi-sama,
Kawasaki-sama,
Nagisa Sato Sensei.

Rei Nanase Sensei,
Arisu Fujishiro Sensei,
Mumi Mimura Sensei,
Masayo Nagata-sama,
Naochan-sama,
Asuka Sakura Sensei
and many others.

Bookstore Dan Kinshicho Branch, Kinokuniya Shinjuku Branch, LIBRO Ikebukuro Branch, Kinokuniya Hankyu 32-Bangai Branch.

Sendai Hachimonjiya Bookstore, Books HOSHINO Kintetsu Pass'e Branch, Asahiya Tennnoji MiO Branch, Kurashiki Kikuya Bookstore.

Salesperson:
Mizusawa-sama

Previous salesperson:
Honma-sama

Previous editor:
Nakata-sama

Current editor:
Shoji-sama

I also sincerely express my gratitude to everyone who picked up this volume.

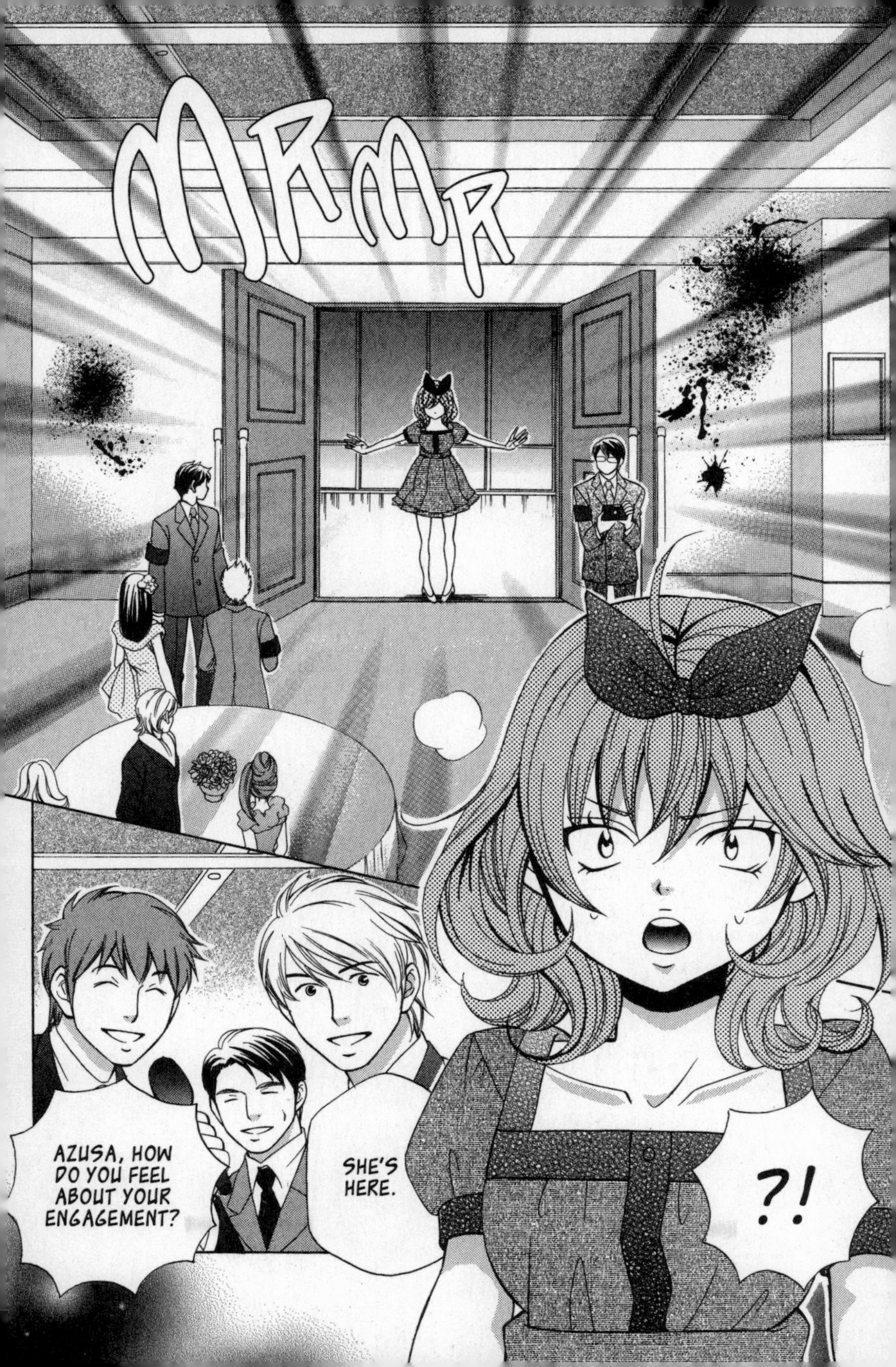
MRMR
?!
SHE'S HERE.
AZUSA, HOW DO YOU FEEL ABOUT YOUR ENGAGEMENT?

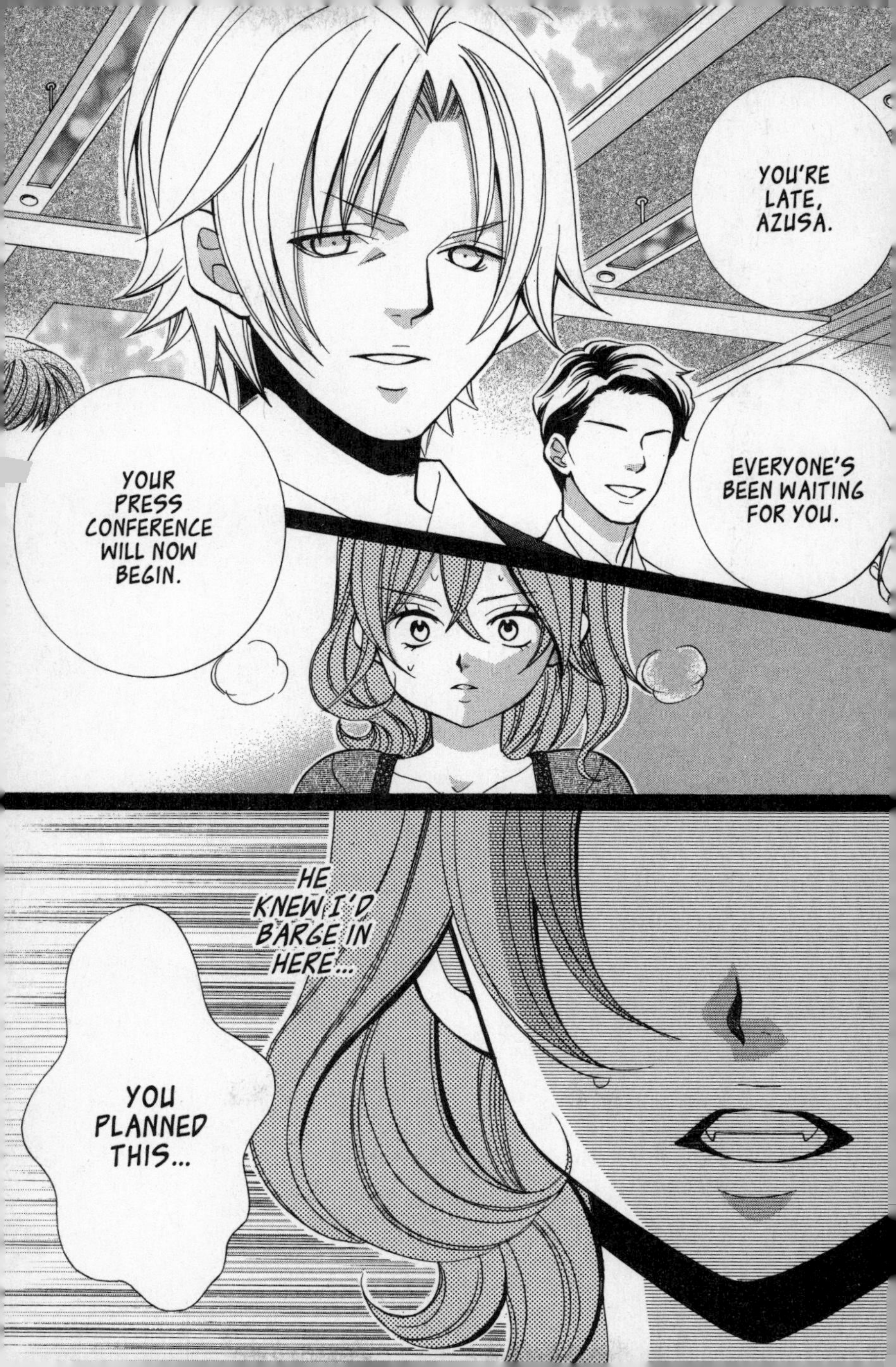
YOU'RE LATE, AZUSA.
EVERYONE'S BEEN WAITING FOR YOU.
YOUR PRESS CONFERENCE WILL NOW BEGIN.
HE KNEW I'D BARGE IN HERE...
YOU PLANNED THIS...

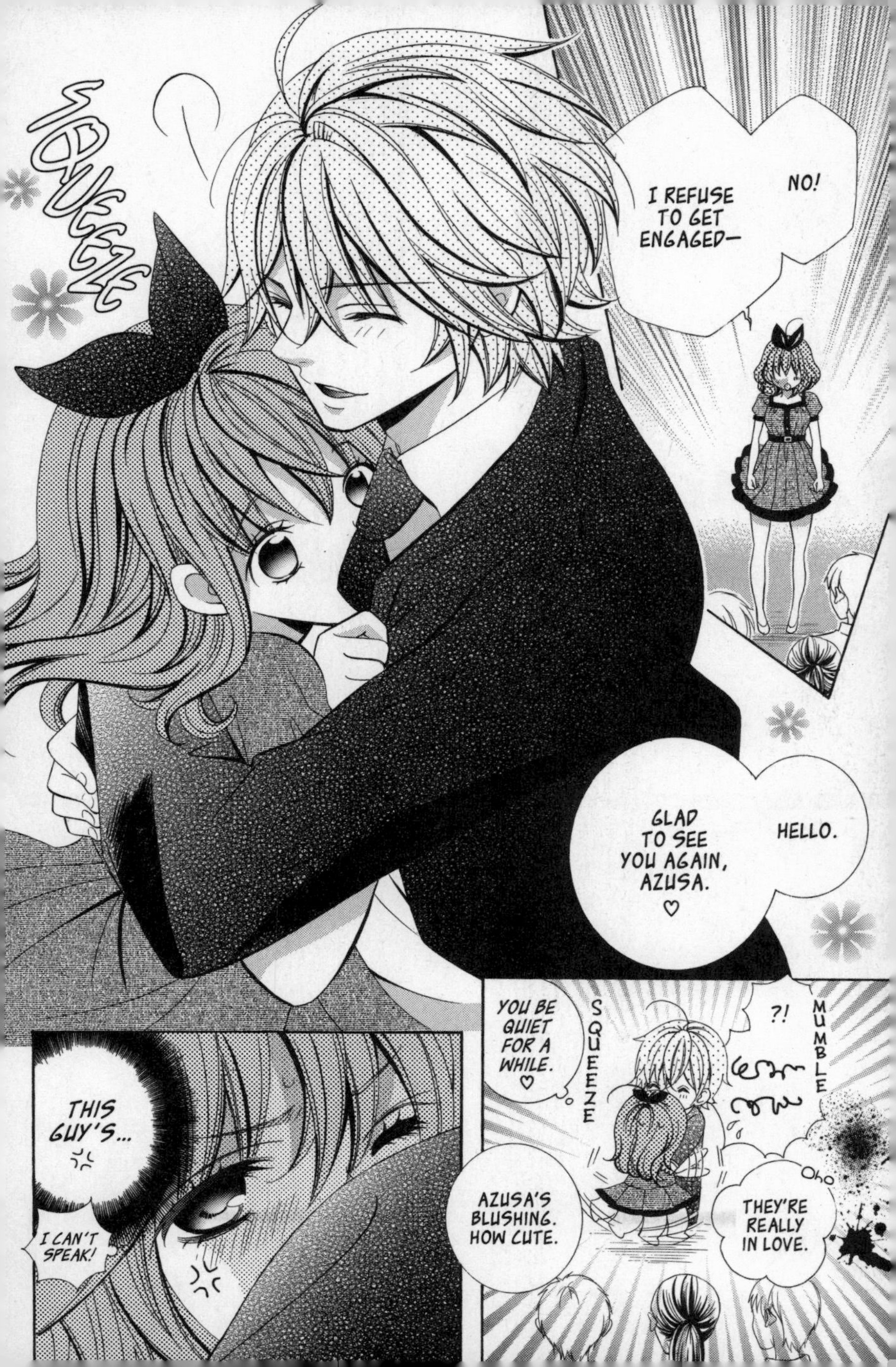

NO!
I REFUSE TO GET ENGAGED—
SQUEEZE
HELLO.
GLAD TO SEE YOU AGAIN, AZUSA. ♡
?!
MUMBLE
SQUEEZE
YOU BE QUIET FOR A WHILE. ♡
Oho
THEY'RE REALLY IN LOVE.
AZUSA'S BLUSHING. HOW CUTE.
THIS GUY'S...
I CAN'T SPEAK!

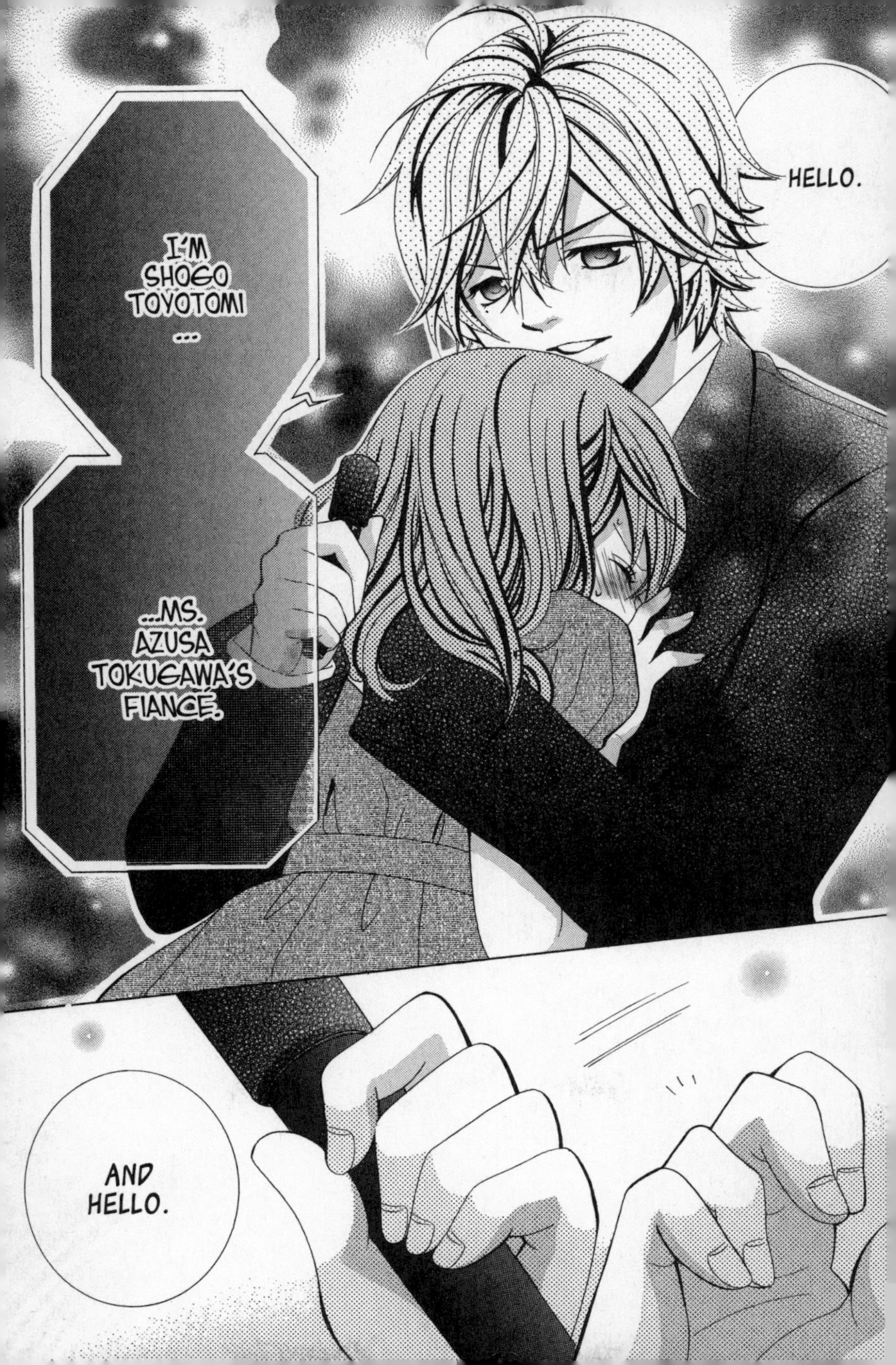
HELLO.
I'M SHOGO TOYOTOMI ...
...MS. AZUSA TOKUGAWA'S FIANCÉ.
AND HELLO.

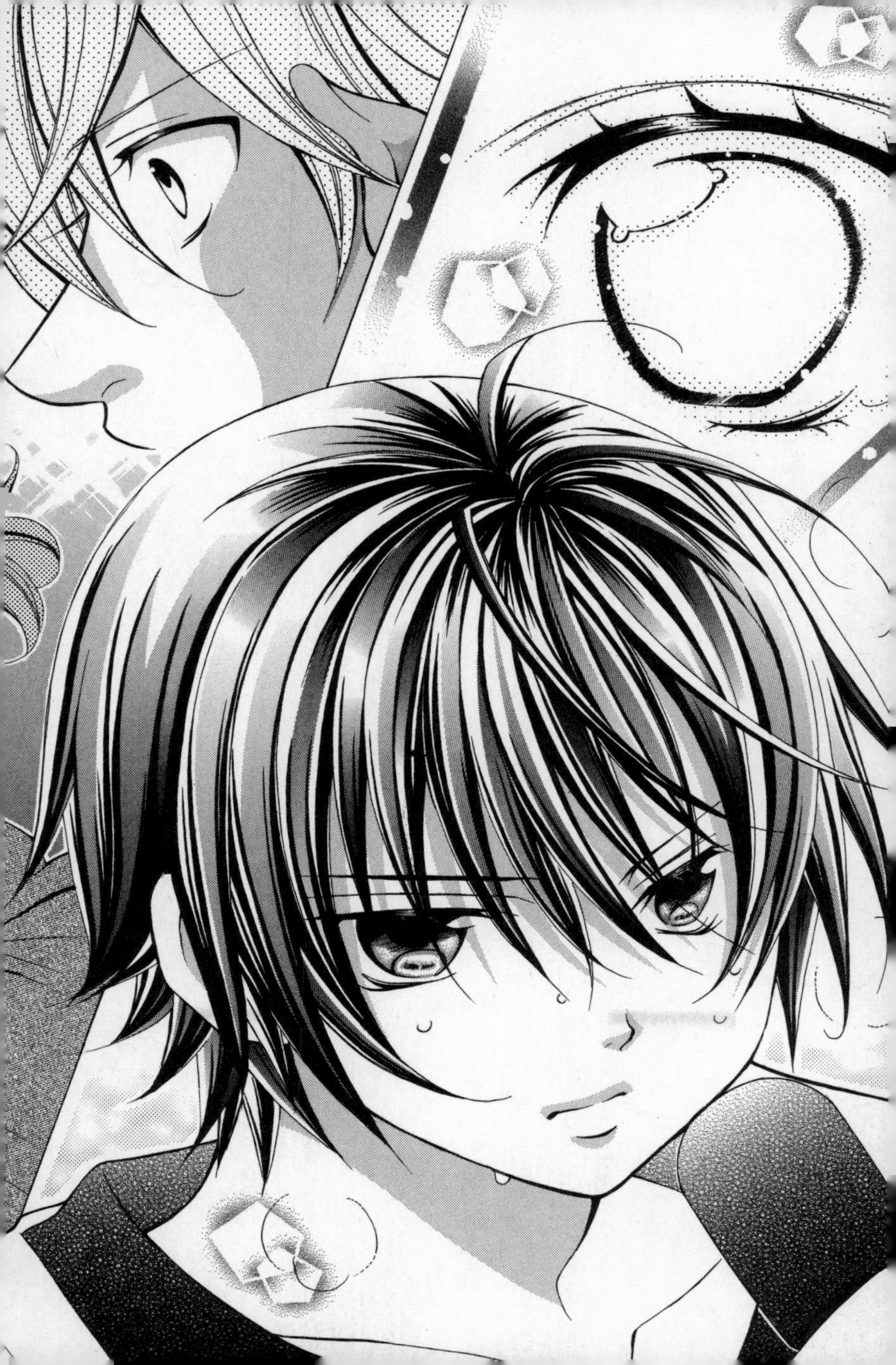

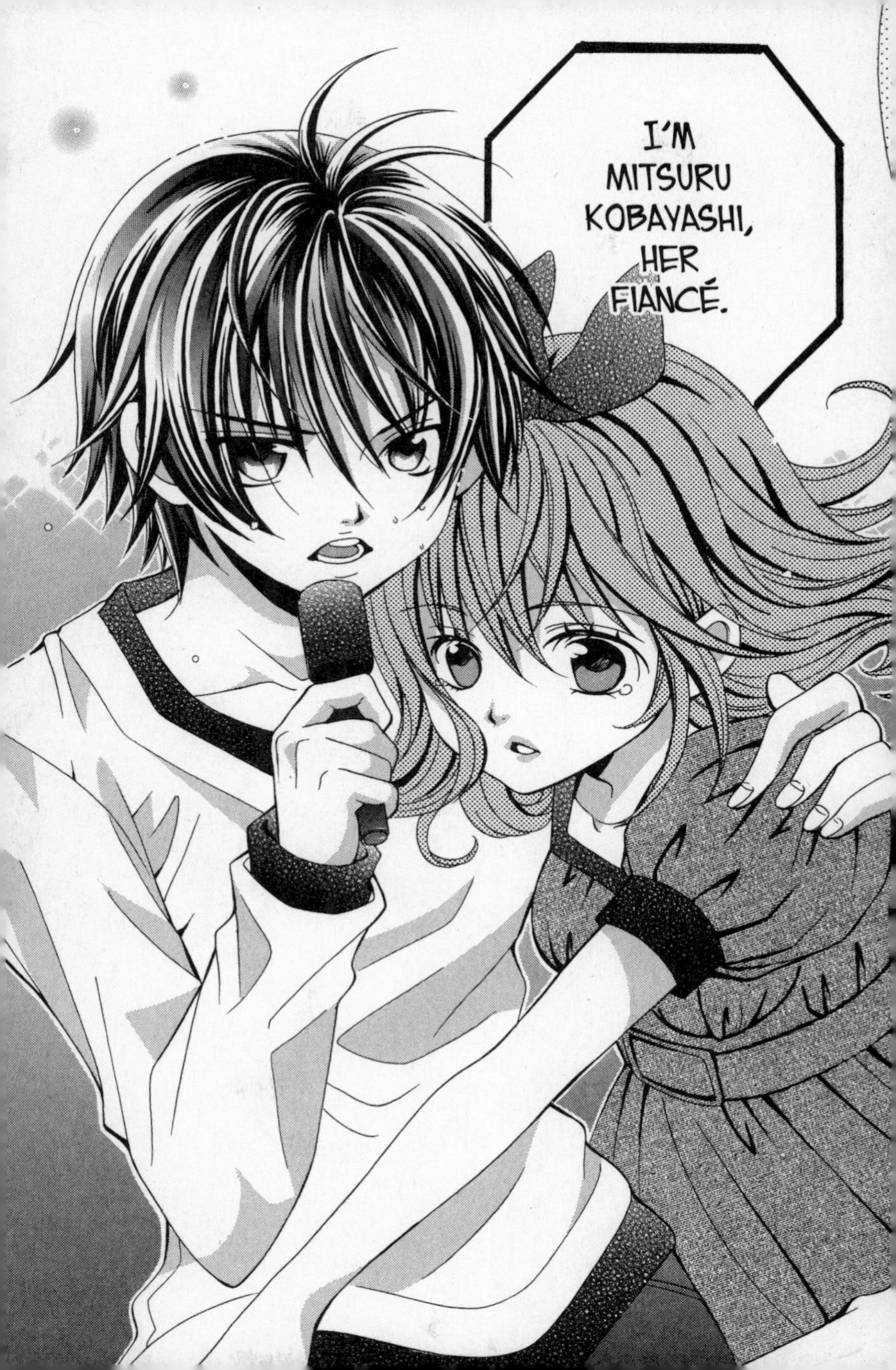
I'M MITSURU KOBAYASHI, HER FIANCÉ.

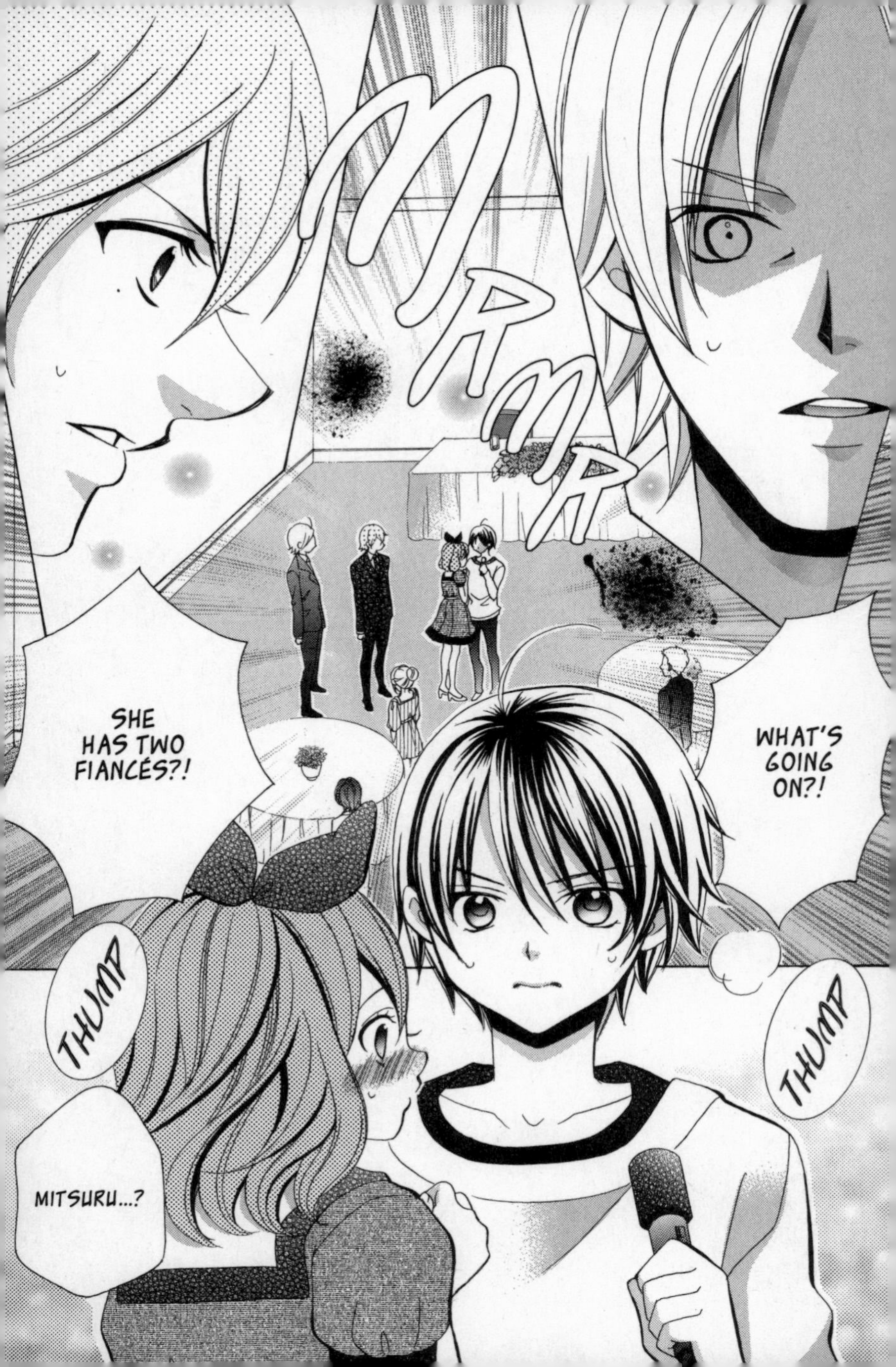
MRMR
WHAT'S GOING ON?!
SHE HAS TWO FIANCÉS?!
THUMP
THUMP
MITSURU...?

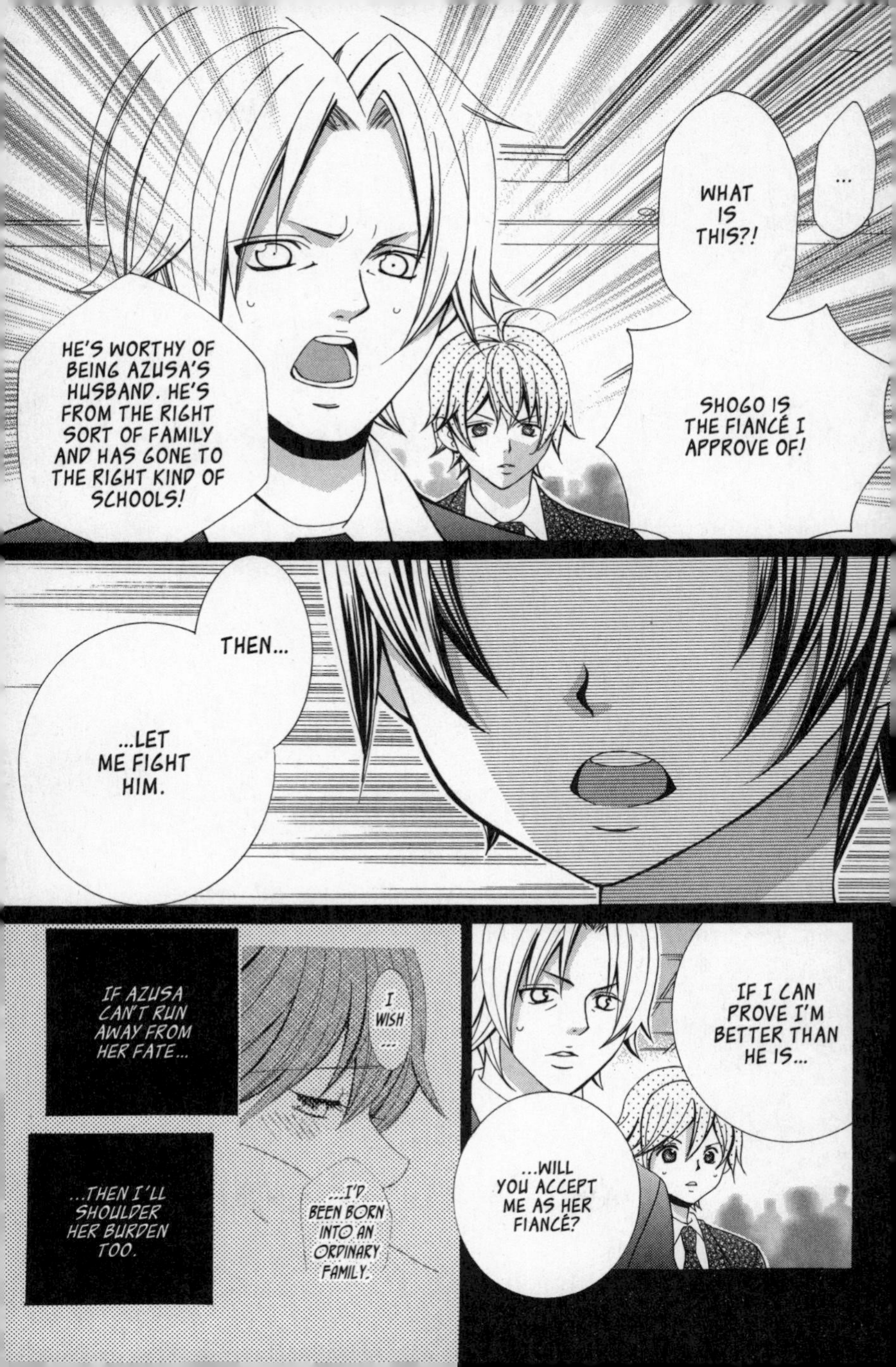
...
WHAT IS THIS?!
SHOGO IS THE FIANCÉ I APPROVE OF!
HE'S WORTHY OF BEING AZUSA'S HUSBAND. HE'S FROM THE RIGHT SORT OF FAMILY AND HAS GONE TO THE RIGHT KIND OF SCHOOLS!
THEN...
...LET ME FIGHT HIM.
IF I CAN PROVE I'M BETTER THAN HE IS...
...WILL YOU ACCEPT ME AS HER FIANCÉ?
I WISH...
...I'D BEEN BORN INTO AN ORDINARY FAMILY.
IF AZUSA CAN'T RUN AWAY FROM HER FATE...
...THEN I'LL SHOULDER HER BURDEN TOO.

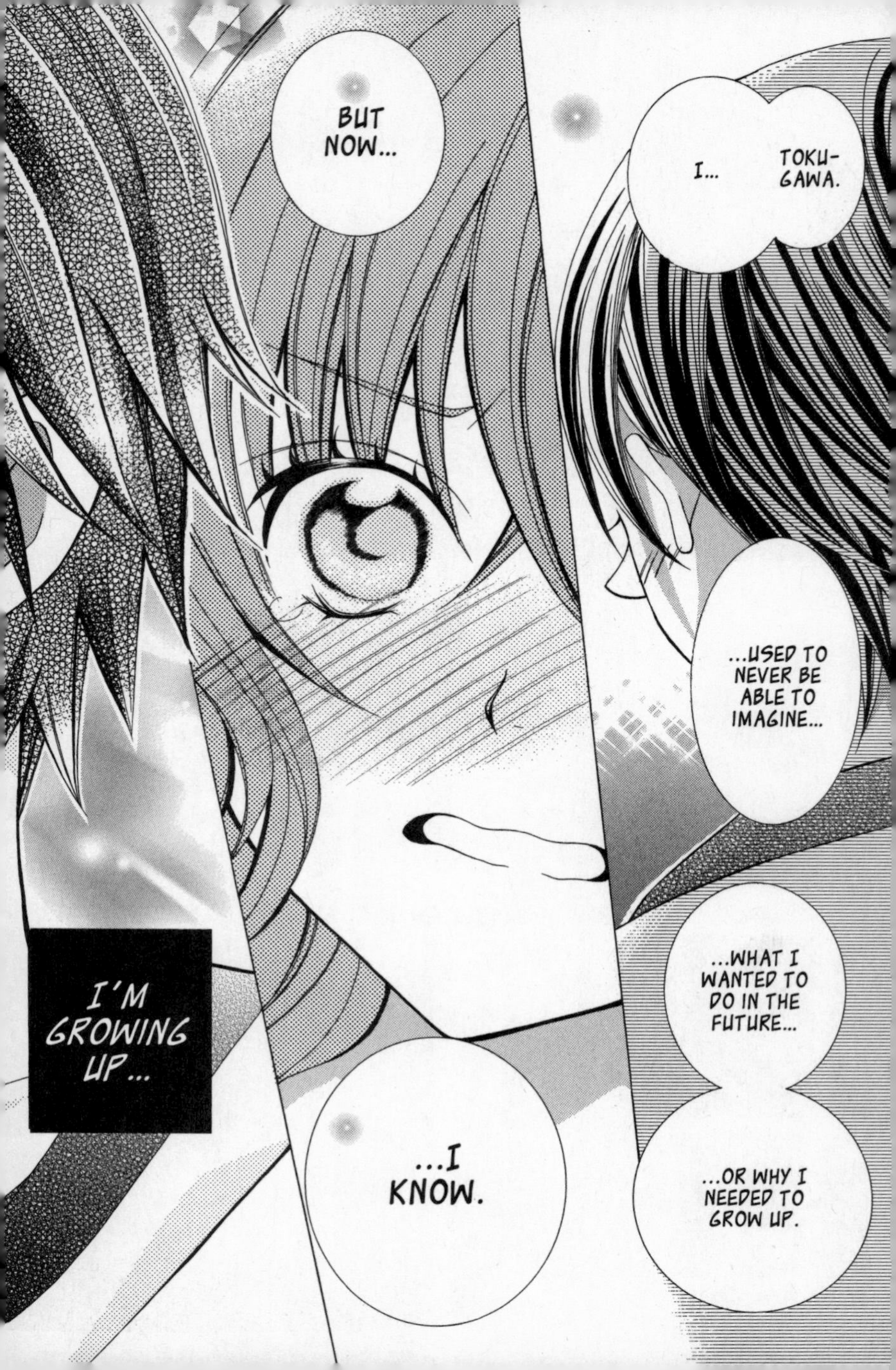
TOKU-GAWA.
I...
...USED TO NEVER BE ABLE TO IMAGINE...
...WHAT I WANTED TO DO IN THE FUTURE...
...OR WHY I NEEDED TO GROW UP.
BUT NOW...
...I KNOW.
I'M GROWING UP...

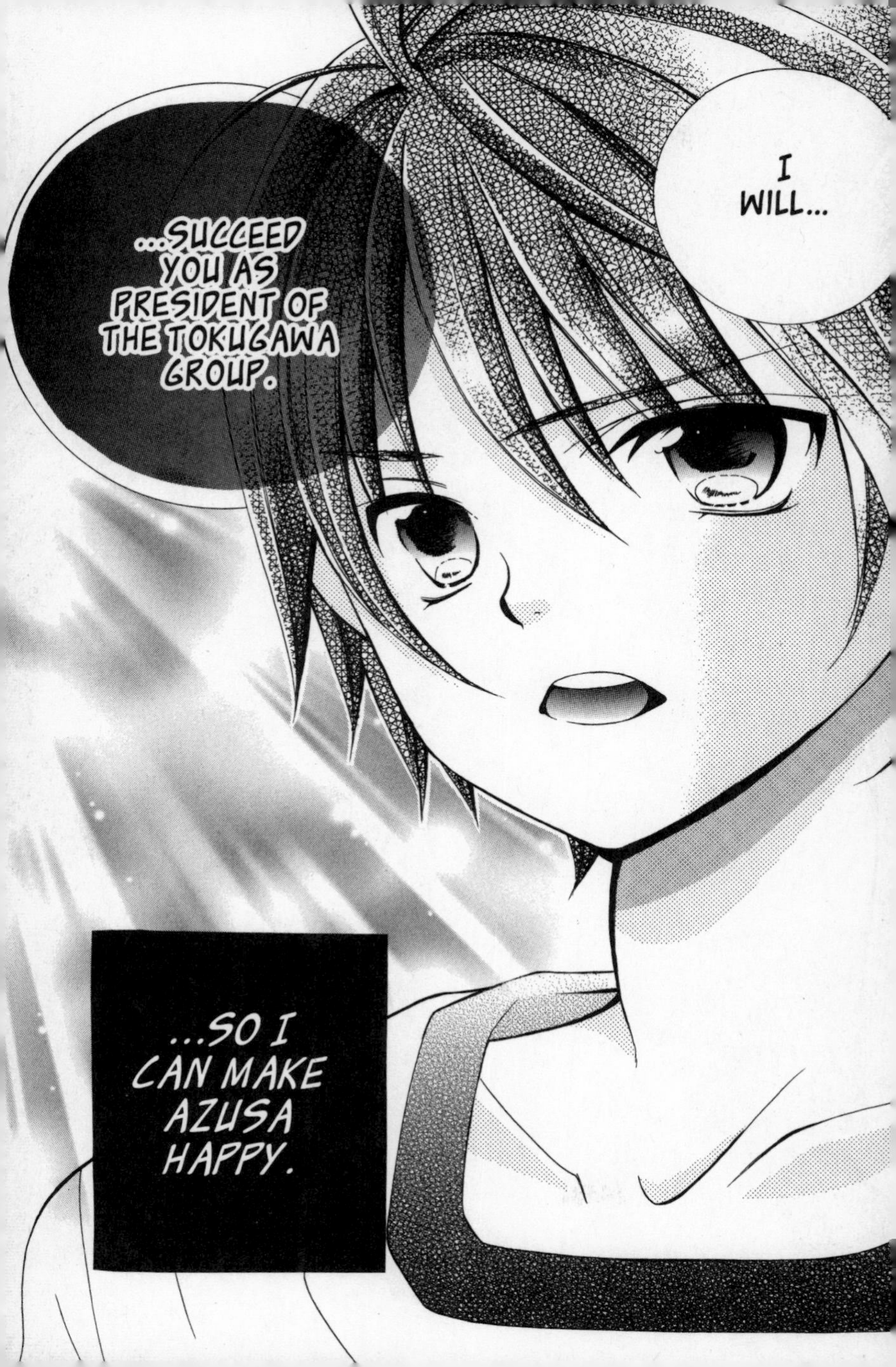
I WILL...
...SUCCEED YOU AS PRESIDENT OF THE TOKUGAWA GROUP.
...SO I CAN MAKE AZUSA HAPPY.

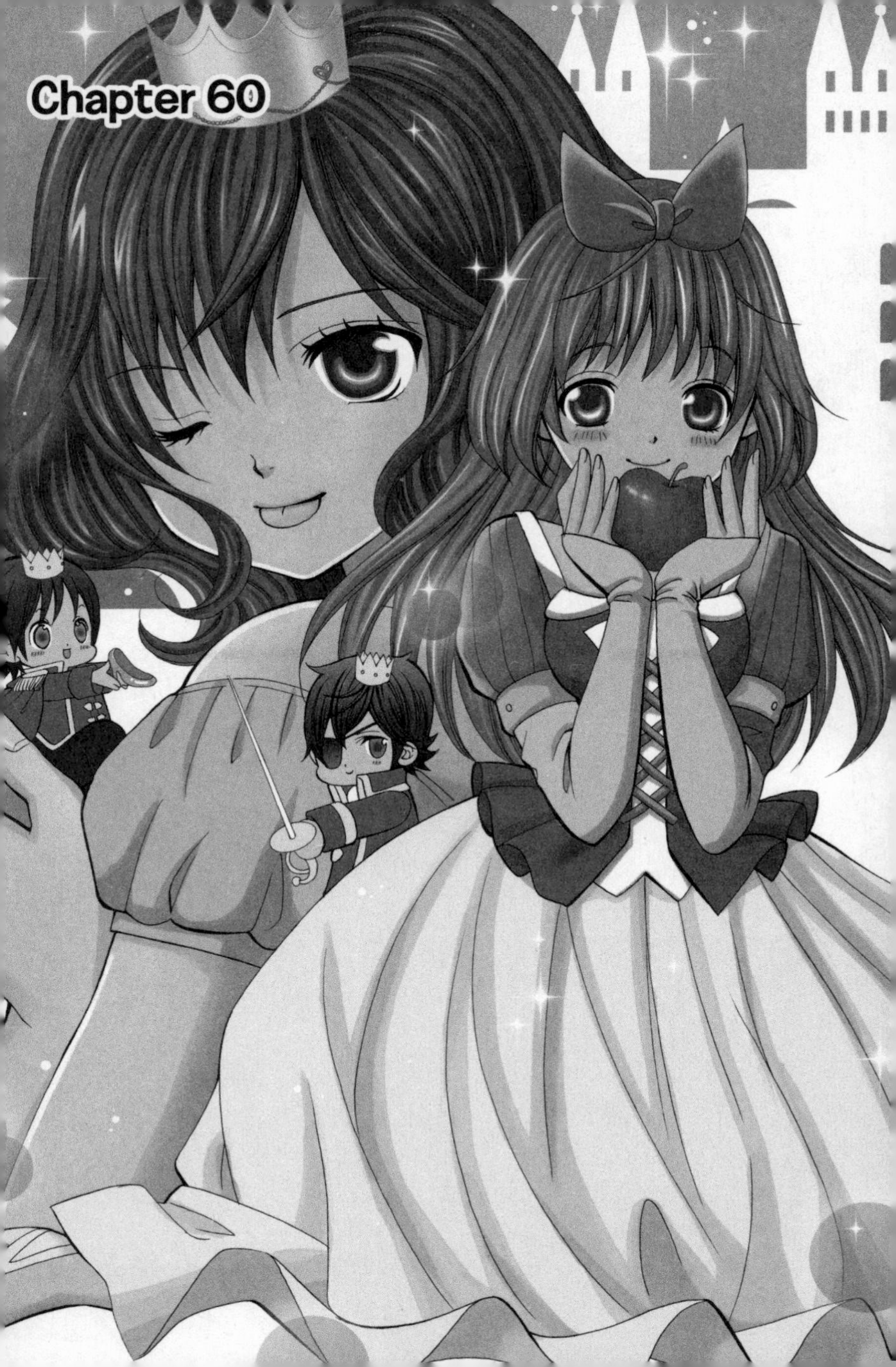
Chapter 60

Chapter 60

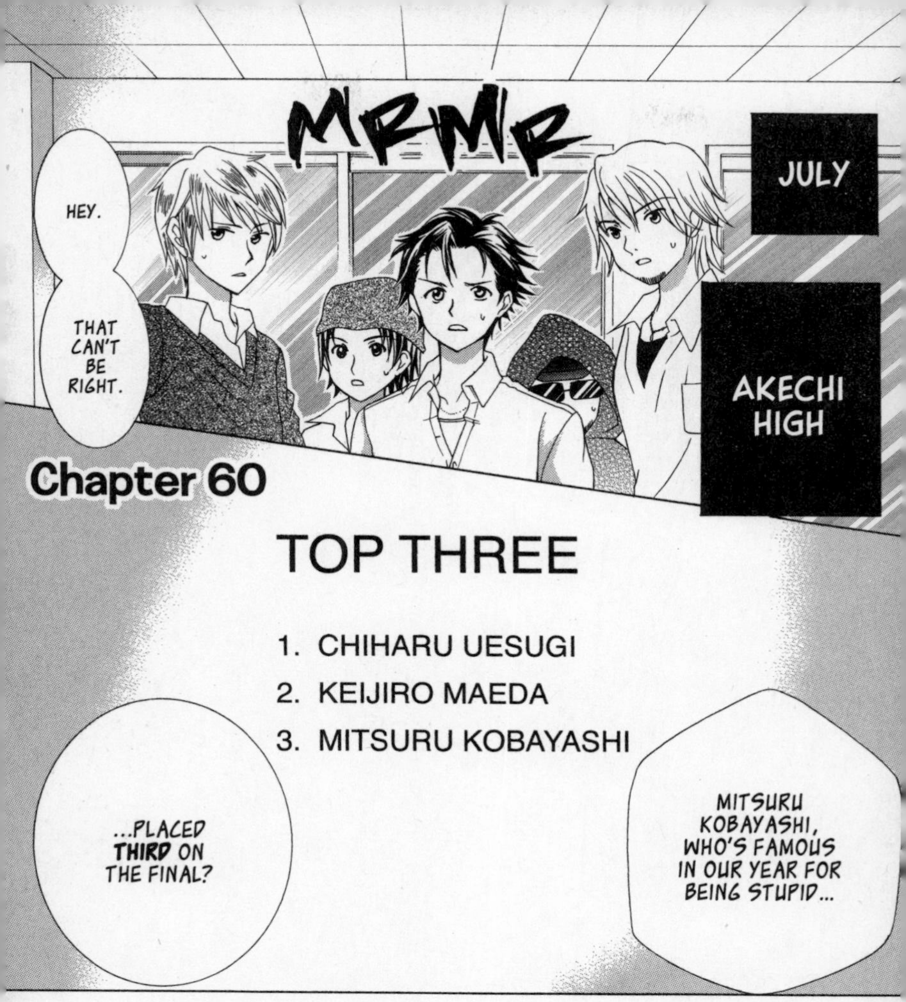
JULY
AKECHI HIGH
MRMR
HEY.
THAT CAN'T BE RIGHT.
MITSURU KOBAYASHI, WHO'S FAMOUS IN OUR YEAR FOR BEING STUPID...
TOP THREE
1. CHIHARU UESUGI
2. KEIJIRO MAEDA
3. MITSURU KOBAYASHI
...PLACED **THIRD** ON THE FINAL?

So Cute It Hurts!!

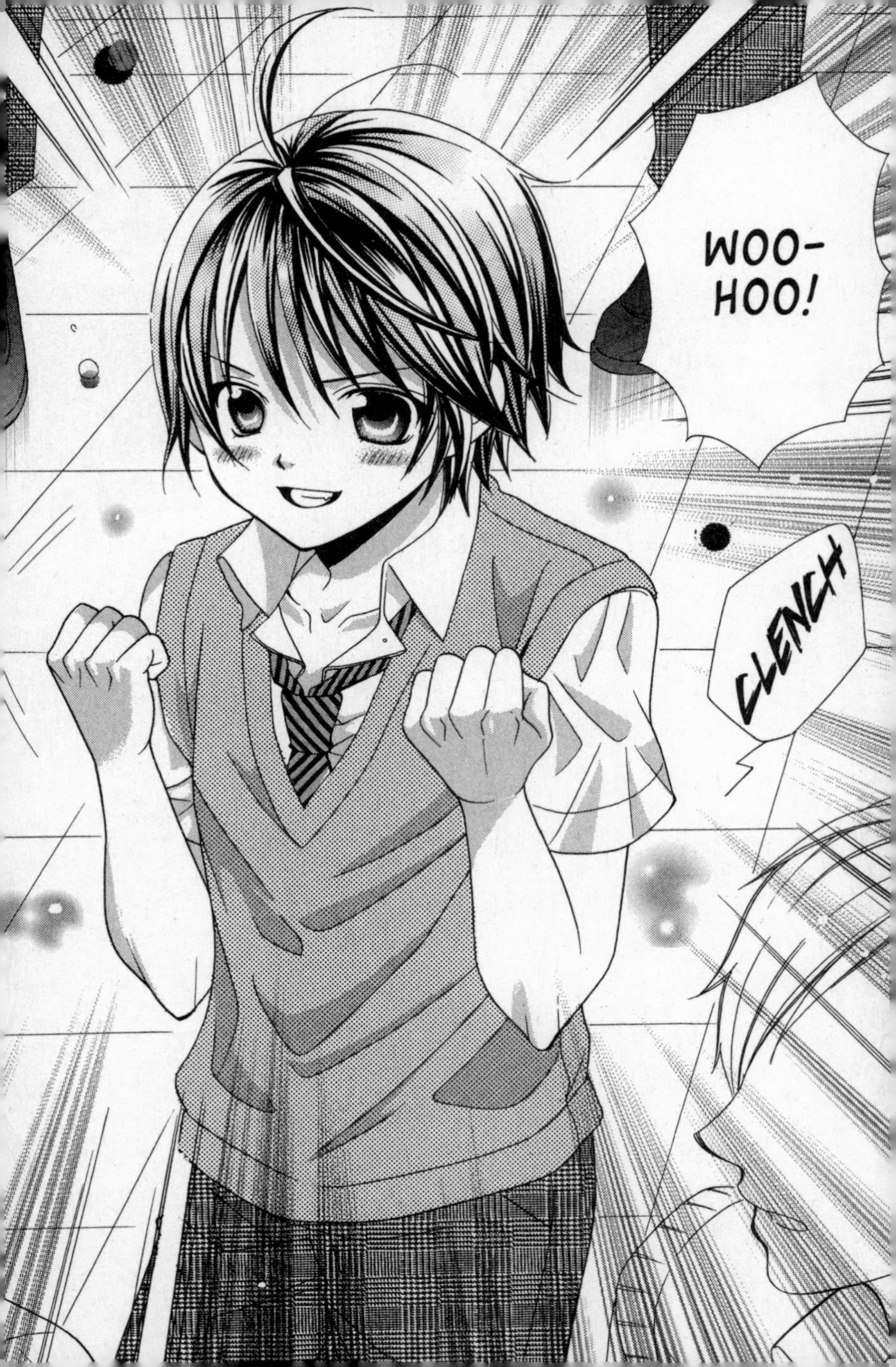
WOO-
HOO!
CLENCH

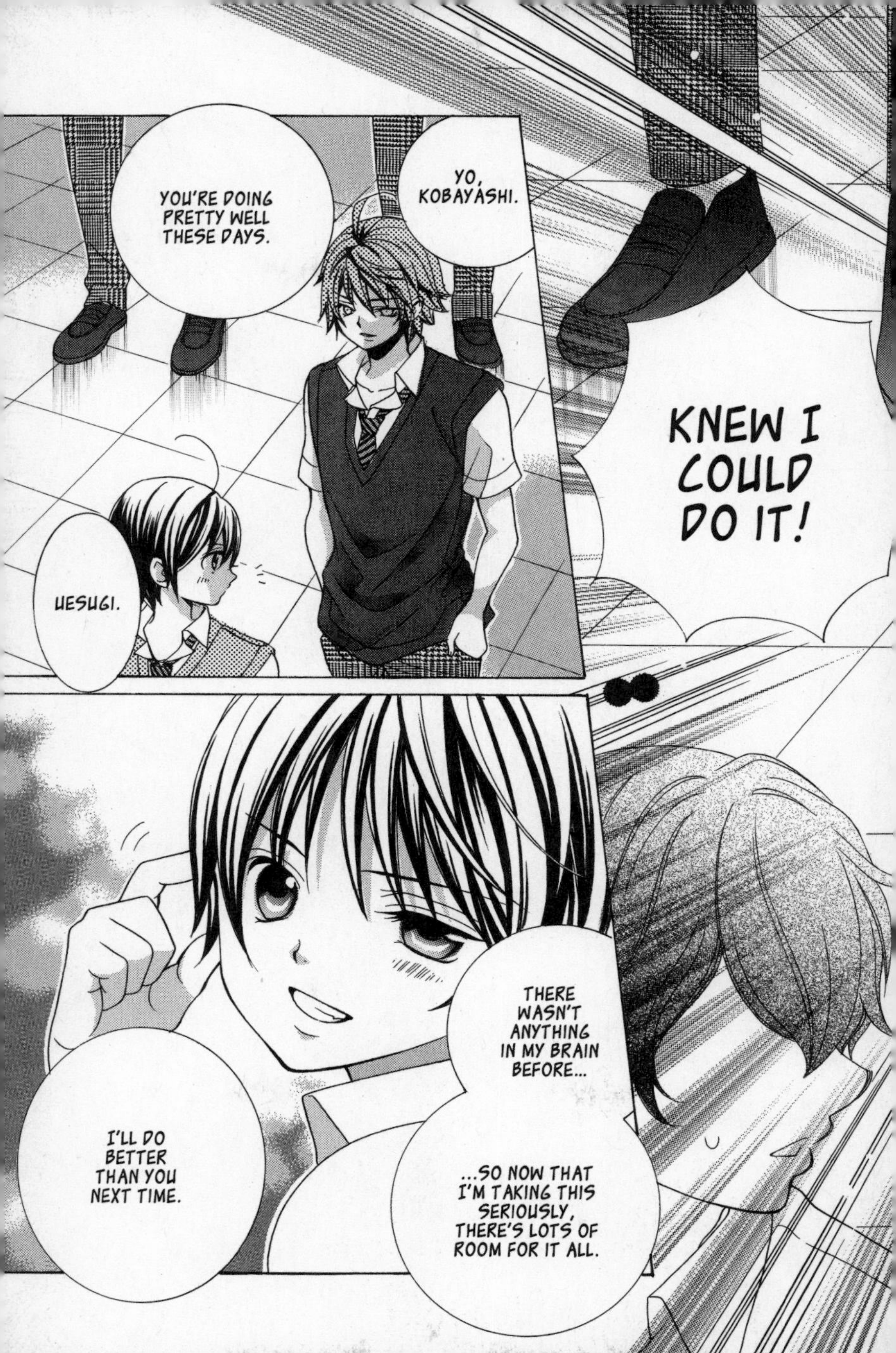
KNEW I COULD DO IT!
YO, KOBAYASHI.
YOU'RE DOING PRETTY WELL THESE DAYS.
UESUGI.
THERE WASN'T ANYTHING IN MY BRAIN BEFORE...
...SO NOW THAT I'M TAKING THIS SERIOUSLY, THERE'S LOTS OF ROOM FOR IT ALL.
I'LL DO BETTER THAN YOU NEXT TIME.

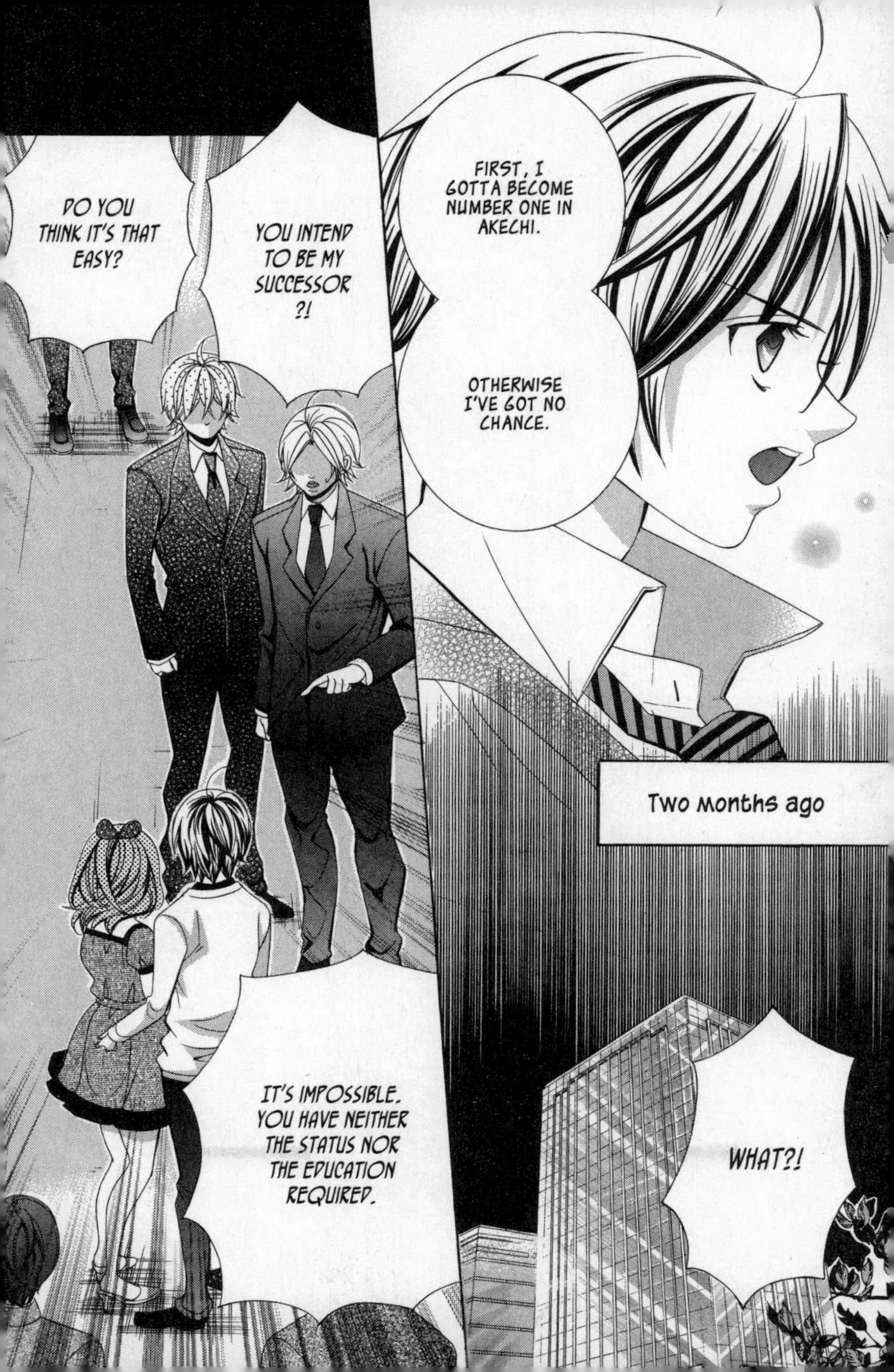
FIRST, I GOTTA BECOME NUMBER ONE IN AKECHI.
OTHERWISE I'VE GOT NO CHANCE.
Two months ago
WHAT?!
YOU INTEND TO BE MY SUCCESSOR ?!
DO YOU THINK IT'S THAT EASY?
IT'S IMPOSSIBLE. YOU HAVE NEITHER THE STATUS NOR THE EDUCATION REQUIRED.

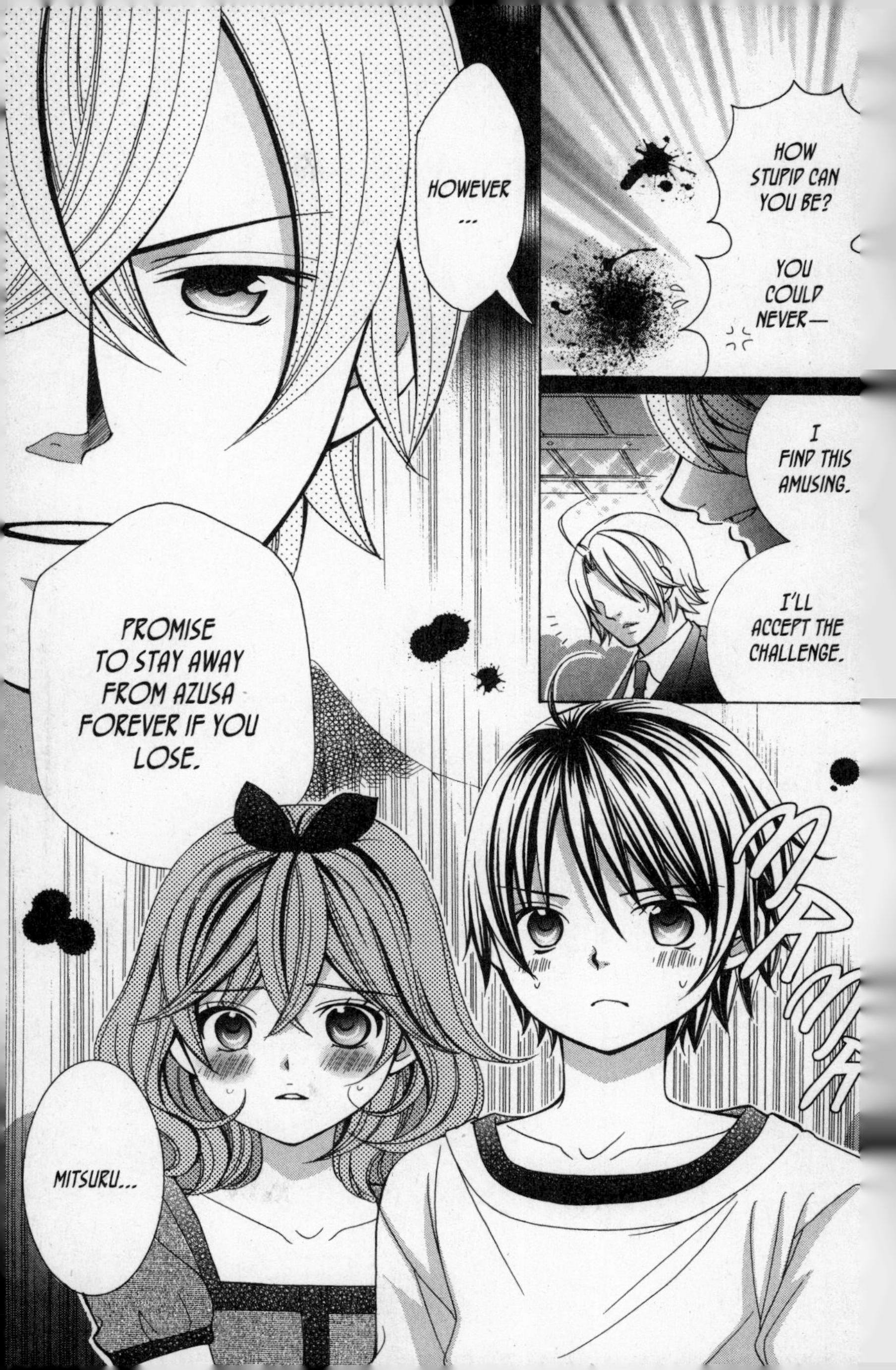
HOW STUPID CAN YOU BE?
YOU COULD NEVER—
I FIND THIS AMUSING.
I'LL ACCEPT THE CHALLENGE.
HOWEVER ...
PROMISE TO STAY AWAY FROM AZUSA FOREVER IF YOU LOSE.
MITSURU...

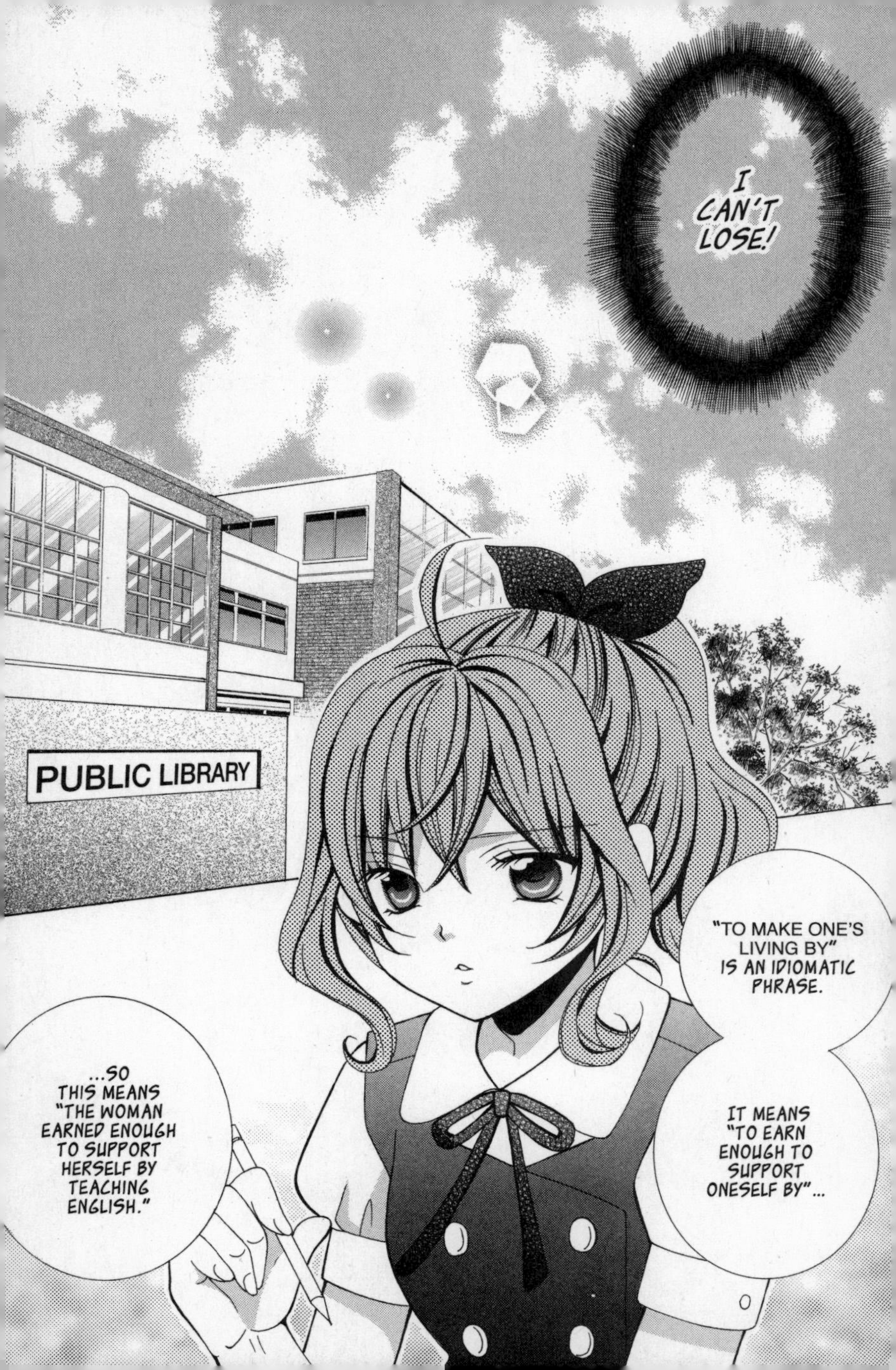
I CAN'T LOSE!
PUBLIC LIBRARY
"TO MAKE ONE'S LIVING BY" IS AN IDIOMATIC PHRASE.
IT MEANS "TO EARN ENOUGH TO SUPPORT ONESELF BY"...
...SO THIS MEANS "THE WOMAN EARNED ENOUGH TO SUPPORT HERSELF BY TEACHING ENGLISH."

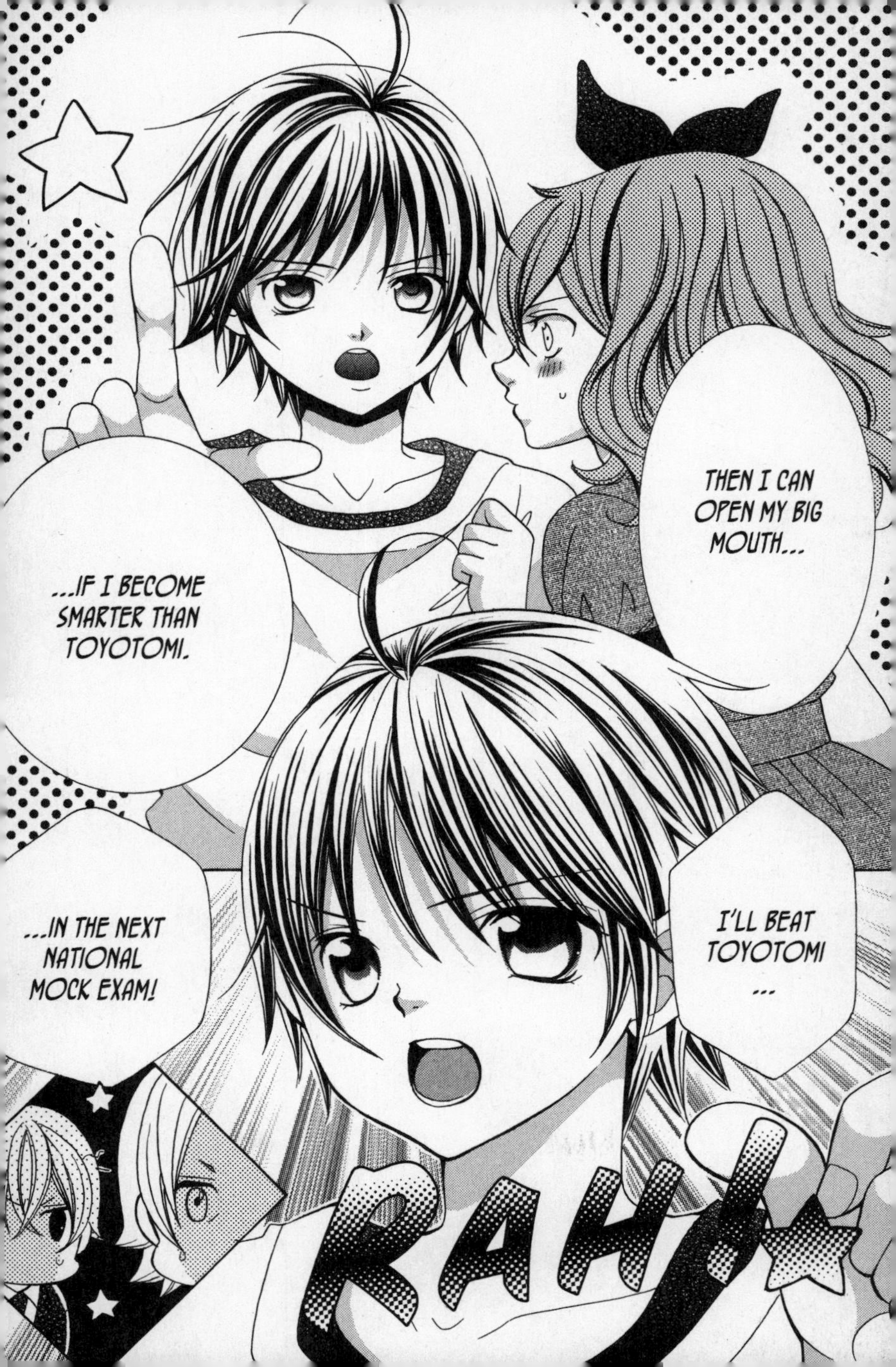
THEN I CAN OPEN MY BIG MOUTH...
...IF I BECOME SMARTER THAN TOYOTOMI.
I'LL BEAT TOYOTOMI ...
...IN THE NEXT NATIONAL MOCK EXAM!
RAH!

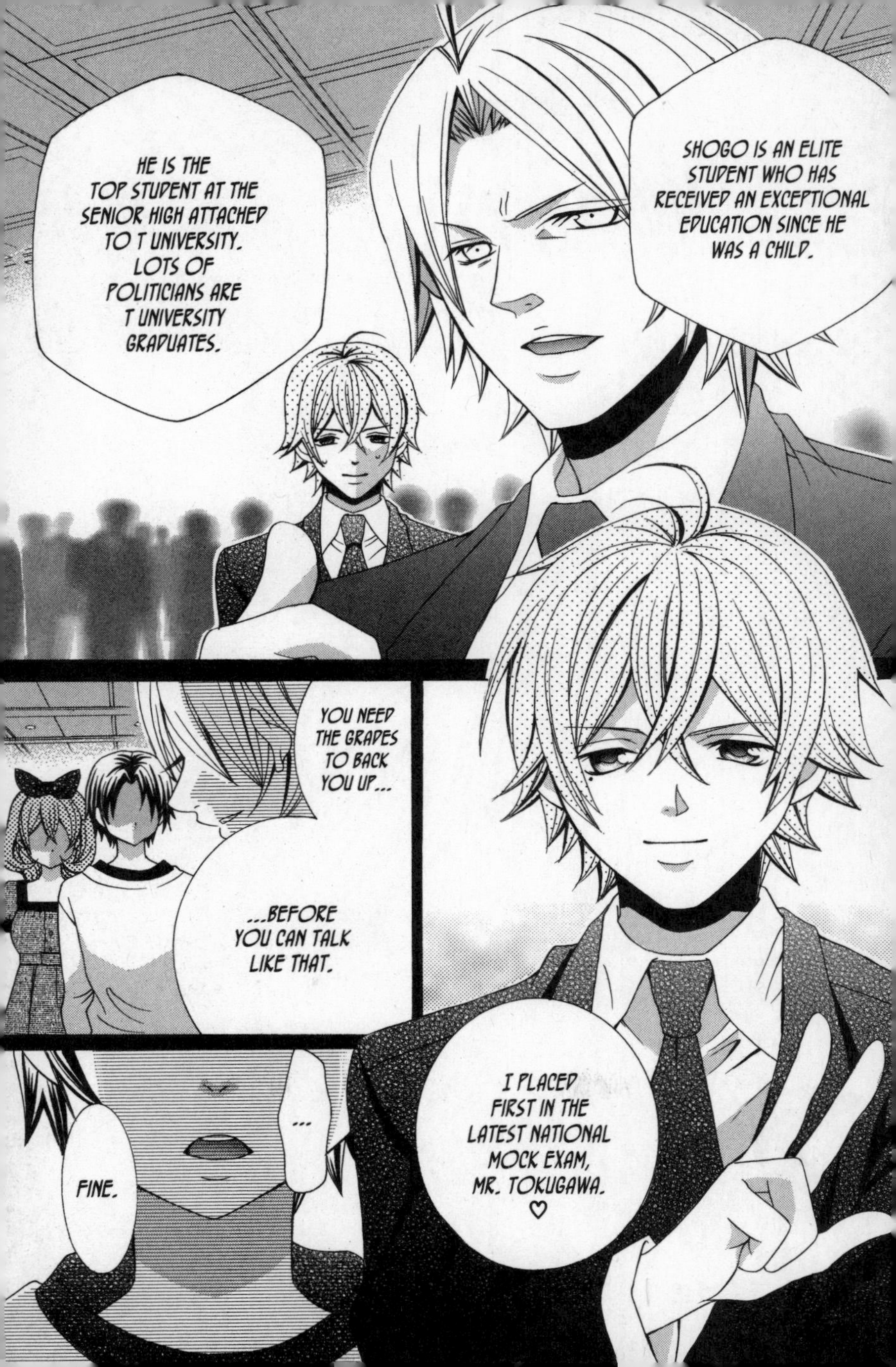
SHOGO IS AN ELITE STUDENT WHO HAS RECEIVED AN EXCEPTIONAL EDUCATION SINCE HE WAS A CHILD.
HE IS THE TOP STUDENT AT THE SENIOR HIGH ATTACHED TO T UNIVERSITY. LOTS OF POLITICIANS ARE T UNIVERSITY GRADUATES.
I PLACED FIRST IN THE LATEST NATIONAL MOCK EXAM, MR. TOKUGAWA. ♡
YOU NEED THE GRADES TO BACK YOU UP...
...BEFORE YOU CAN TALK LIKE THAT.
...
FINE.

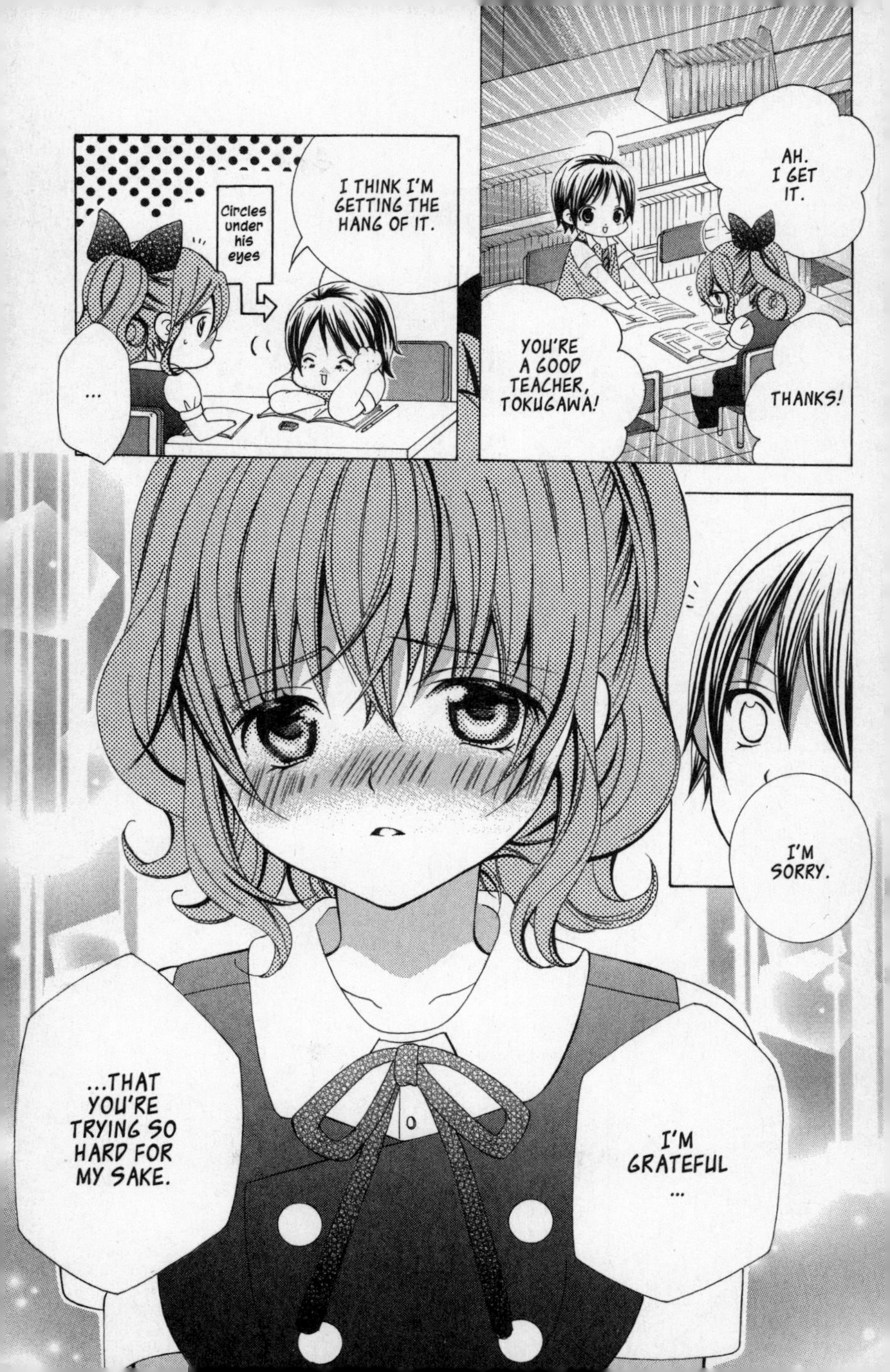
AH. I GET IT.
YOU'RE A GOOD TEACHER, TOKUGAWA!
THANKS!
I THINK I'M GETTING THE HANG OF IT.
Circles under his eyes
...
I'M SORRY.
I'M GRATEFUL ...
...THAT YOU'RE TRYING SO HARD FOR MY SAKE.

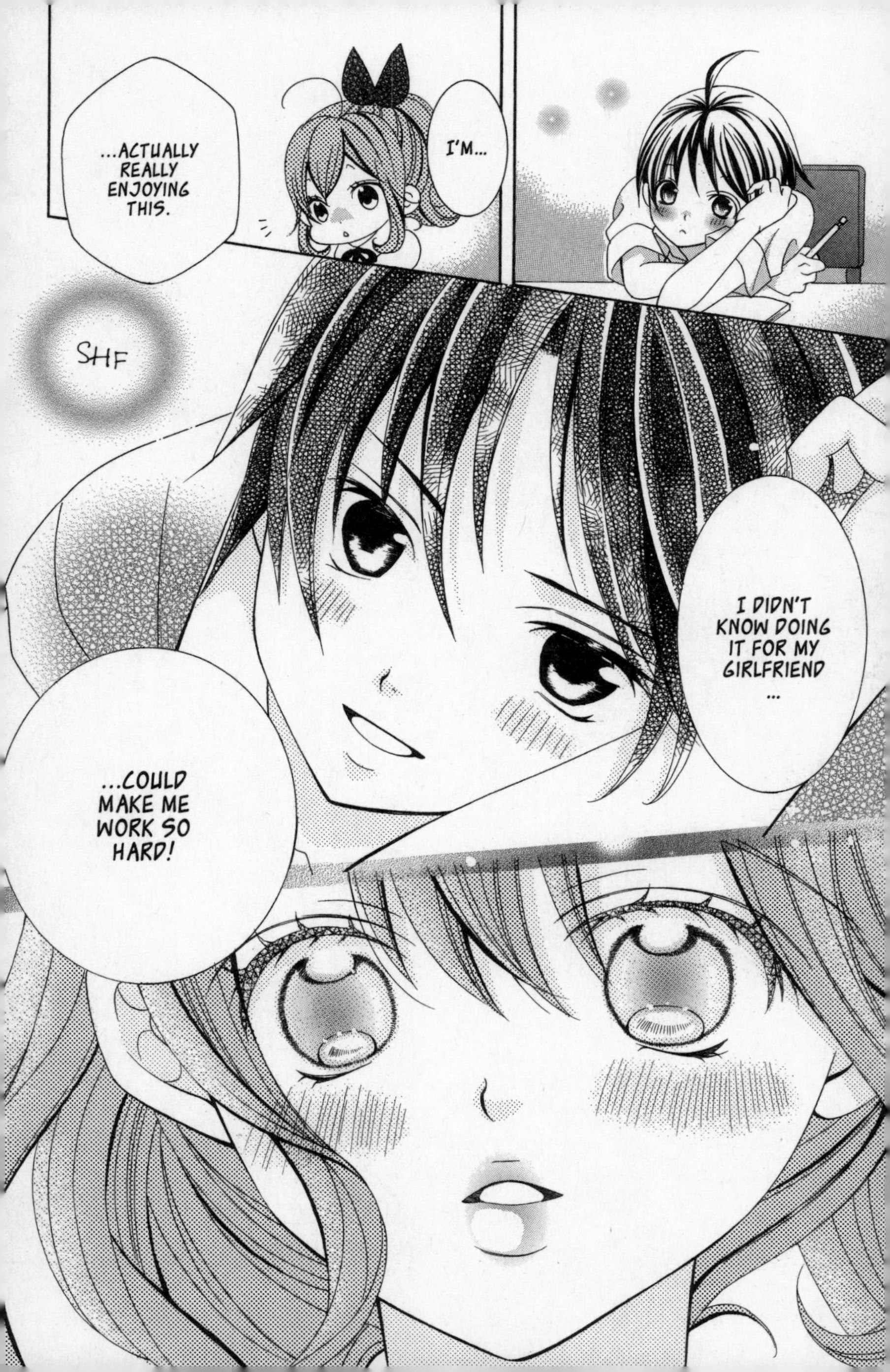
I'M...
...ACTUALLY REALLY ENJOYING THIS.
SHF
I DIDN'T KNOW DOING IT FOR MY GIRLFRIEND ...
...COULD MAKE ME WORK SO HARD!

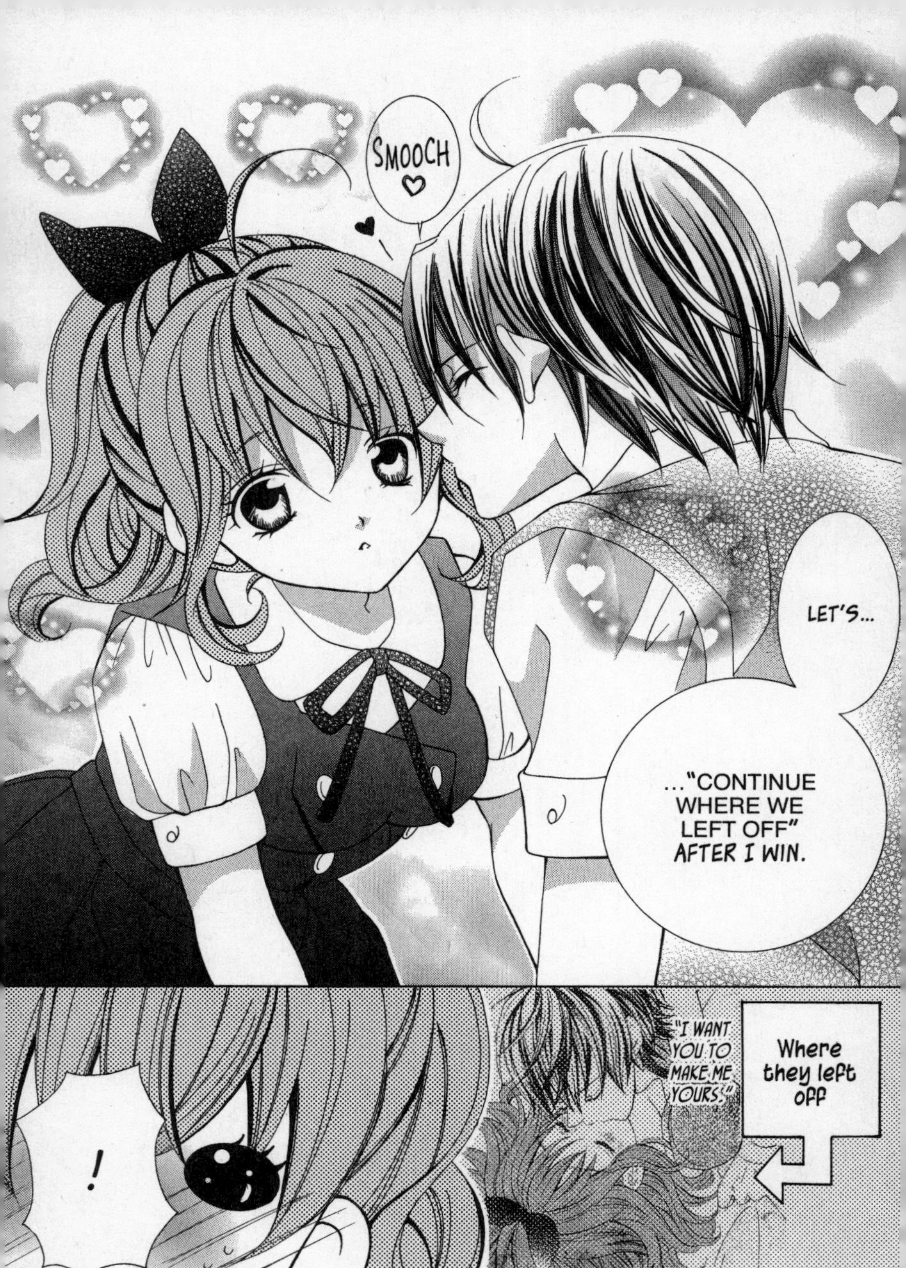
SMOOCH ♡
LET'S...
..."CONTINUE WHERE WE LEFT OFF" AFTER I WIN.
Where they left off
"I WANT YOU TO MAKE ME YOURS."
!

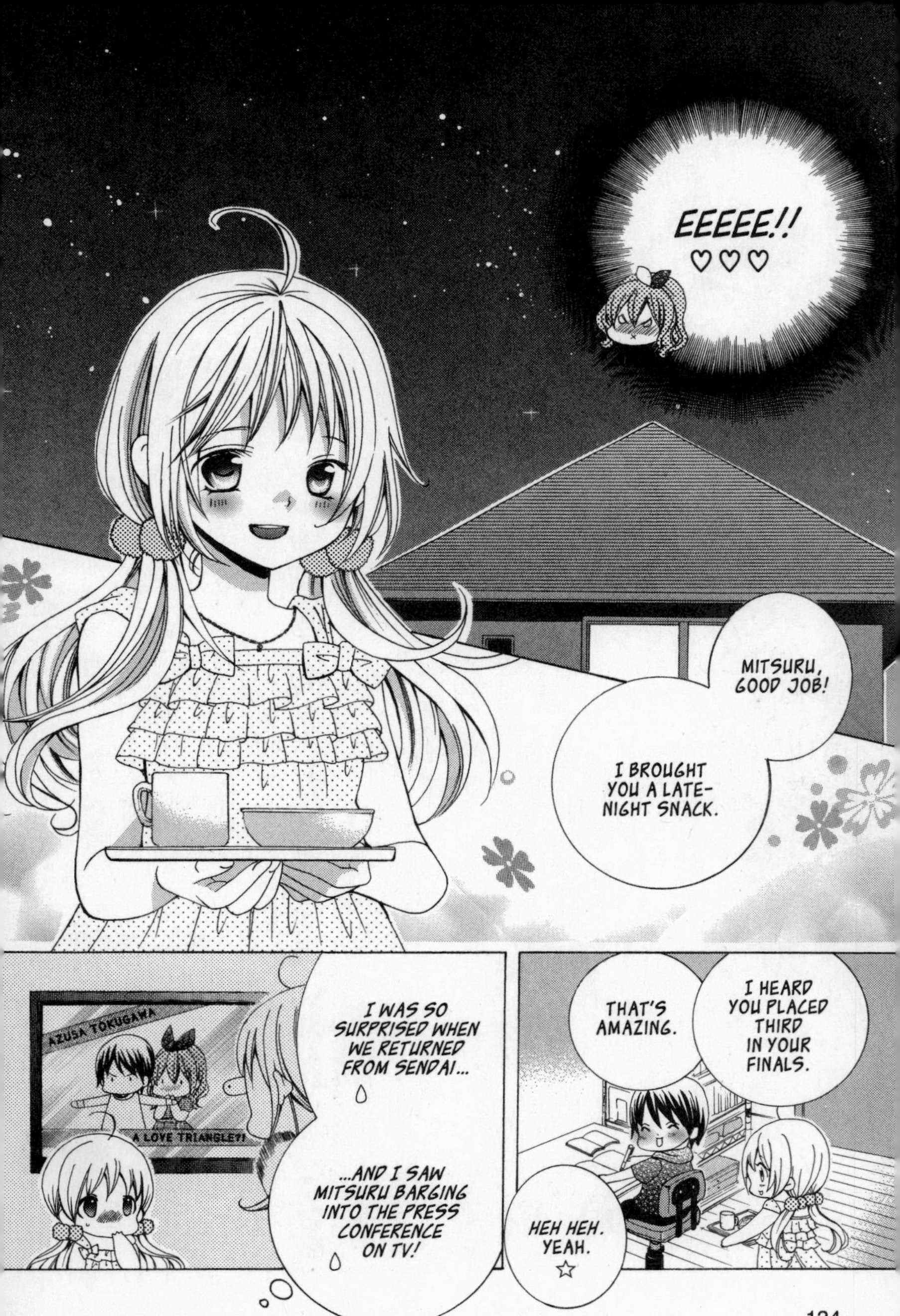
EEEEE!! ♡♡♡
MITSURU, GOOD JOB!
I BROUGHT YOU A LATE-NIGHT SNACK.
I HEARD YOU PLACED THIRD IN YOUR FINALS.
THAT'S AMAZING.
HEH HEH. YEAH. ☆
I WAS SO SURPRISED WHEN WE RETURNED FROM SENDAI...
AZUSA TOKUGAWA
A LOVE TRIANGLE?!
...AND I SAW MITSURU BARGING INTO THE PRESS CONFERENCE ON TV!

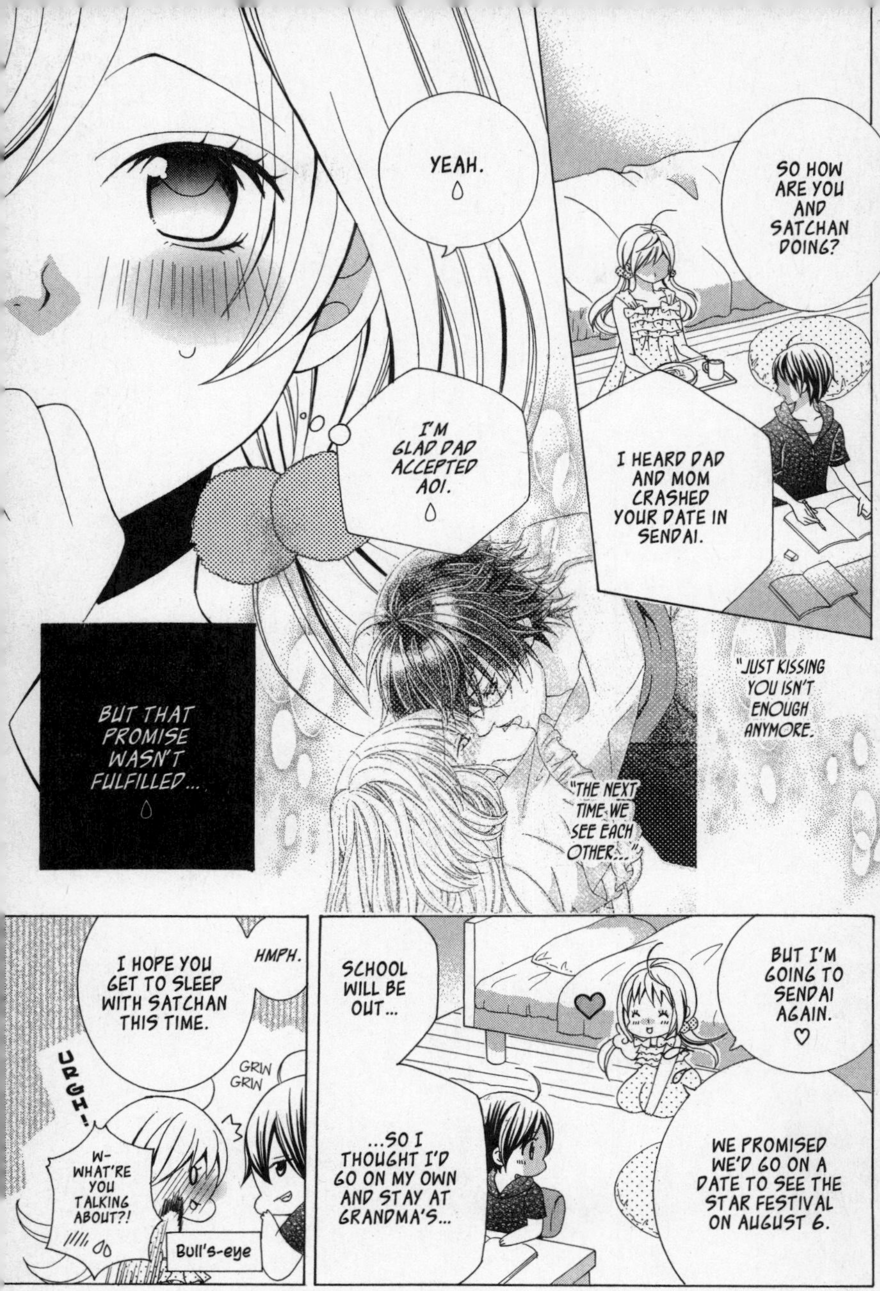
SO HOW ARE YOU AND SATCHAN DOING?
I HEARD DAD AND MOM CRASHED YOUR DATE IN SENDAI.
YEAH.
I'M GLAD DAD ACCEPTED AOI.
"JUST KISSING YOU ISN'T ENOUGH ANYMORE.
"THE NEXT TIME WE SEE EACH OTHER..."
BUT THAT PROMISE WASN'T FULFILLED...
BUT I'M GOING TO SENDAI AGAIN.
WE PROMISED WE'D GO ON A DATE TO SEE THE STAR FESTIVAL ON AUGUST 6.
SCHOOL WILL BE OUT...
...SO I THOUGHT I'D GO ON MY OWN AND STAY AT GRANDMA'S...
HMPH.
I HOPE YOU GET TO SLEEP WITH SATCHAN THIS TIME.
GRIN GRIN
URGH!
W-WHAT'RE YOU TALKING ABOUT?!
Bull's-eye

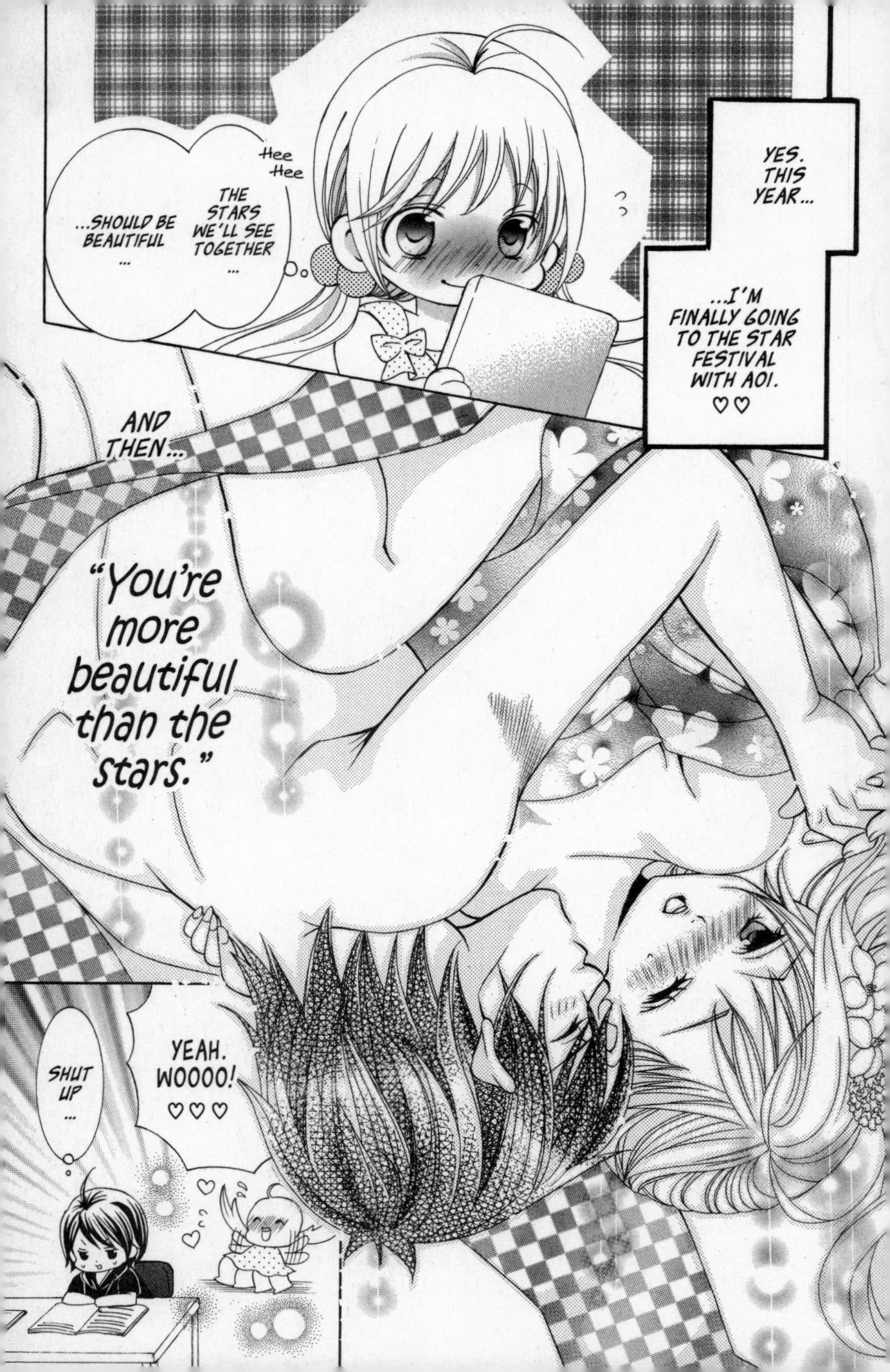
YES. THIS YEAR...
...I'M FINALLY GOING TO THE STAR FESTIVAL WITH AOI. ♡♡
Hee Hee
THE STARS WE'LL SEE TOGETHER...
...SHOULD BE BEAUTIFUL...
AND THEN...
"You're more beautiful than the stars."
YEAH. WOOOO! ♡♡♡
SHUT UP...

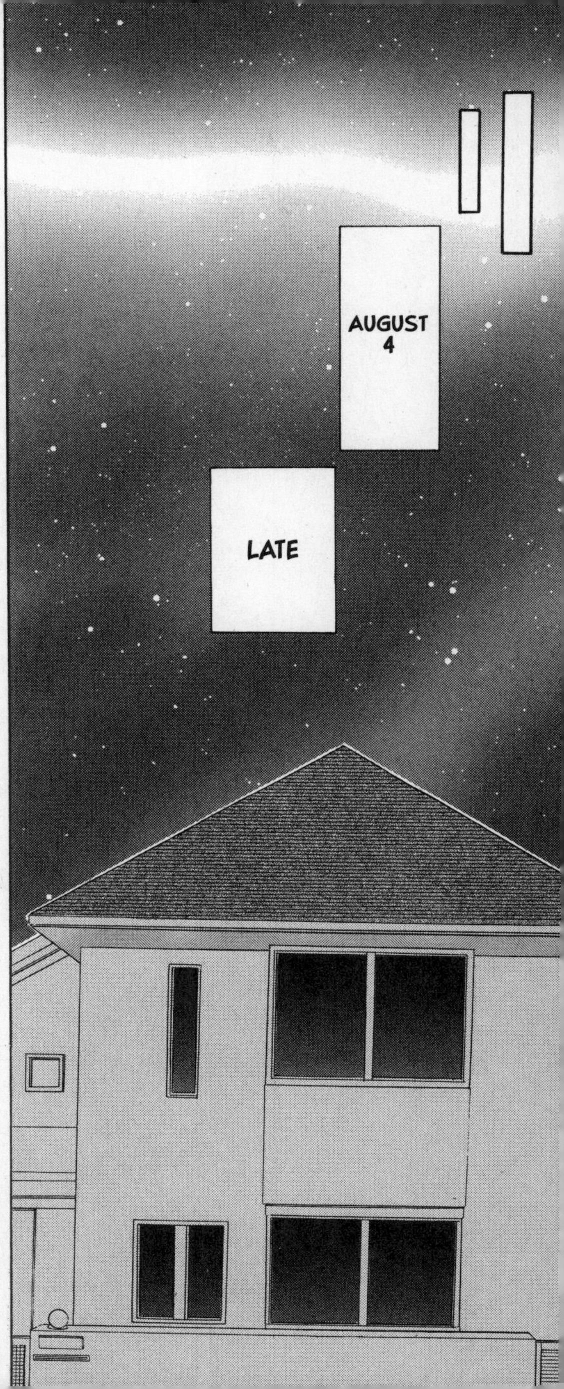
AUGUST 4
LATE

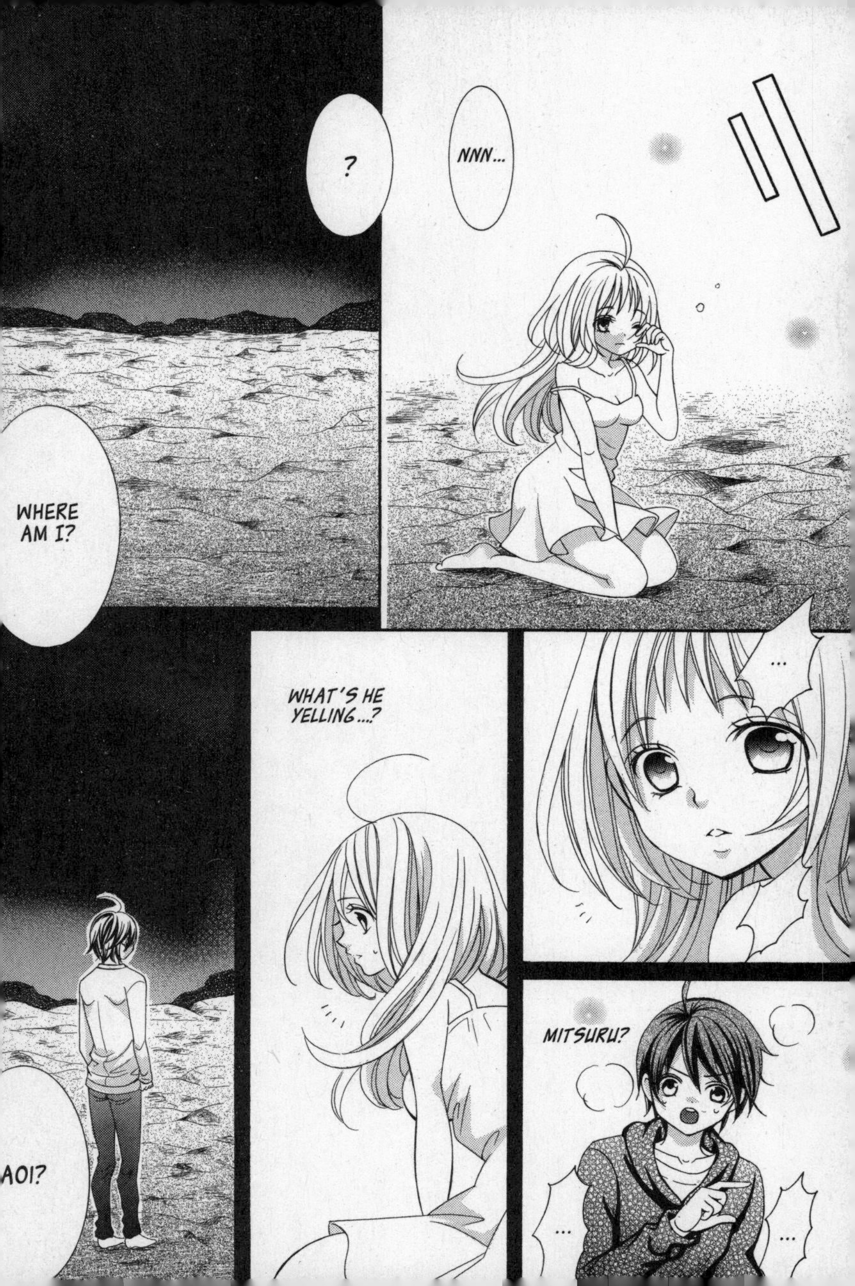
NNN...
?
WHERE AM I?
...
MITSURU?
...
...
WHAT'S HE YELLING...?
AOI?

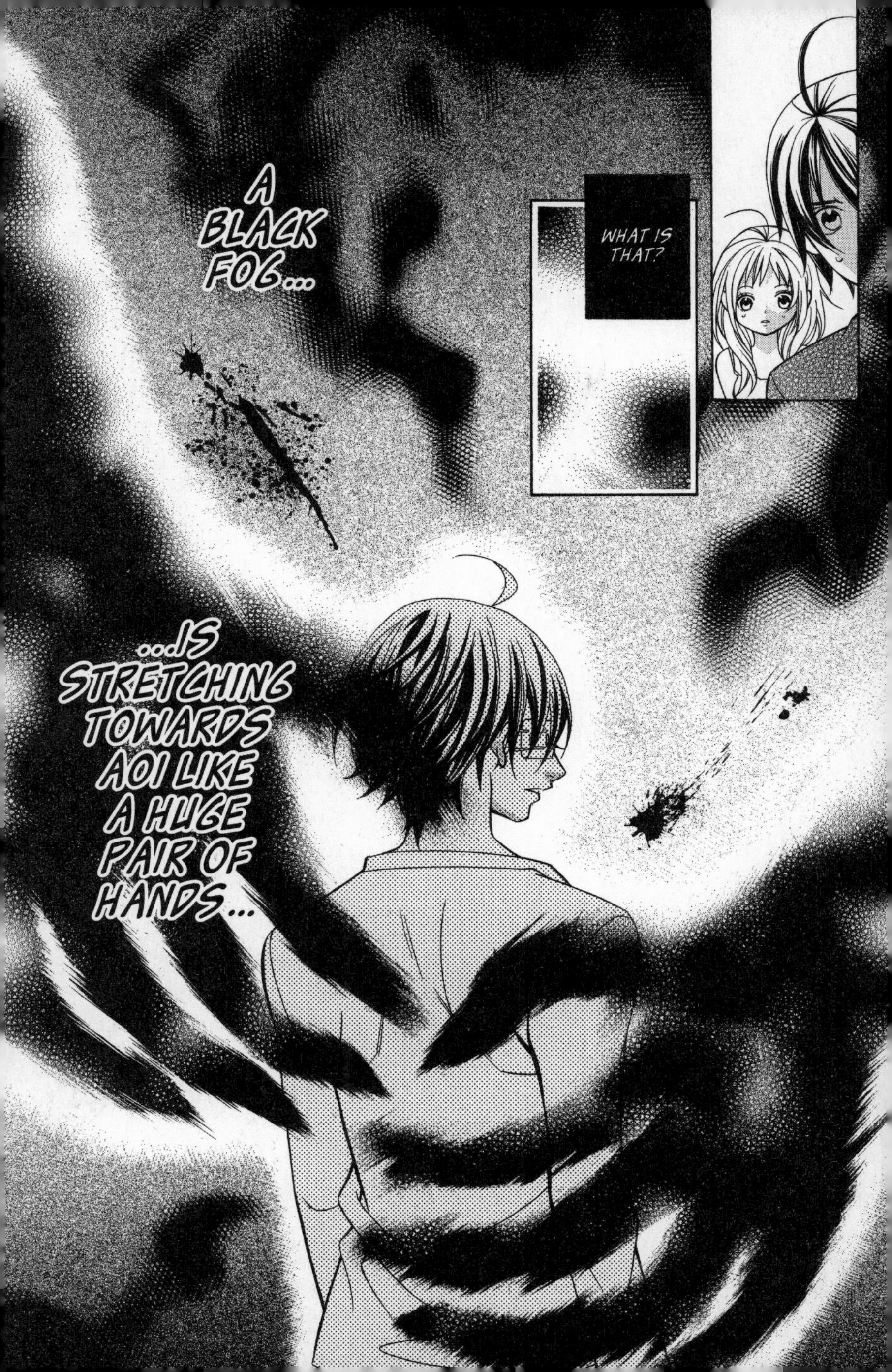
WHAT IS THAT?
A BLACK FOG...
...IS STRETCHING TOWARDS AOI LIKE A HUGE PAIR OF HANDS...

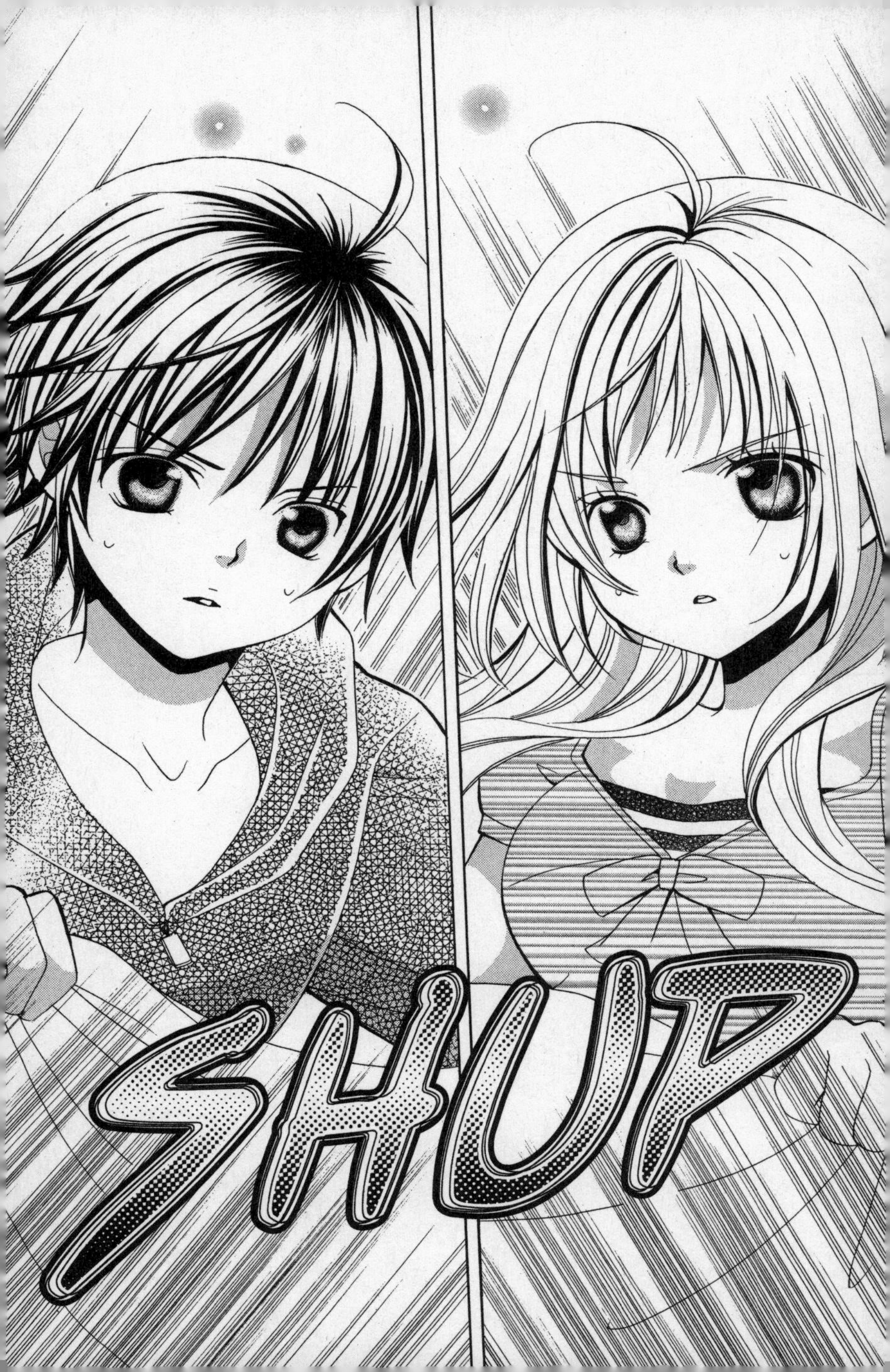
SHUP

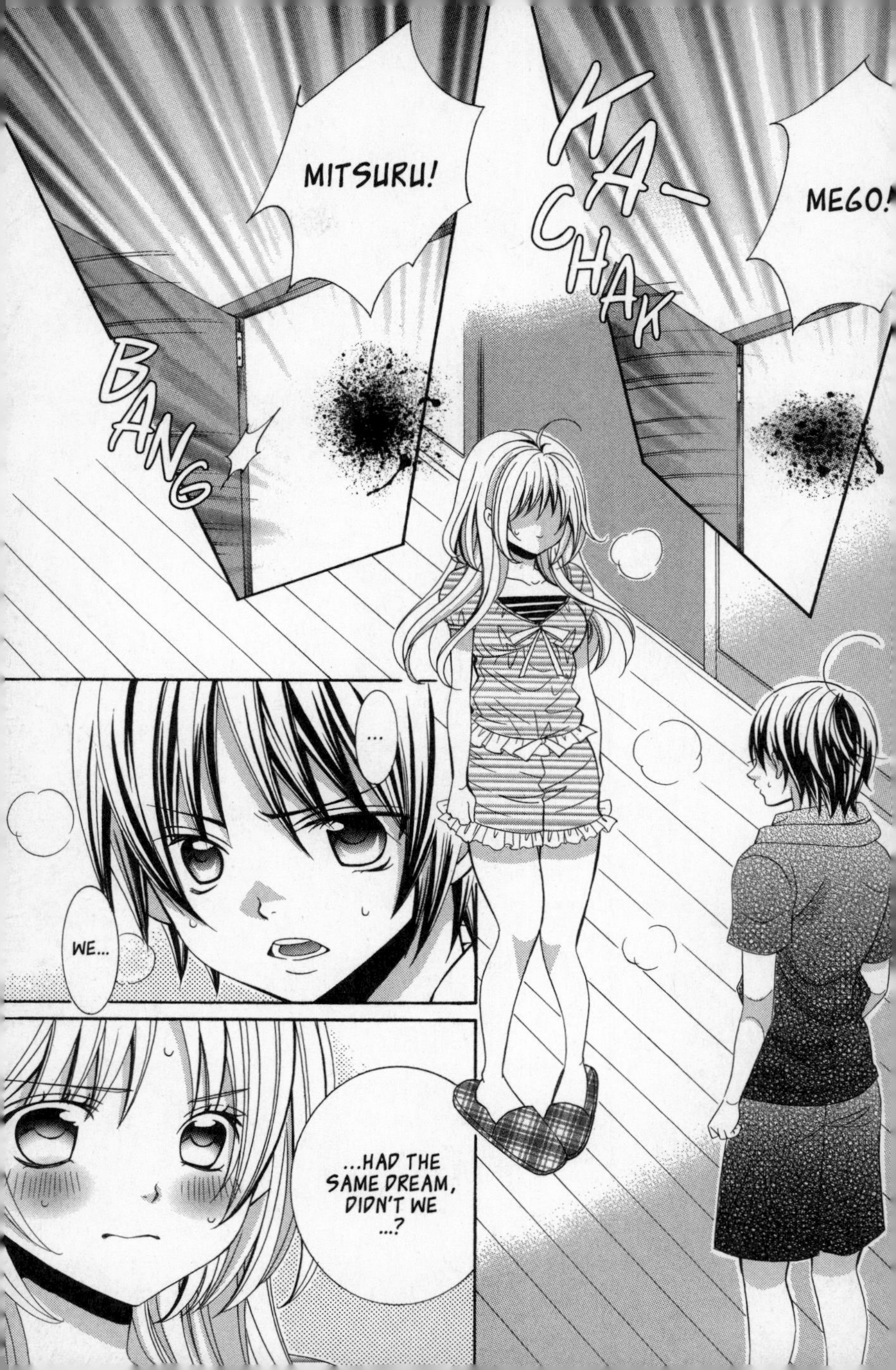
MEGO!
KA-CHAK
MITSURU!
BANG
...
WE...
...HAD THE SAME DREAM, DIDN'T WE ...?

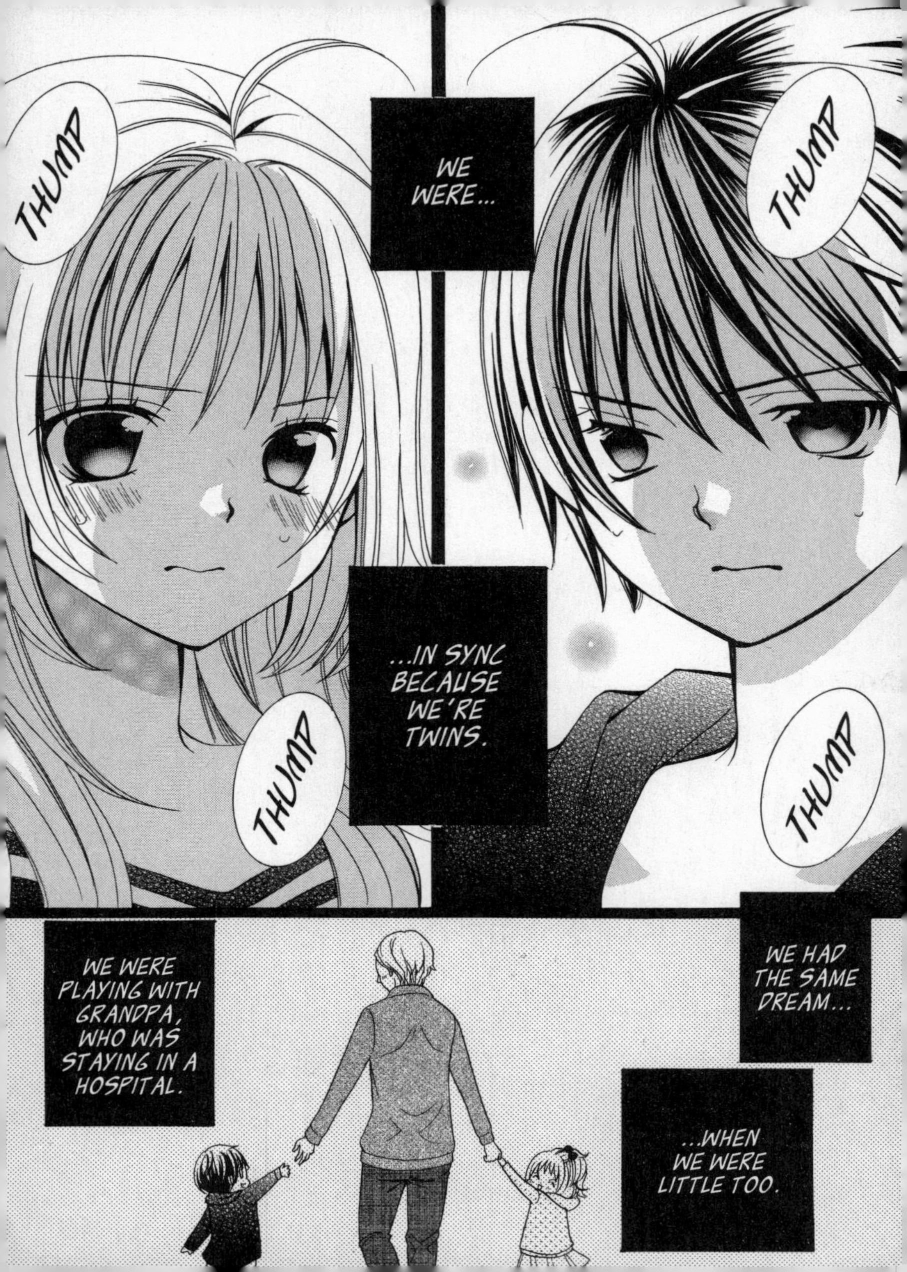
THUMP
THUMP
WE WERE...
...IN SYNC BECAUSE WE'RE TWINS.
THUMP
THUMP
WE HAD THE SAME DREAM...
...WHEN WE WERE LITTLE TOO.
WE WERE PLAYING WITH GRANDPA, WHO WAS STAYING IN A HOSPITAL.

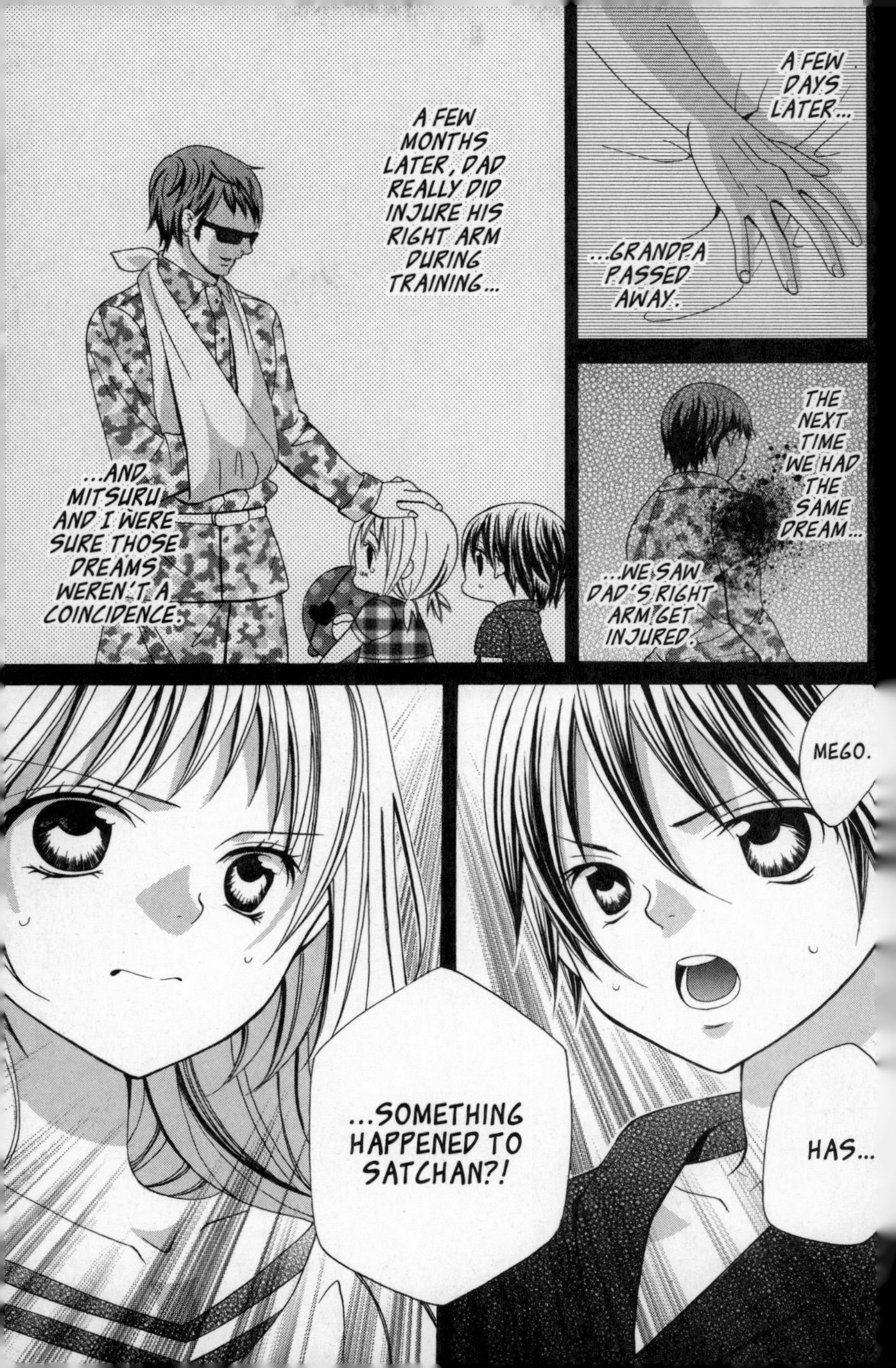
A FEW DAYS LATER...
...GRANDPA PASSED AWAY.
THE NEXT TIME WE HAD THE SAME DREAM...
...WE SAW DAD'S RIGHT ARM GET INJURED.
A FEW MONTHS LATER, DAD REALLY DID INJURE HIS RIGHT ARM DURING TRAINING...
...AND MITSURU AND I WERE SURE THOSE DREAMS WEREN'T A COINCIDENCE.
MEGO.
HAS...
...SOMETHING HAPPENED TO SATCHAN?!

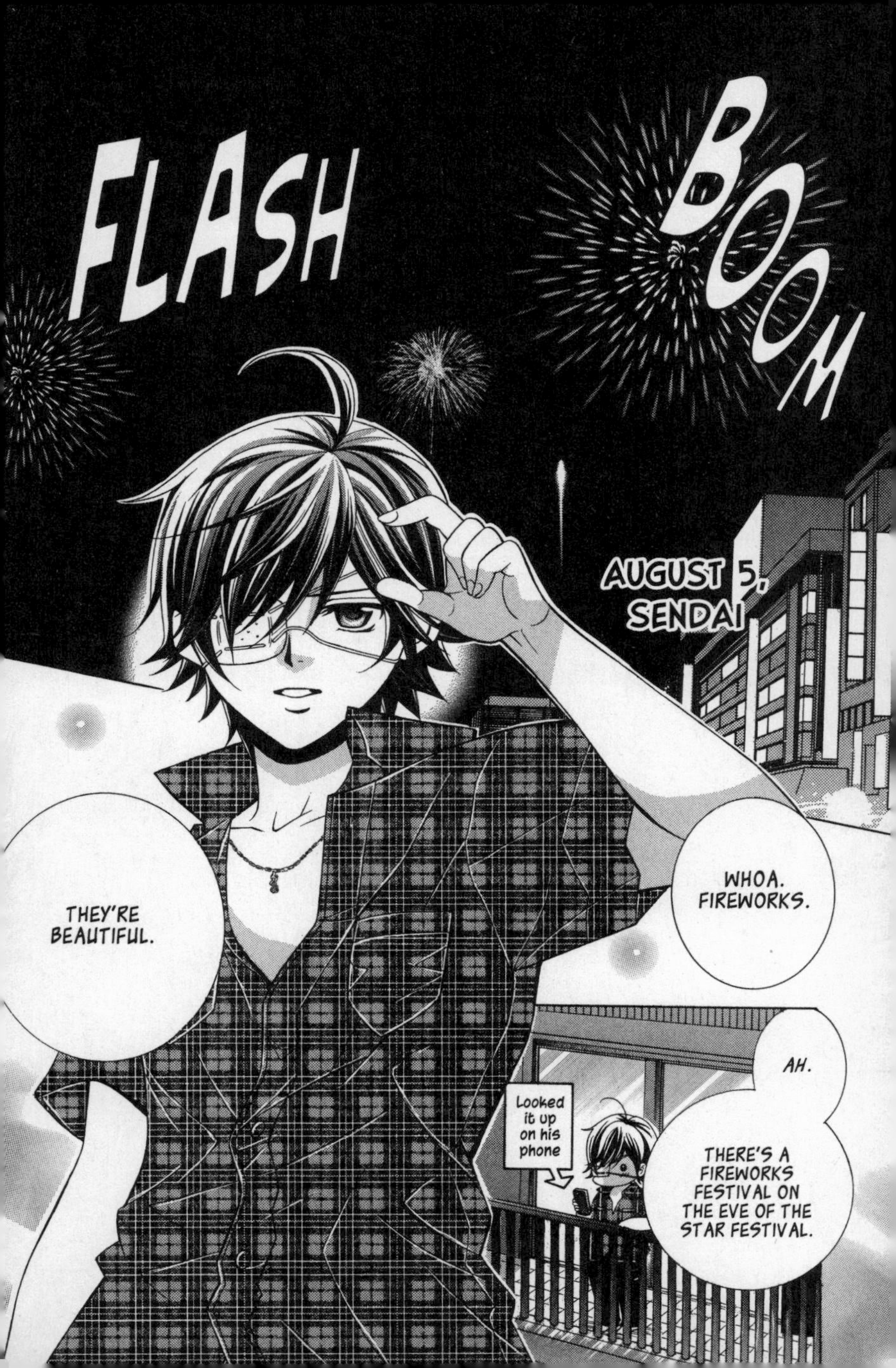
BOOM
FLASH
AUGUST 5, SENDAI
WHOA. FIREWORKS.
THEY'RE BEAUTIFUL.
AH.
THERE'S A FIREWORKS FESTIVAL ON THE EVE OF THE STAR FESTIVAL.
Looked it up on his phone

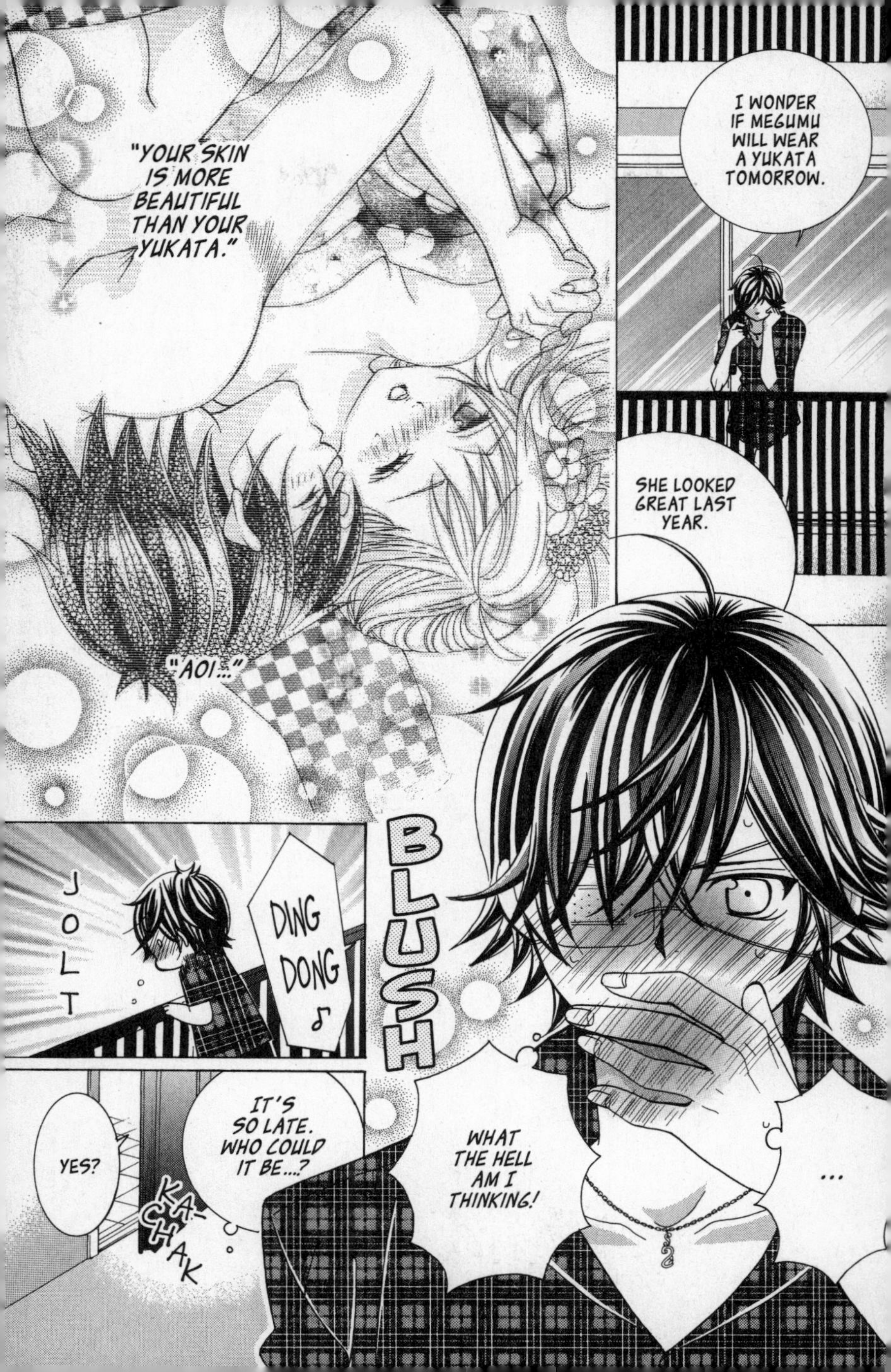
I WONDER IF MEGUMU WILL WEAR A YUKATA TOMORROW.
SHE LOOKED GREAT LAST YEAR.
"YOUR SKIN IS MORE BEAUTIFUL THAN YOUR YUKATA."
"AOI..."
BLUSH
...
WHAT THE HELL AM I THINKING!
JOLT
DING DONG ♪
IT'S SO LATE. WHO COULD IT BE...?
YES?
KA-CHAK

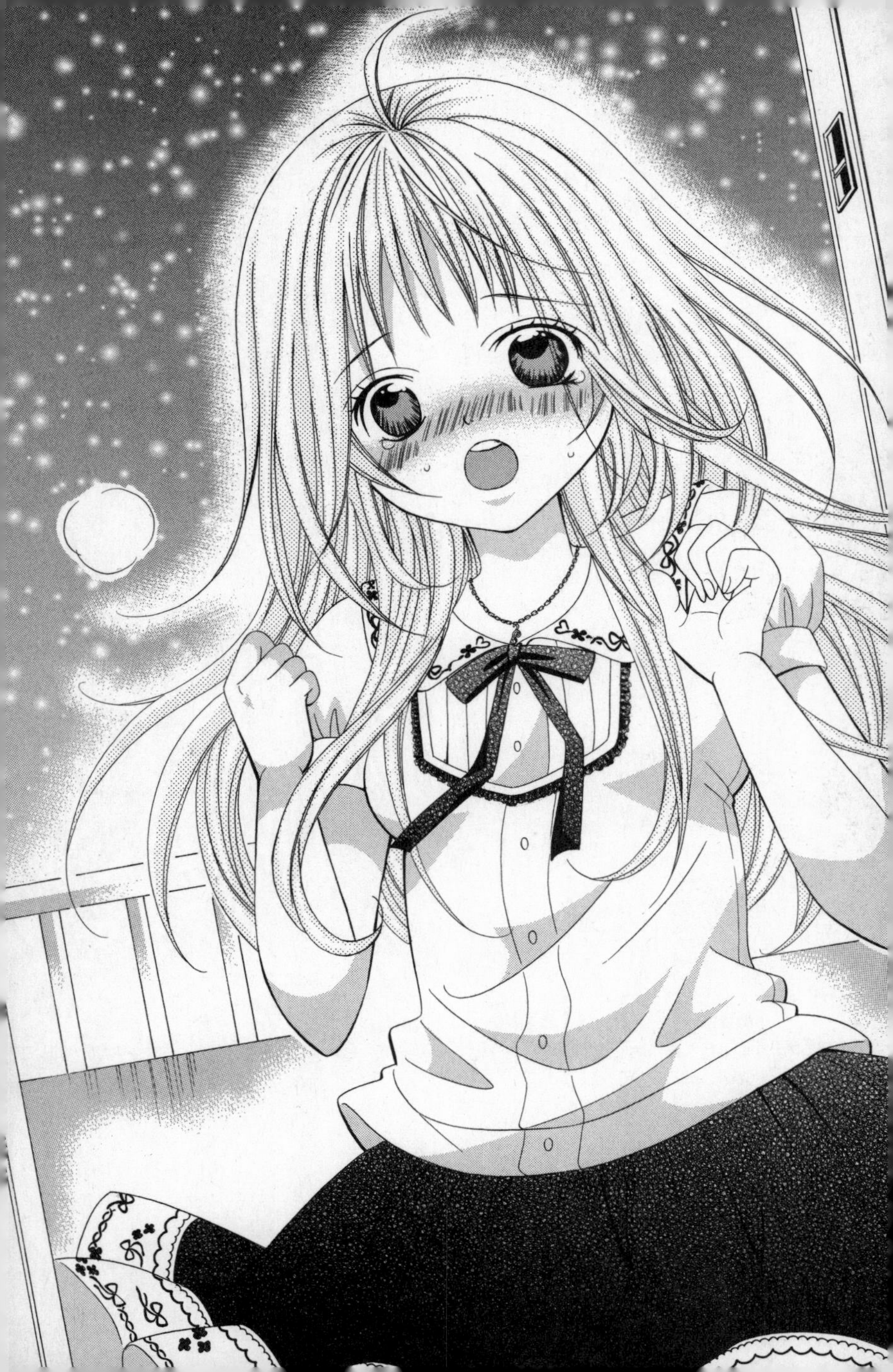

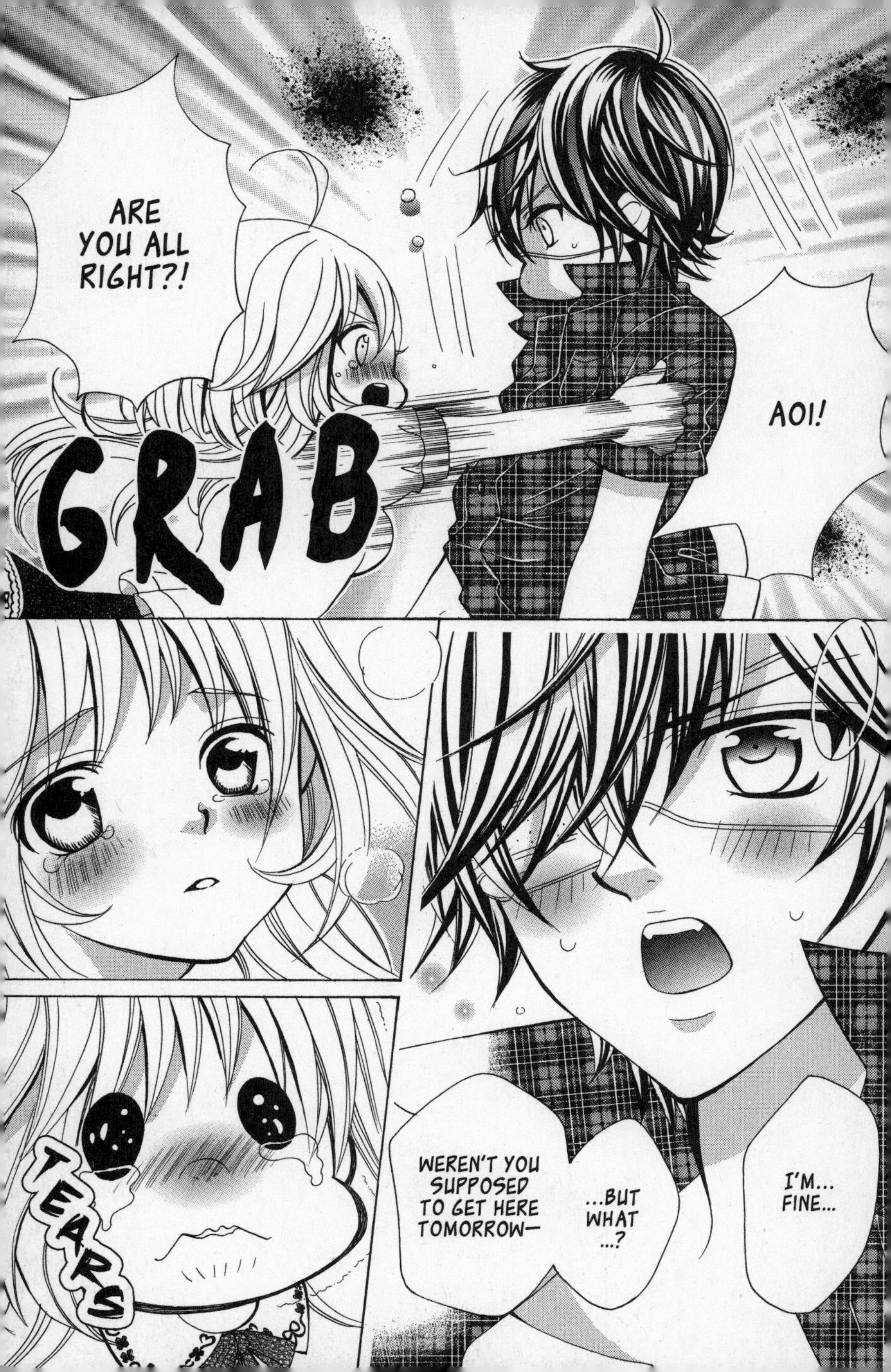
AOI!
ARE YOU ALL RIGHT?!
GRAB
I'M... FINE...
...BUT WHAT ...?
WEREN'T YOU SUPPOSED TO GET HERE TOMORROW—
TEARS

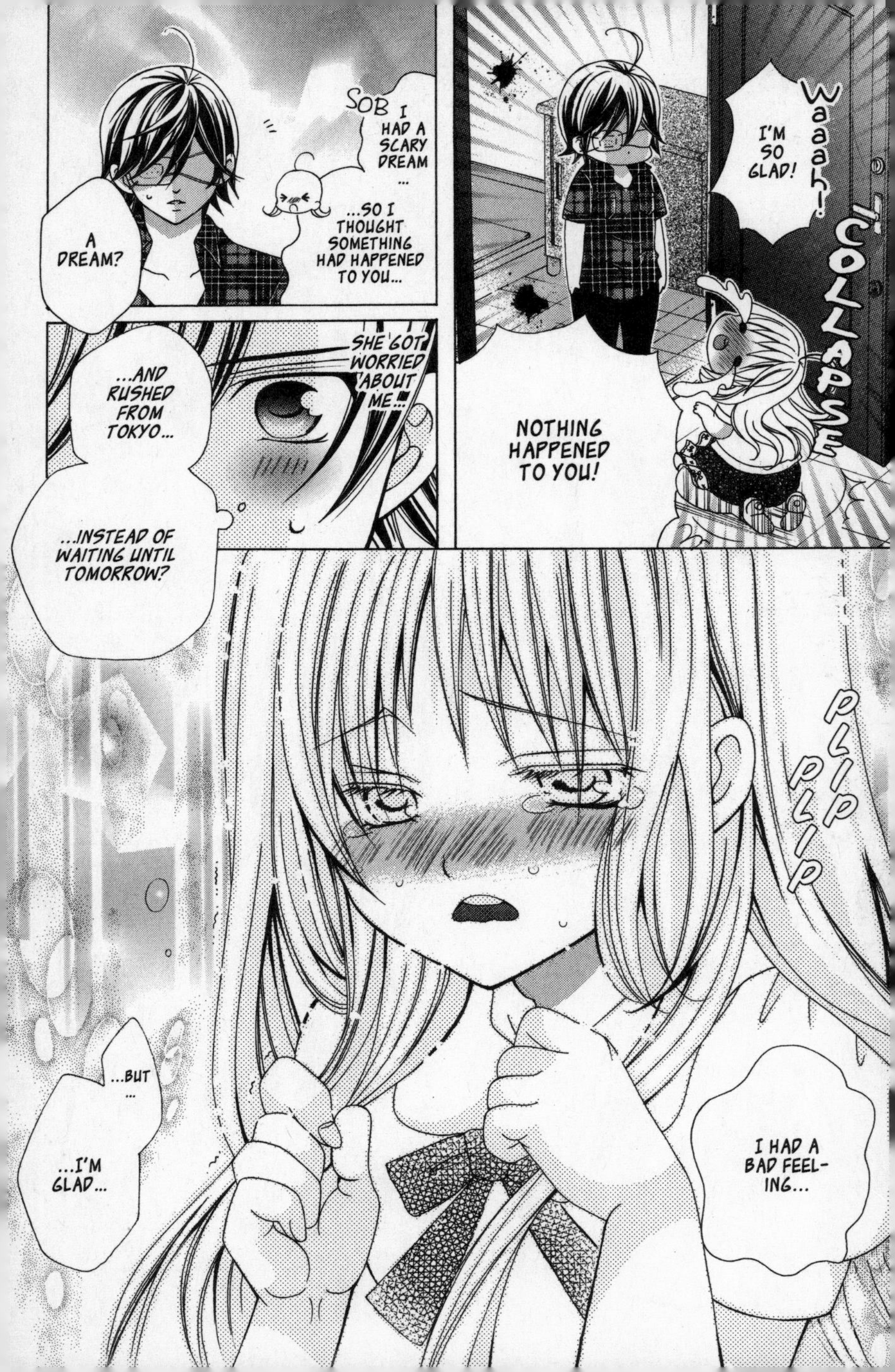
Waaah!
I'M SO GLAD!
COLLAPSE
NOTHING HAPPENED TO YOU!
SOB
I HAD A SCARY DREAM ...
...SO I THOUGHT SOMETHING HAD HAPPENED TO YOU...
A DREAM?
SHE GOT WORRIED ABOUT ME...
...AND RUSHED FROM TOKYO...
...INSTEAD OF WAITING UNTIL TOMORROW?
PLIP PLIP PLIP
I HAD A BAD FEEL-ING...
...BUT ...
...I'M GLAD...

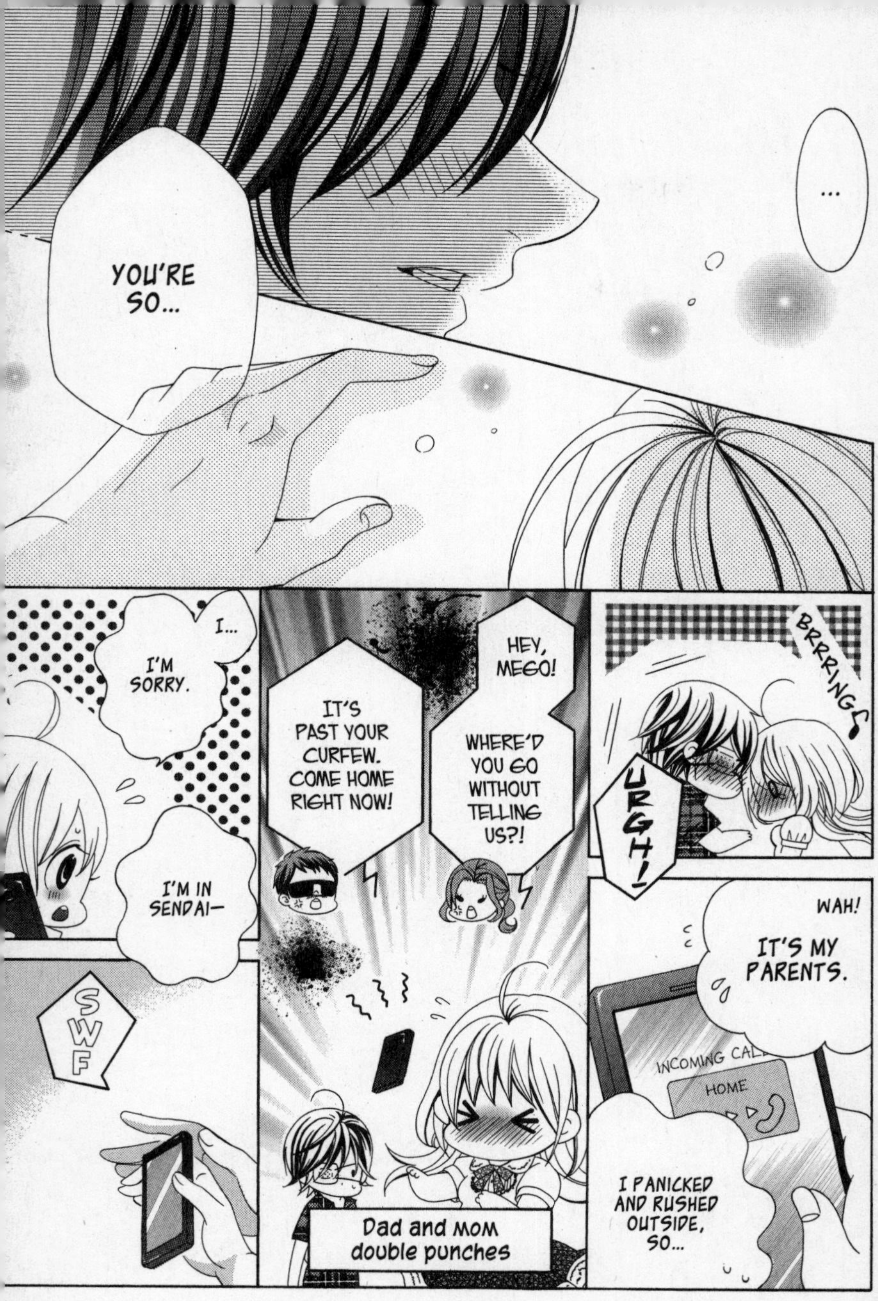
...
YOU'RE SO...
BRRRING
URGH!
WAH!
IT'S MY PARENTS.
INCOMING CAL
HOME
I PANICKED AND RUSHED OUTSIDE, SO...
HEY, MEGO!
WHERE'D YOU GO WITHOUT TELLING US?!
IT'S PAST YOUR CURFEW. COME HOME RIGHT NOW!
Dad and Mom double punches
I...
I'M SORRY.
I'M IN SENDAI—
SWF

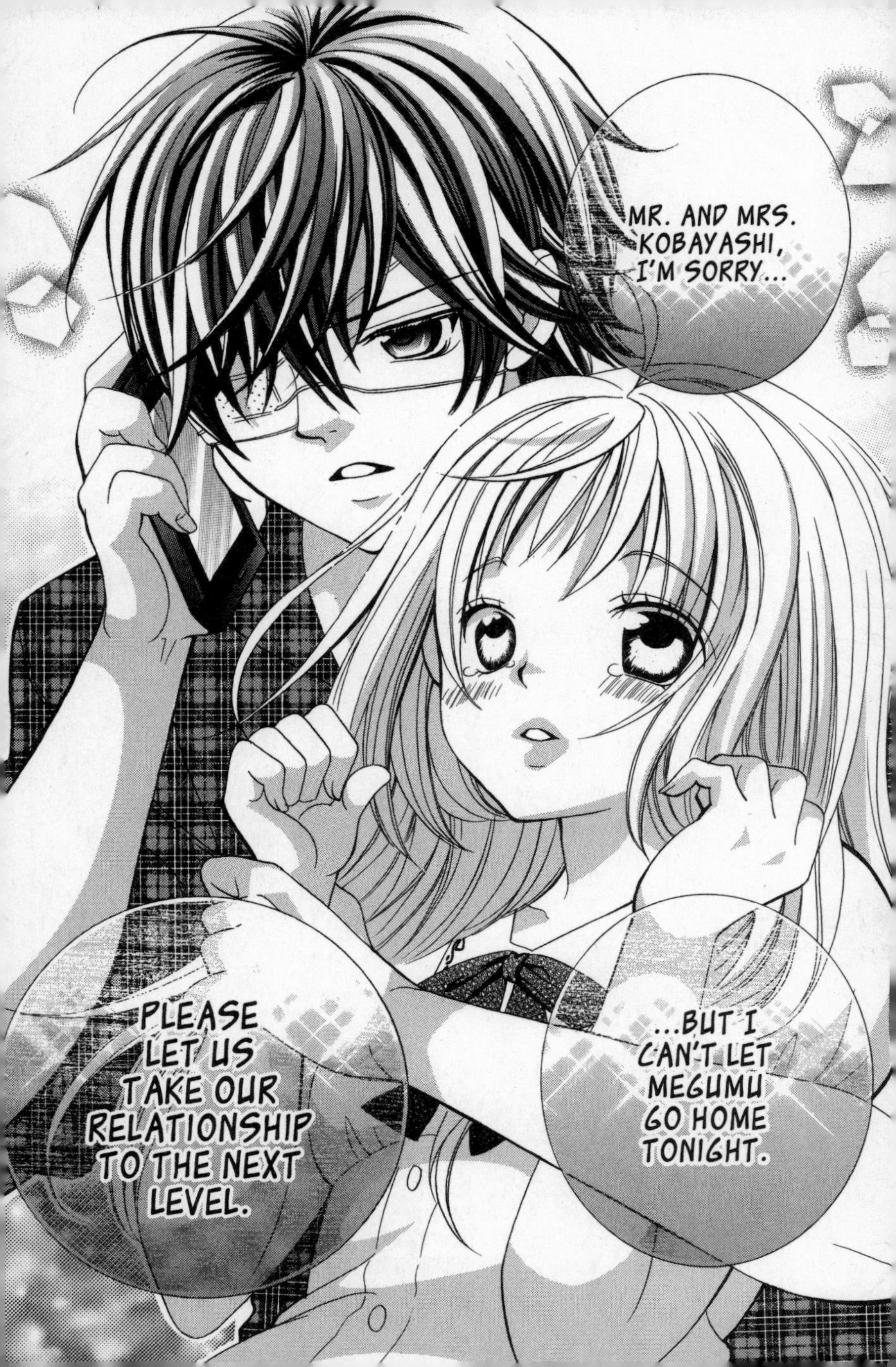
MR. AND MRS. KOBAYASHI, I'M SORRY...
...BUT I CAN'T LET MEGUMU GO HOME TONIGHT.
PLEASE LET US TAKE OUR RELATIONSHIP TO THE NEXT LEVEL.

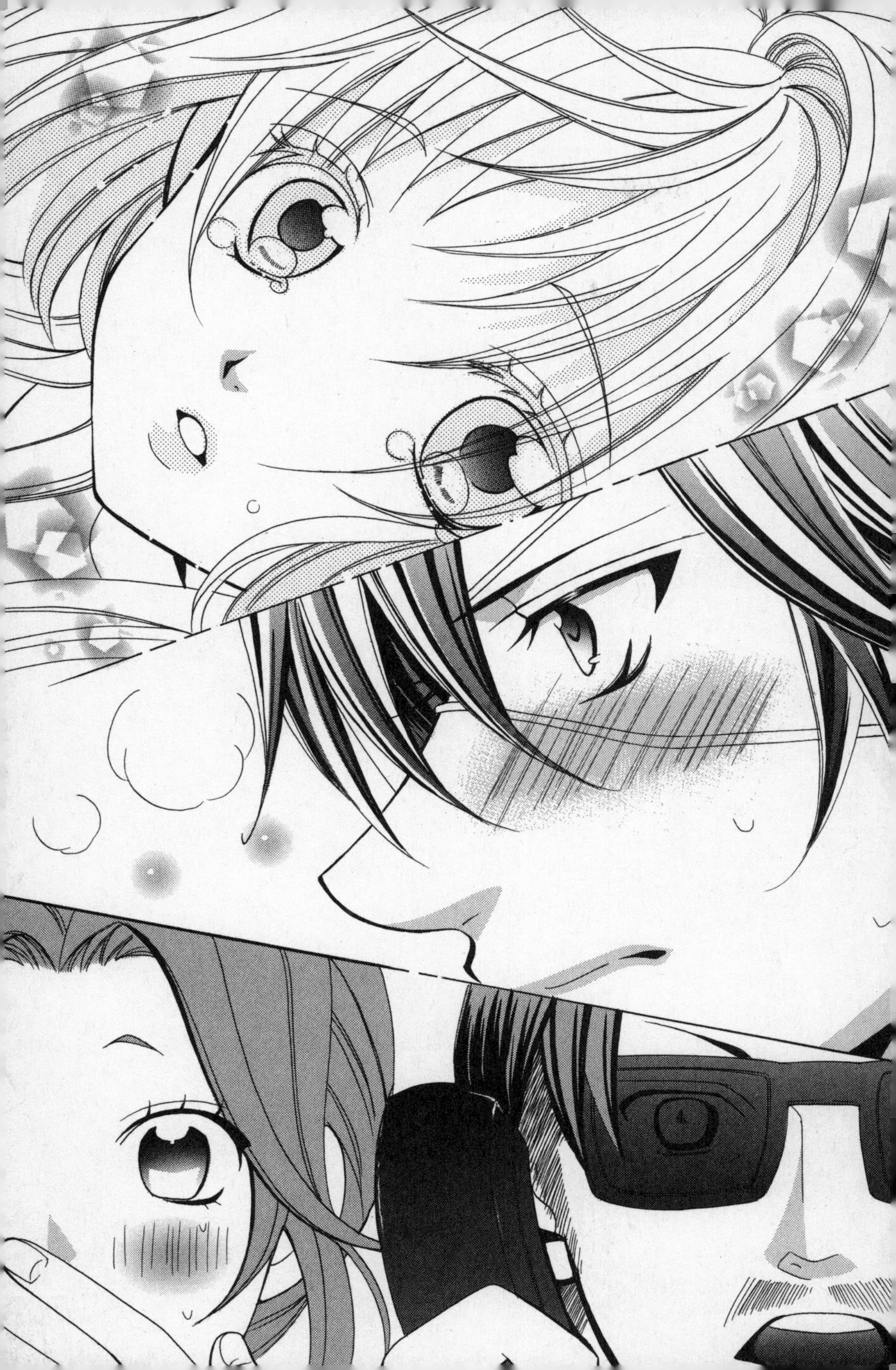

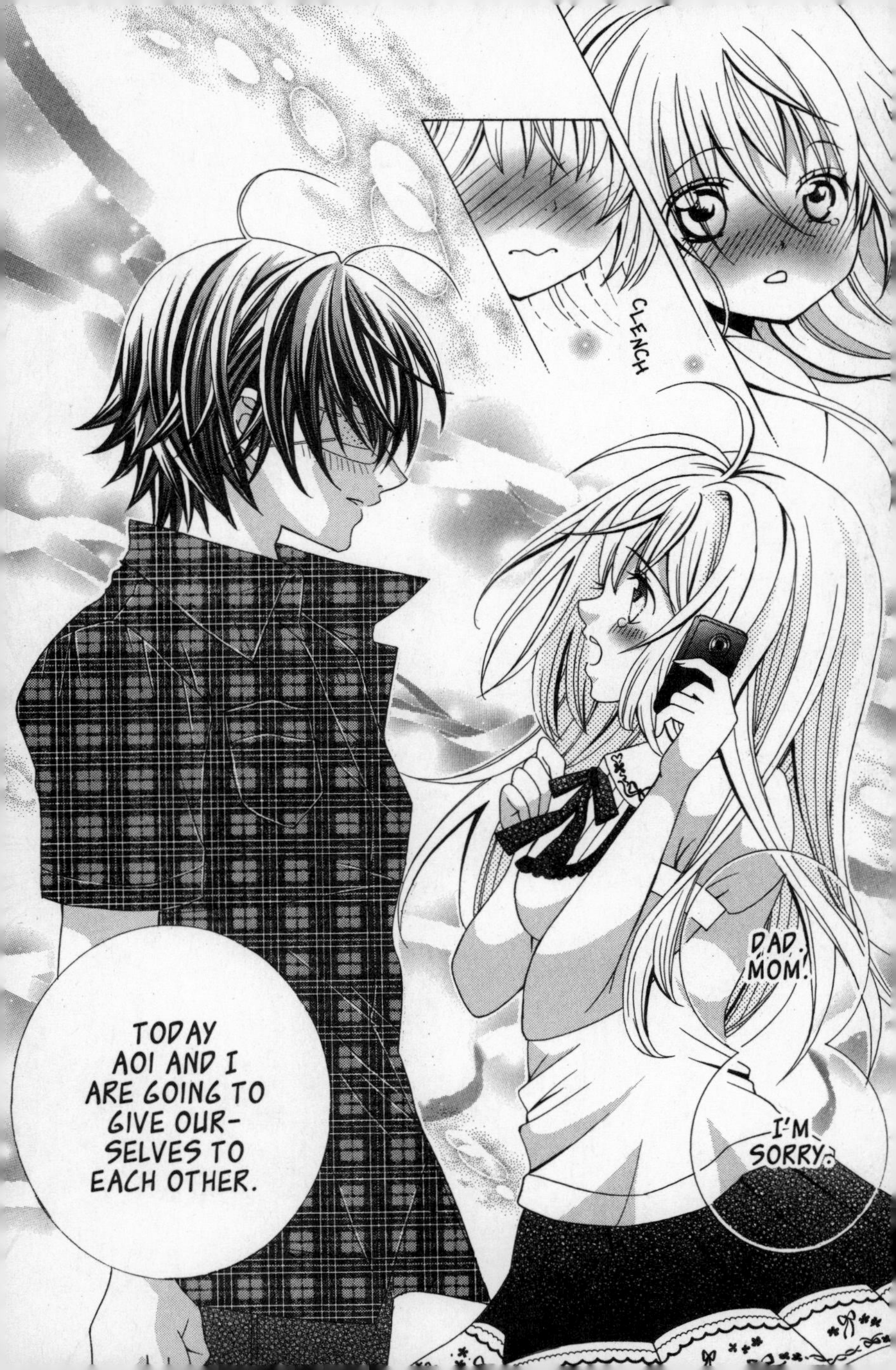
CLENCH
DAD. MOM.
I'M SORRY.
TODAY AOI AND I ARE GOING TO GIVE OUR-SELVES TO EACH OTHER.

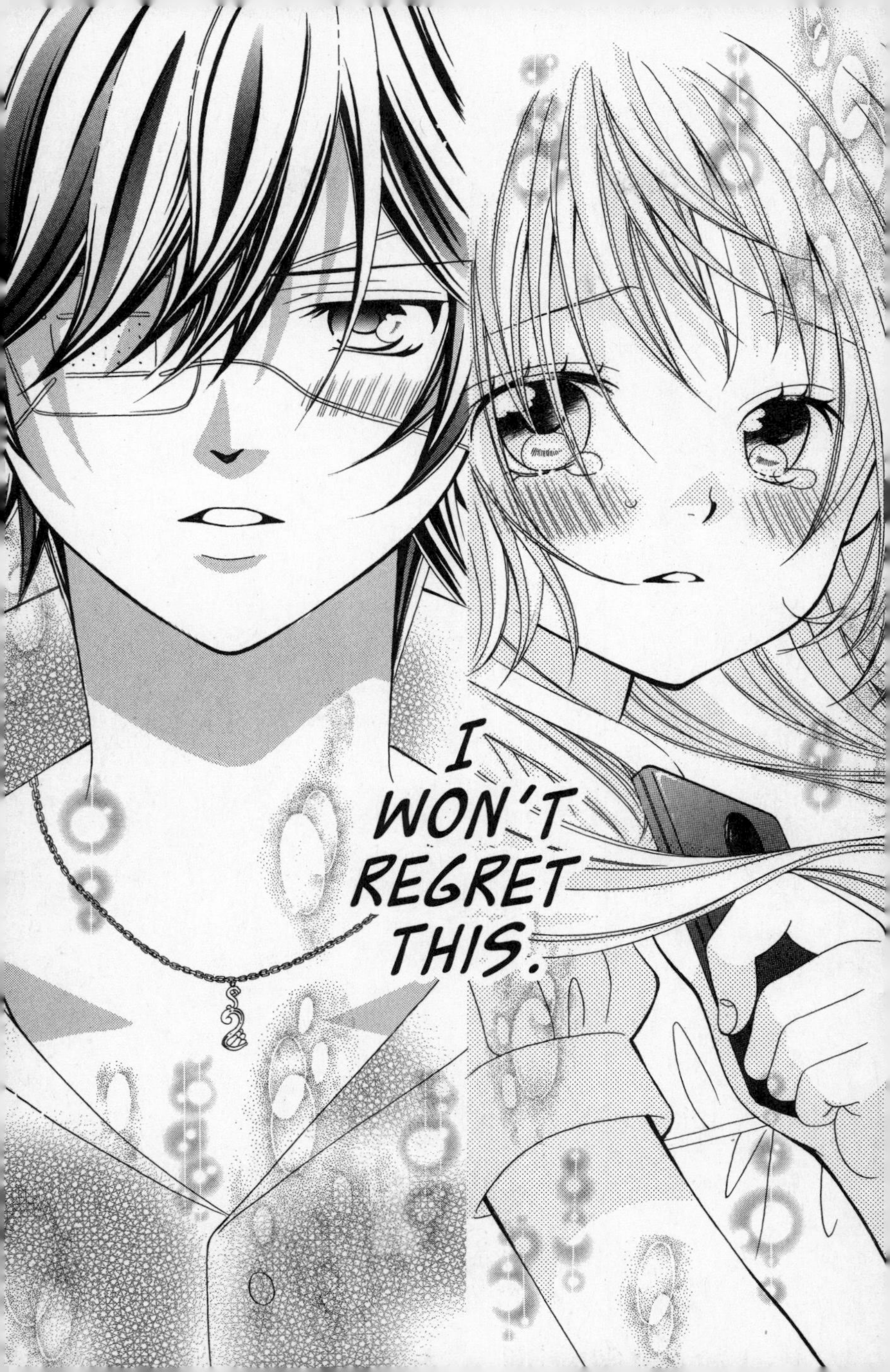
I WON'T REGRET THIS.

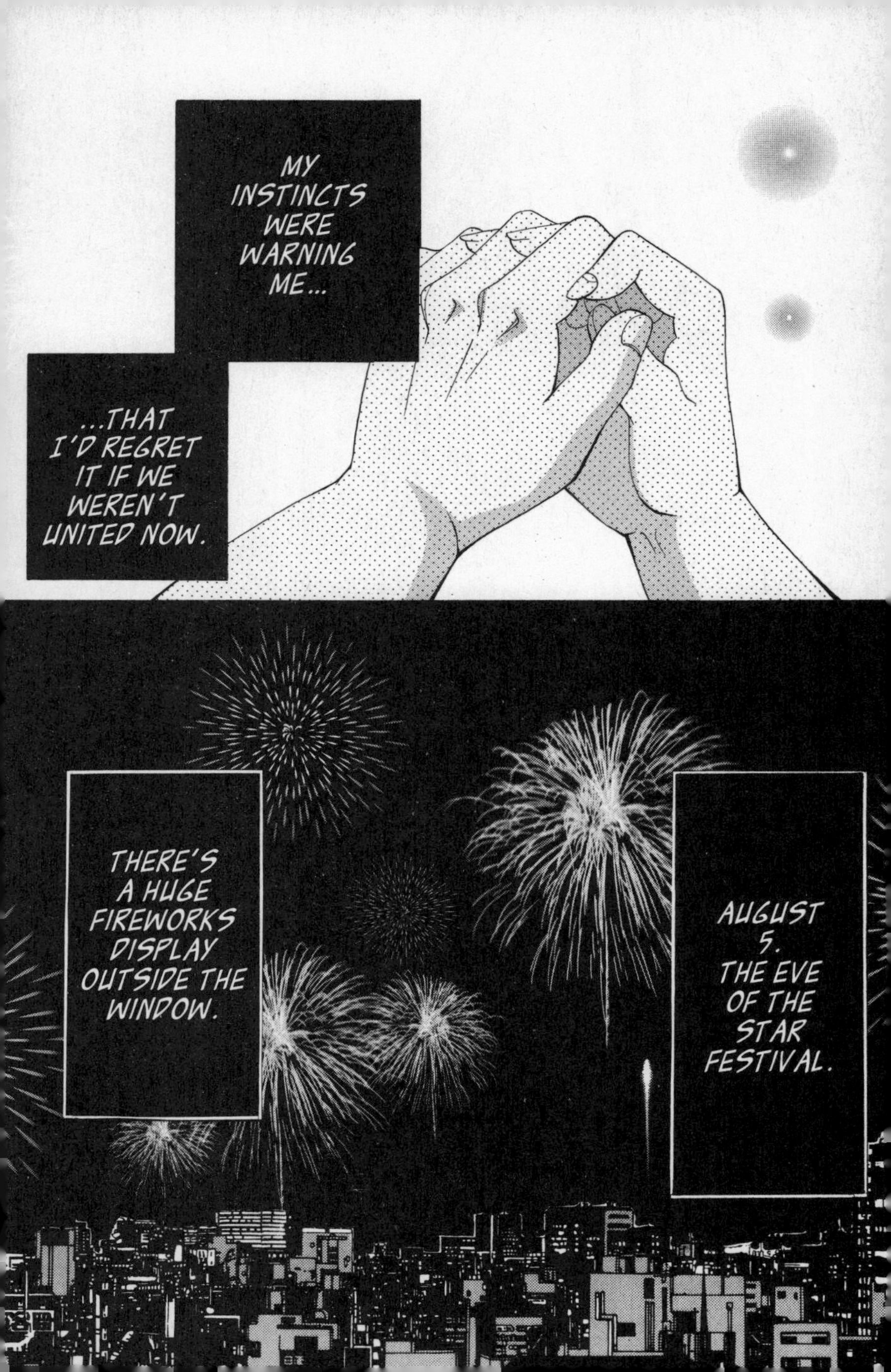
MY INSTINCTS WERE WARNING ME...
...THAT I'D REGRET IT IF WE WEREN'T UNITED NOW.
AUGUST 5. THE EVE OF THE STAR FESTIVAL.
THERE'S A HUGE FIREWORKS DISPLAY OUTSIDE THE WINDOW.

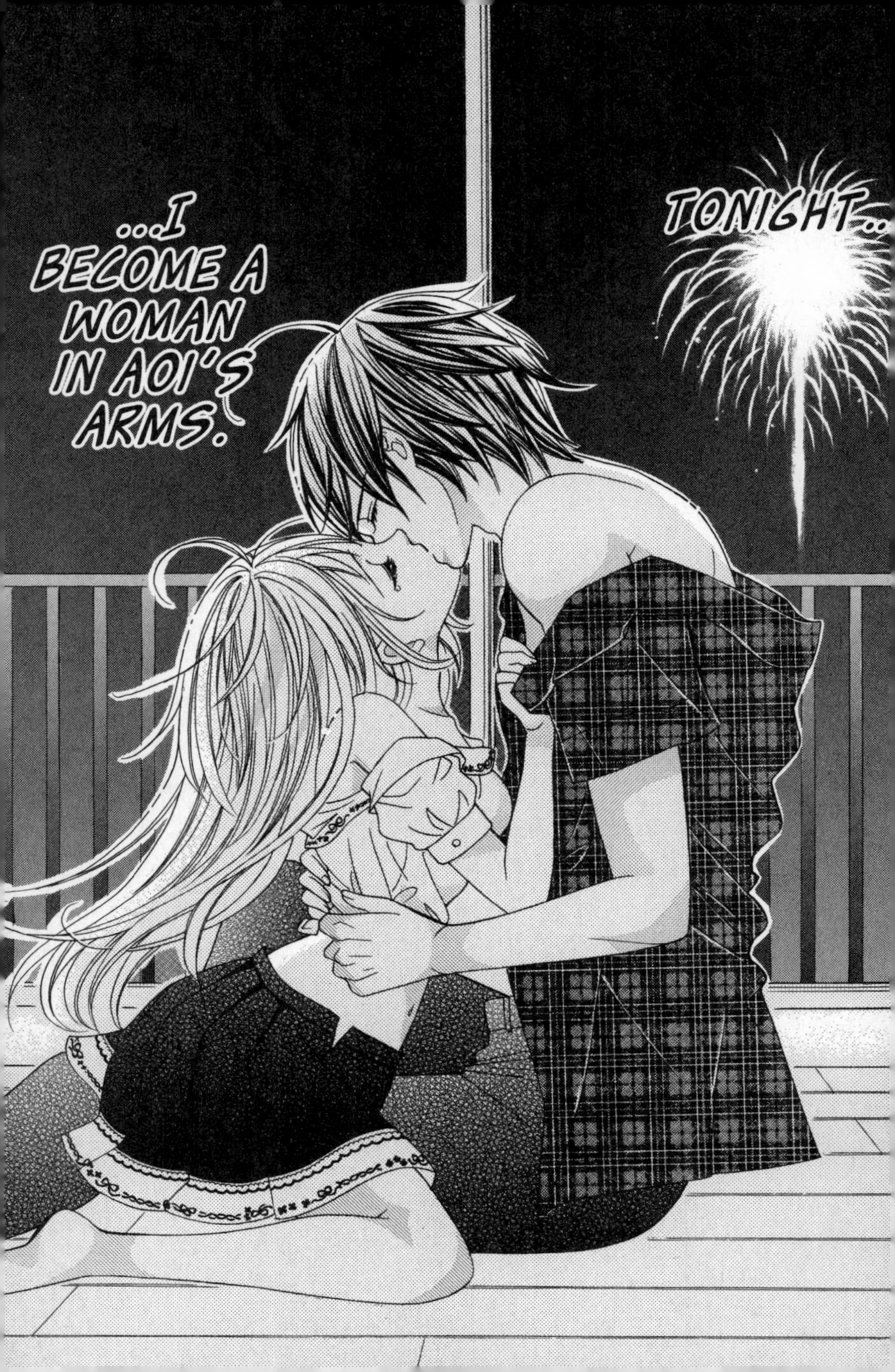
TONIGHT...
...I BECOME A WOMAN IN AOI'S ARMS.

SO CUTE! NINTENDO 3DS GAME

Double scoop!

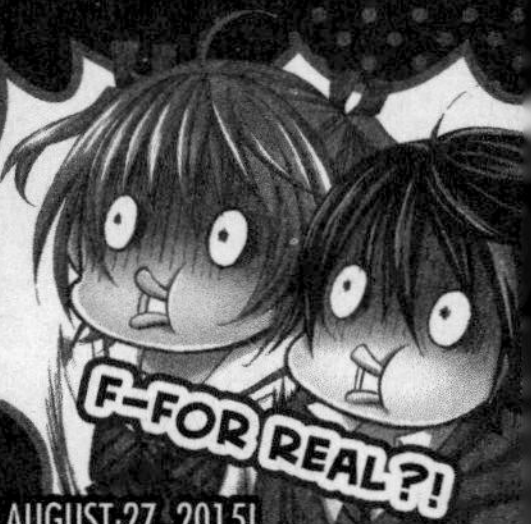
F-FOR REAL?!

HERE'S SOME SPECIAL INFORMATION ABOUT THE SO CUTE! GAME THAT'LL BE OUT AUGUST 27, 2015!

SCOOP 1 WE'VE SECRETLY OBTAINED TWO GAME SCREENSHOTS!

THE GAME FEATURES AN ORIGINAL STORY, SO THERE'RE LOTS OF SCENES YOU CAN ONLY SEE IN THE GAME! TAKE A LOOK AT THESE LOVELY SHOTS.♥

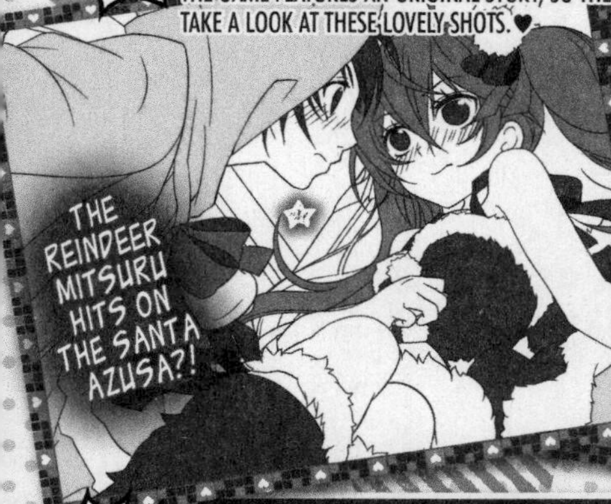
THE REINDEER MITSURU HITS ON THE SANTA AZUSA?!

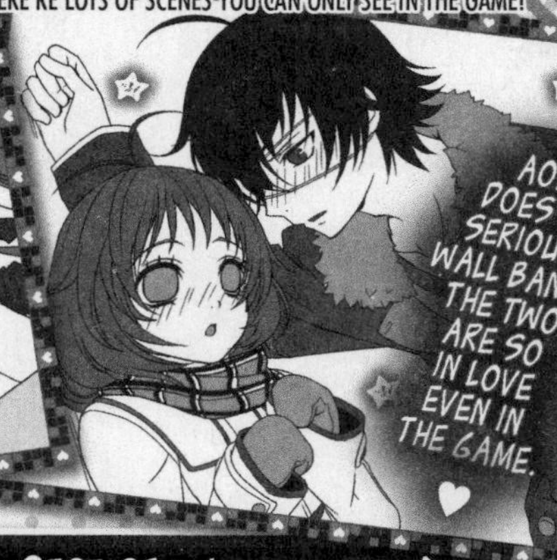
AOI DOES A SERIOUS WALL BANG! THE TWO ARE SO IN LOVE EVEN IN THE GAME.

SCOOP 2 A SUPER-GORGEOUS VOICE CAST!

THE GORGEOUS CAST IS FULL OF SUPER VOICE ACTORS! AND A SUPER-POPULAR VOICE ACTOR PLAYS ELLIO, THE GAME'S ORIGINAL CHARACTER.♥

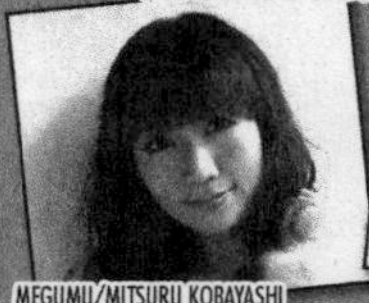

MEGUMU/MITSURU KOBAYASHI
MS. AYAHI TAKAGAKI

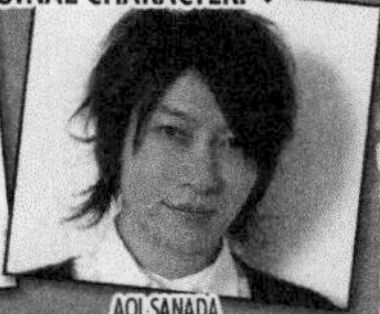

AOI SANADA
MR. DAISUKE ONO

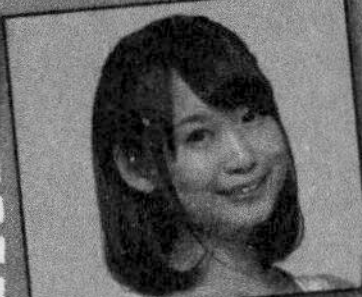

AZUSA TOKUGAWA
MS. YU SERIZAWA

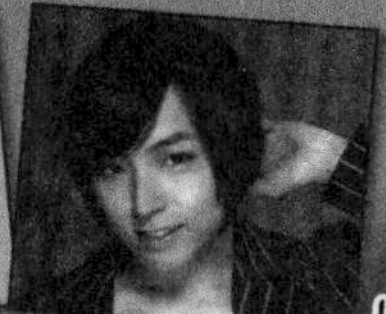

CHIHARU UESUGI
MR. SHOTA AOI

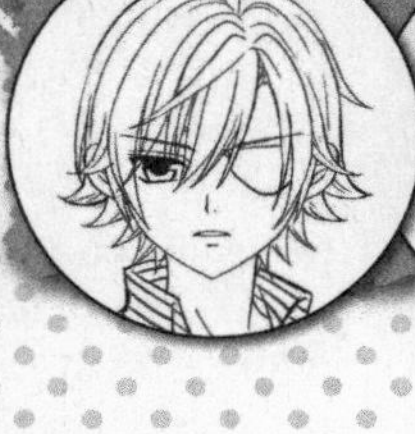

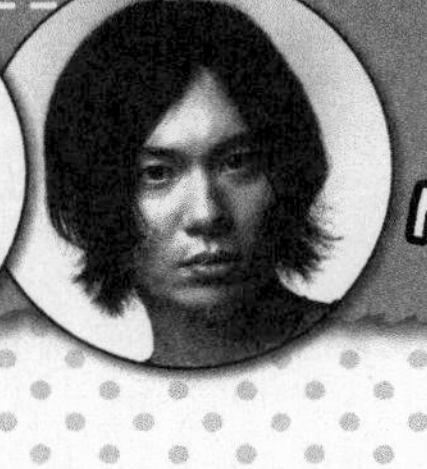

Ellio (ONLY IN THIS GAME)
MR. TATSUO SUZUKI

THE HEART-FLUTTERING VOICES ARE SO CUTE IT HURTS!! (ɔ_ɔ)

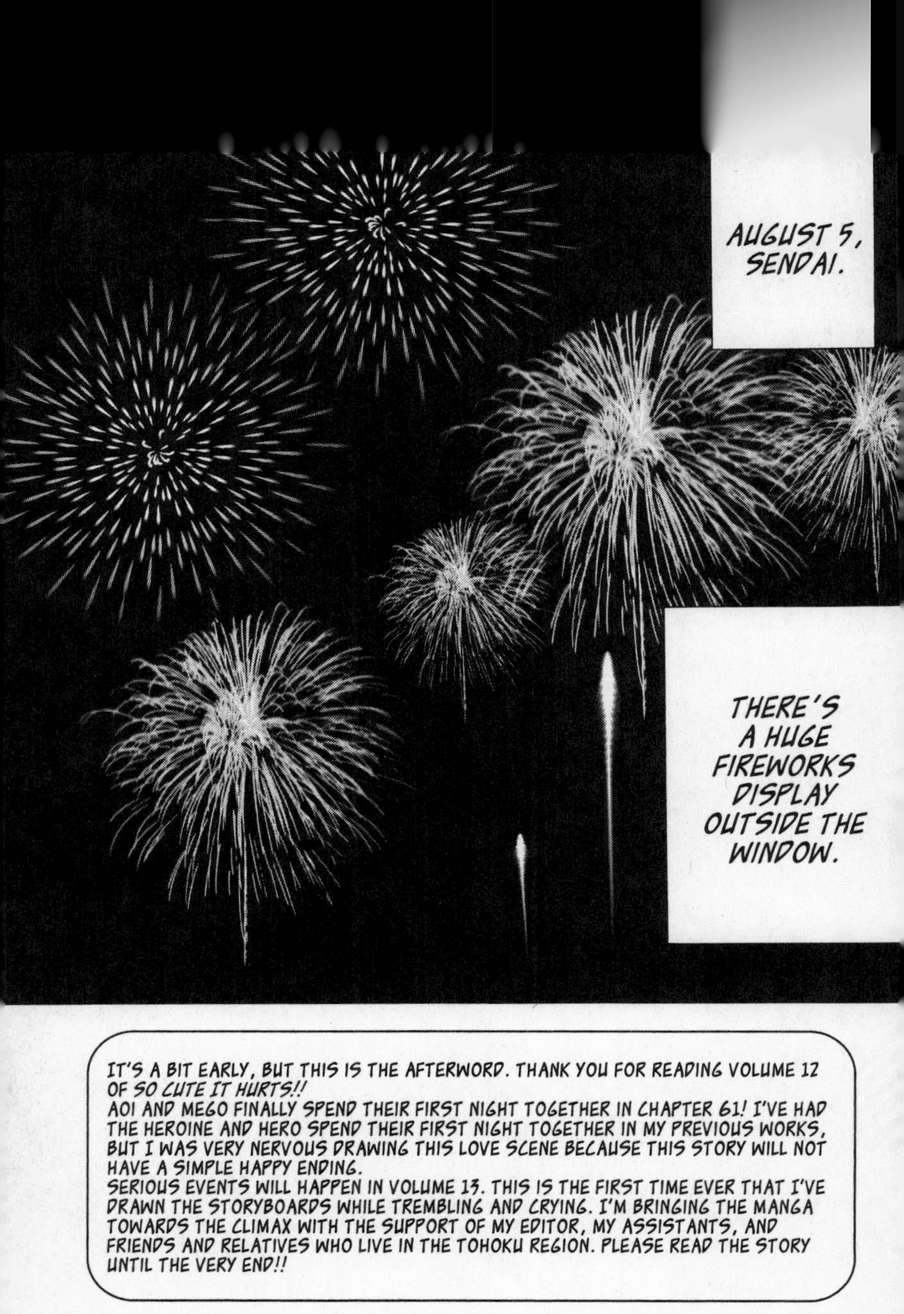
AUGUST 5, SENDAI.
THERE'S A HUGE FIREWORKS DISPLAY OUTSIDE THE WINDOW.

IT'S A BIT EARLY, BUT THIS IS THE AFTERWORD. THANK YOU FOR READING VOLUME 12 OF *SO CUTE IT HURTS!!*
AOI AND MEGO FINALLY SPEND THEIR FIRST NIGHT TOGETHER IN CHAPTER 61! I'VE HAD THE HEROINE AND HERO SPEND THEIR FIRST NIGHT TOGETHER IN MY PREVIOUS WORKS, BUT I WAS VERY NERVOUS DRAWING THIS LOVE SCENE BECAUSE THIS STORY WILL NOT HAVE A SIMPLE HAPPY ENDING.
SERIOUS EVENTS WILL HAPPEN IN VOLUME 13. THIS IS THE FIRST TIME EVER THAT I'VE DRAWN THE STORYBOARDS WHILE TREMBLING AND CRYING. I'M BRINGING THE MANGA TOWARDS THE CLIMAX WITH THE SUPPORT OF MY EDITOR, MY ASSISTANTS, AND FRIENDS AND RELATIVES WHO LIVE IN THE TOHOKU REGION. PLEASE READ THE STORY UNTIL THE VERY END!!

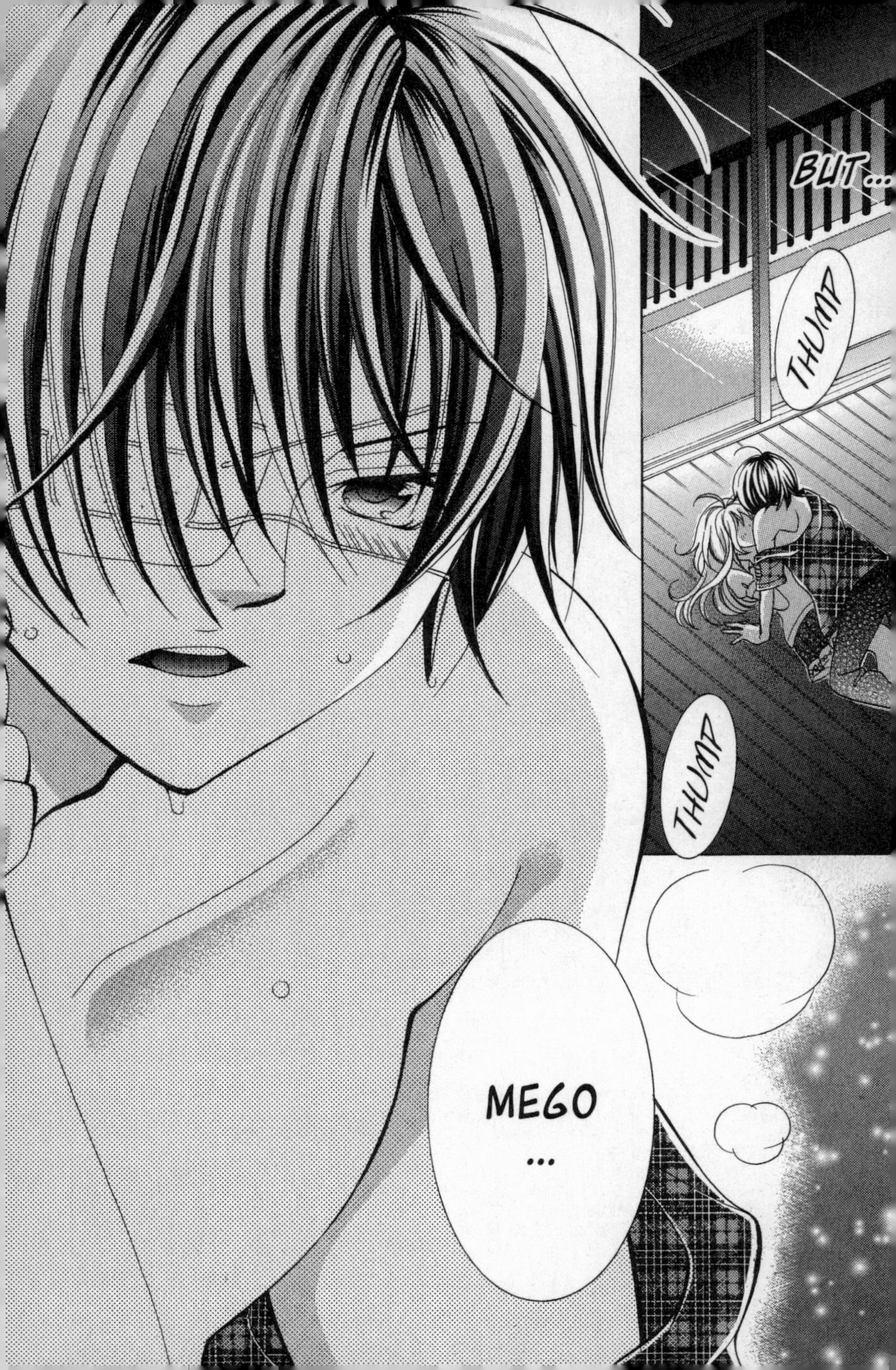
BUT...
THUMP
THUMP
MEGO ...

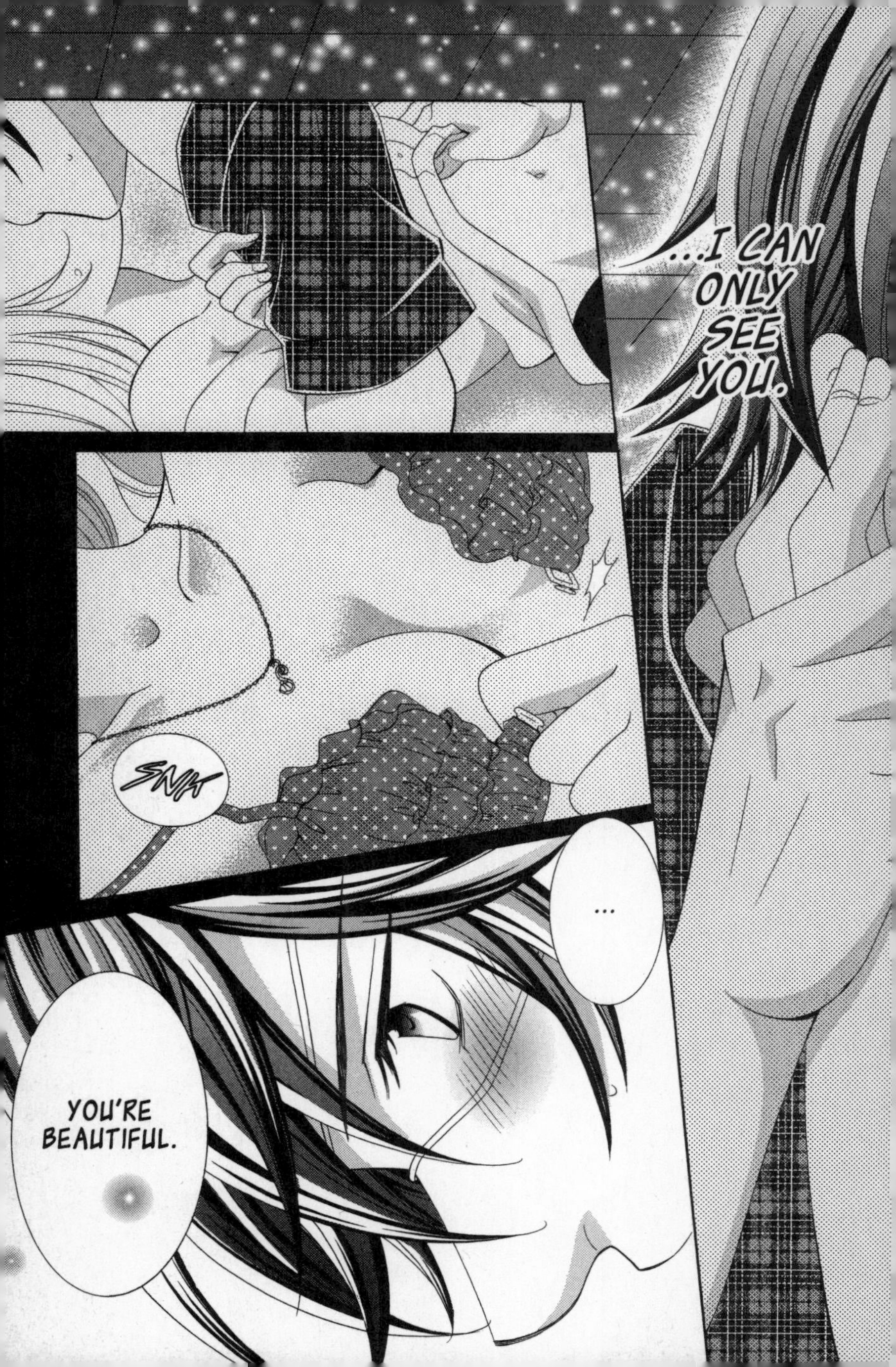
...I CAN ONLY SEE YOU.
SNK
...
YOU'RE BEAUTIFUL.

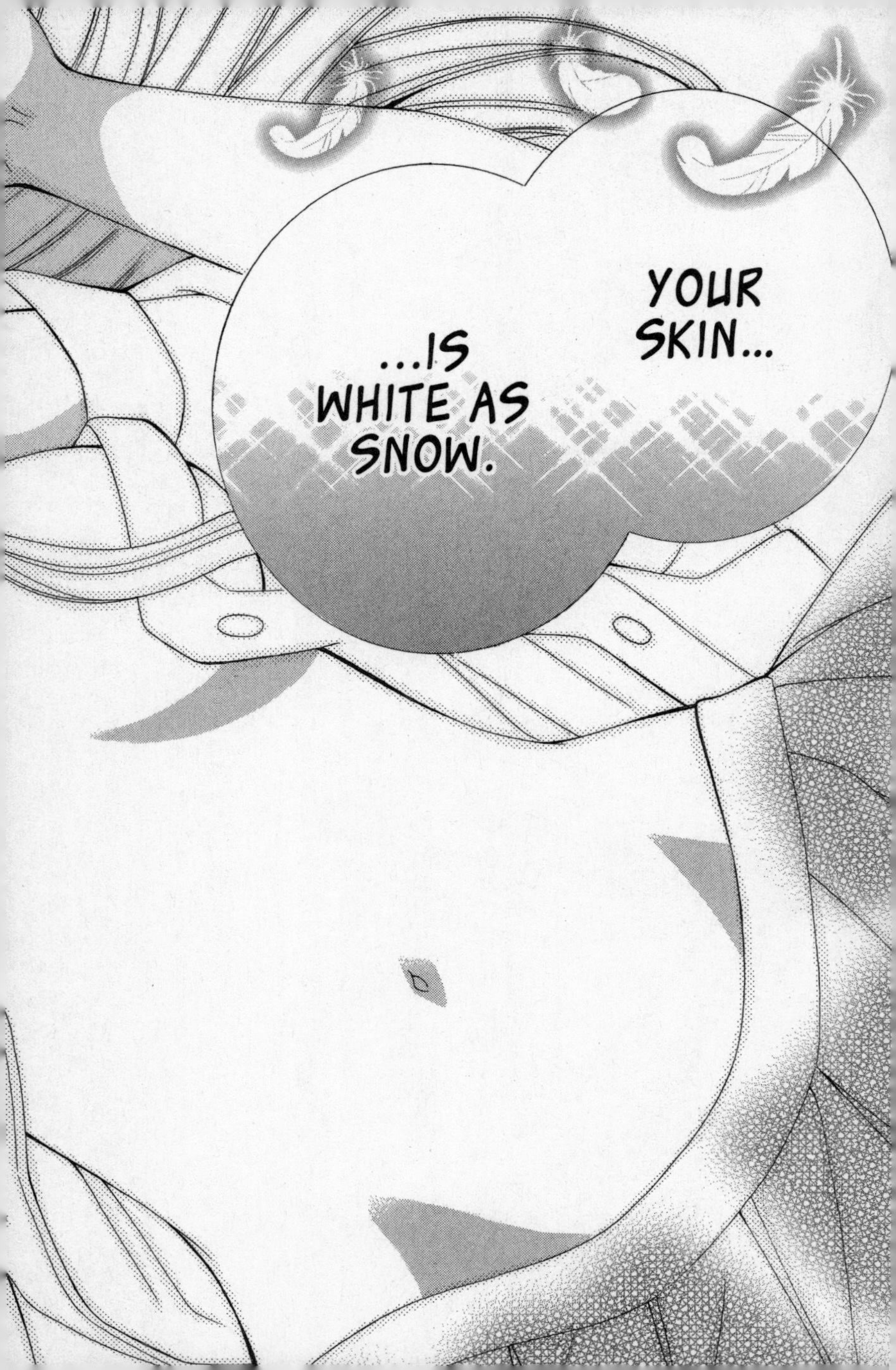
YOUR SKIN...
...IS WHITE AS SNOW.

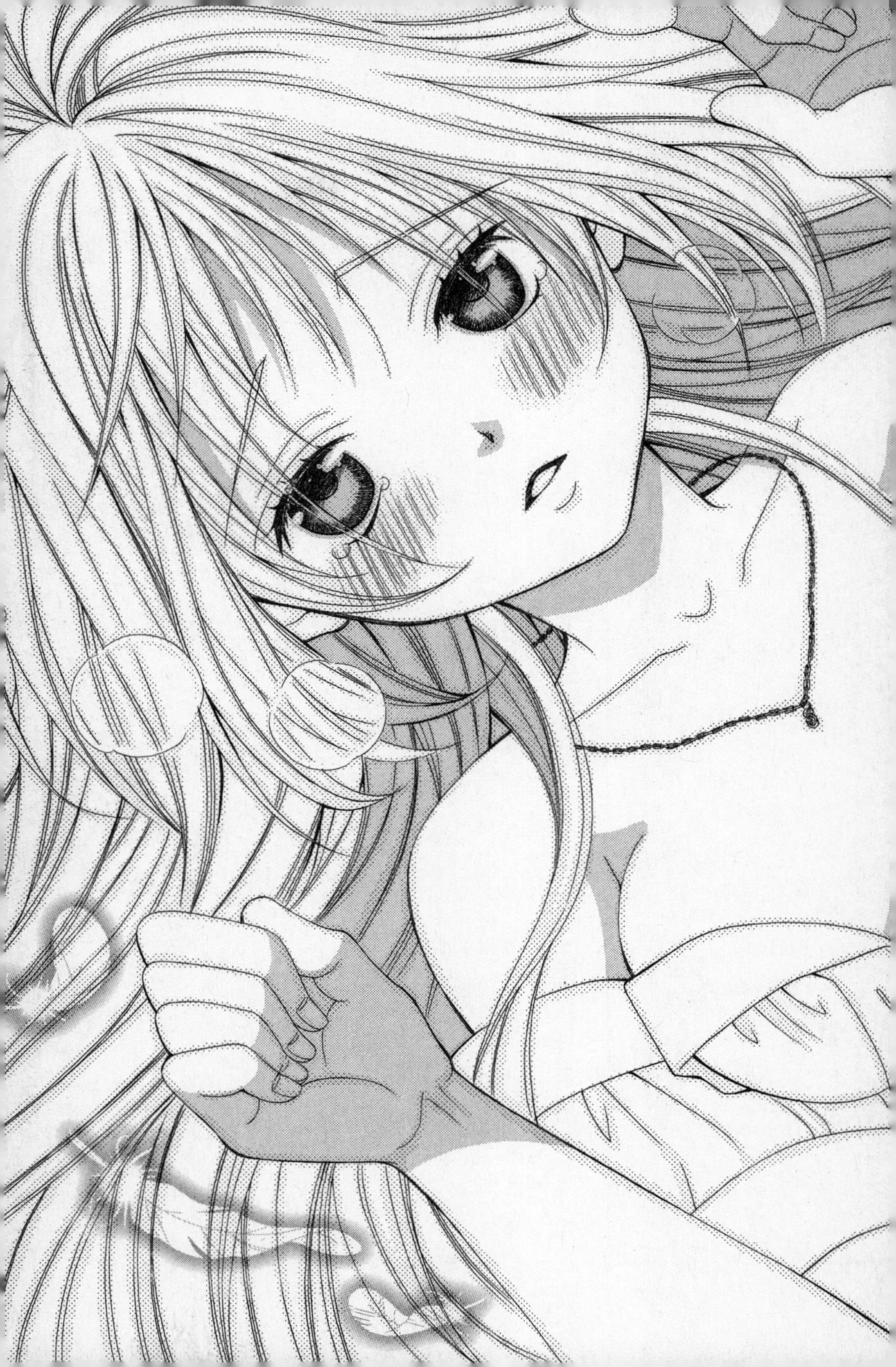

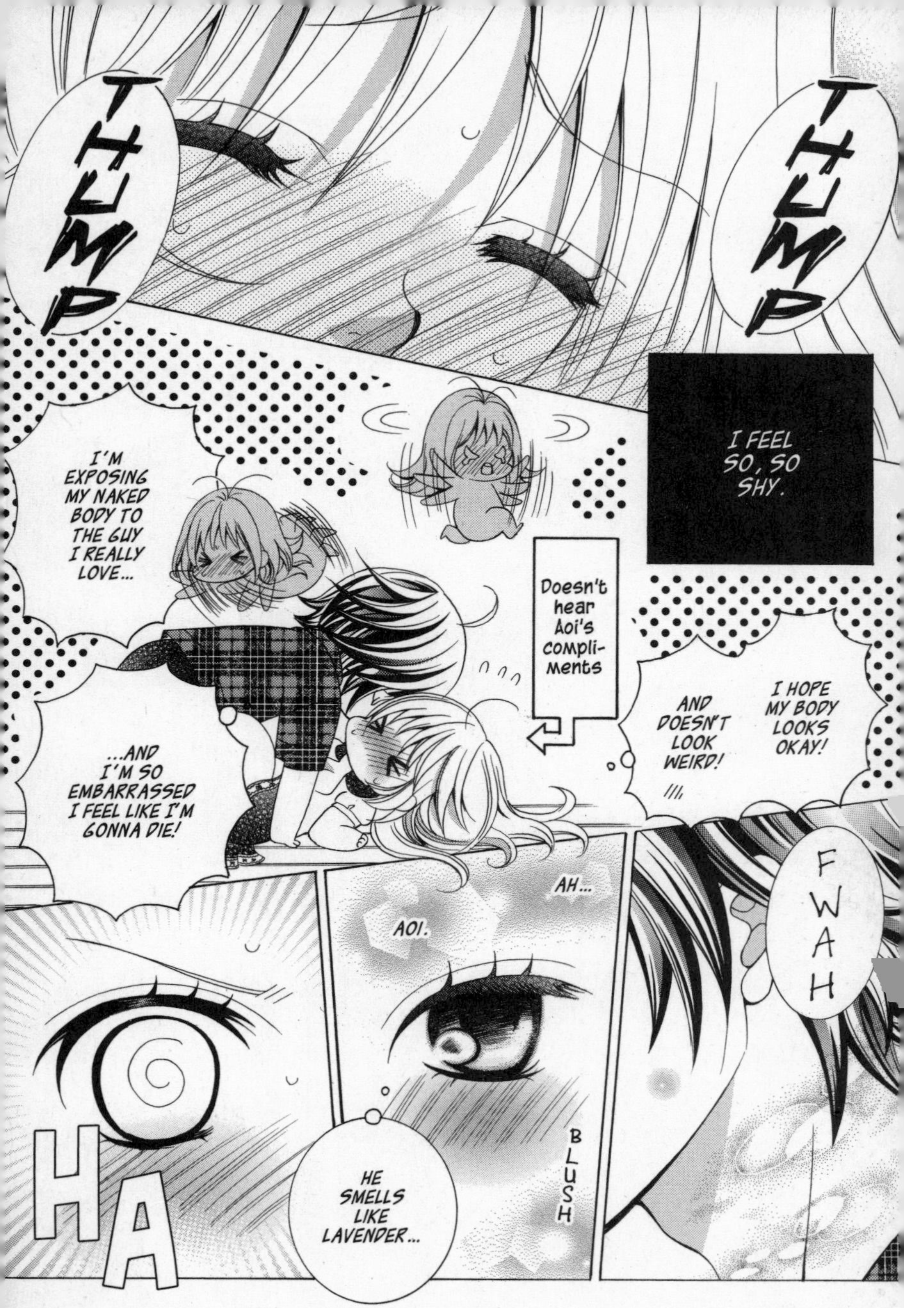
THUMP
THUMP
I FEEL SO, SO SHY.
I HOPE MY BODY LOOKS OKAY!
AND DOESN'T LOOK WEIRD!
Doesn't hear Aoi's compliments
I'M EXPOSING MY NAKED BODY TO THE GUY I REALLY LOVE...
...AND I'M SO EMBARRASSED I FEEL LIKE I'M GONNA DIE!
FWAH
AH...
AOI.
BLUSH
HE SMELLS LIKE LAVENDER...
HA
HA

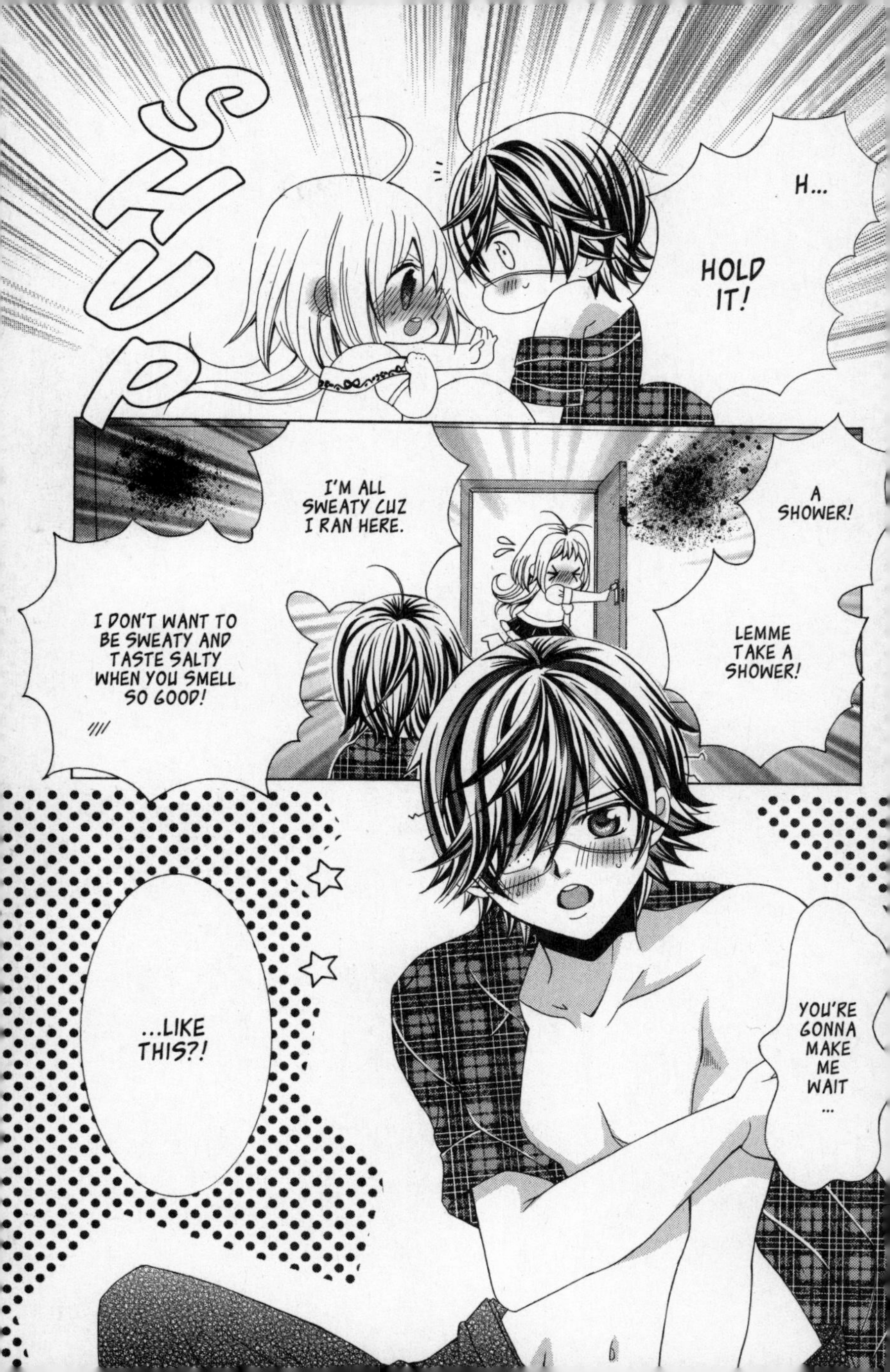
H...
HOLD IT!
SHUP
A SHOWER!
LEMME TAKE A SHOWER!
I'M ALL SWEATY CUZ I RAN HERE.
I DON'T WANT TO BE SWEATY AND TASTE SALTY WHEN YOU SMELL SO GOOD!
YOU'RE GONNA MAKE ME WAIT ...
...LIKE THIS?!

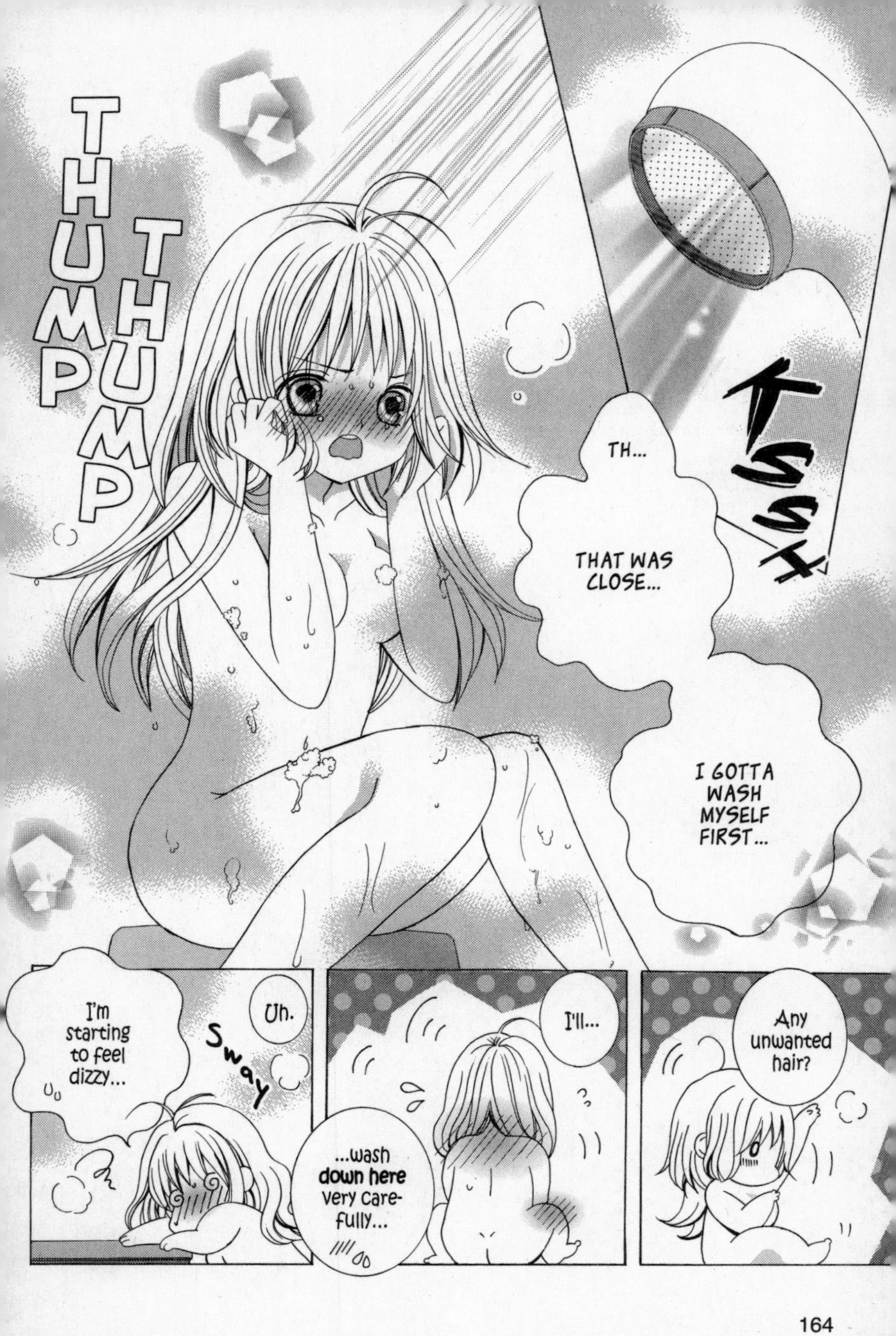
KSSH
TH...
THAT WAS CLOSE...
THUMP THUMP
THUMP THUMP
I GOTTA WASH MYSELF FIRST...
Any unwanted hair?
I'll...
...wash down here very care-fully...
Uh.
Sway
I'm starting to feel dizzy...

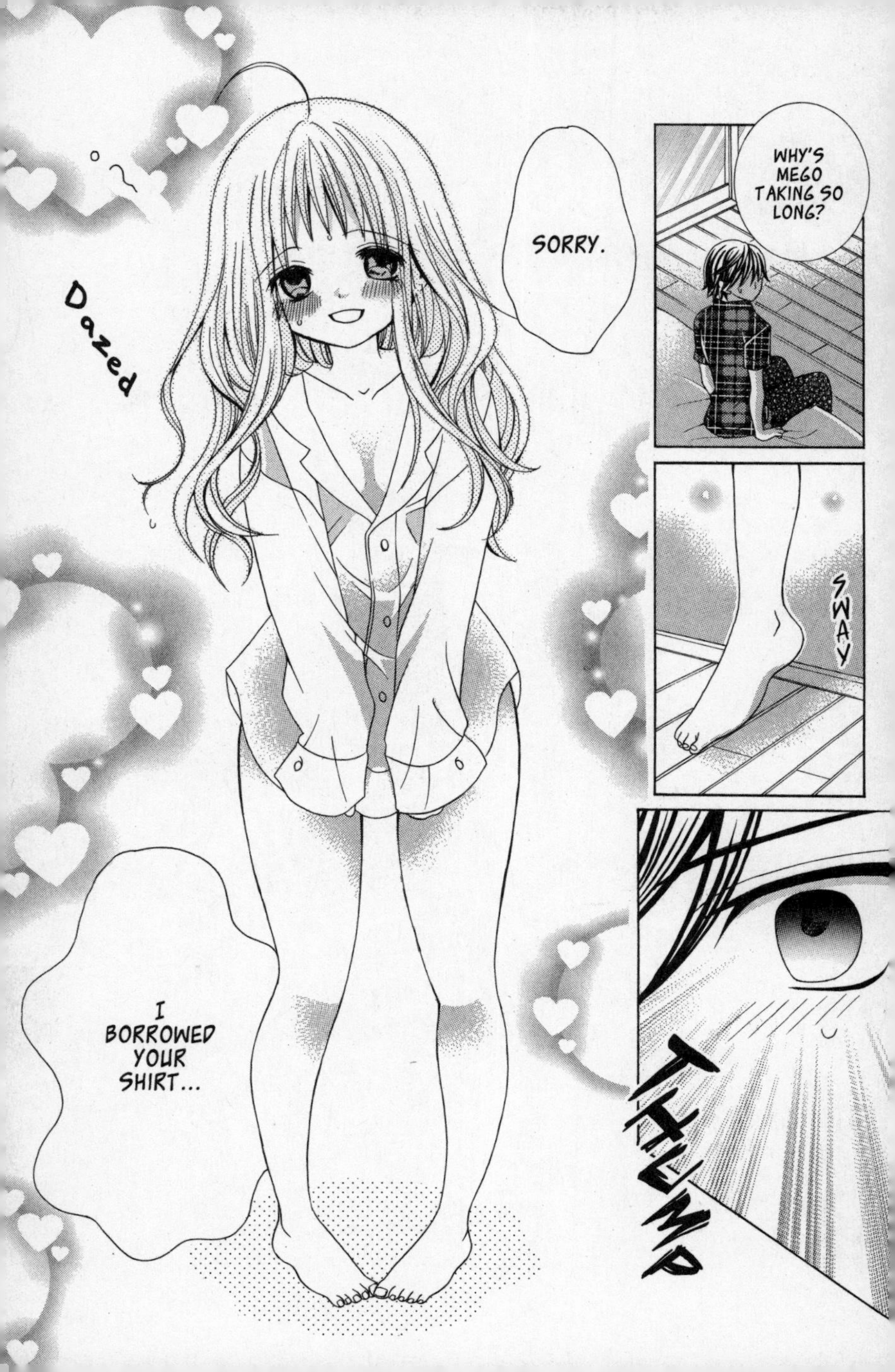
WHY'S MEGO TAKING SO LONG?
SWAY
THUMP
SORRY.
Dazed
I BORROWED YOUR SHIRT...

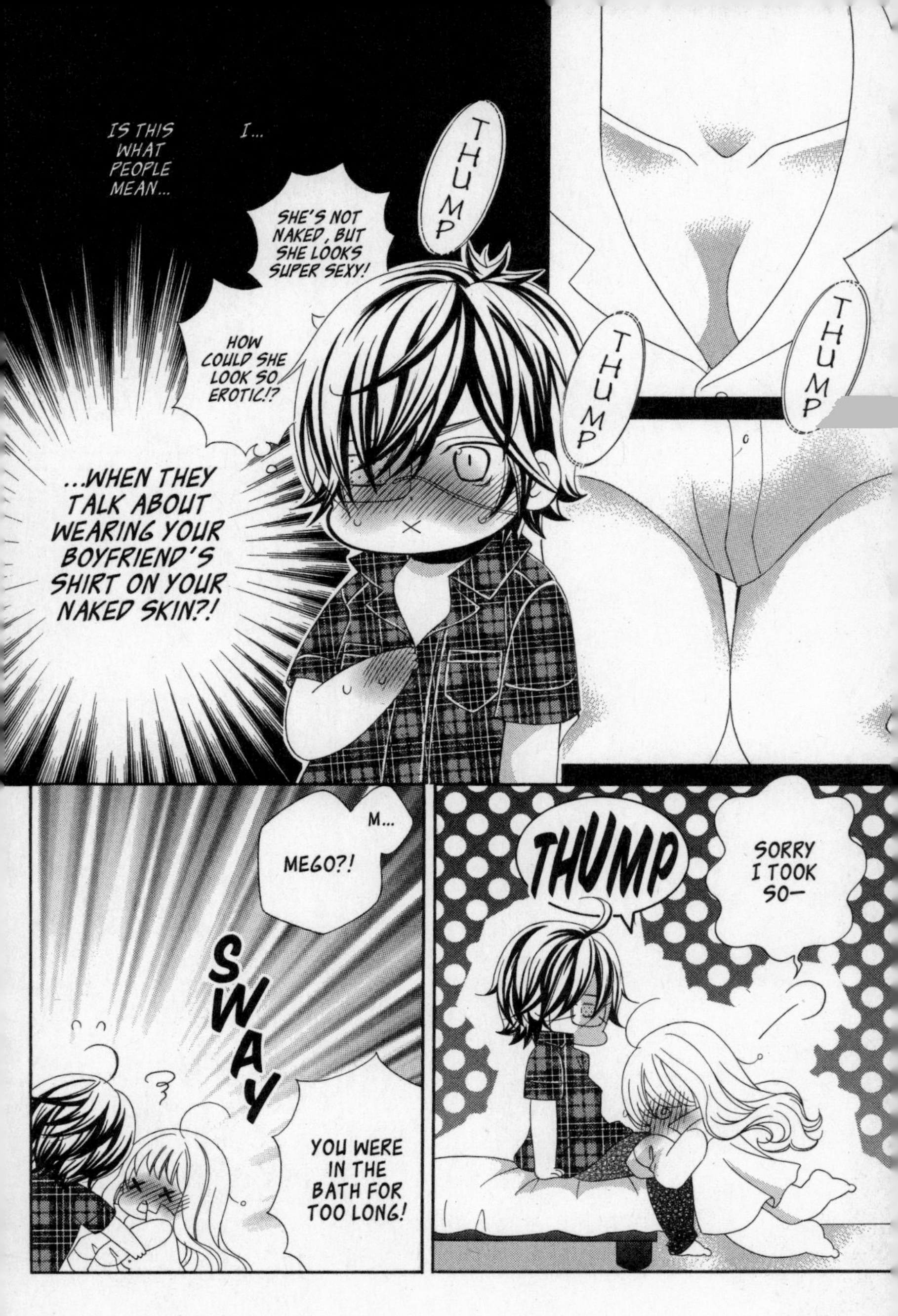
THUMP
THUMP
THUMP
I...
IS THIS WHAT PEOPLE MEAN...
SHE'S NOT NAKED, BUT SHE LOOKS SUPER SEXY!
HOW COULD SHE LOOK SO EROTIC!?
...WHEN THEY TALK ABOUT WEARING YOUR BOYFRIEND'S SHIRT ON YOUR NAKED SKIN?!
SORRY I TOOK SO—
THUMP
M... MEGO?!
SWAY
YOU WERE IN THE BATH FOR TOO LONG!

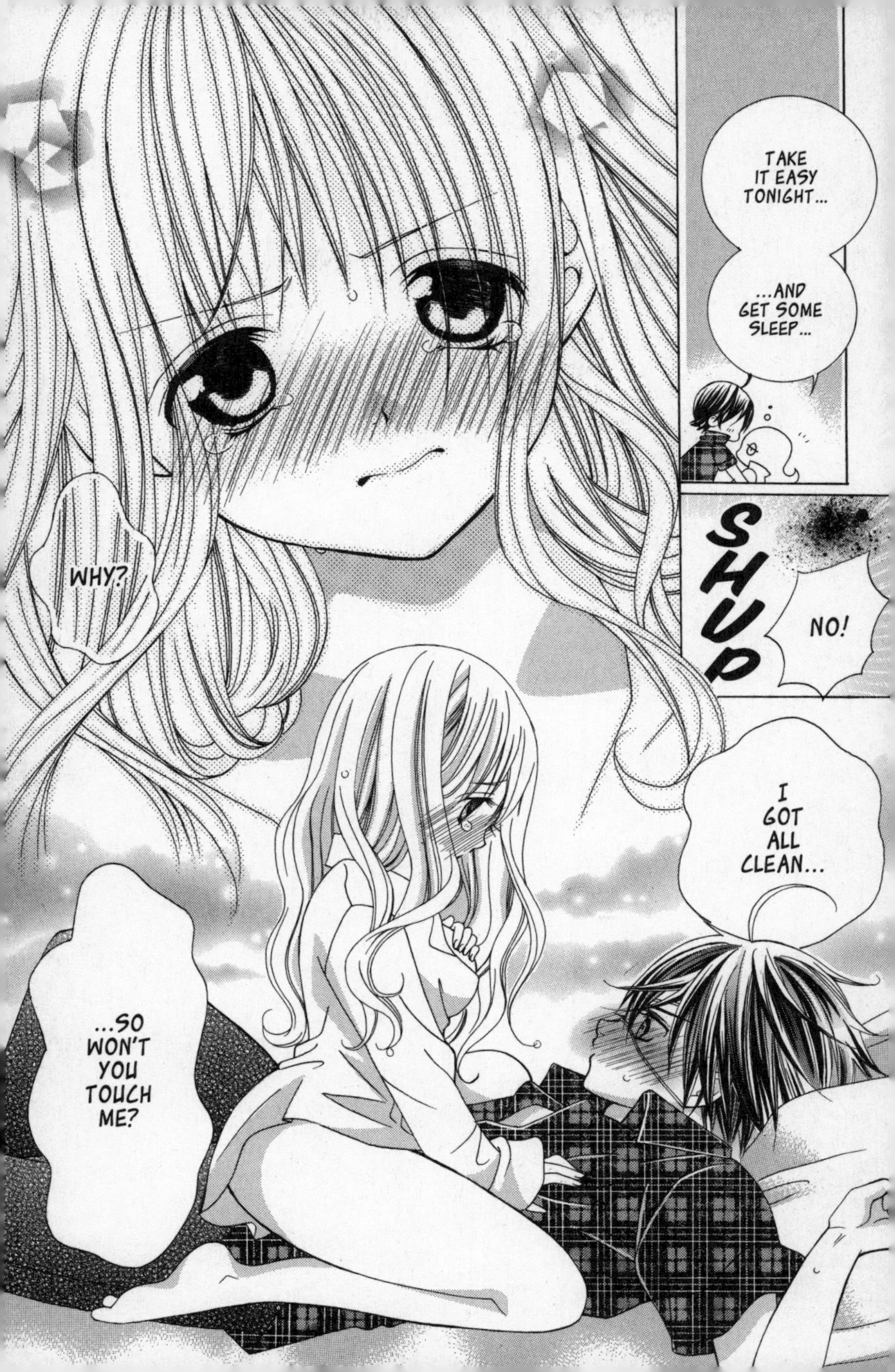
TAKE IT EASY TONIGHT...
...AND GET SOME SLEEP...
SHUP
NO!
WHY?
I GOT ALL CLEAN...
...SO WON'T YOU TOUCH ME?

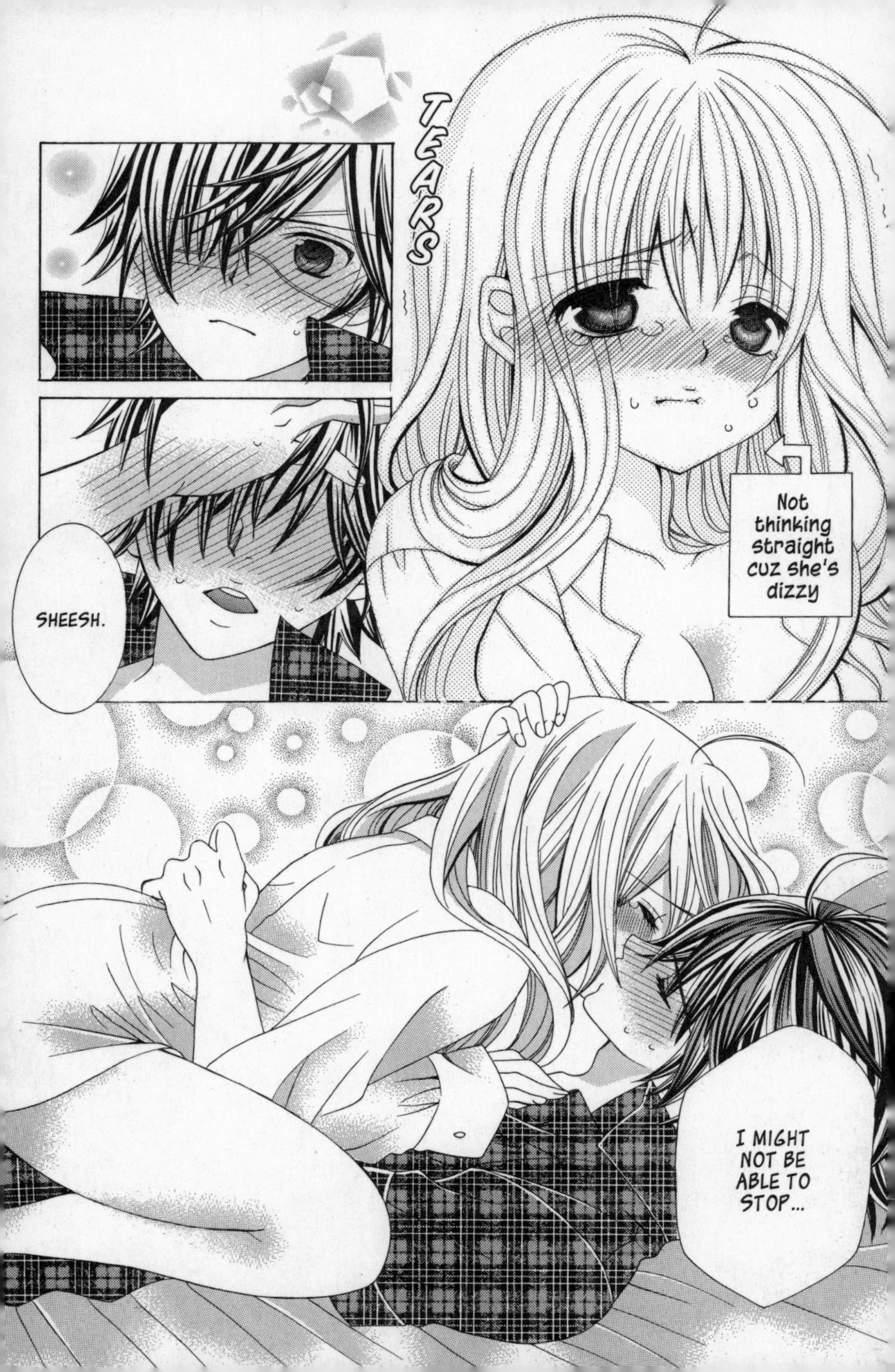
TEARS
Not thinking straight cuz she's dizzy
SHEESH.
I MIGHT NOT BE ABLE TO STOP...

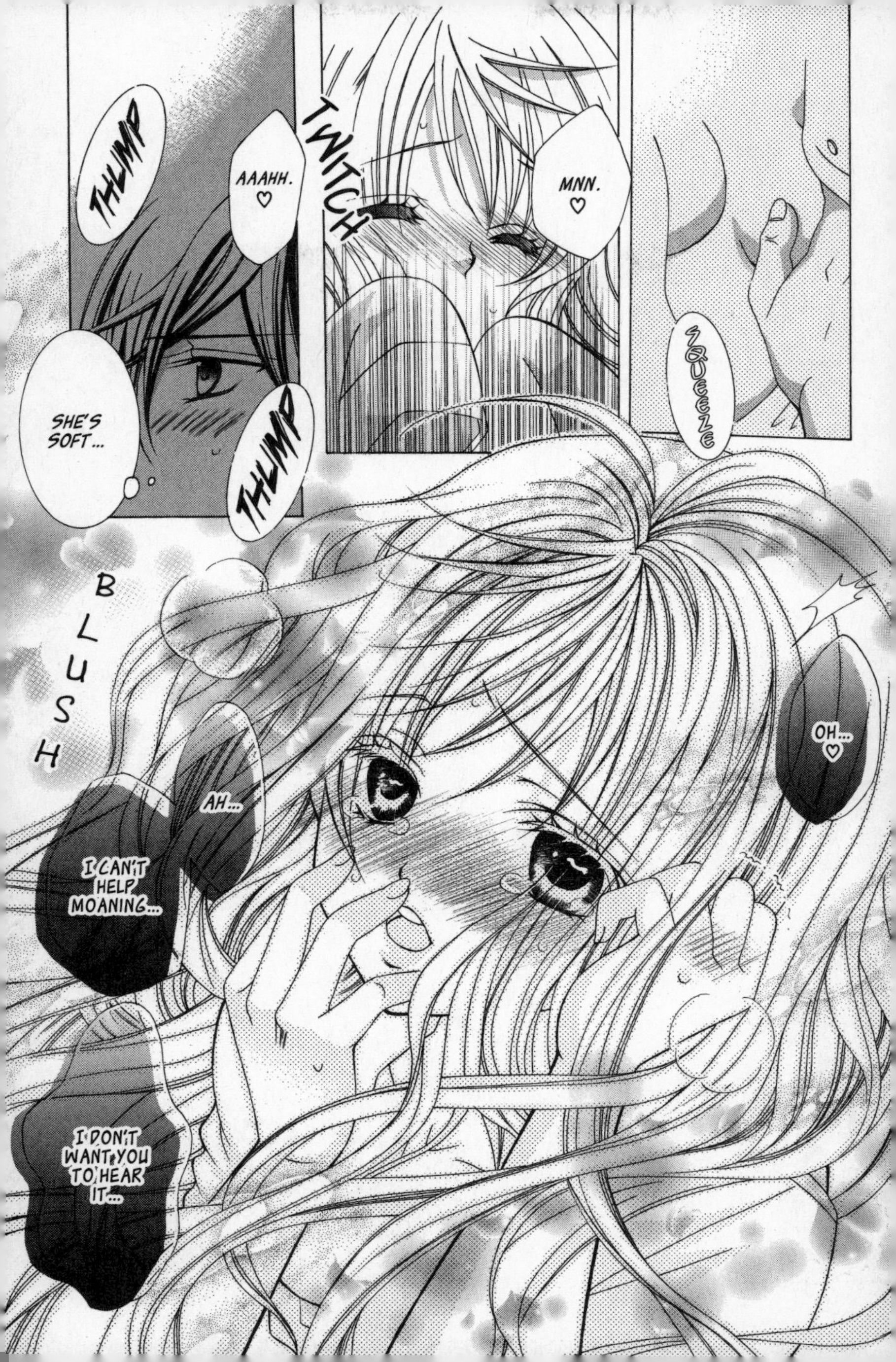
SQUEEZE
MNN. ♡
TWITCH
AAAHH. ♡
THUMP
SHE'S SOFT...
THUMP
OH... ♡
BLUSH
AH...
I CAN'T HELP MOANING...
I DON'T WANT YOU TO HEAR IT...

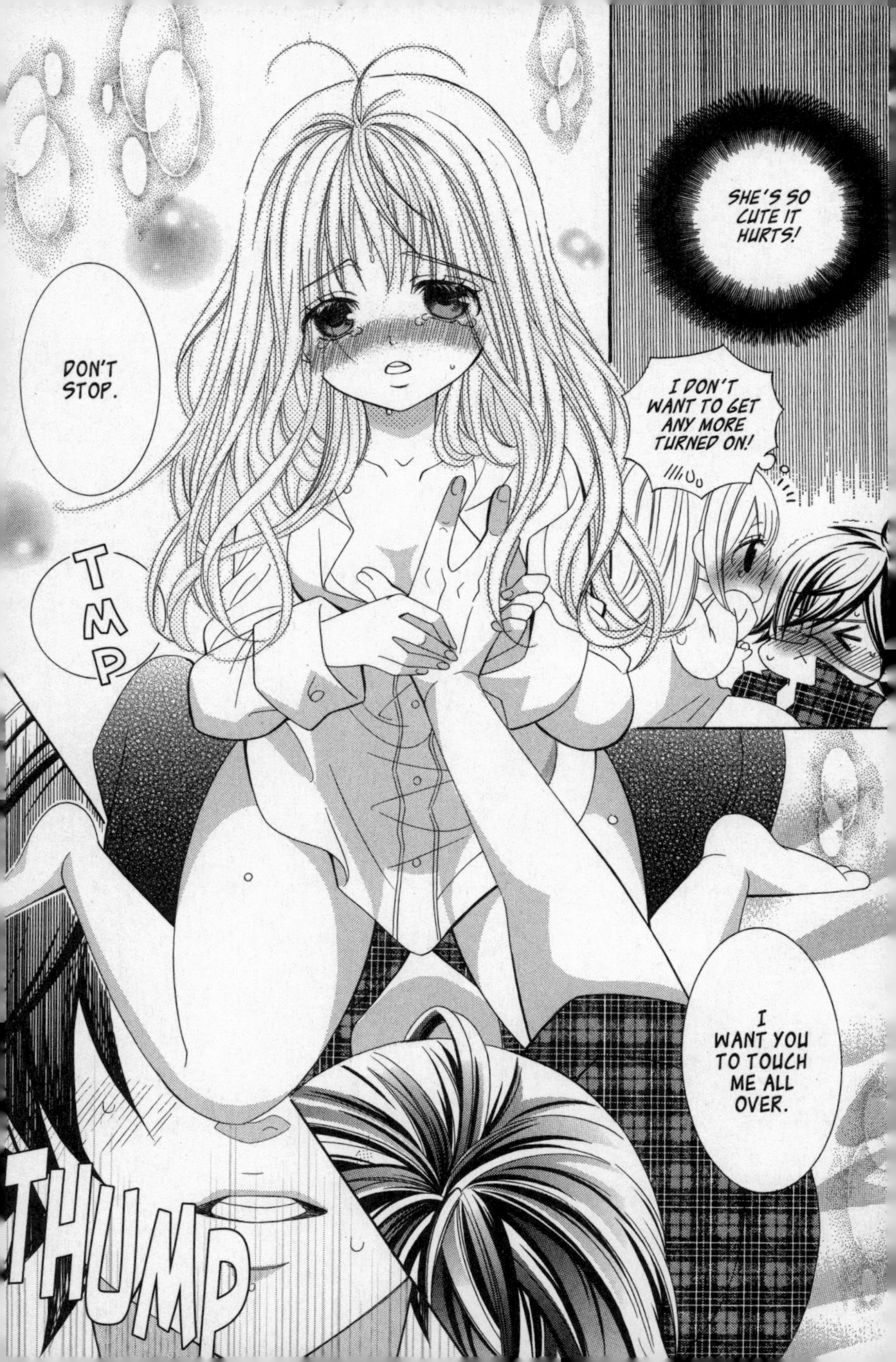
SHE'S SO CUTE IT HURTS!
I DON'T WANT TO GET ANY MORE TURNED ON!
DON'T STOP.
TMP
I WANT YOU TO TOUCH ME ALL OVER.
THUMP

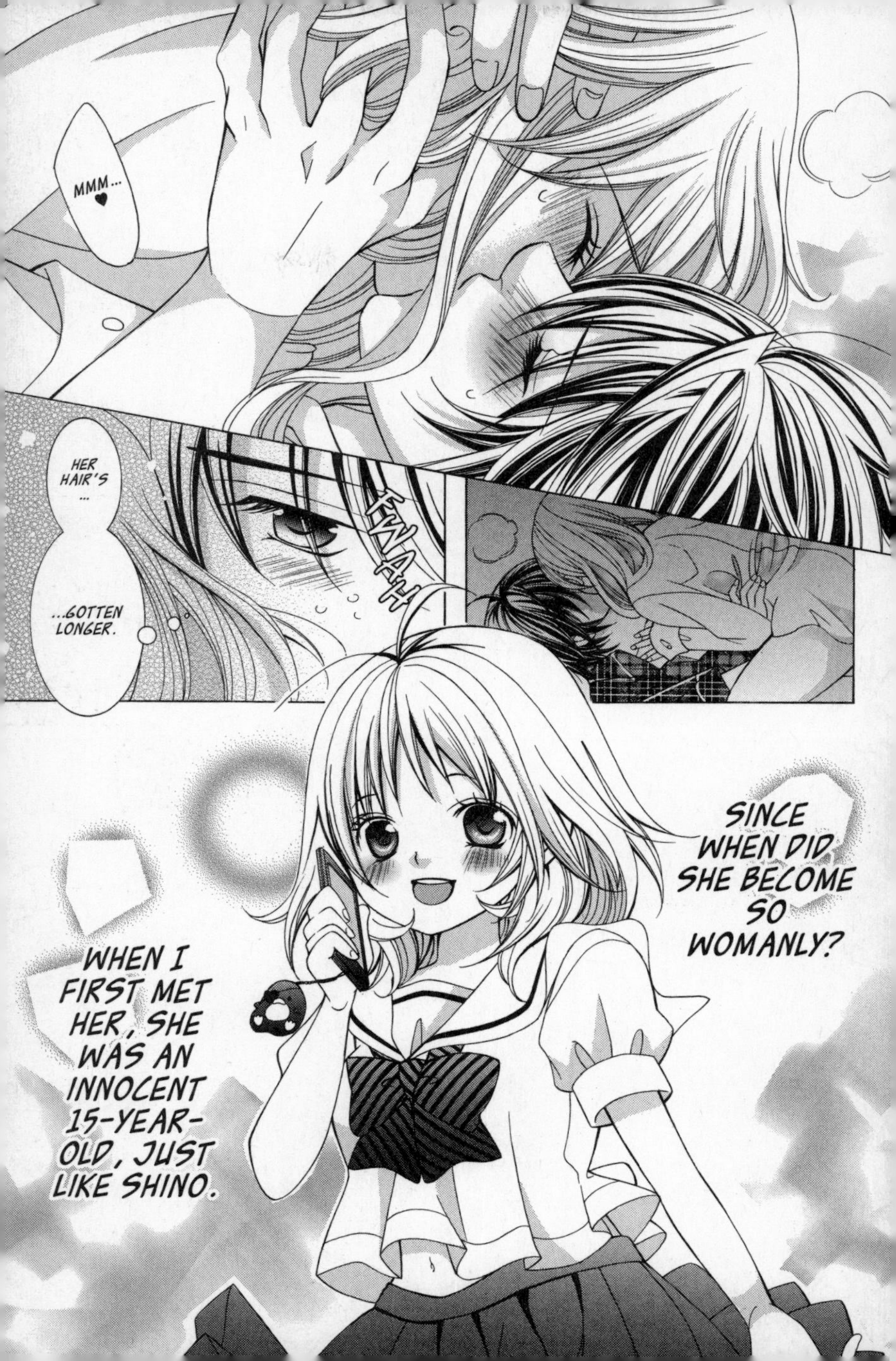
MMM... ♥
KWAH
HER HAIR'S ...
...GOTTEN LONGER.
SINCE WHEN DID SHE BECOME SO WOMANLY?
WHEN I FIRST MET HER, SHE WAS AN INNOCENT 15-YEAR-OLD, JUST LIKE SHINO.

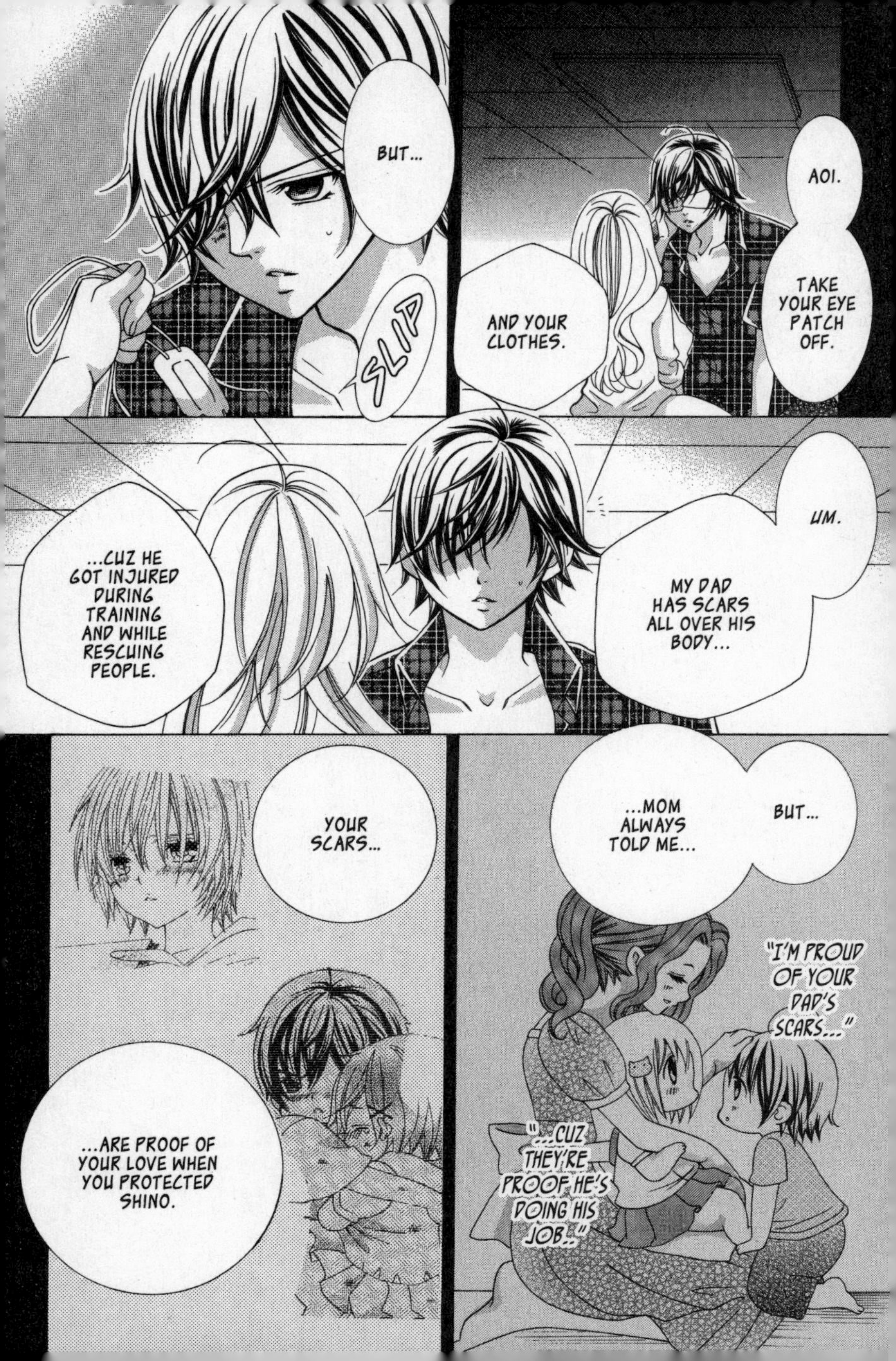
AOI.
TAKE YOUR EYE PATCH OFF.
AND YOUR CLOTHES.
SLIP
BUT...
UM.
MY DAD HAS SCARS ALL OVER HIS BODY...
...CUZ HE GOT INJURED DURING TRAINING AND WHILE RESCUING PEOPLE.
BUT...
...MOM ALWAYS TOLD ME...
"I'M PROUD OF YOUR DAD'S SCARS..."
"...CUZ THEY'RE PROOF HE'S DOING HIS JOB.."
YOUR SCARS...
...ARE PROOF OF YOUR LOVE WHEN YOU PROTECTED SHINO.

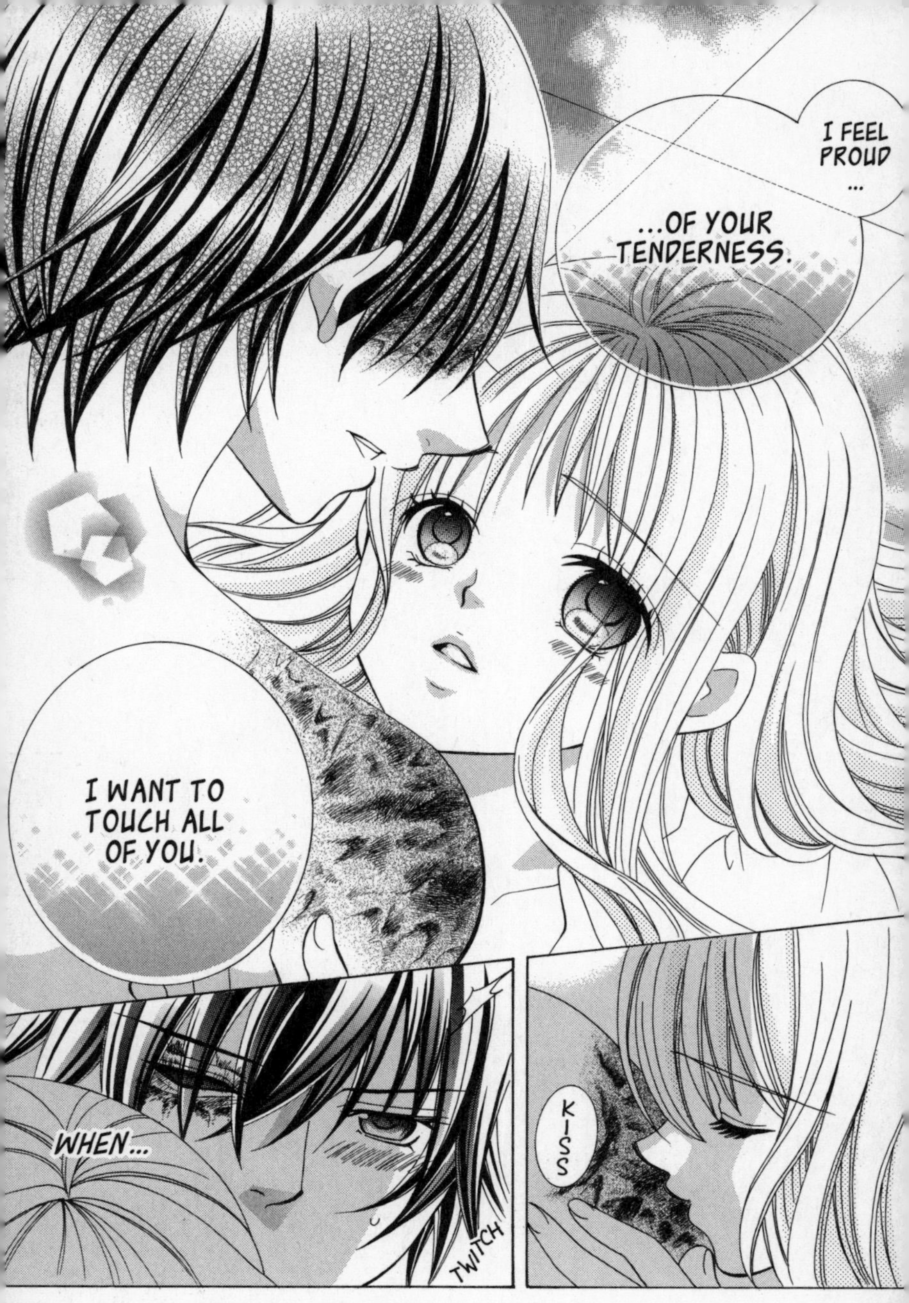
I FEEL PROUD ...
...OF YOUR TENDERNESS.
I WANT TO TOUCH ALL OF YOU.
KISS
TWITCH
WHEN...

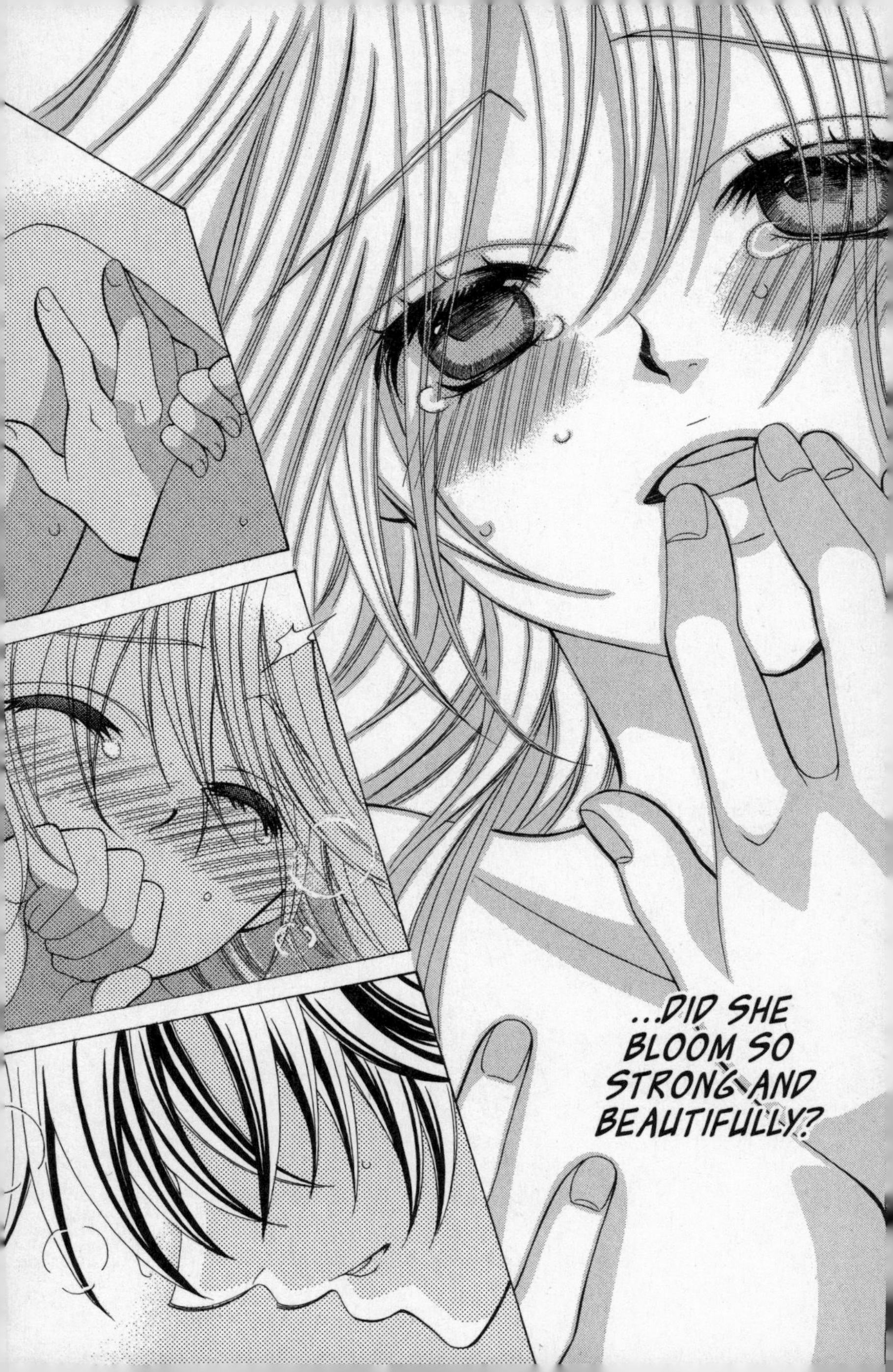
...DID SHE BLOOM SO STRONG AND BEAUTIFULLY?

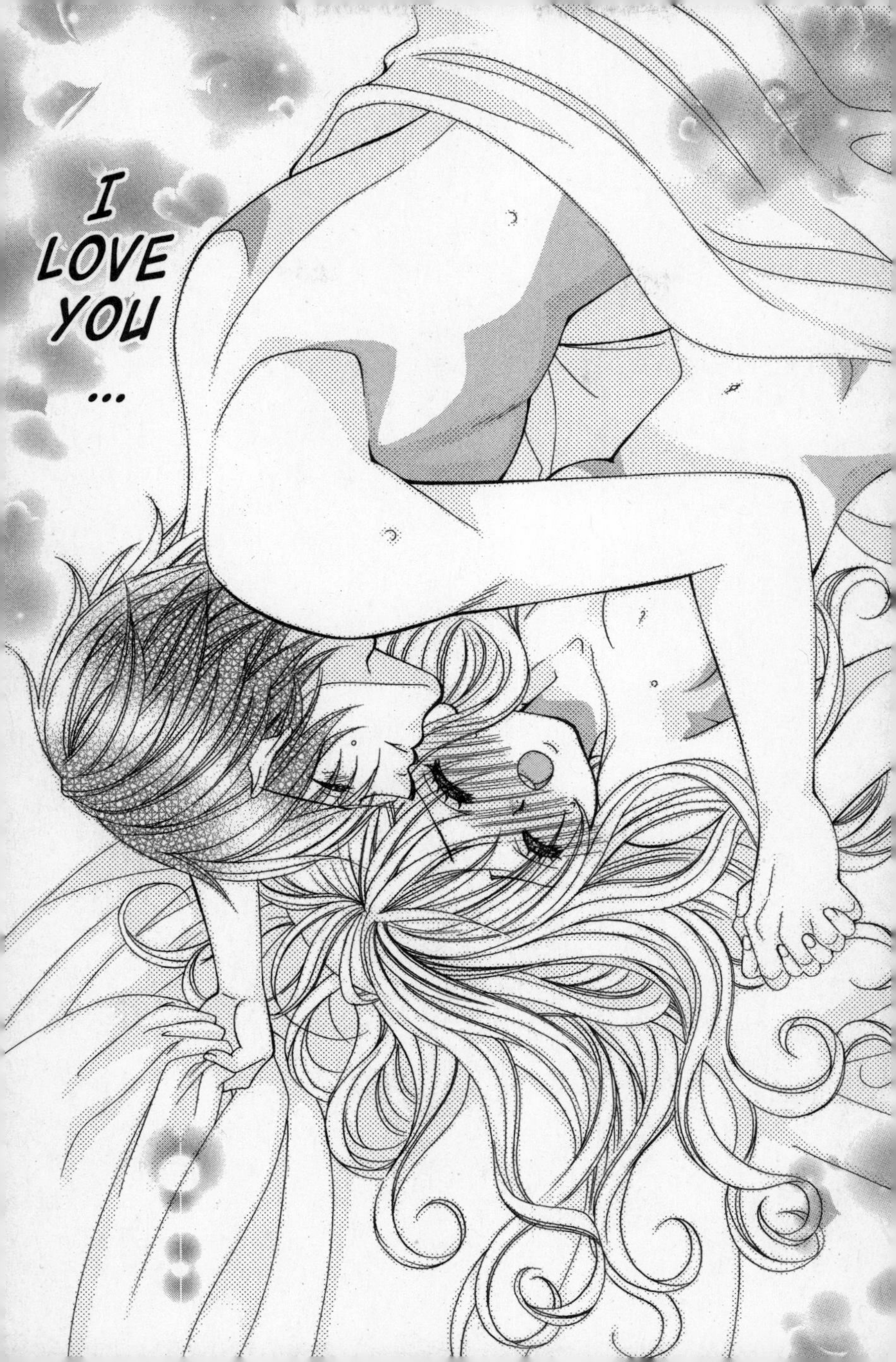
I LOVE YOU ...

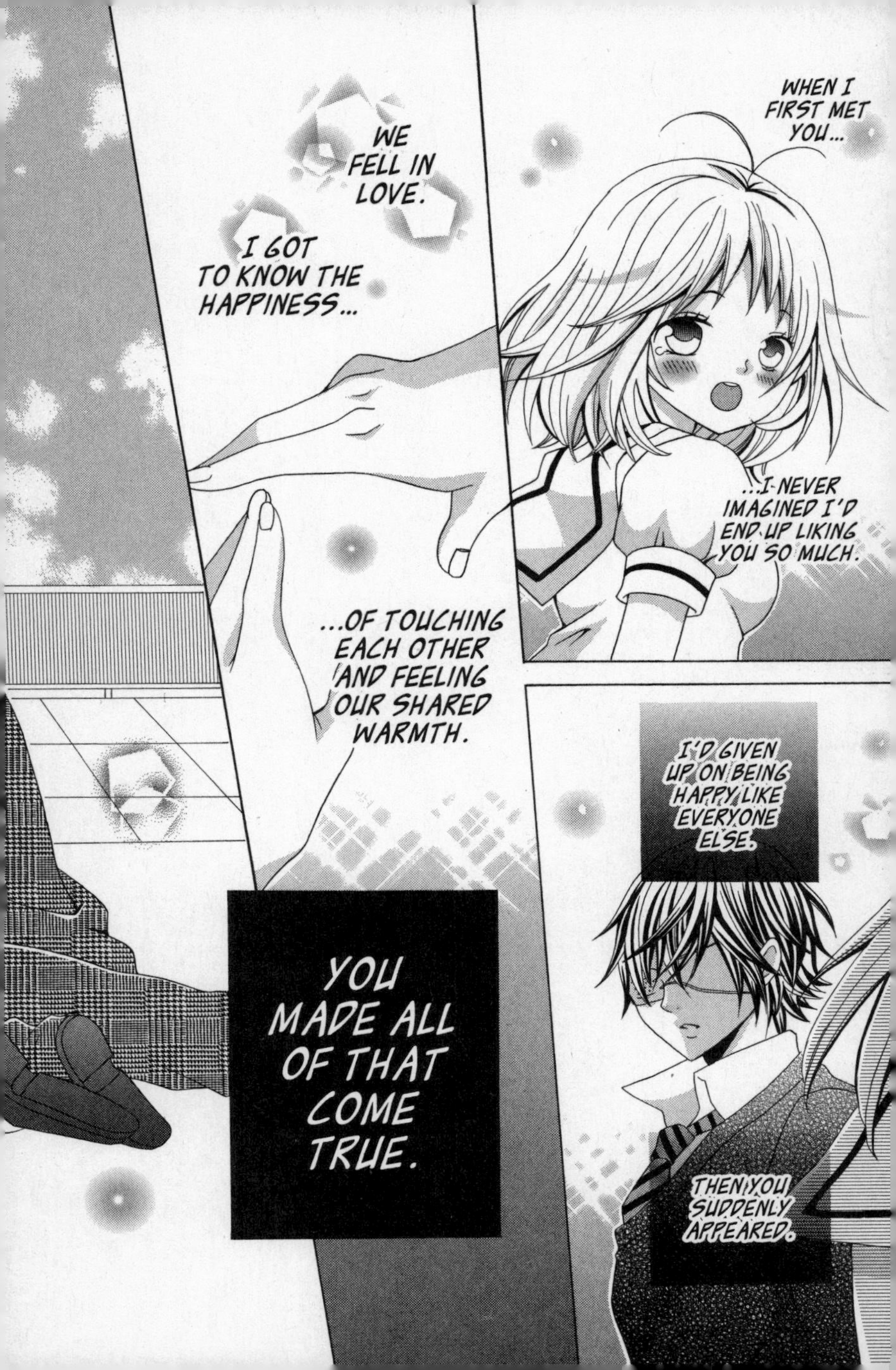
WHEN I FIRST MET YOU...
...I NEVER IMAGINED I'D END UP LIKING YOU SO MUCH.
I'D GIVEN UP ON BEING HAPPY LIKE EVERYONE ELSE.
THEN YOU SUDDENLY APPEARED.
WE FELL IN LOVE.
I GOT TO KNOW THE HAPPINESS...
...OF TOUCHING EACH OTHER AND FEELING OUR SHARED WARMTH.
YOU MADE ALL OF THAT COME TRUE.

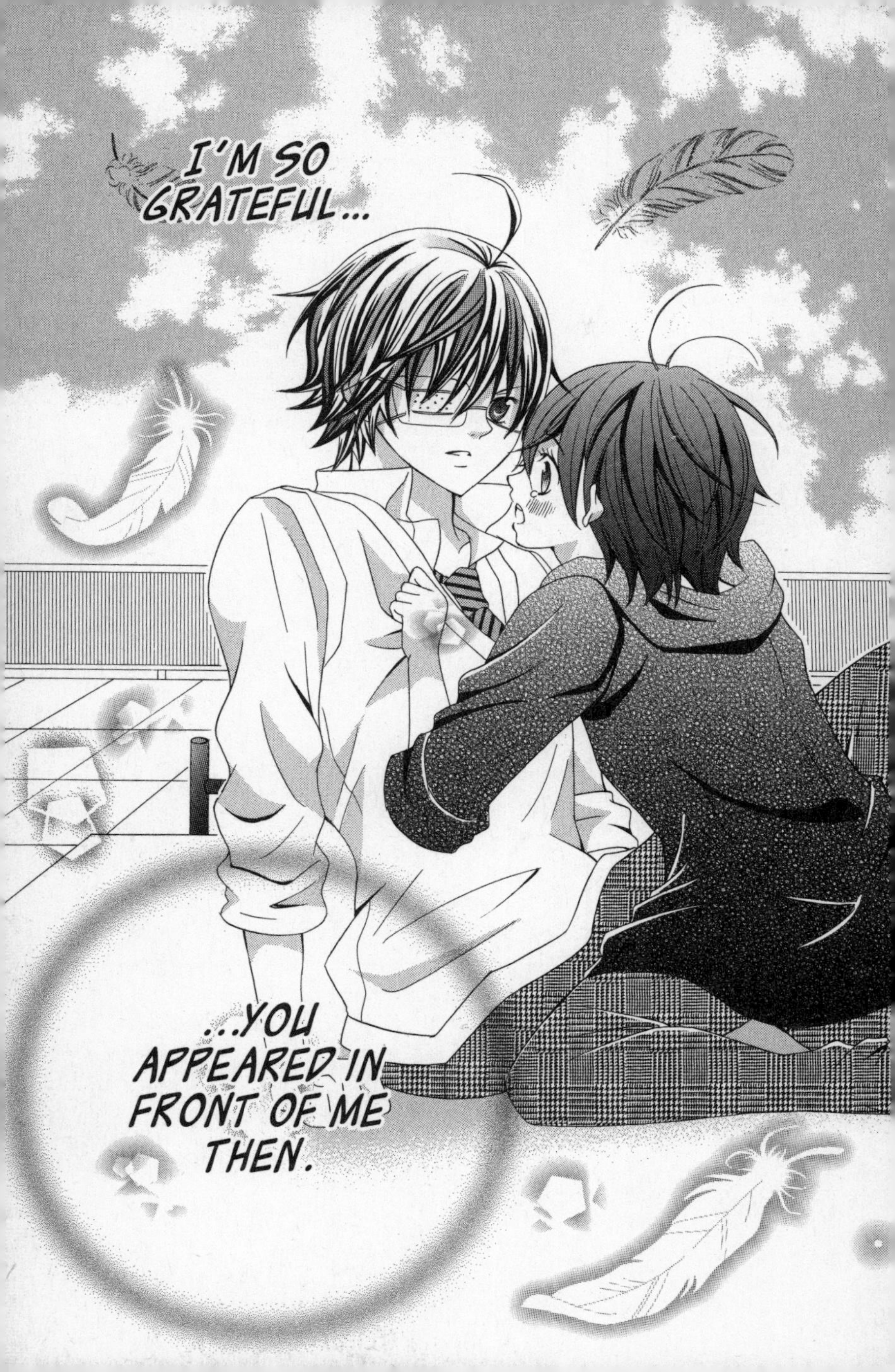
I'M SO GRATEFUL...
...YOU APPEARED IN FRONT OF ME THEN.

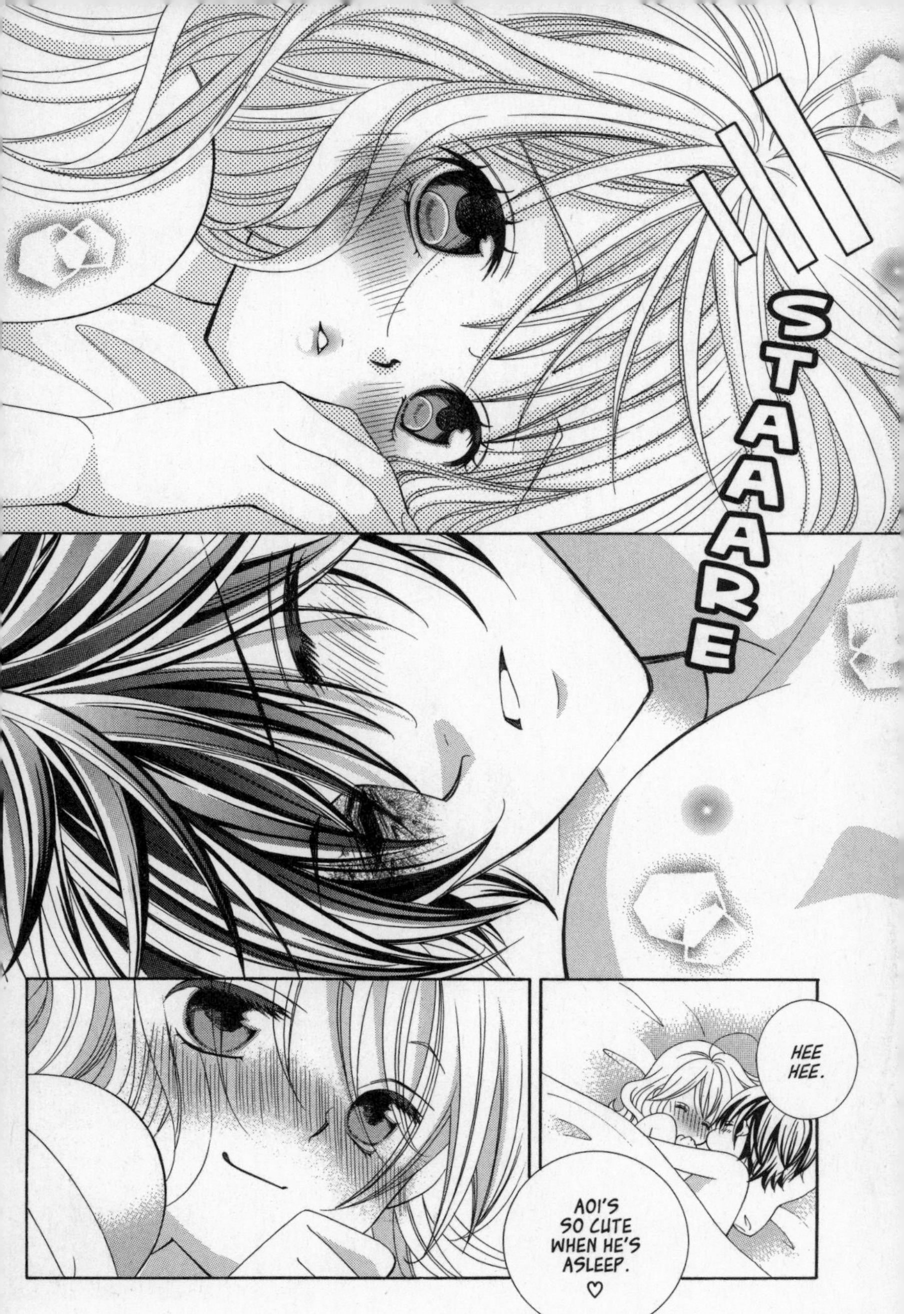
STAAARE
HEE HEE.
AOI'S SO CUTE WHEN HE'S ASLEEP. ♡

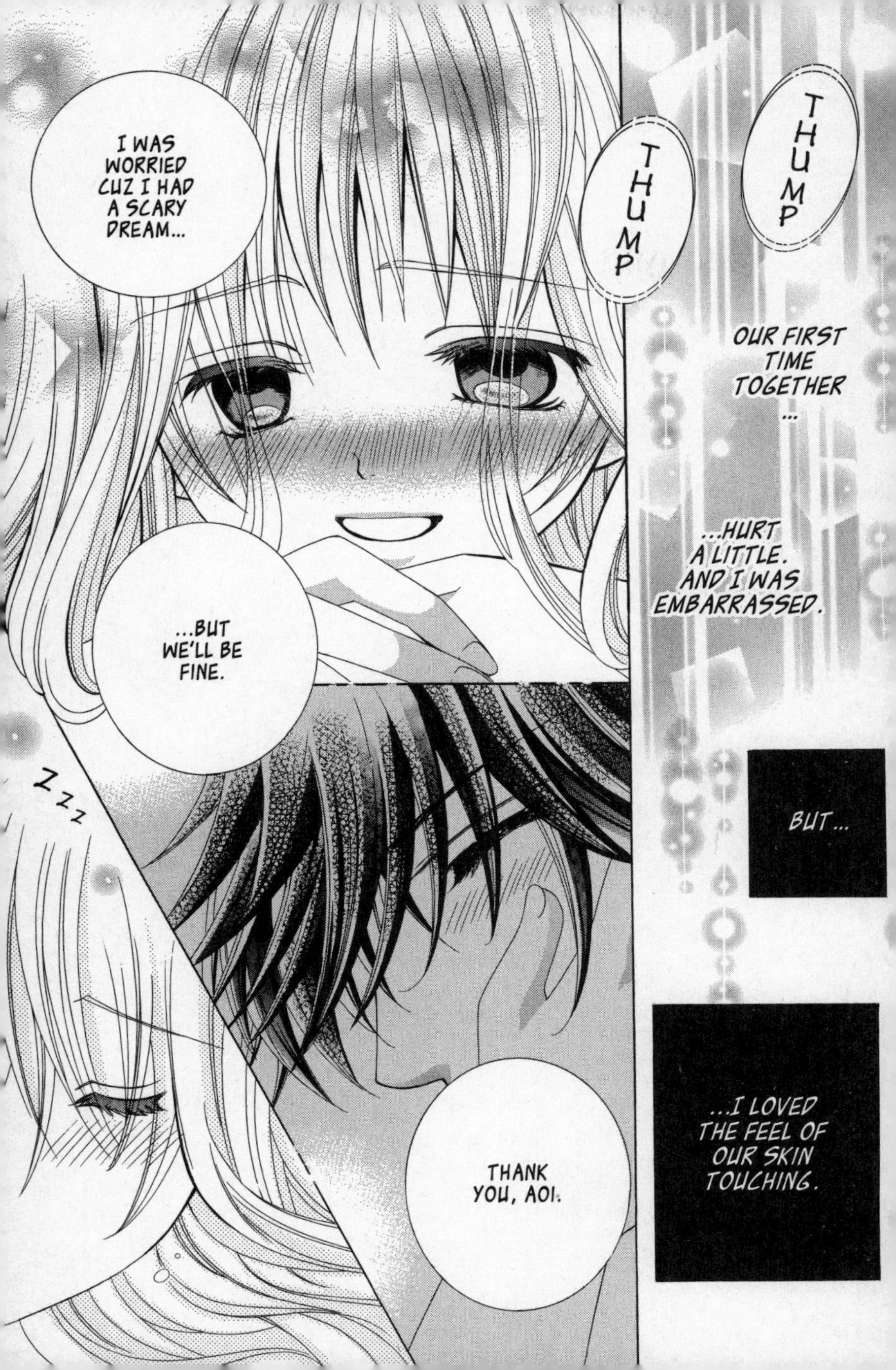
THUMP
THUMP
OUR FIRST TIME TOGETHER...
...HURT A LITTLE. AND I WAS EMBARRASSED.
BUT...
...I LOVED THE FEEL OF OUR SKIN TOUCHING.
I WAS WORRIED CUZ I HAD A SCARY DREAM...
...BUT WE'LL BE FINE.
THANK YOU, AOI.
ZZZ

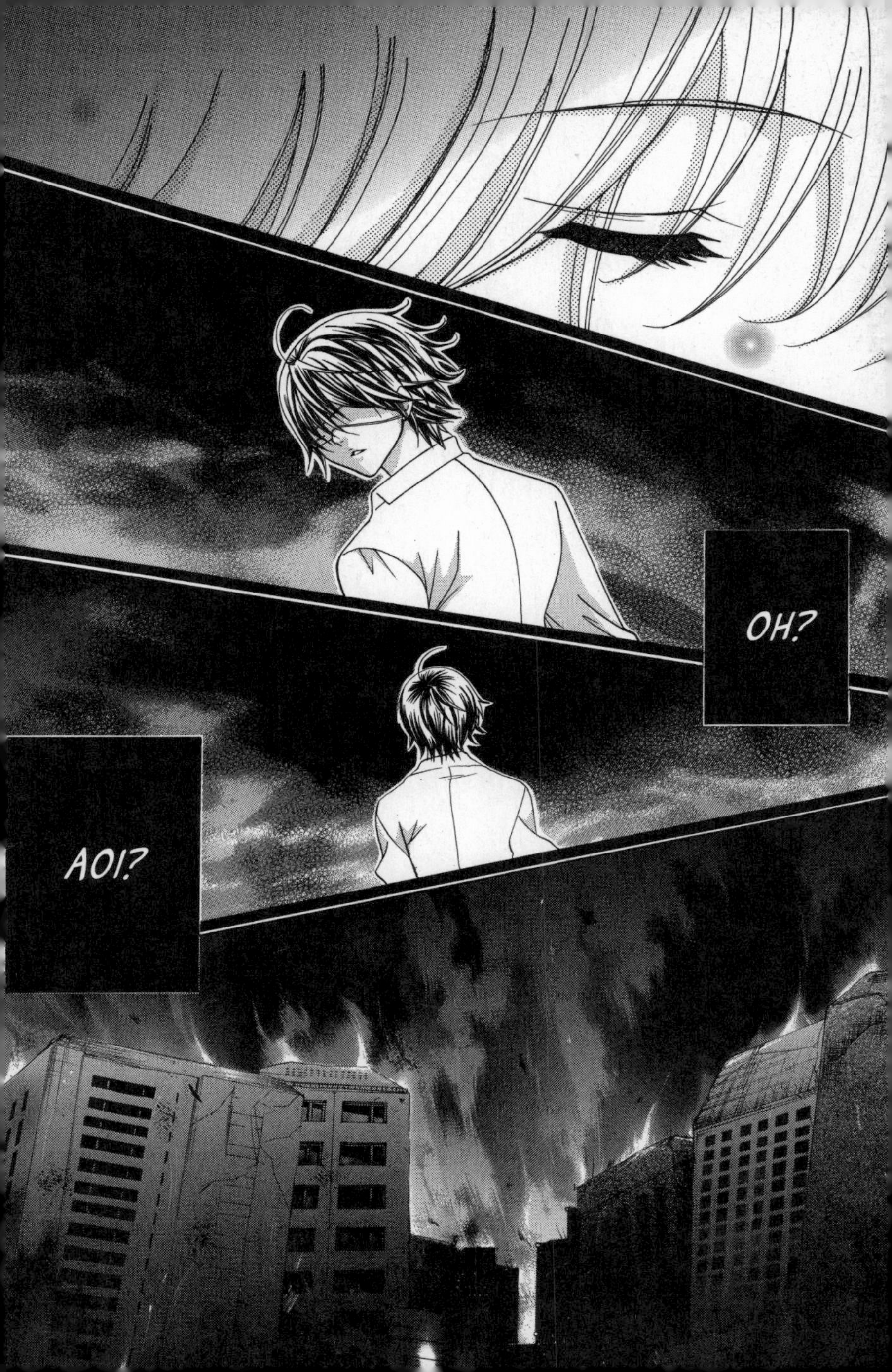
OH?
AOI!?

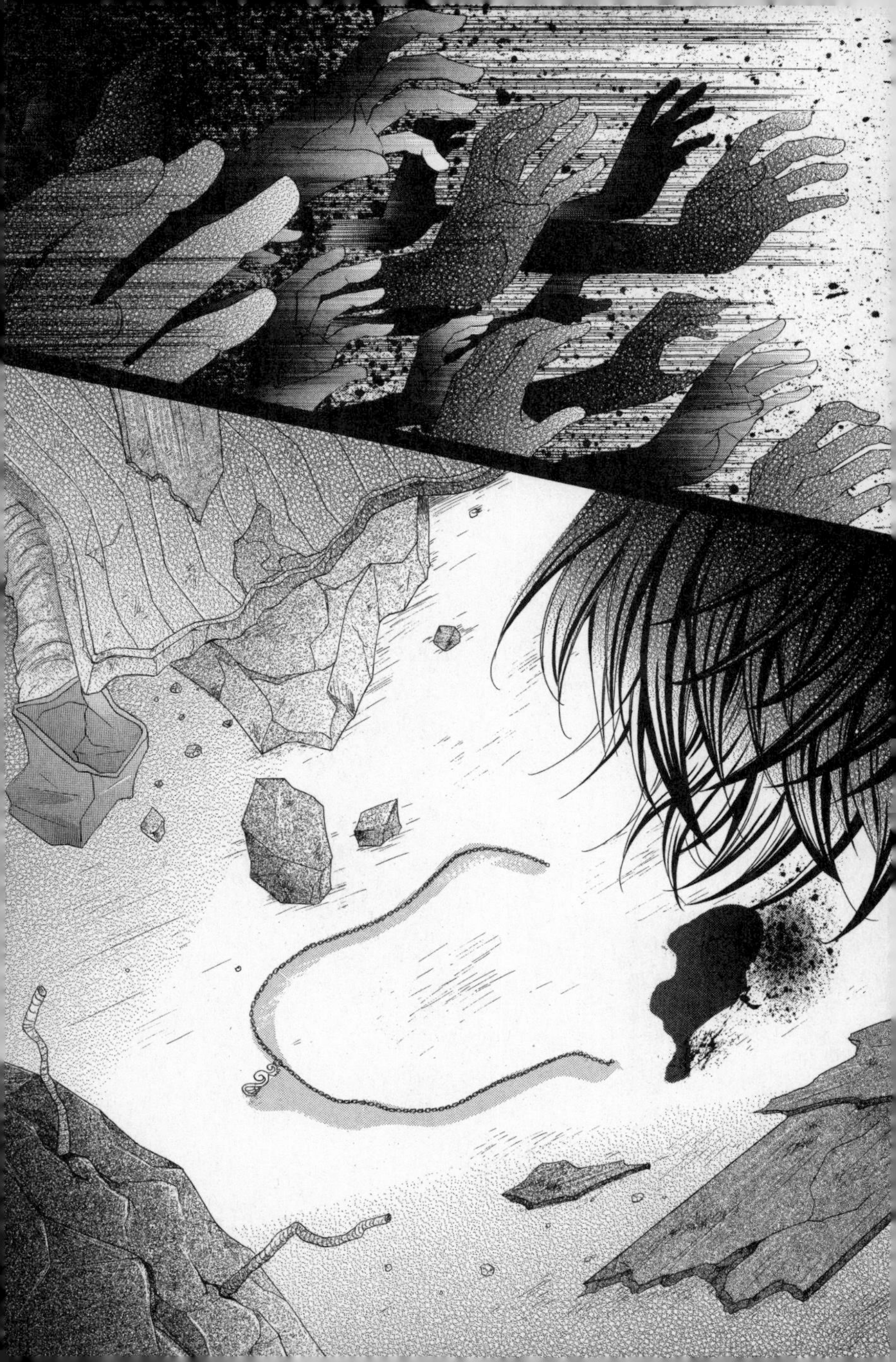

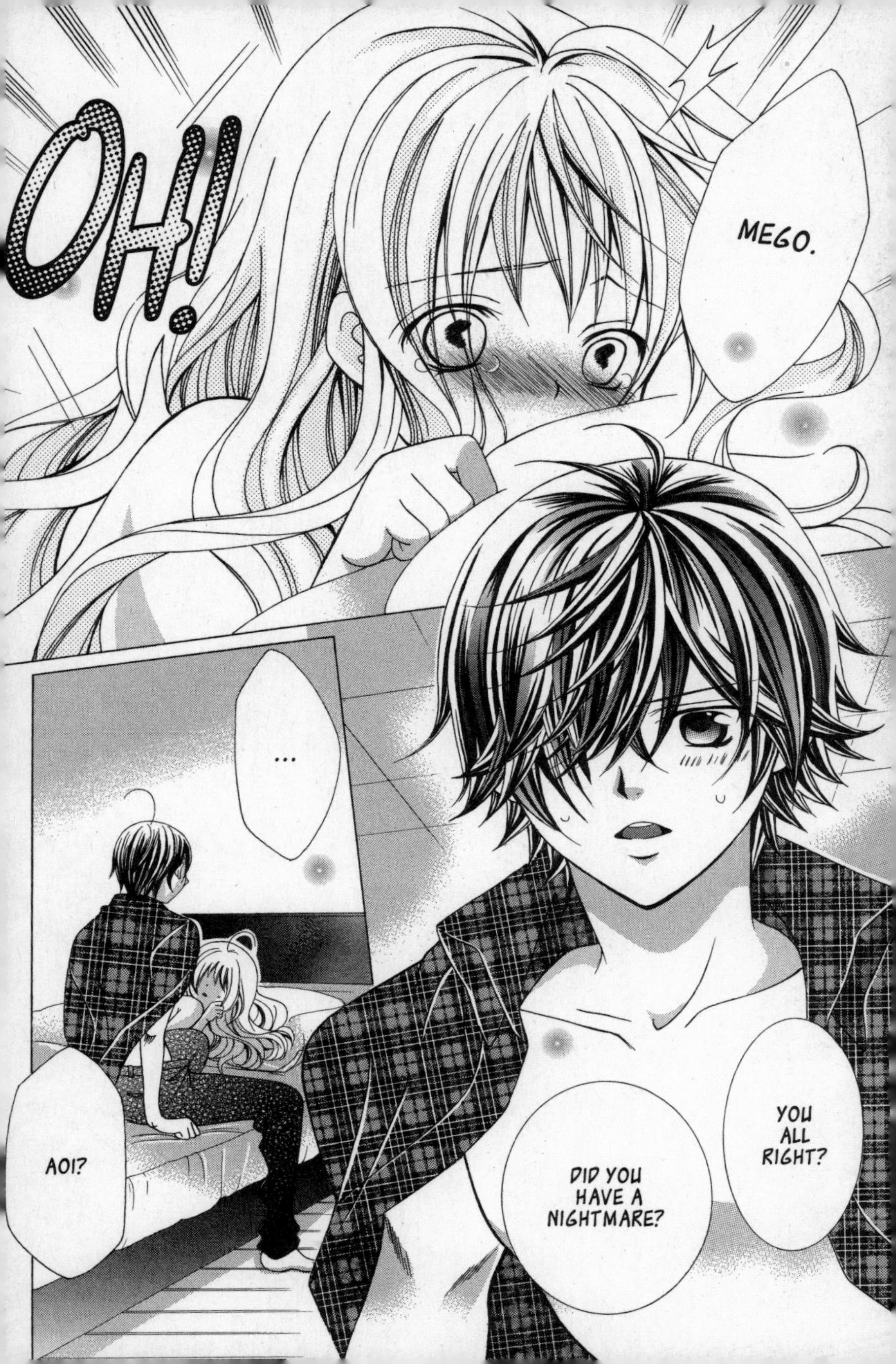

MEGO.
OH!!
YOU ALL RIGHT?
DID YOU HAVE A NIGHTMARE?
...
AOI?

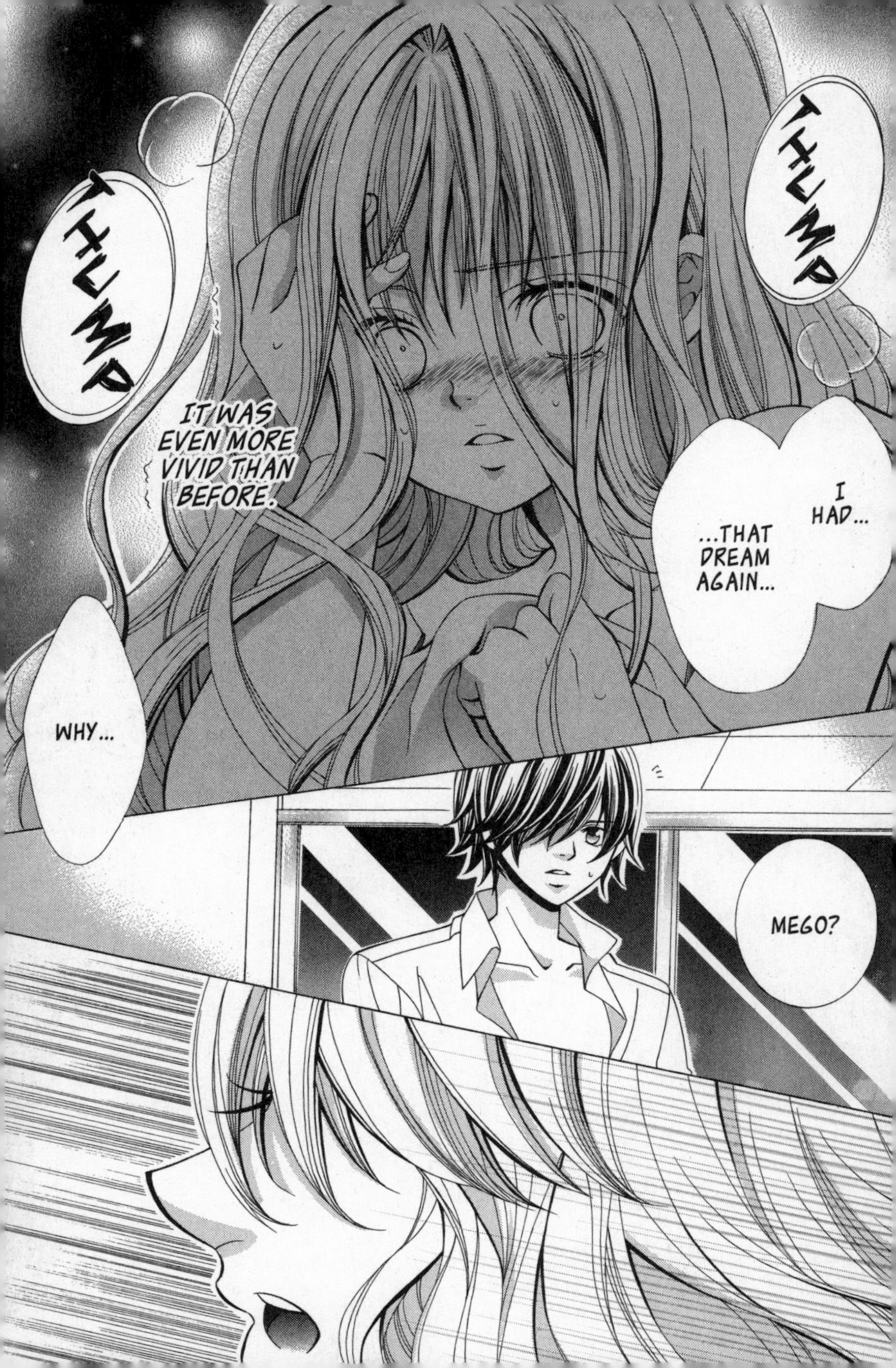
THUMP
THUMP
I HAD...
...THAT DREAM AGAIN...
IT WAS EVEN MORE VIVID THAN BEFORE.
WHY...
MEGO?

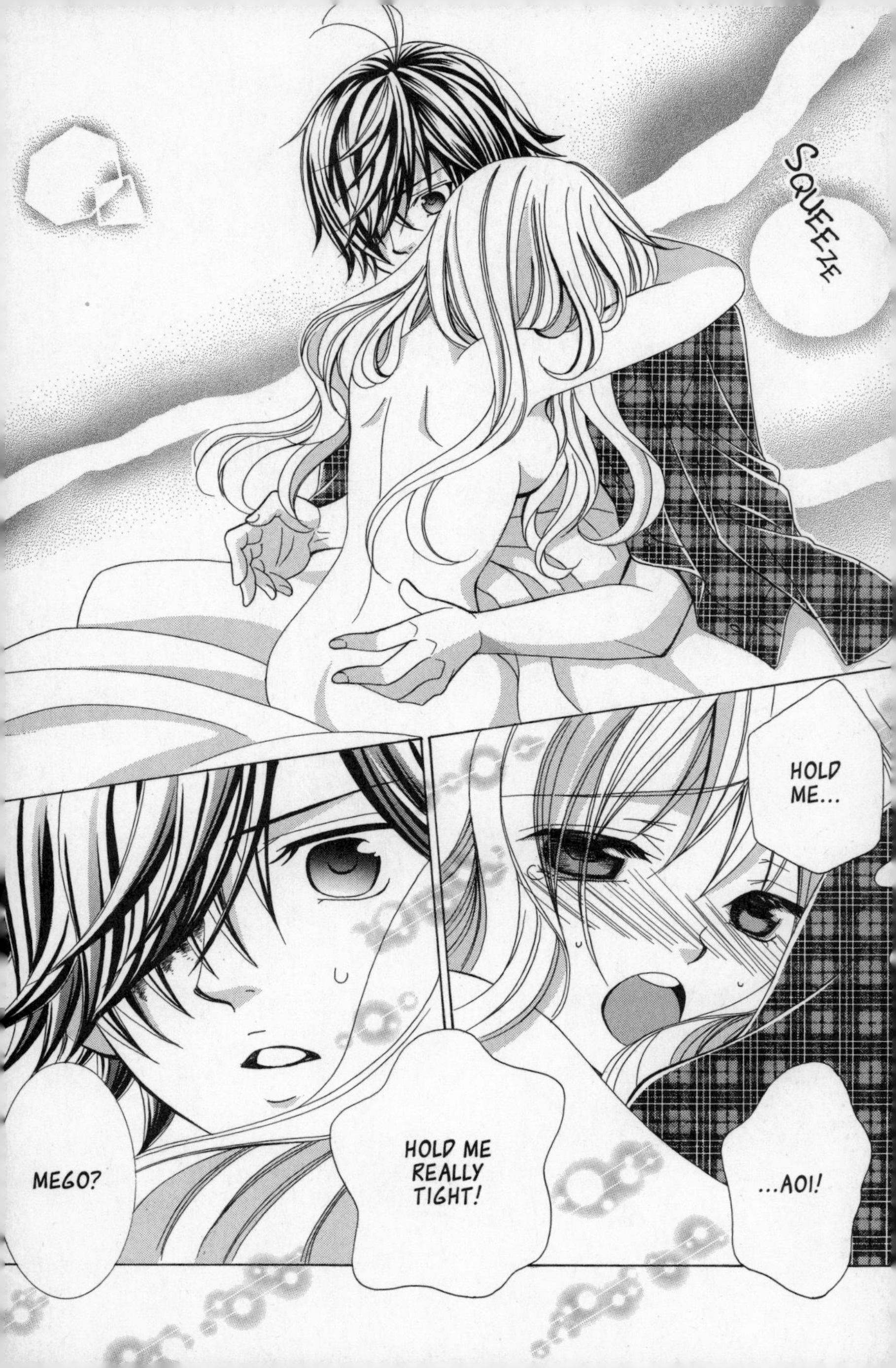
SQUEEZE
HOLD ME...
...AOI!
HOLD ME REALLY TIGHT!
MEGO?

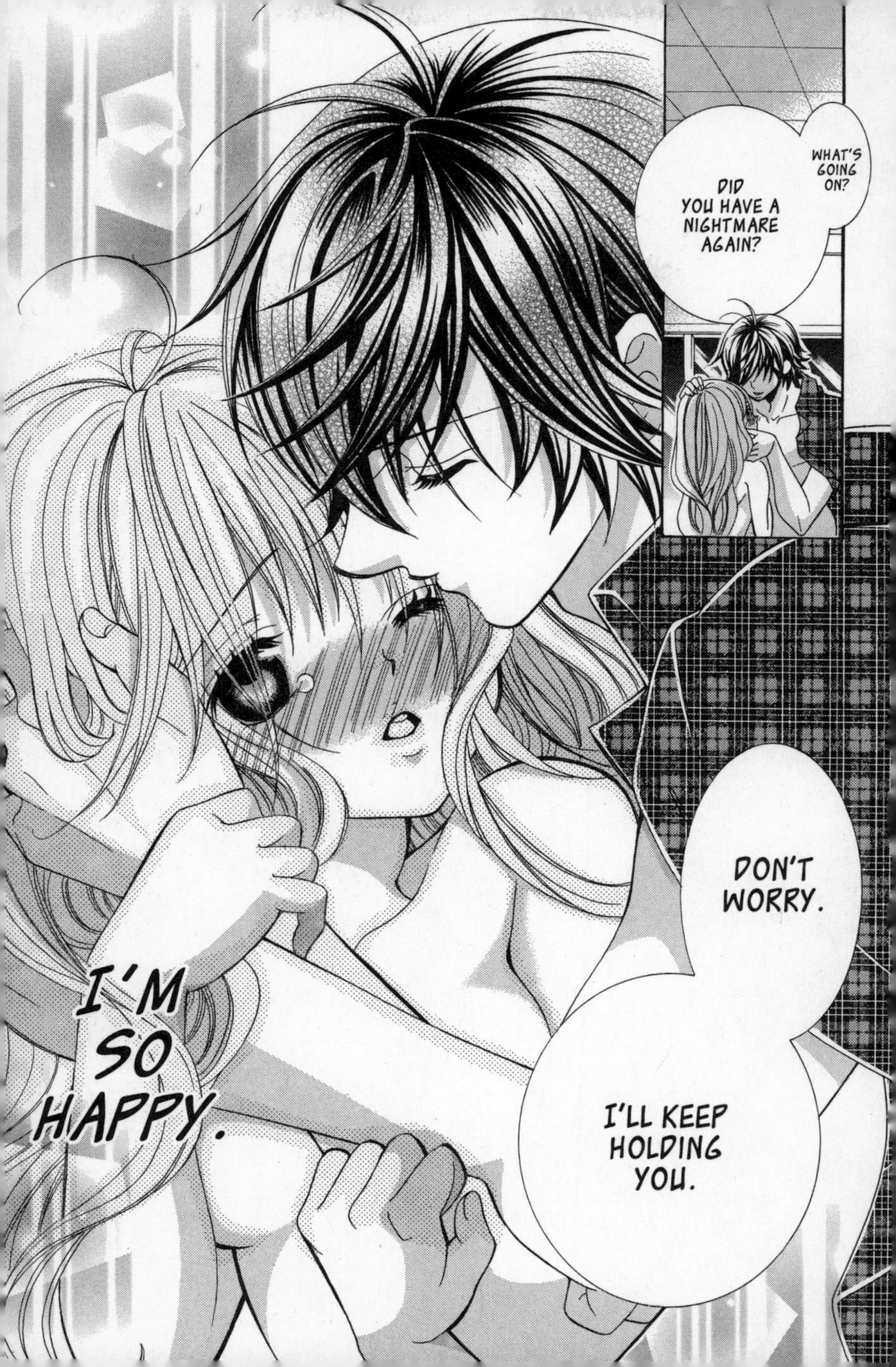
WHAT'S GOING ON?
DID YOU HAVE A NIGHTMARE AGAIN?
DON'T WORRY.
I'LL KEEP HOLDING YOU.
I'M SO HAPPY.

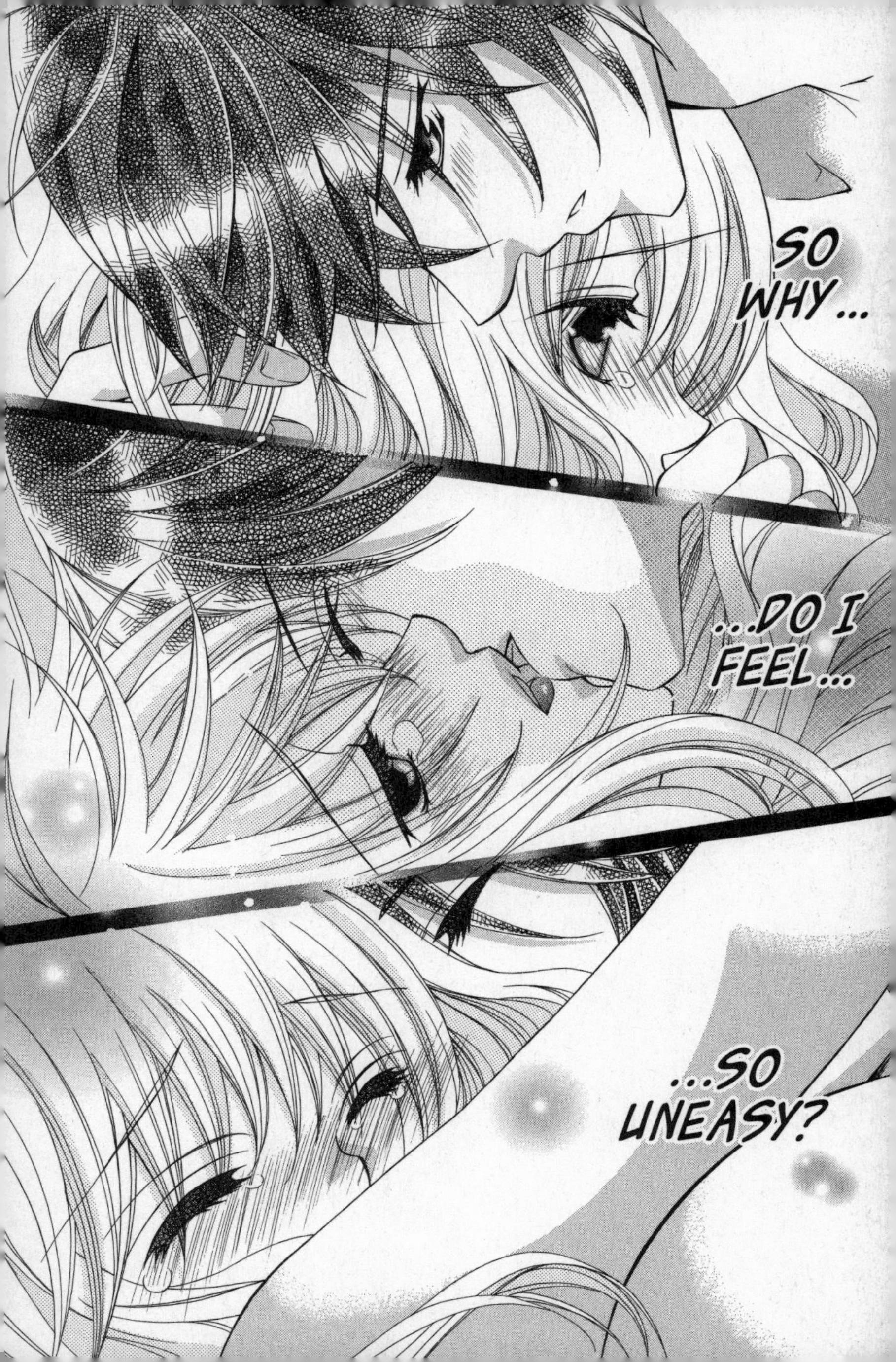
SO WHY...
...DO I FEEL...
...SO UNEASY?

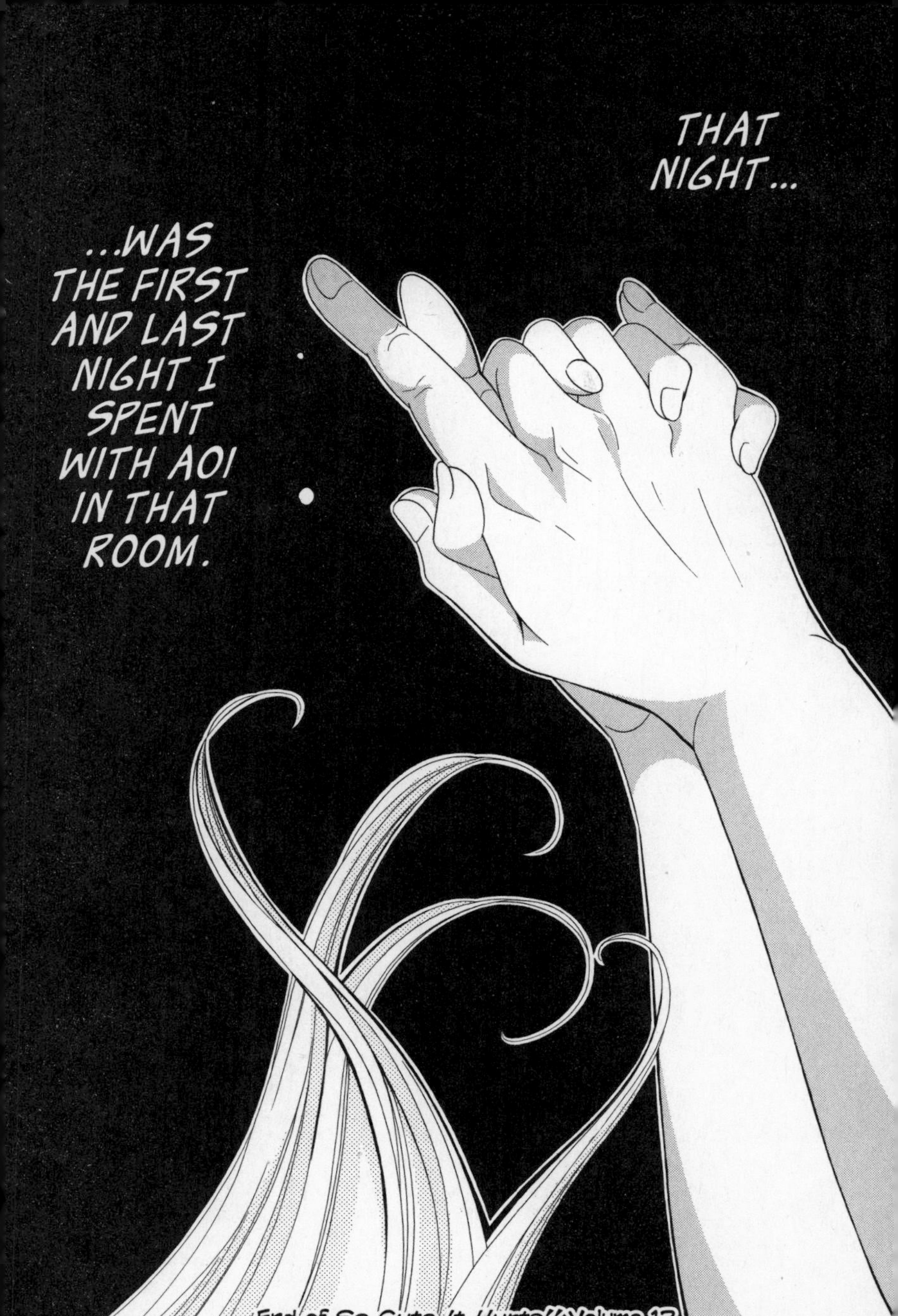
THAT NIGHT...
...WAS THE FIRST AND LAST NIGHT I SPENT WITH AOI IN THAT ROOM.

End of So Cute It Hurts!! Volume 12

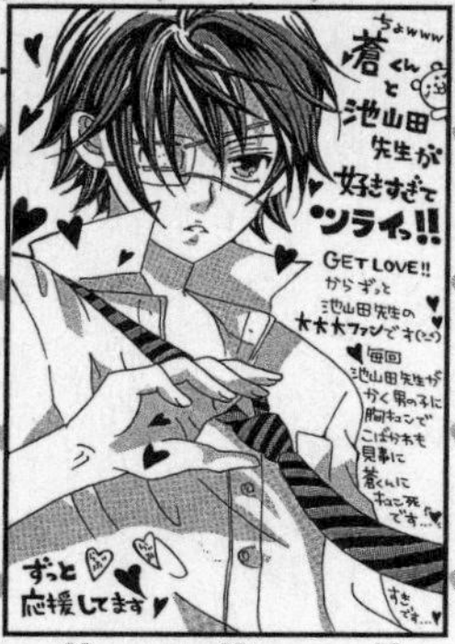

蒼くんと池山田先生が好きすぎてツライっ!!
ずっと応援してます

Aoi-nyan LOVE (Nagano)
←
Ed.: What the... He's cool!!

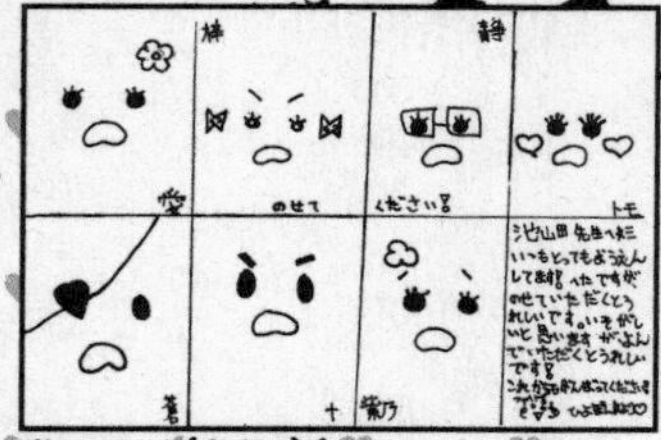

Hiyopon☆ (Shiga) ↑
Ed.: The otaku friends and Shino as penguins are here too. ♡

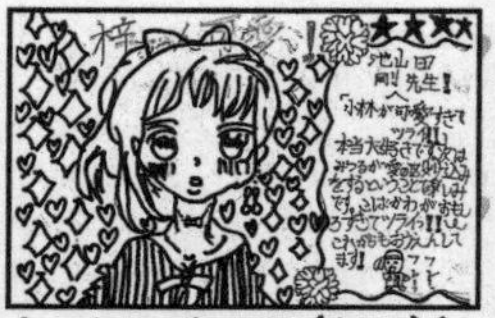

Suzukaze Hayata (Saga) ↑
Ed.: Everyone wants to root for Azusa!

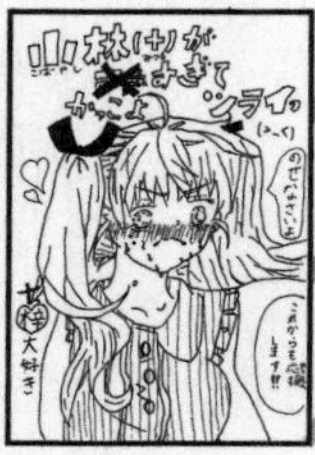

Aoki (Saitama)
←
Ed.: Watch over Azusa and Mitsuru's love!!

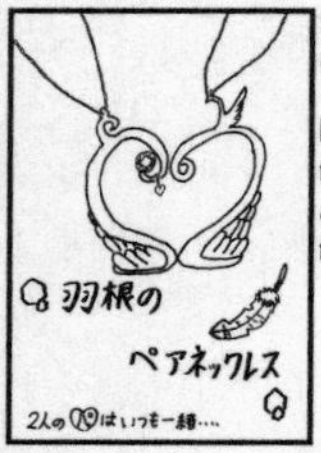

Panda (Mie)
←
Ed.: Yes, their hearts are always together!!

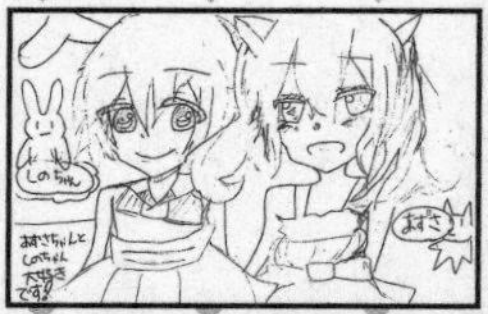

Karin Matsuda (Yamagata) ↑
Ed.: Azusa and Shino with animal ears. ♥

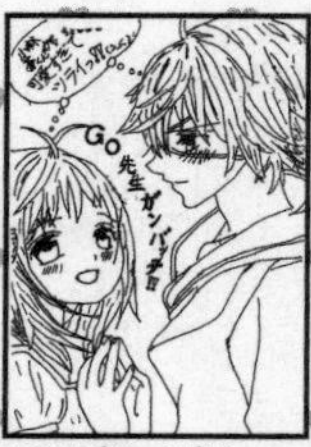

NOAH (Kochi) ↑
Ed.: This lovey-dovey pair is adorable!!

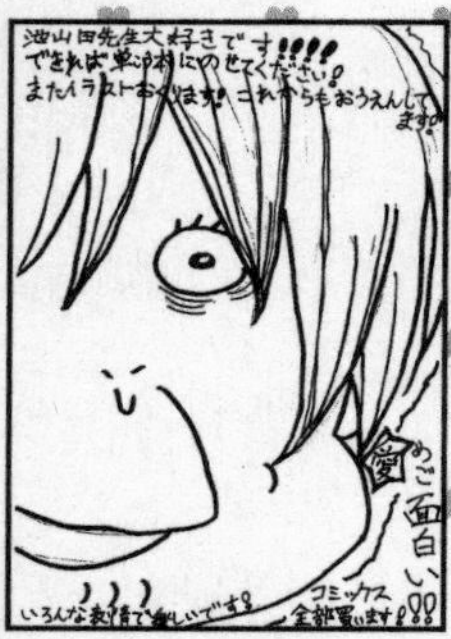

CAT ♥ (Aichi)
←
Ed.: Mego's weird face is ugly but cute!

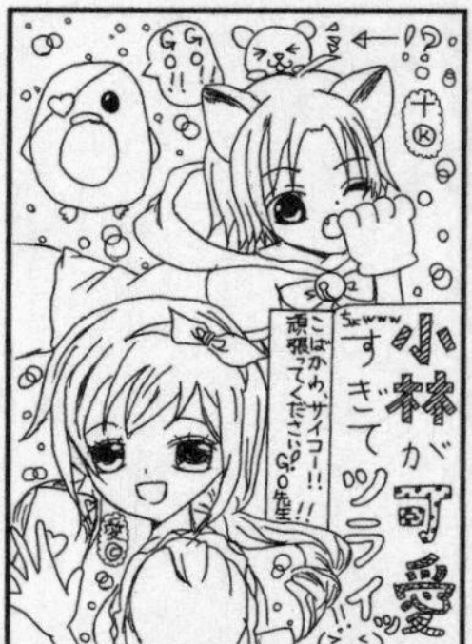

Marina Miyazaki ↑ (Kanagawa)
Ed.: Is that Go-chan sitting on the cat-eared Mitsuru?!

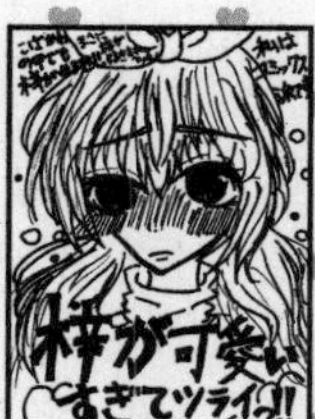

梓が可愛いすぎてツライっ!!

Honoka Sekiguchi (Niigata)
←
Ed.: The blushing Azusa's cute. ♥

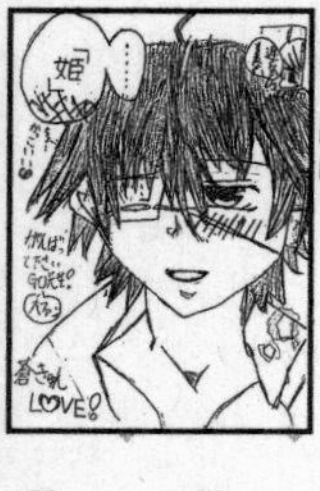

Mai Kikuchi (Hyogo)
←
Ed.: Aoi's blushing... ♥

Send your fan mail to:
Go Ikeyamada
c/o Shojo Beat
VIZ Media, LLC
P.O. Box 77010
San Francisco, CA ☆
94107 (^^)

GLOSSARY

Page 18, panel 2: Golden Week
Golden Week contains four national holidays and is one of Japan's busiest holiday seasons. Depending on what days those holidays fall on, Golden Week can start around late April or early May.

Page 30, panel 3: Bullet train
Called *shinkansen* in Japanese, it is a high-speed train that travels around 200 mph.

Page 56, panel 2: Tohoku
The Tohoku region is in the northeast of the largest Japanese island.

Page 61, panel 2: Ground Self-Defense Force
The land forces of the Japanese Self-Defense Force, similar to the US Army.

Page 63, panel 1: Zuihoden
The mausoleum of Date Masamune.

Page 145, panel 1: Yukata
The *yukata* is a garment that is worn in the summertime in Japan, especially to outdoor festivals and events. Though it resembles the more formal kimono, yukata are made out of cotton rather than silk.

AUTHOR BIO

The *So Cute!* Nintendo DS game will be released in Japan soon! (On sale August 27, 2015.) (^o^) The game is packed with fun stories involving Ellio (who only appears in the game), Mego, Aoi, Mitsuru, Azusa, Shino, Uesugi, Moyuyu, Shizuka and Tomo. ♥♥ Please enjoy the parts of the *So Cute!* world that you can only experience through this game! ♥ ♥ I'm really looking forward to it! (*^ ▽ ^*)

Go Ikeyamada is a Gemini from Miyagi Prefecture whose hobbies include taking naps and watching movies. Her debut manga *Get Love!!* appeared in *Shojo Comic* in 2002, and her current work *So Cute It Hurts!!* (*Kobayashi ga Kawai Suguite Tsurai!!*) is being published by VIZ Media.

SO CUTE IT HURTS!!
Volume 12

Shojo Beat Edition

STORY AND ART BY
GO IKEYAMADA

English Translation & Adaptation/Tomo Kimura
Touch-Up Art & Lettering/Joanna Estep
Design/Izumi Evers
Editor/Pancha Diaz

KOBAYASHI GA KAWAISUGITE TSURAI!! Vol.12
by Go IKEYAMADA
© 2012 Go IKEYAMADA
All rights reserved.
Original Japanese edition published by SHOGAKUKAN.
English translation rights in the United States of America, Canada,
the United Kingdom and Ireland arranged with SHOGAKUKAN.

Printed in the U.S.A.

Published by VIZ Media, LLC
P.O. Box 77010
San Francisco, CA 94107

10 9 8 7 6 5 4 3 2 1
First printing, April 2017

www.viz.com   www.shojobeat.com

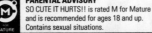

This is the last page.

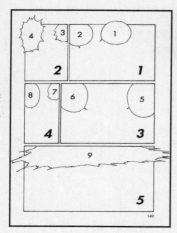

In keeping with the original Japanese comic format, this book reads from right to left—so action, sound effects and word balloons are completely reversed. This preserves the orientation of the original artwork—plus, it's fun! Check out the diagram shown here to get the hang of things, and then turn to the other side of the book to get started!